Ethnic Conflict

Ethnic

Commerce, Culture, and the Contact Hypothesis

Conflict

H. D. FORBES

Yale University Press   New Haven and London

Designed by James J. Johnson and set in Aster
Roman type by Rainsford Type, Danbury,
Connecticut.

Printed in the United States of America by
Thomson-Shore, Inc., Dexter, Michigan.

*Library of Congress Cataloging-in-Publication
Data*

Forbes, H. D. (Hugh Donald)
    Ethnic conflict : commerce, culture, and
the contact hypothesis / H. D. Forbes.
        p.   cm.
    Includes bibliographical references and
index.
    ISBN 0-300-06819-0 (cloth : alk. paper)

    1. Ethnic relations.   2. Culture conflict.
3. Ethnocentrism.   4. Critical theory.
I. Title.
GN496.F67   1997
303.48'2—dc21   96-50343

A catalogue record for this book is available
from the British Library.

The paper in this book meets the guidelines for
permanence and durability of the Committee
on Production Guidelines for Book Longevity
of the Council on Library Resources.

10 9 8 7 6 5 4 3 2 1

To My Sons
MARC and PETER

Je voudrais couler sur une rivière tranquille;
je suis entraîné par un torrent.
—MONTESQUIEU

Contents

Preface

This book tries to define ethnic conflict by showing a pattern in its causes. That pattern has long been obscured by the so-called contact hypothesis and by the reasoning associated with it. By thinking critically about this hypothesis and its rationale, a clearer understanding of ethnic conflict can be attained. In addition, some important features of the modern social sciences can be brought to light.

The contact hypothesis is a broad generalization about the effects of intergroup contact on prejudiced opinions and discriminatory behavior. The idea is that more contact between individuals belonging to antagonistic social groups (defined by customs, language, beliefs, nationality, or identity) tends to undermine negative stereotypes and reduce prejudice, thus improving intergroup relations by making people more willing to deal with each other as equals. For fifty years this hypothesis has occupied a prominent place in social scientists' discussions of prejudice and discrimination. It has influenced the practical remedies for ethnic conflict that they have promoted. Often these have amounted to little more than strong encouragement for more contact in the hope of breaking more stereotypes and thus creating friendlier relations between groups.

The contact hypothesis is an old idea with deep roots in modern liberalism, but it can be best understood in the context of recent social science theories about prejudice and discrimination. Its limitations are most easily seen by carefully examining the results of the empirical research it has inspired and guided. These results show how important it is to distinguish between individual and aggregate levels of analysis when generalizing about the effects of contact on ethnic attitudes and behavior. Less clearly they show how unimportant or misleading are the main distinctions featured in the "contact theory" that social scientists have developed in order to qualify and put limits on the basic idea stated above. Chapters 1–4 of this book deal with the contact hypothesis, the reasoning associated with it, and the findings of the most relevant empirical research.

Only in Chapter 5 do I switch from criticism of contact theory to the exposition of what I regard as a more satisfactory alternative. The linguistic model of ethnic conflict explained in Chapter 5 is the seed from which this book grew—slowly and in unexpected directions because of my reluctance to accept the larger pattern suggested by the model. No hard evidence compels one to see it. The more carefully one examines the question of evidence, the more clearly one sees how difficult it is to determine whether the model is a sound generalization from "the facts" or merely a tendentious interpretation of some of them. The facts summarized in the first half of the book indirectly lend it some support, but the most important considerations seem to be of a more theoretical or philosophical character.

One of my reasons for writing this book has been to explore the strengths and weaknesses of the empiricism that has dominated the modern social sciences. Philosophers have long debated its merits, marshaling powerful arguments for and against. Some maintain that it is necessary if we are to avoid myth-making and ideology; others contend that it is terribly destructive, leading us gradually into tyranny or banality. I know that much light is shed by these heated debates, but I have found it necessary to feel my way like a blind man toward a better understanding of what it means to test hypotheses in the social sciences and to develop theory. The example used here—the contact hypothesis—is complicated enough and has been important enough in practice to make the exercise of testing it worthwhile. By the end of the book I hope that the reader will see that it has been fairly and conclusively tested and that there are important methodological problems in the social sciences that have little to do with the topics usually discussed in courses on methodology.

This book is addressed to social scientists interested in discovering patterns and discussing some basic questions of method or epistemology in the social sciences. It has not been my intention to promote or to discredit any particular practical measures for alleviating ethnic conflict, nor have I tried to show what life is going to be like in the next millennium. Futurologists may find some things of interest here, but it has not been my aim to add to their stock of marketable wares.

In quoted passages, emphasis is in the original unless otherwise noted.

A version of Chapter 5 first appeared as a Working Paper of the Institute for the Quantitative Analysis of Social and Economic Policy, University of Toronto, in 1970. A revision of that paper became a chapter of my dissertation and then, with further revision, a paper published in the proceedings of the Annual Meeting of the Canadian Political Science Association for 1979.

In the many years since I first encountered Karl Deutsch's illuminating and provocative theories about nationalism I have accumulated many intellectual debts. My dissertation supervisor, Robert Dahl, showed me the combination of bold reasoning with careful empirical observation that is the hallmark of social science. His friendship, support, and guidance encouraged me to follow his example. Hayward Alker's infectious enthusiasm for quantitative reasoning added greatly to the impact of his clear explanation of the importance of "ecological fallacies." It is not just nostalgia that makes me look back fondly and with gratitude to the years I spent studying with them. Among the many influences since that time which may not be apparent from my references, the greatest by far were those of Allan Bloom and George Grant, who gave me a new perspective on the social sciences. It may seem strange to suggest that this book—so unlike anything they wrote or encouraged—bears their stamp, but I like to think that it does. For comments on early versions of some arguments, I owe thanks to Stephen Clarkson, Michael Denny, Joseph Fletcher, Jerry Hough, Clifford Orwin, Jone Schoeffel, and Richard Simeon. More recently, the manuscript was reorganized after some conversations with Thomas Pangle and in response to the comments of an anonymous reviewer for Yale University Press who gave me the benefit of some sharp but constructive, detailed, and informed objections to the substance and presentation of its argument. Michael Pratt generously helped me to improve the mathematical part of Chapter 5. To all these teachers, friends, and colleagues I am grateful, but none of them has read all of this book, and several have read none of it. Much as I have benefited from their advice and instruction, they must not be held responsible for its errors and deficiencies.

Introduction

Why *ethnic conflict*? What are its causes? Does it even exist? Conflicts between ethnic groups are a familiar, undeniable fact, but do they have anything to do with ethnicity? The atrocities and injustices of recent years press these questions upon us. Almost any attempt to understand them better must seem worthwhile, but perhaps there is no such thing as ethnic conflict. The term itself may be misleading.

Social scientists often treat cultural differences as merely a pretext for conflict. They find its causes elsewhere, with the help of theories that focus attention on other factors. General theories of social cognition, collective behavior, or civil violence put ethnic groups and their conflicts in the broadest possible explanatory framework. Social systems theory, frustration-aggression theory, or some general theory of cooperation and competition may be used to explain the patterns of order and disorder in society. A few social scientists still turn to psychoanalytic theory for insights into ethnic attitudes and emotions, but a growing number are turning to the economists' rational model of man, *Homo economicus*, for illumination. Many social scientists seem to think that the answer to the riddle will be found in the development of an integrated, comprehensive theory of intergroup relations that does not distinguish between different types of groups. Almost all of these competing theories and approaches draw attention away from cultural differences as a cause of ethnic conflicts.

Many competing theories and approaches mean many different controversies and perplexities. Not all of these can be resolved at once, but perhaps some light can be shed on several of them by examining the correlations between ethnic prejudice and discrimination on one hand and

1

the increasing number of contacts among ethnic groups on the other. Contact is increasing because of mass migration, mass communications, and the growth of global tourism and of a global economy. Some expect this increasing contact to dissolve ethnic conflicts; others say that it just intensifies them. This book tries to dispel some of the puzzlement surrounding ethnic conflict by closely examining one key idea, namely, that more contact between ethnic groups, under the right conditions, even if it increases ethnic consciousness, need not increase conflict. Indeed, according to one statement of the basic idea, more contact, in the right circumstances, means less trouble.

This idea—the contact hypothesis—is explained more fully later. It has deep roots and broad implications. For now, its import can be quickly shown by summarizing an influential theory about economic and political development. Economic development, it is often thought, should undermine narrow ethnic loyalties and thus ultimately reduce ethnic conflict and increase respect for individual rights. After all, the growth of commerce brings previously isolated groups into closer contact and gives them incentives to cooperate with each other in new ways. People drawn into wider networks of exchange are tied together by their practical economic interests. Under the influence of these new interests and engagements, individuals begin to see their clashing cultural commitments (customs and values) in a new and clearer light. By reducing scarcity, economic development reduces the intensity of strictly economic conflicts, and by requiring the development of the modern social welfare state, it reduces the dependence of individuals on kinship ties. Modern technical education and modern means of mass communication such as television modify or displace older systems of socialization. Literacy becomes practically universal, and vast numbers of people acquire a rudimentary knowledge of modern science. New standards of intellectual competence come to the fore, displacing older notions of wisdom or ability. Windows open onto the wider world. Narrow ethnic loyalties tend to give way to a more lively sense of the unity of mankind. Economic or class divisions, always important, begin to cut more sharply across the older ethnic lines of cleavage. People gradually learn to see each other as individual members of a worldwide "family of man" and to recognize their own interest in upholding a common set of basic rights for all.

More than two hundred years ago, in *The Spirit of the Laws*, the great Montesquieu provided the classic statement of this "liberal"—also "Marxist"—view of the dependence of ethnic loyalties and political progress upon economic development. "Commerce cures destructive prejudices," he wrote, as he began the second half (Parts 4 to 6) of his monumental investigation into the laws governing human society. Scattered through his mighty book are all the most important reasons people now give for expecting commercial societies to be relatively just and peaceful. Trade in goods can only with difficulty be separated from the exchange of lore and opinions among the traders, Montesquieu points out, and so trade, generally speaking, fosters skepticism about the demands made by one's own laws and customs. Commerce itself encourages certain values (frugality, economy, moderation, work, tranquillity, order, and rule, for example) that may clash with the more warlike values typically promoted by military or ecclesiastical elites. Written codes of law become more important and more detailed as the growth of commerce produces new conflicts of interest that cannot be resolved by appeal to traditional norms. Commerce habituates people in the careful consideration of their own interests; they become traders with each other, within as well as between their traditional ethnic groupings. Traditions of hospitality and civic virtue may suffer because commerce encourages an exact sense of justice and attention to one's own interests, but at the same time vast numbers of people are being bound together in new and wider networks of reciprocal dependence. As Montesquieu put it, "the natural effect of commerce is to lead to peace."[1]

But this is preposterous, I sense some readers trying to protest. Hasn't Montesquieu's theory been disproved by events? Commerce has grown enormously since the eighteenth century, but the world has become more violent. Indeed, the twentieth century has probably witnessed more suffering from nationalist wars and other eruptions of ethnic violence than any previous century, and not just because technology has made warfare more destructive. Since the eighteenth century, aggressive nationalism and a racism closely akin to it have been added to the older causes of war. These new factors seem to have grown with commerce, and they have generated conflicts within as well as between states. Some of their internal effects have been even more horrible than traditional wars. Millions of innocent people have been deliberately killed in order to "cleanse" national populations. Some great states have broken apart because of the rivalries among their constituent nationalities, or bloody civil wars have been fought to keep them together. The former Soviet Union, long regarded by many as a model of national as well as class harmony, now seems to have been a cauldron of ethnic conflicts temporarily contained by brutal repression and forced ideological enthusiasm. The former Yugoslavia shows that socialism—even workers' control of factories—is no permanent cure for ethnic conflict. But neither backwardness nor socialism nor even totalitarian communism, alone or in combination, can be blamed for ethnic conflict, since it can be found almost everywhere. Warring tribes can be found in Northern Ireland as well as sub-Saharan Africa. Fundamentalism and extremism are major forces not just in the Punjab or in the Middle East but in the United States. Separatist movements such as the movement for Quebec's independence threaten the existence of otherwise stable, peaceful, and prosperous democracies. Even Switzerland, the very model of a modern multinational state peacefully integrating rival nationalities on a commercial basis, has in recent years experienced problems because of prejudice against its "foreign workers."[2]

How should this objection be judged? Some will readily accept it at face value: the facts, they will say, disprove Montesquieu's theory. Case closed! Next hypothesis! Others will be reluctant to dismiss such an eminent theorist so abruptly. Despite the shocking convulsions in some parts of the world, they may say, there is obviously much less prejudice and discrimination now, generally speaking, than there used to be. Perhaps Montesquieu was right to anticipate that the growth of commerce would reduce ethnic prejudice.[3]

Montesquieu's position is certainly more defensible than it may seem at first glance. His generalizations about commerce and prejudice serve his larger purpose, one can say, and they should not be taken out of context. They isolate tendencies and were never meant to be treated as statistical hypotheses—still less taken as a panacea: the more commerce, the less prejudice. Montesquieu may have been a "normative" theorist, but he was not pushing commerce the way some hucksters push headache tablets or, on another channel, salvation. Rather, he was trying to understand the laws of human society, and this meant that he had to try to judge the various goals that different societies have put before themselves. Those that put commercial prosperity ahead of military glory, it seems obvious, will not be as warlike as the ones that are more militaristic. In a commercial culture, the virus of hatred will not be nurtured the way it is in more primitive or religious cultures, which put more value on personal honor or fidelity to religious dogma. Could this generalization not, indeed, be called a "law" of politics? Was it not Montesquieu's basic purpose to isolate just such laws?

Montesquieu began *The Spirit of the Laws* with two broad declarations: that "laws are the necessary relations deriving from the nature of things" and that "all beings have their laws: the divinity has its laws, the material world has its laws, the intelligences superior to man have their laws, the beasts have their laws, man has his laws." Montesquieu's basic idea of law was that of an invariable rule of coexistence or succession in a constantly changing world. "Every diversity is *uniformity*, every change is *consistency*," he wrote (Montesquieu, 1989, p. 4). Among the many rules governing the behavior of intelligent beings he included the laws such beings make for themselves, but behind or before these "positive" laws he assumed that there must be more "primitive" laws that they did not make. The most basic of these laws for mankind, he said, are the so-called laws of nature that governed the behavior of human beings before the establishment of societies.

In this connection, Montesquieu distinguished four elementary motivational or emotional tendencies in human nature—shyness or a tendency to flee from strangers, desire for nourishment, sexual attraction, and sociability in the sense of a desire to share experiences and gain knowledge. Society is built upon these elementary inclinations, he said, and it gives rise to its own propensities for social rivalry and war. Positive laws attempt to harmonize all these conflicting tendencies. Societies have different laws and customs because human beings are finite intelligent beings: they can learn from experience, but they are also subject to error. Different people have different experiences (the necessary effects of dissimilar climates, terrains, histories, and so on), and they draw different conclusions from their experiences, even when these are similar. In fact, human beings show a kind of freakish inventiveness. It is no easy task, then, to analyze their behavior in society. One must look for natural laws or underlying regularities in their behavior, it seems, but these laws will be hard to find and difficult to state properly, for they will always be obscured by the more visible and less orderly outgrowth of positive laws and customs, as the branches of trees are sometimes hidden by the foliage they support.

Difficulties of this sort may well impede the advance of science, I hear some methodologists muttering, but they should not be allowed to halt its progress. Investigators using modern statistical techniques can now, with the help of computers, detect underlying regularities in social data despite errors of measurement (due perhaps to conventions of classification) and very confusing surface variation. A contemporary social scientist schooled in the statistical methods of sociology or economics may therefore have little patience with Montesquieu's hesitant, almost playful attitude toward empirical hypotheses. It is antiscientific, he or she may complain, to put so much emphasis on complexity and surface variation. Empirical hypotheses should be clearly stated and then tested. If the data do not support them, they should be scrapped. Nothing is gained by indulging obviously false or oversimplified generalizations. Montesquieu illustrates the crucial weakness of much "classic political theory": rhetoric is allowed to trump evidence. Excuses somehow carry more weight than observations. Good anecdotes get more attention than sound inferences, and valuable time is wasted exploring statistical backwaters or eddies. Bookish investigators like Montesquieu, rummaging in libraries, come up with strange stories to illustrate remote possibilities, lending plausibility to false hypotheses. Theirs is precisely the kind of quasi-empirical reasoning, a zealous social scientist might well conclude, that *scientific* social science must relegate to the museum of scientific antiquities.

These imaginary disagreements indicate the major themes of the following investigation of ethnic conflict and the contact hypothesis. Only its indirect approach still requires a brief explanation.

Ethnic conflict brings to mind horrible examples far away—in the Balkans or in the heart of Africa—where civilization seems to have collapsed and people again learned what savagery really means. Can simple theories about contact and conflict throw any light on such extreme situations? It seems almost laughable to think of testing the contact hypothesis in the midst of civil war and genocide. Intuitively one looks to religion or to psychiatry for insights into the murky or fiery depths of human nature that are revealed by these horrors. Conventional social science seems powerless before such bewildering phenomena.

Indeed, a profound skepticism about modern empirical social science may result from contemplating its relation to the most disturbing events of our time. The social scientists fiddle while Rome burns, one of their harsher critics once suggested. Their aping of "scientific method" often seems senseless. Can social scientists really *measure* such things as ethnic hatred and violence? What about factors such as history, ideology, culture, personality, leadership, and technology? Surely these cannot be reduced to numbers and taken into account "objectively," using rigorous statistical methods (including factor analysis or causal modeling?) to show their importance. What about long-term trends—are samples of corpses to be raised from the dead to fill out questionnaires? The old-fashioned "casual" empiricism practiced by Montesquieu and his predecessors may have some limitations, but the modern rigorous or systematic empiricism promoted by most social science methodologists has others equally grave. The primary empirical question outlined above—what is the relation between the long-term growth of commerce and the growth or decline of destructive ethnic prejudice?—may be so broad and vague, and so far beyond the reach of any rigorous method, that it may have to be answered on the basis simply of personal insight and experience. Strictly speaking, it may be unanswerable. At the very least it seems to be entangled with difficult secondary questions of theory and method in the social sciences.

Given these difficulties, an indirect approach may in the end produce the best results. Milder conflicts and injustices closer to home, the familiar, even banal versions of the more intense conflicts elsewhere, may provide the best basis for thinking clearly about the nature and causes of ethnic

conflict (compare Billig, 1995). The pattern they suggest—one we somehow already know but have difficulty stating clearly—may hold generally.
In short, some of the disagreements among social scientists about ethnic
conflict may be resolved in a reasonable way by paying close attention to
our simpler intuitions and observations and by carefully considering some
fresh evidence provided by statistical studies of hostile ethnic attitudes
close to home.

My approach to ethnic conflict will be through a minor subdiscipline
of sociology and social psychology, namely, studies of the contact hypothesis. Like most social science hypotheses, the contact hypothesis has many
forms, some more cautious and qualified, others simpler and bolder. It has
no generally recognized source and no truly authoritative statement. Social
scientists almost always emphasize the need for care when stating or applying it. Contact is a necessary condition, they point out, not just for
friendly relations between groups, but also for hostility and violence. Nonetheless, the root idea of the contemporary contact hypothesis is very simple: more contact between individuals belonging to antagonistic social
groups tends to undermine negative stereotypes and thus to reduce prejudice and improve intergroup relations. In relations between groups, familiarity can breed friendliness and appreciation. Commercial exchange,
to the extent that it promotes personal acquaintance, should cure destructive prejudices.

During the past fifty years there have been many careful empirical studies of the contact hypothesis. There is now a substantial literature in sociology and social psychology reporting the results of these studies. A
theory has developed to make sense of them. It is a good example of what
social scientists sometimes call "theory of the middle range." Between the
minor working hypotheses that guide day-to-day research in the social sciences and the "grand" or "classic" social theories provided by speculative
thinkers concerned with every aspect of human society and every phase of
its development, there are a variety of more modest but still far-reaching
theories, many of them now "middle aged," that deserve and get attention.
They consist, according to a classic formulation, not of "general orienta-
tions toward data, suggesting types of variables which need somehow to
be taken into account," but rather of "clear, verifiable statements of relationships between specified variables" (Merton, 1957, p. 9). The theory of
the contact hypothesis is arguably a good example of these middling theories—less than a master conceptual scheme but more than just a simple
hypothesis, yet distinctly empirical in character. Current thinking about
ethnic conflict has been deeply influenced by it. I shall contrast it with three
other theories of similar scope and character, two drawn from social psychology and one from political science. Particularly important, in the end,

will be the theory from political science, which shows how economic development can cause ethnic conflict. By examining all these theories in the light of detailed research that reveals some surprisingly clear empirical uniformities, I shall try to show how the exploration of "higher abstractions" can sometimes be usefully linked to the careful handling of statistical details.

The argument of this book, then, is that studies inspired and directed by the principles of modern empirical social science permit a more definite and rather different answer to the main empirical question above than Montesquieu was able to give on the basis of the evidence available to him. Studies designed to clarify the effects of contact on ethnic prejudice are a surprisingly good source of new, relevant facts. But these studies also clearly show the difficulties of "naturalism" or "empiricism"—the scientific search for causes—in the social sciences. I shall discuss these difficulties at length later, in order to put the main findings of this research in the right perspective.

Ethnic conflict is a huge problem discussed in many disciplines from many different angles. There is no shortage of either empirical materials, particularly case studies, or competing explanatory theories. Unfortunately, no attempt can be made here to survey the abundant empirical literature on ethnic conflict around the world, nor can most of the relevant theoretical literature in sociology, anthropology, and political science be given the attention it deserves. Instead, attention will be focused on a single concept: contact. A single thread of reasoning will be followed to a conclusion. This may seem an unpromising strategy for understanding such a vast and complicated problem, but what more can be said in its defense at this point? The proof of the pudding is in the eating? All roads lead to Rome?

The road we shall follow starts from the assumption that social science theories about prejudice and discrimination offer many insights into the causes and consequences of ethnic conflict.[4] Our task, as the following outline of the book suggests, will be to find a way of stating these insights that is consistent with all that we know from history and our own experience about ethnic conflict.

Chapter 1 begins by explaining the contact hypothesis more fully. The most frequently quoted statement of the hypothesis, provided more than forty years ago by Gordon Allport, says that prejudice may be reduced by equal-status contact between majority and minority groups with common goals, especially when this contact is sanctioned by law or custom (Allport, 1954, p. 281). In short, Allport recognizes that contact has complex effects and prescribes how an analysis of these effects should be conducted: by distinguishing different types of contact that may have different effects in different circumstances. The main conditions for positive effects of contact are now generally thought to be (a) equality of status of the different groups, (b) their cooperative interdependence in the pursuit of common goals, and (c) the presence of supportive social norms. This "contact theory" has clear practical implications: it suggests that contact should be encouraged when it can be expected to have good effects and minimized where it is likely to have bad effects. To the extent possible, situations of contact that increase prejudice (for example, situations of inequality or competition) should be changed into situations in which contact has good effects (situations of equality and cooperation). These are practically important suggestions.

The contact hypothesis cannot be fully understood, however, until its theoretical context and the terms used in stating it are clearly understood. It is not just an isolated empirical generalization or a small set of such generalizations using familiar terms. The major principles underlying the contact hypothesis, like those of any theory, become clearer when they are set alongside the principles of rival theories. Thus the second half of Chapter 1 outlines two alternatives—realistic conflict theory and social identity theory—in order to clarify the ways of thinking about ethnic conflict associated with the contact hypothesis.[5] Throughout the chapter, considerable attention is paid to questions of terminology: a comparison of theories thus begins to resemble a dictionary of the ideas accepted by those who study prejudice and discrimination professionally.

Chapters 2 and 3 shift attention from the words of social scientists to the things they study—what others say and do. These chapters review the existing empirical literature on the effects of contact, sticking close to home. Some "inductive" familiarity with relevant facts may be the best basis for a fruitful discussion of the merits and shortcomings of rival theories. Indeed, sometimes the most important facts come to light only if we temporarily bracket competing explanatory hypotheses and let ourselves be guided simply by the facts.

Chapter 2 examines the great social experiment that began with the 1954 decision of the United States Supreme Court in *Brown v. Board of Education*, which struck down the "separate but equal" principle of American public education. In the years since 1954, contact between black and white children has increased substantially. What effect has this increased contact had on relevant ethnic (or "racial") attitudes? More than one hundred quantitative studies have attempted to answer this simple empirical question. The controversy surrounding school desegregation and busing is the single most important source of research on the contact hypothesis. Unfortunately, no attempt can be made in Chapter 2 to review all the relevant studies in detail. Not only are they very numerous, but many are unpublished. Chapter 2 is thus limited to offering a review of reviews, but such a review clearly establishes that no simple conclusion about the effects of contact on attitudes can be drawn from the available studies. As a social experiment, therefore, school desegregation has failed in this limited sense.

Chapter 3 reviews the remaining quantitative literature on the contact hypothesis, excluding the studies of school desegregation and similar studies of children and adolescents. The remaining studies fall into three broad groups: studies of interaction, studies of proximity, and studies of proportions. This simple scheme is explained; typical studies in each category are described; the main findings of all the studies are summarized; and the most important exceptions or anomalies are noted. More than 150 studies are summarized, and they yield a simple pattern. Moving from studies of interaction through studies of proximity to studies of proportions, the correlation between contact and ethnic prejudice changes sign. Initially negative, it becomes positive. Should this change be explained by methodological factors (that is, defects in research design), or does it have to do with a shift from the individual to the aggregate level of analysis? Can it be explained by contact theory?

Chapter 4 resumes the theoretical discussion of the contact hypothesis. As noted above, contact theory tries to account for different correlations between contact and ethnic prejudice by distinguishing situations of contact. Chapter 4 argues that the theory's two main situational variables, equality of status and cooperative interdependence, are difficult to operationalize and may in the end serve only to throw a confusing light on the patterns they are meant to explain. The competing theories, emphasizing real conflicts of interest between groups and holding that different laws govern interpersonal and intergroup behavior, are more helpful. Their "realism" is valuable, and so is their suggestion that different levels of analysis be clearly distinguished. A simple example is used to illustrate the well known but frequently neglected principle that different statistical relations can exist between the same variables at different levels of analysis.

Chapter 5 revives and revises a "competition theory" of ethnic conflict to clarify the importance of the interpersonal-intergroup distinction. The theory is Karl Deutsch's "communications theory of national development" (Deutsch, 1954, 1966, 1969, 1979). Deutsch outlined a "linguistic" model of nationalism that can be generalized in order to explain conflict based on other cultural traits. A new model, whose main variables are contact, cultural differences, and ethnocentrism, is presented as a means to overcome some of the standard objections to Deutsch's analysis of nationalism and to put the empirical research on the contact hypothesis in a more satisfactory theoretical framework. The model makes clear why contact may have quite different effects at the individual and the aggregate levels of analysis.

The last two chapters tackle some of the broader issues raised by the need to choose between conventional contact theory and the proposed linguistic model of ethnic conflict. How should social science theories be understood? The model suggests an interpretation of the contact hypothesis quite different from the one provided by contact theory. Ethnic conflict may be better understood, and perhaps better managed, I shall try to make clear, if the desire to understand it is allowed to take priority over the felt need to eliminate its evils quickly from our society.

Chapter 6 discusses statistical testing as a basis for choosing between rival theories. The statistical methods that could in principle be used to test contact theory and the linguistic model of ethnic conflict are briefly explained, and their limitations are made clear. Skepticism about statistical reasoning as a foundation for the social sciences is of course nothing new: indeed, in the past generation it has become once again a mark of sophistication among social scientists. More data are being analyzed and more statistics calculated than ever before, but with a less aggressive faith than formerly in "scientific method." Social scientists are perhaps more open today than they were a generation ago to the insights of their critics. Philosophers using the history of the natural sciences to show the limitations of positivism have persuaded some social scientists to adopt a "critical" or "hermeneutic" orientation methodologically. Rival theories cannot really be evaluated, many now say, without reckoning with their practical political implications. Statistical "goodness of fit" is not the only or even a very important criterion of acceptability. Social life is not independent of its theoretical interpretations, it seems, nor does theory dwell in some ivory tower above the hurly-burly of politics. Social scientists are not just holding up mirrors to nature. They are not just objective spectators of events: they are value-loaded participants in a vast process of social transformation and the conquest of nature. Their active role in this process needs to be critically examined.

Perhaps it remains true, however, that broad admonitions to "think critically" are of little help unless they are accompanied by cogent illustrations. "A critical attitude needs for its raw materials, as it were, theories or beliefs which are held more or less dogmatically" (Popper, 1962, p. 50).

Chapter 7 brings together these various lines of argument and draws some conclusions about the nature or causes of ethnic conflict and the limitations of contemporary social science theories about it. Montesquieu may well have been too sanguine about the pacifying effects of the growth of commerce, I shall conclude, but his twentieth-century successors, despite their better data and more powerful computers, have yet to overcome the limitations of his perspective. Indeed, these limitations now seem to be built into our culture.

1 Defining Terms

Much confusion results from trying to reason about complicated matters of fact without paying sufficient attention to the words we use to describe our thoughts and impressions. "Define your terms!" is an old injunction as valid now as when Thomas Hobbes wrote, "A man that seeketh precise truth had need to remember what every name he uses stands for, and to place it accordingly, or else he will find himself entangled in words, as a bird in lime twigs, the more he struggles the more belimed" (Hobbes, 1960, p. 21). Yet to grasp the meaning of general terms, especially the most general terms in our language (such as *truth* and *meaning*), is no easy task. Philosophers from Socrates to Wittgenstein have advised friendly argument or a dialectical approach to their clarification. A "scientific" approach emphasizing clear stipulations, undeniable facts, and strict deductions easily becomes narrow and dogmatic when it is not simply powerless. The present investigation starts slowly, therefore, with an attempt to restate what others have said about contact and conflict. Too much of a good thing can be wearisome, however, and readers who find their attention wandering after the explanation of the contact hypothesis should jump to Chapter 2. The remainder of this chapter will remain conveniently available as a reference.

Ethnic Conflict

Adults are rarely puzzled when they see children fighting over toys. They may be frustrated or annoyed, they may even lose their patience and rebuke the little ones too harshly, or they may be amused as they watch them squabbling over their possessions. But there is nothing very mysterious or perplexing about what is going on. The conflict—the crying, shouting, and hitting—has a simple explanation: it is rooted in conflicting desires to own or use particular things. There are similar conflicts in adult life—between homeowners and burglars, for example, or between separating spouses—when there are no generally accepted rules to govern the division of valued things or when these rules are no longer respected. Even two lovers sharing a dessert after a wonderful meal at a beautiful restaurant may feel tiny twinges of conflict as they each eye the last bit of the chef's art on the plate between them. Conflicts of material interests sometimes end in violence, on a small scale with children, on a larger scale with adults. But no one finds them very puzzling.

Ethnic conflict—the adult equivalent of shouting and hitting, between ethnic groups—is often more puzzling because it is less "realistic." Ethnic groups are sets of individuals distinguished from one another by their cultural identities and characteristics. Thus different groups speak different languages, wear different clothes, eat different foods, tell different stories, cultivate different virtues, have different courtship rituals and kinship rules, worship different gods or worship the same one differently, and so on. Such groups sometimes fight over the possession of land or other natural resources (water, oil, fish) or over jobs or housing, but the most typical ethnic conflicts seem to have remarkably little to do with clashing material or economic interests. They center on conflicting desires for more intangible goods such as power, respect, or social status. Unlike children, ethnic groups are disposed to fight about abstractions such as recognition and identity. Their conflicts may appear to arise out of, or at least they are closely connected with, their distorted images of each other. Negative stereotypes are a problem in relations among ethnic groups, and deep emotions, reflected in painful embarrassments, extreme opinions, and unpredictable explosions of anger, seem to be the most striking feature of ethnic conflicts. Human nature shows itself at its most primitive in the unbelievable brutality of some ethnic conflicts. But ethnic conflicts can also be surprisingly quiet and peaceful. A pattern of social discrimination involving little or no violence may be the most important manifestation of an ethnic conflict. In short, there is something strange, even mysterious about ethnic conflict, unlike class conflict or other conflicts of economic interests, which are more open to inspection, more compatible with reasonableness, and much easier to understand.

Contact

Global commerce has grown enormously in the past century or two, and it continues to grow, drawing people everywhere into larger and more complicated networks of exchange. Contact among different peoples or ethnic groups is increasing. The world is shrinking, and we are now living in a global village. What effects flow from the growing-shrinking-globalizing trend of recent decades? Should we expect it to reduce ethnic prejudice and discrimination? Has it tended to pacify relations among ethnic groups? In fact, in our present age of global technology and electronic enlightenment, ethnic conflict seems to have become a bigger problem than it was a generation ago or even a century ago.

Among the theories offering insights into these trends, the most directly relevant is "contact theory," which derives from the contact hypothesis. The work of Gordon Allport, who was a professor of psychology at Harvard University from 1930 to 1967, best represents this theory. For the past forty years almost all discussions of the contact hypothesis have followed the lines laid down in his magisterial study *The Nature of Prejudice* (Allport, 1954).[1] Allport did not invent contact theory; he did not even try to explain what he meant by contact, apart from distinguishing a great many different types of it. His achievement was rather to systematize and consolidate an existing body of research and theorizing. Since 1954 other writers have modified some details of Allport's framework or stated its principles in their own words. But a review and critique of contact theory can best begin with Allport's book, which will be examined in some detail.

Prejudice and Reason

Contact theory rests upon a definition of prejudice that sharply distinguishes it from the negative attitudes resulting from realistic conflicts. Allport begins his book by describing some easily recognizable examples of prejudice—nasty comments about blacks by white Rhodesians, similar comments about (white) Americans by West Indians and Englishmen, complaints about Ukrainians by Poles or about Poles by Germans, and so on. No corner of the world, it seems, is free from "group scorn," since we are all "fettered to our respective cultures" and so "are bundles of prejudice" (Allport, 1954, p. 4).

Allport highlights two essential features of the examples he cites: (1) hostility toward and rejection of individuals and (2) faulty, unwarranted generalizations about groups. A third feature sets prejudice, in the precise sense, apart from ordinary unfavorable prejudgments, namely, its incorrigibility. Unlike simple misconceptions, prejudices resist the evidence that would unseat them. Prejudiced people get emotional when their preconceptions are threatened with contradiction. "Thus the difference between ordinary prejudgments and prejudice is that one can discuss and rectify a prejudgment without emotional resistance" (p. 9). Allport combines these three essential features in his formal definition of prejudice: "Ethnic prejudice is an antipathy based upon a faulty and inflexible generalization. It may be felt or expressed. It may be directed toward a group as a whole, or toward an individual because he is a member of that group" (p. 9). The most important effect of prejudice, he points out, is to place the individuals against whom it is directed at some disadvantage not merited by their own misconduct. Like any sensible definition of an obscure but widely used term, Allport's definition of prejudice takes account of the term's everyday use.

The remaining chapters of *The Nature of Prejudice* try to explain why individuals tend to accept, to cling to, and to act upon unwarranted, unfavorable generalizations about groups when dealing with individuals. These chapters provide a practically oriented analysis of a dangerous and unpleasant form of human irrationality.

The analysis begins with a chapter recognizing that human beings live in groups that speak different languages, adhere to different customs, and honor different values. Such differences lead people to associate with their own kind, a tendency that need not be ascribed to a "gregarious instinct" or a "consciousness of kind." Nor need it be ascribed to prejudice. "The fact is adequately explained by the principles of ease, least effort, congeniality, and pride in one's own culture" (p. 19). Difficulties arise, however, when individuals with limited experience outside their own groups try to generalize about the characteristics of other groups. Lacking relevant experience, they easily exaggerate the differences between themselves and others and readily misunderstand the reasons for them. Living apart, linked by few channels of communication, they create real conflicts on the basis of imaginary differences.

When there are genuine conflicts of interest between groups, however, the resulting antipathies are not prejudices. When defining prejudice Allport had carefully distinguished it from realistic social conflict. The negative views of Nazis held by most Americans during World War II, for example, were not prejudices, because the Nazi party had evil policies: "True, there may have been good individuals in the party who at heart rejected the abominable program; but the probability was so high that the Nazi group constituted an actual menace to world peace and to humane values that a realistic and justified conflict resulted" (p. 8). Likewise, gangsters suffer from the justified hostility of good citizens, not from the prejudices of bigots, for the evidence of their antisocial conduct is conclusive. Ex-convicts represent a true borderline case. There is some justified hostility and some irrational prejudice. Many prisoners are never reformed, so it may make sense to refuse a man employment who has a criminal record, "but there is also an element of unwarranted prejudgment involved" (p. 8).

Allport also recognizes the obvious connection between affirming one way of life and denigrating a rival one, since the affirmation alone takes us "to the brink of prejudice": "As partisans of our own way of life, we cannot help thinking in a partisan manner. Only a small portion of our reasoning is what psychologists have called 'directed thinking,' that is, controlled exclusively by outer evidence and focused upon the solution of objective problems. Whenever feeling, sentiment, values enter we are prone to engage in 'free,' 'wishful,' or 'fantasy' thinking. Such partisan thinking is entirely natural, for our job in this world is to live in an integrated way as value-seekers. Prejudgments stemming from these values enable us to do so" (p. 25). Many examples might suggest that negative opinions of others are just reflexes of our own cultural commitments, and although clashes of interests and values do occur on this basis, they are not in themselves instances of prejudice (pp. 26, 229, 352, 444–46). Prejudice in the true sense begins when our natural partisanship threatens other people's interests or safety. The basic "love-prejudice" toward our own way of life gives rise to a reciprocal "hate-prejudice" when the dislike of outsiders goes beyond what is rationally justifiable, as it often does, according to Allport, in wartime. An enemy who threatens our "positive values" makes us "stiffen our resistance and exaggerate the merits of our cause." If we did not feel that we were wholly right, we could not marshal all our energies for our defense. "And if we are wholly right then the enemy must be wholly wrong. Since he is wholly wrong, we should not hesitate to exterminate him." There may be such things as "just wars"—ones in which the threats to our values are genuine and must be resisted—yet even in these cases there is some degree of prejudice. "The very existence of a severe threat causes one to perceive the enemy country as wholly evil, and every citizen therein as a menace. Balance and discrimination become impossible" (p. 27).

Prejudice is an enormous practical problem because balanced and discriminating thinking about groups is surprisingly rare.

Why is this so? Allport's answer is long and complicated. Underlying much of the discussion, however, is a simple contrast between two kinds of thinking, one more efficient, the other less so. The first kind of thinking is "realistic," the second, "autistic."

The aim of all thinking, according to Allport, is to anticipate and adjust to reality. "By thinking we try to foresee consequences and plan actions that will avoid whatever threatens us and will bring our hopes and dreams to pass" (p. 167). An individual who does this efficiently, taking the objectively known properties of stimulus objects into account and advancing along his way to important goals in life, is said to reason. "He may, of course, make errors in his reasoning, but still if the total direction is realistically oriented, we affirm the basically rational character of his thought" (p. 168). This normal, problem-solving process is called "directed thinking."

As this summary suggests, the problem solved by directed thinking need not be the attainment of the most "objective" possible description of every possible stimulus object. Good thinking has to help the individual achieve his goals, and this may sometimes require the support and cooperation of others. Agreeing with their prejudices may sometimes be a practical way of getting them to cooperate. "Common prejudices create common bonds," as Allport points out (p. 154).

Moreover, an individual who thinks a lot about some stimulus object without any practical, realistic engagement with it is likely to think inefficiently. Allport calls this less rational form of mental activity "autistic thinking." Our minds run on, turning over one idea after another, in a kind of daydream, without making any progress whatsoever toward any definite goal. Problems may seem to get solved, but the successes are only imaginary.

In autistic thinking, since there is no practical engagement with reality, private obsessions easily come to the surface and color perceptions. The resulting biases and distortions are generally accompanied by rationalizations. People do not like to admit that their "free" thinking, which is not checked by any practical engagement with reality, is prejudiced and autistic, so they cook up some respectable reasons for their strange opinions. They offer plausible reasons for their opinions rather than the real reasons. And as Allport admits, "it is not possible always to distinguish between reasoning and rationalization, especially between *errors* in reasoning and rationalization." Rationalizations frequently look very much like reasons. "They tend to conform to some accepted social canons. . . . [And] they tend to approximate as closely as possible the canons of accepted logic" (p. 169).

Inefficient thinking about ethnic groups could, in principle, produce many different unreasonable (though carefully rationalized) theories about them, some "positive," others "negative," and still others just strange. But for a great variety of reasons explained in detail by Allport, such thinking generally produces hostile stereotypes that are used to justify discriminatory behavior. (Favorable attitudes and friendly behavior tend to be the result of realistic thinking and accurate perceptions.) The basic fact about intergroup prejudice is that people often jump to unfavorable conclusions about groups to which they do not belong. (That is what prejudice is, by definition.) People seem to think that because, in strict logic, an "in-group" always implies a contrasting "out-group," they cannot be loyal to one without denigrating the other. They fail to see that humanity is a possible in-group for all human beings and that loyalty to humanity can override the narrower loyalties to its conflicting parts, which cause so much trouble today (compare pp. 41–46).

Restricted Communication

An article by Theodore Newcomb (Newcomb, 1947), cited by Allport, throws some light on his reasons for thinking that inefficient thinking tends to produce negative "hate-prejudice" rather than positive "love-prejudice." Newcomb separates social relations in which communication is spontaneous and unrestricted from relations in which it is inhibited and incomplete. In situations of restricted communication, he argues, our hostile impulses tend to be projected onto those we know only slightly, and the result is the development of hostile attitudes, which are rationalized by mistaken beliefs about the aggressive intentions of the unknown others. Newcomb contends that the hostile attitudes will change only if the mistaken beliefs are corrected. When channels of communication are opened, the hostile person discovers that his "enemies" do not, in fact, wish him harm, and he comes to see the aggressiveness in his own behavior. As a result, he becomes less defensive and less hostile. The same remedy applies, according to Newcomb, in the case of intergroup hostilities: "The shared defensiveness of hostility toward others as members of groups is essentially like the private defensiveness of inter-personal hostility" (Newcomb, 1947, p. 78). Institutionalized barriers to communication, such as segregation and discrimination, guarantee that each group's impressions of other groups will be shaped more by its own psychic needs than by the demands of reality. In particular, such barriers encourage the projection of hostility onto out-groups. Hostile stereotyping flourishes. Hostile opinions rationalize the segregation and discrimination that are themselves essential conditions for channeling hostility into intergroup conflict. (According to a recent account of this process, "the result is a self-amplifying cycle of antagonism, separation, and unrealistically negative attributions," Rothbart and John, 1993, p. 33.) In order to reduce hostility, the barriers to communication between the groups must be broken down so that each group can form a realistic view of the intentions and characteristics of the other groups.

Allport follows Newcomb, arguing that casual, impersonal contacts encourage hostile stereotyping, whereas prolonged, personal contacts make people aware of their common humanity. High levels of prejudice can coexist with frequent contact only when the contact is impersonal: in the southern states, for example, the contact between blacks and whites has been arrested at the stage of fleeting, impersonal encounters. To reduce prejudice it would be necessary for the members of each group to have a chance to know the members of the other group intimately, as individuals. The practical problem of contact, therefore, is to distinguish the conditions under which greater proximity and more frequent interaction will lead to genuine acquaintance, followed by a reduction of prejudice, from the conditions under which proximity and interaction will just encourage stereotyping.

Types and Situations of Contact

In a chapter titled "The Effect of Contact" Allport begins by noting the need for a theory of contact that will go beyond the simplest contact hypothesis. "It has sometimes been held that merely by assembling people without regard for race, color, religion, or national origin, we can thereby destroy stereotypes and develop friendly attitudes" (p. 261). But the case is not so simple, as he says. There may indeed be a tendency for groups to progress peacefully from sheer *contact* through *competition* to *accommodation* and then finally to *assimilation*, but "this progression is far from being a universal law." Whether the law will hold "seems to depend on the *nature of the contact* that is established." The effects of contact "obviously" depend upon "the kind of association that occurs, and upon the kinds of persons who are involved" (pp. 261–62). Allport then distinguishes roughly thirty independent variables that could be used to define different types or situations of contact and that ideally deserve study, "both separately and in combination," but he focuses on the simple dichotomy between casual contact and true acquaintance.

Casual contact is the kind that is practically inescapable whenever two or more groups live intermingled in a common territory. People's paths cross, and they come to know each other at least superficially, exchanging goods and sometimes more; but they will never get beyond superficial knowledge of each other, Allport points out, if they are segregated in daily life or else "firmly frozen into superordinate-subordinate relationships." Mere proximity without familiarity, jostling in stores and in subways, just brings stereotypes to mind.[2] Indeed, the evidence suggests that casual contact increases prejudice rather than dispelling it. Allport cites a number of studies showing that prejudice increases directly with the numerical density of a minority group. He endorses a "sociocultural law" relating the probability of ethnic conflict to minority density (pp. 227–29). With respect to casual contact, then, the rule seems to be "the more contact the more trouble" (p. 263).

True acquaintance is the second major type of contact, and in contrast to casual contact, research shows that it lessens prejudice. Allport summarizes a questionnaire study of student attitudes in Georgia (Gray and Thompson, 1953) that is discussed in Chapter 3. After summarizing a number of similar studies, Allport concludes that "contacts that bring knowledge and acquaintance are likely to engender sounder beliefs concerning minority groups, and for this reason contribute to the reduction of prejudice" (p. 268).

Allport then reviews the literature on residential, occupational, and social (or "goodwill") contact, making the basic point that simply living or working side by side with minorities is much less important than the forms of communication that result from such proximity. For example, the studies of public housing, also discussed in Chapter 3, lend no support to the idea that integrated housing automatically solves the problem of prejudice. Integration does, however, create a situation in which friendly contacts and accurate social perceptions can develop. By removing barriers to effective communication, it encourages the reduction of fallacious stereotypes and the substitution of a realistic view for one of fear and autistic hostility. "There is ordinarily a net gain of friendship" (p. 273).

Studies of contact on the job suggest that prejudice is created and maintained by an ethnic division of labor in which minorities occupy positions at or near the bottom of the status hierarchy. In order for contact on the job to reduce prejudice, representatives of the oppressed minority must be employed at higher occupational levels, so that the contacts between majority and minority individuals are contacts between equals or between superior "inferiors," so to speak, and inferior "superiors."

Allport's review of the literature stresses the importance of common objectives to unite the individuals in contact. "The nub of the matter seems to be that contact must reach below the surface in order to be effective in altering prejudice. Only the type of contact that leads people to *do* things together is likely to result in changed attitudes" (p. 276). This principle is best illustrated by the studies of integrated companies in the American army in World War II that are summarized below. A certain amount of segregation (by platoon) remained in these mixed companies, as Allport notes, but "still it brought the two races into close contact *on an equal footing in a common project* (of life and death importance)" (p. 277). Subsequent studies by the Research Branch of the Information and Education Division of the army showed that this contact under combat conditions had a pronounced effect on attitudes: generally speaking, cooperation with blacks in killing Germans reduced the prejudice of white Americans.

Finally, Allport recognizes that there is a personal as well as a situational factor in prejudice. Citing a study of children at an interracial summer camp that showed equal gains and losses in prejudice as a result of the camping experience, Allport stresses that "it was the anxious and the aggressive boys who failed to develop tolerance as a result of their equal-status contact with Negro boys" (p. 280). The relation between contact and prejudice is at best a statistical rule: even equal-status contact in the pursuit of common goals does not reduce prejudice among all the individuals concerned, since some personalities resist the effects of contact. Their personal disorders may run too deep to permit them to benefit from equal-status contact. Despite acquaintance, they *need* scapegoats.

Allport concludes his chapter on the effects of contact with a broad but carefully qualified generalization: "Prejudice (unless deeply rooted in the character structure of the individual) may be reduced by equal status contact between majority and minority groups in the pursuit of common goals. The effect is greatly enhanced if this contact is sanctioned by institutional supports (i.e., by law, custom or local atmosphere), and provided it is of a sort that leads to the perception of common interests and common humanity between members of the two groups" (p. 281). This frequently quoted passage is as close as one can get to a succinct and generally accepted statement of the contact hypothesis as understood by social scientists.

Contact Theory

Several writers had made similar points before 1954 (for example, Watson, 1947; Williams, 1947), and many have since followed in Allport's footsteps, particularly his student, Thomas Pettigrew. In fact, the reasoning just outlined is now sometimes called the "Allport-Pettigrew contact hypothesis." Like Allport, Pettigrew dismisses what may be called the layman's contact hypothesis—that if only different groups could experience more contact with each other, their relations would automatically improve. "Unfortunately, the case is not so simple," he writes (Pettigrew, 1971, p. 275). Africans and Europeans, he points out, have more contact in the Republic of South Africa than anywhere else on the African continent, and black and white Americans have more contact in the South than in any other region of the country; yet neither of these areas is conspicuous for its interracial harmony. "It almost looks as if contact between two peoples exacerbates, rather than relieves, hostility; but this conclusion would be just as hasty and fallacious as the naive assumption that contact invariably lessens prejudice." Contact must instead be seen as a factor that amplifies or reduces the effects of other factors. Its effects depend on the other factors present in the situations in which it occurs. "Increasing interaction, whether of groups or individuals, intensifies and magnifies processes already underway. Hence, more interracial contact can lead either to greater prejudice and rejection or to greater respect and acceptance, depending upon the situation in which it occurs. The basic issue, then, concerns the types of situations in which contact leads to distrust and those in which it leads to trust (p. 275)."

Pettigrew summarizes Allport's conditions for a positive effect of contact as follows: "Prejudice is lessened when the two groups (1) possess equal status, (2) seek common goals, (3) are cooperatively dependent upon each other, and (4) interact with the positive support of authorities, laws, or customs" (p. 275).

Yehuda Amir has published two useful reviews of the literature that use Allport's conditions as a framework for analysis of contact and prejudice (Amir, 1969, 1976). In them he discusses the principle of equal status, cooperative and competitive factors, casual as opposed to intimate contact, institutional support, and personality factors. Some of his observations will be discussed in more detail below. His overall conclusion is best represented by the following remark from his second review: "Most writers agree with and even stress the point that contact per se cannot be considered an unqualified tool or a general panacea for changing prejudice or promoting better intergroup relations: only in specific situations or under special conditions will intergroup contact achieve this end" (Amir, 1976, p. 286; compare Ben-Ari and Amir, 1988, pp. 153–54).

Stuart W. Cook, one of the earliest and most dedicated students of the contact hypothesis, reworked the broad question "Does intergroup contact reduce prejudice?" into the more complex question "In what types of contact situations, with what kinds of representatives of the disliked group, will interaction and attitude change of specified types occur—and how will this vary for subjects of differing characteristics?" (Cook, 1962, p. 76). With respect to the contact situation, Cook identified five major conditions: (1) the degree of proximity between the groups provided by the situation, (2) the direction and strength of the norms of one's own group within the situation with regard to intergroup association, (3) the direction and strength of the expectations with regard to intergroup association believed to characterize authority figures in the situation, (4) the relative status within the situation, and (5) the interdependence requirements of the contact situation in terms of competition and cooperation (compare Cook, 1969, pp. 186–87; Cook, 1978, p. 97; Miller and Brewer, 1984, p. 2).

Two recent reviews of the literature, Harrington and Miller (1992) and Jackson (1993), confirm the importance of the "situational" qualifications Cook and others, following Allport, have put on the simplest contact hypothesis. The first of these reviews "revisits the contact hypothesis" using the headings of cooperative interdependence, equal-status contact, stereotype disconfirmation, normative support, and acquaintance potential. The second states the "basic principles" of the hypothesis by discussing equality of status, cooperative interdependence, institutional support, invalidation of stereotypes, and interpersonal versus intergroup contact. Although generalization is hampered by "inconsistencies in conceptualizations," the research of many decades can be summed up, it seems, in a simple "law of contact"—"favorable contact tends to reduce ethnic prejudice" (Jackson, 1993, p. 56).

How to distinguish favorable from unfavorable contact is the central problem of contact theory. In the most thorough and thought-provoking of the recent reviews of the relevant literature, Walter Stephan emphasizes the shift since the early 1970s from a purely "situational" to a more "cognitive" orientation in research on the contact hypothesis: "The more recent cognitive approaches are concerned with how the information available in contact situations is processed. For the most part, the additions made to contact theory by the cognitive approach consist of explanations of ways in which biases enter into the processing of intergroup information" (Stephan, 1987, p. 18). But as Stephan shows, these more recent cognitive studies fit into an expanded "contact model" in which the main determinants of different outcomes continue to be differences in "situational antecedents" and "societal antecedents" such as "relative statuses," "goals interdependence," and "social norms and roles" (pp. 24–25; compare Stephan and Brigham, 1985, pp. 6–7). In the most recent of the reviews, Stephan and Stephan (1996), the "evidence concerning the original contact hypothesis" is summarized under the headings of cooperation, equal status, individualized contact, and support by authority figures.

As Donald Taylor and Fathali Moghaddam testify in a recent textbook, the themes of contact theory have remained unchanged for almost fifty years. "Briefly stated, intergroup contact will be associated with harmony to the extent that it involves interaction that is intimate, where there is equal status between the interlocutors, where the surrounding social climate is supportive, and where the purpose of the interaction is cooperative rather than competitive" (Taylor and Moghaddam, 1994, p. 180).

Contact theory—the contact hypothesis as understood by social scientists—is an attempt to account for different correlations between contact on one hand and ethnic attitudes and behavior on the other by distinguishing different situations of contact. Pettigrew summed up matters as follows: "My teacher, the late Gordon Allport, outlined 'the contact hypothesis' in his volume, *The Nature of Prejudice*. He pointed out that the naive belief that mere contact between groups will improve intergroup attitudes is clearly wrong. What matters are the conditions of the contact" (Pettigrew, 1991, p. 169). The most important situational variables are now generally said to be equality or inequality of status, cooperative or competitive interdependence in the pursuit of common goals, and the presence or absence of normative support.

Individualism

Contact theory is misunderstood if it is construed as a straightforward empirical hypothesis, like the layman's contact hypothesis, that could be tested by some simple observations and then accepted or rejected. As will be explained later, the theory embraces a great many empirical hypotheses. The evidence bearing on these hypotheses from surveys and experiments will be reviewed in Chapters 2 and 3. The conditions for positive effects of contact will be examined again more closely in Chapter 4, when some directly relevant evidence will be discussed in detail. The more closely the theory is examined, however, the more difficult it will be to imagine how it could possibly be falsified.

Before considering these empirical materials and this curious difficulty, the reader may wish to get a clearer idea of some standard alternatives to contact theory or the contact hypothesis. Two alternatives in particular—realistic conflict theory and social identity theory—help to clarify how it may be misleading. The most noticeable difference between these two theories and contact theory is the emphasis the former put on groups rather than individuals. Their main tenets will be explained in a moment, but first let me try to clarify what their proponents are objecting to when they object to the "individualism" of contact theory.

Character Structure.

When Allport separated ethnic prejudice from realistic group conflicts, he cut it off from any source other than the mechanisms of individual psychology. He made it necessary to find the roots of prejudice in defects of character rather than in the relations between groups. As Allport himself declared, "prejudice is ultimately a problem of personality formation and development" (Allport, 1954, p. 41).

Allport conceded that realistic conflicts of interest can cause apparently prejudiced behaviors (antilocution, avoidance, segregation, discrimination, physical attack, even extermination), but he maintained that prejudice and realistic conflict are quite different things because they have different causes. Prejudice may provide some "excess baggage" in some realistic conflicts, clouding the issues and hindering a realistic solution of the core conflict: "In group disputes it is—we must admit—exceedingly difficult to distinguish realistic conflict from prejudice proper" (p. 230). But prejudice proper is not an effect of realistic conflicts; it typically exists apart from any such conflicts. Rather than being an effect of conflict, it creates imaginary conflicts—real hatreds rationalized in terms of imaginary conflicts of interest. Contact can cure these destructive prejudices because it can show people that their stereotypes lack any basis in fact.

According to Allport, prejudice ultimately arises from such features of human nature as the tendency to overgeneralize, to misinterpret foreign customs, to hold rigidly to what is familiar, to harbor hostile feelings, to use differences as an excuse for rejection, to be greedy and unjust, and to blame others for one's own problems. The fundamental causes of prejudice thus lie deep within the human soul, and "the most momentous discovery of psychological research in the field of prejudice" he thought might be the discovery that "the cognitive processes of prejudiced people are *in general* different from the cognitive processes of tolerant people. . . . Research shows that the prejudiced person is given to two-valued judgments *in general*" (pp. 174–75). Prejudiced people, according to this account, tend to dichotomize when they think of nature, human institutions, and moral or psychological phenomena. They tend to be intolerant of ambiguity, showing a marked need for simple, definite categories. They persist in old ways of reasoning, whether or not this reasoning has anything to do with human behavior. They weave "a single and unitary style of life" from the cognitive and emotional strands of their personalities, and this style sets them apart from tolerant people. The prejudiced repress their impulses rather than consciously facing and mastering their conflicts. They fail to integrate the myriad of impulses that arise within the personality and the myriad of environmental pressures without. There are sharp cleavages between their conscious and unconscious layers. In short, they have weak egos in need of psychological crutches. "The [prejudiced] individual cannot face the world unflinchingly and in a forthright manner. He seems fearful of himself, of his own instincts, of his own consciousness, of change, and of his social environment. Since he can live in comfort neither with himself nor with others, he is forced to organize his whole style of living, including his social attitudes, to fit his crippled condition. It is not his specific social attitudes that are malformed to begin with; it is rather his own ego that is crippled" (p. 396).

Here Allport echoes the basic idea of *The Authoritarian Personality* (Adorno et al., 1950), which analyzed ethnic prejudice as the expression of "deep-lying trends in personality."[3] Allport's contact theory is now sometimes said to have encouraged a cognitive approach in studies of prejudice (Katz, 1991), but its roots are in psychodynamic theories of personality. Like the Berkeley group, and indeed like Jean-Paul Sartre (1948), Allport strove to distinguish two contrasting patterns of personality, one being that of the natural bigot who has refused to accept his own freedom, who lives inauthentically, and who uses difference as a pretext for resentful rejection of others. Allport presents ethnic prejudice as the characteristic expression of this kind of psychological disorder. Tolerance, or more positively, acceptance and approval of others, reflects the opposite, healthier condition of the psyche.

Group Position.

The most telling objection to contact theory is the same as the standard objection to the theory of the authoritarian personality, namely, that it exaggerates personality as a cause of ethnic prejudice and therefore neglects its social causes. The theory tends to make something that is very common or even normative—social prejudice—look like something quirky and unusual. The theory evidently rests upon assumptions about the nature of prejudice that deny or at least greatly downplay its collective aspects. By personalizing the problem, the theory may tend to encourage reliance upon inefficient psychotherapeutic manipulations to deal with it.

Herbert Blumer provided one of the clearest and most persuasive statements of this objection. In a justly famous article published only a few years after Allport's book appeared, and at the height of the controversy about *The Authoritarian Personality*, he raised a strong objection to their common focus on the individual. According to Blumer, "race prejudice exists basically in a sense of group position rather than in a set of feelings which members of one racial group have toward the members of another racial group" (Blumer, 1958, p. 3). Most social scientists, he conceded, approach prejudice as fundamentally a matter of individual feelings—of antipathy, hostility, hatred, intolerance, aggressiveness, and so on. But in fact, he maintained, it is a matter of the relationships among groups. Individuals belong to groups; they necessarily come to identify themselves with particular groups; and their identifications provide the framework for their prejudices. Consequently, prejudice can be understood only by investigating the process by which groups form images of themselves and others. This is fundamentally a *collective* process, not a matter of individual quirks of personality: "It operates chiefly through the public media in which individuals who are accepted as spokesmen of a racial group characterize publicly another racial group. To characterize another racial group is, by opposition, to define one's own group. This is equivalent to placing the two groups in relation to each other, or defining their positions vis-à-vis each other. It is the *sense of social position* emerging from this collective process of characterization which provides the basis of race prejudice" (pp. 3–4).

Various typical feelings develop in those belonging to a dominant group (feelings of superiority, distinctiveness, insecurity, and so on), but the sense of group position transcends the feelings of its individual members, so that "the locus of race prejudice is not in the area of individual feeling but in the definition of the respective positions of the racial groups." As already suggested, this definition occurs within the dominant group. "The process of definition occurs obviously through complex interaction and communication between the members of the dominant group" (p. 5). Its leaders and ordinary members exchange opinions about the outsiders, presenting definitions and expressing feelings. Currents of opinion and emotion sweep through the group. If there are no serious internal clashes, these currents grow, fuse, and gain strength. "It is through such a process that a collective image of the subordinate group is formed and a sense of group position is set." Thus the source of racial prejudice is to be found not in the individual, according to Blumer, but in "a complicated social process in which the individual is himself shaped and organized" (p. 6).

Group Psychologies.

Like Blumer, the theorists to be discussed in the remainder of this chapter shift attention from the individual to the group, which is said to have a reality of its own. They insist that individual behavior is profoundly affected by identification with groups and by conformity to group norms. Some even distinguish two fundamentally different kinds of behavior—interpersonal and intergroup (for example, Brown and Turner, 1981; Hewstone and Brown, 1986). Their analyses of prejudice and discrimination emphasize conflict between groups (and intergroup behavior) rather than individual irrationality (and interpersonal behavior). Without denying that contact can sometimes have beneficial effects on the attitudes of individuals, they contend that such effects are much more limited than contact theorists such as Allport and Pettigrew usually suggest. "To the extent that the contact takes place on an 'interpersonal' basis it is unlikely to modify intergroup attitudes and behaviour since the two domains are controlled . . . by different processes" (Brown and Turner, 1981, p. 60). In order to change intergroup attitudes, it seems, intergroup relations must first be changed, not just the relations between some of the individual members of each group. "Whenever the underlying structure of social divisions and power or status differentials is fairly resilient, it is not likely to be substantially affected by piecemeal attempts at reform in selected situations of 'contact' " (Tajfel, 1982, p. 29).

Realistic conflict theory and social identity theory provide competing versions of this standard criticism. Focusing as they do on groups and group loyalties or social identifications, they bring out, by contrast, the individualism of contact theory. But how exactly does a focus on groups help to explain the prejudices of individuals? Both theories point to (a) the conflicts between groups and (b) the identifications that individuals have with groups. The two theories make different assumptions about individual motives, however. Through the process of identification, they link different conflicts to different forces or elements within individual psyches. Realistic conflict theory emphasizes conflicting "realistic" interests, which are generally understood to be *material* interests. To simplify and exaggerate, realistic conflict theory suggests that groups are like children fighting over toys: they all want the same ones and they have not yet understood the need for some elementary rules. Social identity theory, by contrast, emphasizes motives having to do with self-esteem and social status. Groups, from its perspective, are more like adolescents—unsure of themselves, sensitive to slights, craving the approval of others, but apt to flare up at any restrictions on their freedom and very concerned about the social pecking order. These caricatures draw too sharp a distinction between the two theories, but they clarify a real difference. There is a simple common sense about realistic conflict theory that is lacking in social identity theory. Realistic conflict theorists point to the importance of possessions, strikes, and revolutions. Social identity theorists seem more concerned with snubs, smiles, and sneers. They seem to inhabit an orderly but uncomfortable world like that described by Rousseau: one's amour propre is continually being affronted by the disrespectful behavior of others, and conflicts have more to do with pride than with greed. Thus the intergroup conflicts in terms of which social identity theory explains individual prejudices can perhaps be linked directly to the individual distempers that Allport had in mind when he wrote about weak egos and psychological crutches.

Realistic conflict theory and social identity theory are similar in that they both shift attention from individuals to groups and both emphasize conflicts between groups, but they differ in that one is more "economic," whereas the other is more "psychological." The following brief summaries of these theories will show their similarities and differences more clearly. The basic problem they raise is how to combine a sound methodological individualism with a proper recognition of the importance of groups.

Realistic Conflict Theory

Morton Deutsch and Muzafer Sherif pioneered the experimental research on intergroup relations that emphasizes group rather than individual variables (Deutsch, 1949; Sherif, 1966). Their experiments showed that individual attitudes vary as a function of the personal involvement of individuals with groups and the "functional relations" between these groups and other groups. Intergroup attitudes are positive or negative depending upon the incentives for competition or cooperation in the situations in which the groups find themselves.

Sherif's most famous experiment showed that some of the main features of intergroup conflict—such as loyalty to in-groups, hostility against out-groups, and stereotyping—could be created experimentally in the absence of ethnic differences (Sherif and Sherif, 1953; Sherif et al., 1961). His subjects were unacquainted eleven- and twelve-year-old boys, all white, middle-class, and Protestant, who were attending three-week summer camps in Oklahoma. Before leaving for the campsite, the boys were divided by the experimenters into two groups roughly matched for camping experience, popularity, and intellectual and athletic ability. During the first week of camping, the two groups were kept apart. During the second, they were brought together in such competitive team sports as baseball, football, and tug-of-war and in competitions for the neatest and cleanest cabins and for the best songs and skits. During the third week, the groups engaged in common activities that were noncompetitive or that required cooperation—fixing broken water supply equipment, renting a movie, and pulling together to free a stuck truck. The children were not, of course, told that their activities had been carefully planned to show how their attitudes and behavior would respond to changes in the situational incentives for either competition or cooperation. Observation of the children (their name-calling, friendship choices, food fights, and so on) suggested that competitive situations create "ethnocentric" stereotyping and hostility and that contact alone has no effect on attitudes. Far from reducing conflict, it may only give rival groups a chance to berate each other. Common or "superordinate" goals (securing drinking water, viewing a movie, traveling to Arkansas in the unstuck truck) are needed to dissolve hostility and to promote intergroup friendships.

Now some readers may be inclined to dismiss this experiment and others like it as irrelevant. All such exercises prove, one could argue, is something that everyone already knows: that competition tends to create bad feeling between the competitors. We see it all the time—for instance, in professional sports, if not close up, in our own lives. Nonetheless, such experiments have encouraged social scientists to develop and to take more seriously "realistic conflict theory" (Taylor and Moghaddam, 1994). The label was provided by Campbell (1965), who traced the ancestry of the view and analyzed its main elements, highlighting two basic principles: first, that "real conflict of group interests causes intergroup conflict," and second, that intergroup conflict—awareness of and action in relation to the underlying conflict of group interests—generates "the whole syndrome of ethnocentrism" (Campbell, 1965, pp. 287, 291; compare LeVine and Campbell, 1972). The novelty of a "realistic" approach along these lines should not be exaggerated, however. Social scientists of various stripes have long used it when discussing relations among states. There are usually exceptions to any generalization, but journalists, historians, and other commentators, along with most politicians and diplomats, have generally attributed most international conflicts to the divergent interests and clashing political ideologies of rival states rather than to the emotional difficulties and misperceptions of their leaders or citizens. For example, in the 1950s, when Allport and Sherif were writing, most Americans thought that the Cold War had more to do with Soviet aggression than with the autistic thinking of John Foster Dulles and his officials in the State Department or in the Pentagon.

Perhaps the only interesting question is whether this realistic perspective has any role to play in explaining prejudice and discrimination *within* a society like the United States, where the relevant ethnic groups are not organized for competition as rival states are (with armies, navies, and so on) and do not have clear territorial or ideological ambitions. In the view of many social scientists, international conflicts may have a realistic basis, but domestic ones are best understood as the by-product of irrational prejudices and stereotyping.

Sherif's experiments with children do no more than remind readers of a possibility. They obviously do not prove that there are any genuine, naturally occurring conflicts of interest between ethnic or cultural groups, whether within or between states. They do not disprove the assumptions of contact theory that ethnic prejudice is something psychological rather than economic or political in its motives and that ethnic discrimination has economic and political costs rather than benefits.

Real Interests

The economics of ethnic conflict is too important a topic to be dealt with properly in passing, but a word must be said here about economic motives for ethnic prejudice and discrimination. Do dominant groups denigrate and oppress subordinate groups in order to exploit them economically? There is no denying that some members of a dominant group always benefit economically from the kinds of discrimination practiced within and between such societies as Canada and the United States. Consequently these individuals have an economic motive for maintaining the prejudices that rationalize their benefits. To take the simplest case, which has been studied in the most detail, the domestic manufacturers of a commodity protected by a high tariff generally gain from "ethnic" discrimination against "foreign" goods. They have an economic interest, therefore, in cultivating negative stereotypes of their foreign competitors (perhaps as child abusers, brainless automatons, or environmental hazards). But some of their fellow citizens suffer economically because of these prejudices and the resulting discrimination: consumers of the commodity generally have to pay higher prices so that the manufacturers can enjoy higher profits, and the gains of those whose profits increase are generally smaller than the losses of those who pay higher prices. So much is elementary economic analysis, and the same reasoning applies generally. If people have a "taste for discrimination," they are likely to suffer economically for it, even if others benefit (Becker, 1957; Sowell, 1981). Similarly, if jobs or housing were like pies to be divided, then whites or Christians might stand to benefit on the average from discrimination against blacks or Jews—setting aside the question of whether the average would cover those who actually did the discriminating. But the economy is not a zero-sum game: cooperation can make the pie grow. Is there any reason to think that whites or Christians have higher incomes, on the average, because of the discrimination practiced against blacks or Jews in the United States? Yet there is prejudice against these groups. So we seem to be driven back from a realistic analysis of the situation to the more psychological analysis underlying the contact hypothesis.[4]

Social Identity Theory

The basic objection to a group-level, "realistic" analysis of domestic prejudice and discrimination has been met in recent years by the work of European social psychologists who have shifted the emphasis from economic and political motives for conflict to those having to do with self-esteem. Their approach and their ideas are generally labeled "social identity theory." Before considering the theory itself, consider the observations that seem to be at its root and that are used to explain it.

Two simple observations seem to undermine any realistic interpretation of conflict between such groups as blacks and whites in the United States: first, that self-derogation is common among members of oppressed groups, and second, that competitive behavior exists even in "minimal" group situations. In other words, it seems *not* to be generally true that intergroup attitudes are positive or negative depending upon the incentives for competition or cooperation in the situations in which groups find themselves.

No simple theory of realistic group conflict can explain the self-denigration and acceptance of out-group superiority frequently observed among members of oppressed groups. The real conflicts between these groups and their oppressors should "realistically" lead them to hate their oppressors. Sherif's experiments, although they were not designed to clarify the motives of the children, leave the impression that any competitive interdependence will produce the commonly recognized symptoms of intergroup conflict (such as hostile stereotyping of out-groups and overvaluation of in-groups) on *both* sides of the conflict. The experiments reinforce the expectation that groups in unequal relations of power and status (who are in conflict because the "superiors" refuse to recognize the equality of the "inferiors") should develop strong mutual antipathies. But in fact, as Tajfel and Turner (1979, p. 36) point out, "decades of research into inter-group relations suggest that ethnocentrism among stratified groups [has been] very much a one-way street." Thus black children sometimes prefer white dolls. Some women play dumb and helpless with men. A surprising number of Jews accept anti-Semitic stereotypes. Lower-class people generally admire the rich and the famous. And—a bit more *recherché*—French Canadians often rate bilinguals more favorably when they speak English than when they speak French (Lambert et al., 1960). In short, it seems that dominant groups can openly denigrate groups below them in status, whereas the subordinate groups eagerly display positive attitudes toward their oppressors. This is a remarkable fact. Some forms of political, economic, and social subordination seem able to eliminate or even reverse the natural ethnocentrism or competitiveness of subordinate groups. Why is inequality so frequently associated with acquiescence rather than rebellion? Realistic conflicts of interest are not, it seems, *sufficient* to evoke hostile attitudes and antagonistic behavior in relations among groups.

Nor does it seem that realistic conflicts of interest are *necessary* for intergroup antagonism. In a classic series of experiments, Henri Tajfel and his associates examined the widespread propensity to favor in-groups over out-groups, demonstrating that it exists even when these groups are "minimal," that is, lack any history or meaning outside the experimental situation. (For good summaries of this European social psychological literature, see Tajfel, 1982, and the literature cited there; Brown, 1986, pp. 541–74; and Taylor and Moghaddam, 1994, pp. 61–94.) For example, individual subjects were randomly assigned to one of two categories, "chronic overestimators" and "chronic underestimators," following a "test" of their ability to estimate the numbers of dots shown on slides projected for a fraction of a second each. In another experiment, subjects were "tested" for their preferences in modern art and randomly assigned to either a Klee or a Kandinsky group, depending upon their supposed preferences. Others were simply assigned at random to an A group and a B group. Then these subjects were really tested, using a simple procedure in which they gave points or small amounts of money to anonymous members of their new in-group or its complementary out-group (for example, "Member No. 74 of the Klee group" or "Member No. 44 of the Kandinsky group"). The procedure allowed the experimenters to vary at will the "functional relations"—the competitive or cooperative interdependence—between these arbitrary groupings. The subjects could respond to these different situations in different ways, following a strategy of fairness between groups, for example, or one of discrimination in favor of their in-group or even the out-group. They could maximize one particular group's winnings or maximize the total winnings of the two groups (playing against the experimenter). Statistical methods were developed for detecting which strategy subjects tended to use. In fact, they almost always favored their in-groups, though generally not as much as the tests permitted them to do: in-group favoritism was usually mitigated by considerations of fairness. But evidence of generosity toward out-groups was notably lacking, and there was strong evidence of a desire to maximize the differences in winnings between in-groups and out-groups, even if that meant giving less to the in-groups than the maximum allowed. Many subjects were willing to give less than the maximum possible to their own group, provided they could deprive the relevant out-group of even more.

Tajfel's experiments evidently engaged a latent competitiveness having to do with groups, even though the groups in question had no prior significance for the individuals involved, no formal organization or generally recognized existence, no history whatever of conflict or competition, and no realistic differences of interest. The experiments pointed to the conclusion that realistic conflicts of interest are not a necessary condition for competitive intergroup attitudes and behavior. These attitudes appear even among minimal groups not divided by any genuine conflicts—whose relations one would expect to be governed by elementary norms of fairness and empathy or compassion.

Social identity theory is best understood as an attempt to state the necessary and sufficient conditions for overt intergroup conflict (Brown, 1986, p. 543). It emphasizes an important source of conflict that realistic conflict theory tends to neglect or obscure, namely, rivalry for social status. The theory postulates a powerful desire in each individual for the esteem or admiration of others, and it recognizes that the satisfaction of this desire depends in large measure on the groups or social categories to which an individual belongs, together with the reputation of these groups among other individuals. Those who belong to groups or categories with high prestige (such as whites or males) enjoy a gratifying, positive social identity and high self-esteem, whereas those who belong to groups or categories in disrepute suffer from a negative social identity and are deprived of self-esteem. There is, of course, nothing unrealistic, abnormal, or pathological about the desire to feel good about oneself. Its importance as a motive is sometimes forgotten, however, when attention is focused on supposedly realistic clashes of interest between groups.

In the interest of attaining a positive social identity, any group may try to distinguish itself from its complementary group or groups on shared value dimensions. Some groups may try to improve or defend their overall position vis-à-vis other groups by changing their group's attributes (its wealth, average education, generosity) without challenging the generally accepted criteria of prestige or their relative weights. Others will try to change the dimensions of evaluation, so that the in-group appears in a more favorable light without undergoing any change in its attributes (as in the movement whose rallying cry was "Black is beautiful"). Generally speaking, individuals and groups will simultaneously pursue a mixture of strategies, all directed at improving their social standing. "The basic hypothesis . . . is that pressures to evaluate one's own group positively through in-group/out-group comparisons lead social groups to attempt to differentiate themselves from each other. . . . The aim of differentiation is to maintain or achieve superiority over an out-group on some dimensions" (Tajfel and Turner, 1979, pp. 40–41).

According to social identity theory, *all* groups or categories are in principle rivals for esteem or status—not just blacks and whites, or men and women, but also Christians and Jews, blondes and brunettes, endomorphs and ectomorphs, the sick and the well, overestimators and underestimators, and even those born on even-numbered days or under particular signs of the zodiac as against those born on odd-numbered days or under other signs. Every society must somehow decide which groups are better and which worse. Who should admire whom? It is childish to suppose that the problem can be solved by having everyone admire everyone else, so that all are special. Not only are there obvious differences among people that invite invidious comparisons, but such a rule would require tolerant and law-abiding citizens to admire rapists, racists, sexists, and homophobes. Social life is inconceivable without gradations of merit and differences in power and status. The question is, who should be on top?

The desire for a positive social identity is in principle an inexhaustible source of conflict among groups. (Is a positive identity ever positive enough?) Every group or category is potentially at odds with every other one, as each tries to improve its ranking in the social hierarchy. This jockeying for position is obviously entangled with realistic conflicts generated by material scarcity (and moderated by increasing affluence), but it is not simply a function of "the situation" as understood in the older realistic theory. In situations with realistic incentives for cooperation, intergroup competition can nonetheless be observed. The desire for a more positive social identity may be even stronger than the desire for material rewards.[5]

But *which* groups will actually compete for social status? The problem cannot be solved by simply pointing to "the situation," since "the situation" is seen as fundamentally the same for all groups—one of potential rivalry for a more positive social identity. What factors, then, determine when this latent conflict will come to the surface? Why is there overt conflict and considerable bad feeling between blacks and whites in the United States, but not between Geminis and Libras? This is in essence the novel question answered in a novel way by social identity theory.

Why Ethnic Identifications?

Social identity theory highlights *identification*, or *self-categorization*, as the necessary and sufficient condition for intergroup conflict. The theory introduces "social identity processes" between situations of contact and the behavior observed there that has to be explained. This theoretical innovation is best understood by contrasting social identity theory with the realistic conflict theory discussed earlier.[6]

Realistic conflict theory treats the attitudes of individuals toward different groups, including their identifications, as *effects* of the underlying conflicts of interest among the groups. An individual's awareness of belonging to a particular group, his or her identification with the fate of that group, and his or her willingness to behave as a loyal group member are all said to reflect the situation of conflict or cooperation among groups. Campbell (1965, pp. 288–89) states the relevant principles as follows: "Real threat [that is, conflict of interest in the situation] causes ingroup solidarity," and "real threat causes increased awareness of own ingroup identity" (compare LeVine and Campbell, 1972, pp. 31–32).

Social identity theory, by contrast, treats identification with groups as a *cause* of conflict (compare Tajfel, 1974, pp. 66–67). Identification with a group is said to trigger a process of social comparison. The broad, unfocused desire for a positive social identity becomes the more specific desire for the positive distinctiveness of the group in question. Individuals who identify with the group cease to deal with other individuals simply as individuals—in terms of their individual characteristics and interpersonal relations (whatever these are). Instead they begin to deal with them as group members, "standing in certain defined relationships to members of other groups" (Tajfel and Turner, 1979, p. 35). The more individuals identify with these in-groups and out-groups, the more they will deal with each other in stereotyped ways determined by the "functional relations" among the groups. Norms will develop to govern the relations among the groups, and all individuals will have to conform more or less to these norms. Life will begin to take on the character of something determined by consciousness (rather than consciousness being determined by life). But the propensity of individuals to identify with groups will, of course, be influenced by objective social, economic, and political structures: social identity theorists carefully avoid the error ("idealism") of claiming causal "primacy" or "priority" for "subjective" variables. They insist only that social identity variables have a "relative autonomy" worth investigating. "Just as the effects of these variables are powerfully determined by the previous social, economic, and political processes, so they may also acquire, in turn, an *autonomous* function that enables them to deflect in one direction or another the subsequent functioning of these processes" (Tajfel and Turner, 1979, p. 65).

The minimal group experiments described earlier illustrate the theory. They show that categorization itself, *even explicitly random categorization*, is sufficient to evoke competitive behavior between the resulting groups, despite their lack of a common history or realistic common interests. The experiments demonstrate not only how easy it is to trigger group comparisons and intergroup competition but also how social behavior varies with the salience of group membership. When subjects were told by the experimenters only that the subjects preferred Klee or Kandinsky but nothing about *groups* defined by such preferences, very little in-group favoritism was observed. Most subjects allocated rewards evenhandedly between Klee fanciers and Kandinsky fanciers (Billig and Tajfel, 1973).

But to repeat the question, Why do individuals identify with some groups rather than others? Social identity theory is relatively undeveloped as a theory about the conditions that create strong group loyalties outside the psychological laboratory. In their attempts to make "social identifications" less mysterious, proponents of the theory point to a variety of considerations: "objective" conflicts of interest among groups; opportunities (or the lack of them) for individual mobility across group boundaries; physical, cultural, and ideological similarities and differences among groups; and even information processing strategies of the cognitive systems of their members and the ideas they have about who they are or who they would like to be. Indeed, in social identity theory it sometimes seems that "thinking makes it so," or as Tajfel puts it, that social identification or categorization functions in the theory as a kind of "haphazardly-floating 'independent variable' which strikes at random as the spirit moves it" (Tajfel, 1981, p. 51). How can such an airy, immaterial variable be explained by hard material realities?

With respect simply to conflicts of interest among groups, the new "European" theory differs from the older American one only insofar as it emphasizes self-esteem as a motive for conflict. It deepens Sherif's economic and political "realism" by putting a greater emphasis on "subjective" conflicts rooted in the processes of social comparison explained earlier. Subjective conflicts of this sort, it suggests, are less likely to occur the more the groups resemble each other and the lower the barriers to individual social mobility. An egalitarian society or system of inequality that permits "passing" from one group to another encourages individuals to interact as individuals rather than as members of groups (or, more precisely, as members of the groups that define individuality, rather than as members of the groups that define groupyness), other things being equal. And other things being equal, individuals able to leave low-prestige categories will dissociate themselves psychologically from other members of these categories more easily and more frequently than individuals not able to leave (Tajfel and Turner, 1979, pp. 35–36, 43–46; Brown and Turner, 1981, pp. 42–43). But exactly how these generalities should apply to "races," classes, cultures, and the thousands (or hundreds of thousands) of sets of human beings we routinely distinguish remains very unclear: "What is relatively absent from social identity theory, and self-categorization theory, is a link between people's everyday lives, social networks, routines and relationships and their behaviour as group members. Individuals and groups do not merely stand in relation (in terms of status, power, etc.) to one another, but they have continuing *relationships* with one another. . . . Relationships require various forms of contact, coordination and negotiation over time" (Abrams, 1992, p. 85). This book as a whole, and Chapter 5 in particular, may be seen as an attempt to explain ethnic identifications without falling into the traps of individualism and idealism.[7]

Primordialism

Among social scientists of the past generation, there has been a division between different approaches to ethnicity that roughly parallels the difference between realistic conflict theory and social identity theory. On one hand are analysts who emphasize the mysterious and deeply "psychological" sources of attachment to ethnic groups; on the other are those who insist that the ordinary processes of socialization and ordinary motives of self-interest are sufficient to account for ethnic loyalty (Scott, 1990; Williams, 1994, pp. 57–58).

Some social scientists, following the lead of Edward Shils and Clifford Geertz, have treated ethnic loyalty as something "primordial" that binds groups together in a mysterious way. "For virtually every person, in every society, at almost all times, some attachments seem to flow more from a sense of natural—some would say spiritual—affinity than from social interaction" (Geertz, 1973, pp. 259–60). These attachments are rooted in the "assumed givens" of social existence, such as being born into a particular family and a particular religious community, speaking a particular language, and following particular social practices. "These congruities of blood, speech, custom and so on, are seen to have an ineffable, and at times overpowering coerciveness in and of themselves" (p. 259). One is bound to one's primordial groups "as the result not merely of personal affection, practical necessity, common interest, or incurred obligation, but at least in great part by virtue of some unaccountable absolute import attributed to the very tie itself" (p. 259). Individuals simply *identify* with their primordial groups—to use the language of social identity theory—and there is no point trying to explain their identifications in terms of their current social interactions, for these interactions all take place within frameworks provided by the identifications. To the extent that "primordial" identifications prevail over "civil" ones, Geertz argues, interactions are likely to be tempestuous, because individuals meet as rivals for recognition. Their dominant motive is the desire to be "noticed" favorably by others or "to maintain a socially ratified personal identity" (pp. 258, 268, 309). This is not a desire that all can easily satisfy, for it is difficult to organize a society in which all are being noticed while none are just noticing.

"Primordialist" accounts of ethnicity collide with "situationalist" or "circumstantialist" ones that downplay the emotional or nonrational sources of ethnicity. Instead, they stress its socially constructed, variable, flexible, and basically unmysterious nature. At the root of ethnicity are no ineffable spiritual ties, no deep psychological longings or fundamental flaws in human nature, just elementary social and economic processes that are amenable to rational sociological analysis. Ethnic loyalties compete with other group loyalties, such as class loyalties, and they may ultimately be subservient to material conditions. They are created by social circumstances, and they can be modified or destroyed by changing these social circumstances. Ethnicity should be regarded not as a permanent feature of society but as one that may eventually fade away in response to changes in the situations in which people find themselves. This emphasis on the flexibility and the derivative character of ethnic ties is in the spirit of realistic conflict theory—at least in comparison to social identity theory.

Social identity theorists do not of course write as stodgy opponents of fluidity and change, but between the lines of their theory can be found a latent primordialism. The theory emphasizes the desire for recognition, as noted above, and it gains relevant empirical content by relying on unexplained processes of identification or self-categorization to attach its theoretical generalities to the facts of social life. The attention given to the effects of identification in the theory, and the neglect of its causes, may seem strange until one realizes that the theorists are taking for granted some uncontroversial assumptions about natural affinities and the givens of social existence. Their reliance on mysterious spiritual processes is obscured by their implicit acceptance of common opinions about which identities or self-categorizations are in practice really important—the primordial ones.

Science and Ethnicity

The similarities among the three theories outlined in this chapter are at least as important as their differences. For example, all three tend to downplay ethnicity—in the sense of ethnic or cultural differences—as a cause of ethnic conflict. Allport's contact theory, let me repeat, rests upon a definition of prejudice that makes it a kind of mistake and that separates it from the natural partisanship that people have for their own way of life. Prejudice and discrimination may arise from a misperception of ethnic differences or from the creation of purely imaginary differences between groups, but prejudice has nothing to do with real ethnic differences. Similarly, realistic conflict theory separates conflict from ethnicity. To be sure, the theory could be spelled out in many different ways, since it is almost a pure formalism. Some of its interpretations could emphasize ethnic differences. But in fact it has been spelled out in experiments that downplay ethnicity. The main point of Muzafer Sherif's famous experiments with children at summer camps was to show that "ethnocentrism" could exist without ethnic differences. Similarly, the experiments used to test and develop social identity theory typically create situations of competitive or cooperative interdependence simply by manipulating material "payoffs" in artificial situations: the "winnings" of the experimental subjects are made to depend upon how they play the game, and the relevant groups have nothing to do with ethnicity. The experiments demonstrate the central contention of social identity theory: that in-group favoritism is a perfectly general tendency that does not depend upon the existence of ethnic or cultural differences between the groups or even upon any real conflicts of interest between them. In practice, the processes revealed by the experiments are attached by the theorists to primordial ethnic identities and conflicts, but without any account of specifically *ethnic* identities.

Another important similarity has to do with the empirical or scientific character of all three theories. They all aim to clarify and to explain relevant facts and patterns of facts. Following Montesquieu and the other pioneers of modern empirical social science, Allport, Blumer, Sherif, and Tajfel have tried to discover some of the natural laws or empirical regularities of human behavior. They have quietly restrained whatever impulses they may have felt simply to preach particular norms of conduct or to prescribe different remedies for ethnic conflict. They have certainly not argued for any particular hierarchy of values—that freedom should rank above equality, for example, or that loyalty is more important than tolerance. All the theories considered so far are "value free" in the sense that they are theories about facts, not values.[8]

Many different facts are relevant for judging the merits and shortcomings of these theories. The relevant facts include the broad historical trends noted above as well as the detailed information produced by social surveys and psychological experiments. Unfortunately, generalizations about historical trends are notoriously difficult to verify, even before one tries to sort out their causes. Such generalizations may seem to prove or disprove a particular theory, but their status as facts is often very questionable. In constituting these "facts," intuition seems to play a larger role than observation, counting, or measurement. Thus, while it may be plausible to link the growth of commerce over the past several centuries to an increase in violence or a decline in prejudice, a more careful inspection of the historical record for a particular part of the world and over a better-defined period of time may well reveal some other combination of trends—perhaps even a decrease in violence together with an increase in prejudice. Social scientists arguing about the relative merits of different empirical theories tend, therefore, to focus on the clearer, more elementary, or less controversial facts—the "brute facts"—produced by surveys and experiments. This is certainly true of the discussion surrounding the contact hypothesis during the past generation. Broad historical trends have been almost completely ignored. It is best, therefore, to defer further discussion of the rival theories outlined in this chapter until some of the most relevant facts, from the standpoint of contemporary social science, have been summarized. The next two chapters review the existing empirical literature on the attitudinal effects of greater or less contact between ethnic groups.

2 A Social Experiment

The desegregation of American education during the past forty years has provided many opportunities to test the contact hypothesis. Before 1954, when the United States Supreme Court handed down its historic decision *Brown v. Board of Education* (347 U.S. 483), separate white and "colored" schools existed by law in seventeen southern and border states and in the District of Columbia. Even in the northern and eastern states with substantial black populations, black and white children rarely attended the same schools, despite the absence of any formal requirement or provision for racially segregated schooling.[1] In these states, de facto educational segregation was an effect of residential segregation and the tendency of school authorities to define school districts in such a way as to create racially homogeneous schools. After 1954, and especially after the Supreme Court's school busing decisions of the early 1970s, many children who had previously attended all-white or all-black schools were moved abruptly into racially mixed schools. As a result of a change in government policy, in other words, the contact between black and white children increased dramatically in many localities.

Desegregation was promoted in the belief that greater contact would quickly produce more positive attitudes. What were the attitudinal effects of these sudden changes in the level of interracial contact? I will not try to summarize each study that deals directly with this apparently simple question. Fortunately, their results have been widely discussed, and several excellent reviews of the literature have been published during the past thirty years. I shall describe two of the studies in some detail to illustrate the difficulties typically encountered when doing research on the contact hypothesis in schools. For the rest, I shall rely upon the reviews, since they all point to the same conclusion.

Before examining the representative studies and the reviews of the literature, however, it is important to understand their historical context. As several writers have pointed out (for example, Dworkin, 1977), the decisions of the Supreme Court do not ultimately depend for their legitimacy upon any debatable social science hypotheses. In 1954 the demand for desegregation was a simple demand of justice. Social science seems to have entered the dispute only as a way of getting around a legal technicality, but this technicality must be understood before the significance of the subsequent studies can be fully appreciated.

Policy and Rationale

The American experiment in desegregation began as a dispute about the true meaning of the equality guaranteed all American citizens by the Fourteenth Amendment to the United States Constitution. This amendment was one of three adopted shortly after the Civil War whose general purpose was to abolish slavery and to enfranchise the black populations of the southern states. Section 1 of the Fourteenth Amendment reads as follows:

> All persons born or naturalized in the United States, and subject to the jurisdiction thereof, are citizens of the United States and of the State wherein they reside. No State shall make or enforce any law which shall abridge the privileges or immunities of citizens of the United States; nor shall any State deprive any person of life, liberty, or property, without due process of law; nor deny to any person within its jurisdiction the equal protection of the laws.

In the years following the Civil War, section 1 gave rise to much important constitutional litigation, and for many years its basic purpose was frustrated by the decisions of the Supreme Court.

The landmark case for present purposes was *Plessy v. Ferguson* (163 U.S. 537), decided in 1896, which established the principle of "separate but equal" facilities. The Court upheld a Louisiana statute requiring railway companies operating within the state to provide equal, but separate, accommodations for their white and colored passengers, either by providing two or more coaches for each passenger train or by dividing a single coach by a partition. Plessy, following an altercation with the employees of a railway company who were trying to enforce this law, had challenged its constitutionality. The lower courts had upheld the law, and eventually Plessy's case had reached the Supreme Court. The justices there drew a distinction between civil or political rights and social rights. The Fourteenth Amendment guaranteed the former (for example, the right to vote or to serve on juries), they said, but not the latter.

> The object of the amendment was undoubtedly to enforce the absolute equality of the two races before the law, but in the nature of things it could not have been intended to abolish distinctions based upon color, or to enforce social, as distinguished from political, equality, or a commingling of the two races upon terms unsatisfactory to either. Laws permitting, and even requiring, their separation in places where they are liable to be brought into contact do not necessarily imply the inferiority of either race to the other, and have been generally, if not universally, recognized as within the competency of the state legislatures in the exercise of their police power. The most common instance of this is connected with the establishment of separate schools for white and colored children, which has been held to be a valid exercise of the legislative power even by courts of States where the political rights of the colored race have been longest and most earnestly enforced. (p. 544)

The justices neglected the obvious implication of inferiority associated with segregation and used a weak analogy to evade the point of the Fourteenth Amendment. Just as children and adults, or men and women, can be treated differently under the law without thereby being deprived of the equal protection of the law, they claimed, so can blacks and whites. In making distinctions between classes of citizens, legislatures must act reasonably, they acknowledged, but courts must allow legislatures wide discretion "to act with reference to the established usages, customs and traditions of the people, and with a view to the promotion of their comfort, and the preservation of the public peace and good order" (p. 550). If some citizens are offended by the resulting distinctions, they said, this is not a reason for denying the validity of the offending legislation. Blacks, despite their civil or political equality with whites, were not accepted by them as their social equals, and the justices denied that they had the power to compel such acceptance. "If one race be inferior to the other socially, the Constitution of the United States cannot put them upon the same plane" (p. 552).

The justices were accommodating the dominant political forces of the time by permitting an obvious breach of the fundamental principle of equality that they claimed to uphold. But the distinction they were using is still widely accepted today. In the public sphere, all citizens, black and white, male and female, rich and poor, young and old, must be treated equally, even if they are sometimes treated differently. (For example, all must be able to vote, and their preferences must be given equal weight, even if they are required to vote in different constituencies or at different polling stations depending upon where they live.) In the private sphere, however, citizens are permitted to make invidious distinctions on the basis of characteristics such as age, race, sex, creed, national origin, or annual income that the state is obliged to disregard. (An individual may, for example, choose to associate in his private life only with people of his own nationality, religion, political affiliation, sexual orientation, or income level.) What has changed since 1896 is the exact location and management of the boundary between public and private, or state and society. Many business transactions previously considered private are now considered public—for example, those having to do with the selection of clients for hotels and restaurants.

So far as American education is concerned, the landmark case was *Brown v. Board of Education* in 1954, when the Supreme Court declared that "separate educational facilities are inherently unequal" (347 U.S. at 495). The cases before the Court on that occasion had been decided by lower courts in conformity with the then prevailing separate-but-equal doctrine. The black and white schools in question, like the earlier railway carriages, were deemed substantially equal (or were being made so) with respect to such tangible factors as physical plant, transportation, curricula, and teacher qualifications. Nonetheless, the Supreme Court accepted the cases because it was concerned about the effects of separation itself and of its intangible symbolism. In its historic decision, the Court held that separating black children from other children of similar age and qualifications "solely because of their race generates a feeling of inferiority as to their status in the community that may affect their hearts and minds in a way unlikely ever to be undone" (p. 494). Contrary to what the Court had declared in 1896, real equality of education required the elimination of state-enforced segregation by race.

What the Court had in mind as an alternative to segregation was, it seemed, "a system not based on color distinctions" (p. 495). In a follow-up decision the next year (*Brown v. Board of Education*, 349 U.S. 294), the justices explained that their objective was to effectuate a transition to "a racially nondiscriminatory school system." One of the methods lower courts were directed to consider as a means to that end was "revision of school districts and attendance areas into compact units to achieve a system of determining admission to the public schools on a nonracial basis" (p. 296). Henceforth, one might have concluded, American public education was going to be "colorblind."

American society was not colorblind, however. Residential segregation was a fact of life, and it was the basis for a substantial separation of the races educationally, even in states with no history of slavery or enforced segregation. Thus many school systems that had never formally discriminated on the basis of race still had schools that were exclusively or almost exclusively attended by children of only one race.

Beginning in the late 1960s, the Court began to chip away at the edifice of social segregation. In a series of decisions stretching from *Green v. County School Board of New Kent County* (391 U.S. 430) in 1968 to *Milliken v. Bradley* (418 U.S. 717) in 1974, the Court obligated local school officials to do away with "socially" segregated schools. The cumulative effect of these cases was to reintroduce race as a formally acceptable criterion for assigning students to schools, provided that the effect of such assignment was to mix the races rather than to separate them. In other words, the Court went significantly beyond what seemed to be its earlier position, namely, that state-enforced segregation (contrary to the mixing tendency of society) is an evil condemned by the Constitution. It advanced to the position that state-enforced mixing (contrary to the separating tendency of society) is a positive good required by the Constitution.

The research to be described presently was conducted against the background of these changes in law and policy. It was meant to throw light on their *effects*. But, as already suggested, the hypothesis tested in the various studies must also be counted among the *causes* of the changes in policy just summarized.

In 1954 the Supreme Court needed grounds for rejecting the separate-but-equal principle, which had been proclaimed by an earlier Court and which had been used in deciding cases for more than fifty years. No doubt the Court had many reasons for rejecting the authority of *Plessy v. Ferguson*, but it did not want to undermine its own authority by flatly declaring that an earlier set of Supreme Court justices had been devious and unjust. The reason the Court gave for setting aside *Plessy* was the increase in psychological knowledge since 1896: "Whatever may have been the extent of psychological knowledge at the time of Plessy v. Ferguson, this finding [that segregation has a tendency to retard the educational and mental development of Negro children and to deprive them of some of the benefits they would receive in a racially integrated school system] is amply supported by modern authority" (347 U.S. 483, at 494). The principal modern authority cited—in the famous "footnote 11" appended to this sentence—was Kenneth B. Clark, who had served as an expert witness and who was one of three psychologists responsible for a "social science statement" about the effects of segregation that was eventually signed by thirty-two social scientists who had worked in the field of American race relations (Kluger, 1976, pp. 553–57).

The signers of this document were mainly concerned with the intellectual and emotional damage done by enforced segregation, but several paragraphs of the statement dealt with the relation between segregation and racial attitudes, and they provide a version of the contact hypothesis: "Segregation leads to a blockage in the communication and interaction between two groups. Such blockages tend to increase mutual suspicion, distrust and hostility. Segregation not only perpetuates rigid stereotypes and reinforces negative attitudes toward members of the other group, but also leads to the development of a social climate within which violent outbreaks of racial tensions are likely to occur" (Allport et al., 1953, p. 432). Desegregation might initially increase rather than reduce interracial tensions, the social scientists recognized, but in light of the available evidence they dismissed predictions of violent opposition as unrealistic. Experience showed that after a short period of adjustment, given favorable circumstances, desegregation generally produced "more favorable attitudes and friendlier relations between races." The statement indicated a number of the relevant conditions, which, it concluded, "can generally be satisfied in . . . public schools" (pp. 437–38).

Social science was thus drawn into the controversy about desegregation. In 1954 the Supreme Court seemed to endorse the general principle that governments must not discriminate on the basis of race, but in doing so the Court relied upon a justification for changing the law that was provided by social science (Kluger, 1976, pp. 705–7; Rosen, 1972, pp. 134–72). Within fifteen years the contact hypothesis and the other theories outlined in the social science statement were being invoked, indirectly, to justify the deliberate use of racial distinctions to encourage integration.

The later Supreme Court decisions, starting with *Green*, never spelled out a clear rationale for their departure from what *Brown* seemed to require, namely, the elimination of race as a basis for assigning children to schools. The Court's opinions emphasized instead the desirability of eliminating racially unbalanced schools. This substantive goal was given priority over the "semantic" principle of nondiscrimination. Local authorities were charged with quickly devising realistic plans that would eliminate or at least mitigate racial segregation. The link with *Brown* was the underlying belief that separation of the races is an evil that the state has a duty to overcome, not just by forbidding racial discrimination but by achieving the greatest possible measure of actual desegregation (compare Graglia, 1976). The justification for this belief included the social science research on the contact hypothesis, which seemed to show that good effects would flow from greater interracial contact.

From the outset, however, social scientists understood that the decisions of the Supreme Court, justified in part by the presumed validity of the contact hypothesis, provided valuable opportunities for the experimental testing of the hypothesis outside the psychological laboratory (for example, Williams, Fisher, and Janis, 1956, p. 583).

The Effects of Desegregation

Since the start of desegregation of American schools in the 1950s, there have been considerably more than one hundred quantitative studies of its effects on intergroup attitudes and behavior, about half of them published. This substantial literature has been reviewed more than a dozen times in the past thirty years (Carithers, 1970; Cohen, 1975; McConahay, 1978; Proshansky, 1966; St. John, 1975; Schofield, 1978, 1986, 1991; Schofield and Sagar, 1983; Stephan, 1978, 1986, 1991; and Weinberg, 1977; see also Armor, 1972, 1995; Braddock, 1985; Cook, 1979; Gerard, 1983; Hawley and Smylie, 1988; Longshore, 1982; Longshore and Prager, 1985; Miller, 1981; Schofield, 1993, 1995; Stephan and Stephan, 1996; and Wells, 1995). No attempt will be made here to review it once again. Rather, two of the best studies will be described in some detail in order to clarify the issues in this area of research, and then the reviews themselves will be reviewed.

The Bay Area Study.

Among the early studies, Webster (1961) stands out because of its sound design and its surprising results. The study analyzed the effect of desegregation on the "social acceptance attitudes" measured by a nine-item social distance scale. It involved 104 experimental subjects and 108 controls.

The opportunity for the study arose when a high school district in the San Francisco Bay area decided to change the acceptance zones for some of its schools. As a result, a previously all-white junior high school became about 20 percent black. The experimental subjects were drawn from two of its feeder elementary schools, one black, the other white. The attitudes of these subjects were first measured in June 1959, when they were finishing grade 6, and then again in March 1960, after six months at the newly desegregated school. The control subjects were grade 7 pupils in black and white junior high schools in neighboring cities. They were roughly matched with the experimental subjects in socioeconomic characteristics. The attitudes of these control subjects were measured only once, in the spring of the second year.

The main results of the study are shown in table 2.1. Statistical analysis of these averages revealed that the white experimental subjects were significantly less socially accepting of blacks than were their controls and that the negative trend in the attitudes of the experimental subjects was statistically significant. The difference between the black experimental and the black control subjects was not significant, but the *positive* trend in the black experimental subjects was significant. Thus the main hypothesis of the study was not confirmed in the case of the white subjects and not clearly

Table 2.1   Desegregation and Social Acceptance

Race of Respondents	Experimental Groups		Control Groups
	1959	1960	1960
White	1.85	1.48	2.54
		(N = 60)	(N = 55)
Black	6.05	6.32	5.98
		(N = 44)	(N = 53)

Source: S. W. Webster, "The Influence of Interracial Contact on Social Acceptance in a Newly Integrated School," *Journal of Educational Psychology*, 52 (1961), p. 294.
Note: Scale scores ranged from 0 to 9, with higher scores representing greater acceptance.

confirmed in the case of the black subjects. "Contact had a negative effect upon the white subjects; they became significantly less accepting of Negroes. The findings were inconclusive in the case of the Negro subjects, but did tend to indicate that change was greater in the direction of more acceptance of whites" (Webster, 1961, p. 296).

These mainly negative results may be explained, as the author points out, by the relatively short duration of the contact between the black and the white pupils. "A 6-month period of time could very well be inadequate to allow for the necessary intergroup adjustment of the subjects" (p. 295). Another possible explanation might be the weakness of the social distance scale used as a test of individual attitudes. Responses to such a scale, when averaged, may clearly indicate a group's place in a social pecking order but reveal very little about individual differences in attitudes. "While social distance measures have proven to be both reliable and valid, it is possible that they are not sensitive enough to measure less noticeable changes within individual attitude structures. Methods and instruments which assess interracial attitudes with greater depth and precision would seem to be needed" (p. 295).

The Delaware Study.

Among more recent studies, Parsons (1985) deserves attention because of its scope, its simple long-term design, and its focus on more general racial attitudes. It was part of a much larger study by a team of researchers who observed the progress of school desegregation in New Castle County, Delaware (which includes Wilmington) from 1976 to 1981.

In 1978, following prolonged litigation, the eleven school districts in the county (the inner-city Wilmington district and ten suburban districts) were ordered to implement a metropolitan school desegregation plan. Data

Table 2.2   Racial Attitudes of Parents and Children

	Year of Test			
Group Tested	1978	1979	1980	1981
Black Parents	3.93	3.90	3.90	3.89
White Parents	3.45	3.38	3.35	3.33
Black Students	4.23	4.36	4.28	4.28
White Students	3.74	3.53	3.46	3.41

Source: M. A. Parsons, "Parents' and Students' Attitude Changes Related to School Desegregation in New Castle County, Delaware," in *Metropolitan Desegregation*, ed. R. L. Green (New York: Plenum, 1985), pp. 195, 197.
Note: Data reported are mean scale scores ranging from 1.00 (least positive) to 5.00 (most positive). Sample sizes are about 42 for the black parents and students and 245 for the white parents and students.

were gathered by the researchers on the attitudes of both parents and students in 1978, before the implementation of the plan, and each year thereafter from 1979 to 1981, following its implementation. The measures of parental and student attitudes were Likert scales composed of statements of opinions about relations and interactions between blacks and whites with which the respondents agreed or disagreed on five-point scales. Higher scores on these composite measures indicate more positive attitudes toward race relations. The main results of the study are shown in table 2.2. Statistical analysis of these averages revealed significant differences between blacks and whites but no significant trends over time. "Overall, the answer [regarding trends] was that racial attitudes did not improve. In fact, during the first year, racial attitudes became slightly less positive for both students and parents, and the decreased level remained constant as desegregation continued" (p. 206).

This study, too, unfortunately suffers from some methodological weaknesses. For example, there is a problem with sampling: only five of the eleven districts cooperated in the study, and the ultimate return rate for the questionnaires mailed to parents and students in these five districts (over a period of four years) was only about 2 percent. Moreover, opposition to desegregation, including litigation, continued in the community during the three years following the initial court order. "This opposition centered around the issue of district organization, with the county finally being redistricted to form four school districts rather than one. The ongoing turmoil made more difficult the attempts by teachers, staff, administrators, students, parents, and the community to move forward with the business of education under desegregation" (p. 206). In short, the negative attitudes of parents and other adults toward desegregation may have swamped the positive effects of greater interracial contact on the racial attitudes of the children involved.[2]

These two studies are typical of many others in the literature, not just in their results but in what they reveal about the obstacles to methodologically sound research in communities undergoing desegregation. A fully satisfactory study would have to observe developments over a relatively long period of time (perhaps five to ten years); it would have to secure the cooperation of a truly random sample of school officials, parents, and students; it would have to use unquestionably valid measures of racial attitudes; and it would have to avoid the contamination of its attitude measures by "history"—and perhaps the contamination of children's responses by the opinions of their parents and teachers. Because these conditions have never been fully satisfied, it is very difficult to draw firm conclusions about the attitudinal effects of desegregation from the available literature. The difficulties have been repeatedly described and increasingly emphasized in the thirteen reviews of the literature that will now be summarized.

Reviews of the Literature.

The first relevant review, Proshansky (1966), discusses all the literature then available on the development of intergroup attitudes during childhood, including eight studies that deal directly with interracial contact in schools. From these it draws a cautiously optimistic conclusion: "Cooperative and equal-status interracial contacts in the school setting can, but will not necessarily, reduce ethnic prejudice. How much of a reduction will occur, how generalized it will be, and indeed whether it will occur at all very likely depends on a host of factors internal to the school (e.g., attitudes of teachers, racial distribution in the classroom), as well as external to it (e.g., community atmosphere, parental attitudes)" (p. 356).

The next review, Carithers (1970), focuses specifically on patterns of racial cleavage and association under different conditions of school segregation and desegregation. Its reference list of eighty-nine items includes several unpublished doctoral dissertations. The section of the review that deals with contact and attitude change summarizes twenty directly relevant studies. It reports inconsistent results. "There is no general agreement about the effects of interracial contacts on attitude change. Some studies have found heightened tolerance; some heightened resistance; some no change. There seems to be, however, a general agreement that interracial contact *per se* will not bring about increased tolerance or acceptance" (p. 41). The review concludes with the broad statement that "we simply do not know what happens to whom under what conditions of school desegregation" (p. 43).

Five years later two reviews appeared, Cohen (1975) and St. John (1975), which called for a significant change in the direction of research effort. In the future, according to these authors, the first priority of research should be to clarify the conditions for successful desegregation by concentrating on the differences among desegregated schools. They found that most earlier studies that compared segregated and desegregated schools suffered from various methodological weaknesses, but they did not urge that these weaknesses be corrected, for that would only perpetuate the tendency to focus obsessively on "the effects of desegregation." Henceforth the quality, not the quantity, of contact should be the main concern. Nevertheless, the two reviews in question provide some "quantitative" insights gleaned from the earlier literature.

St. John (1975) systematically analyzes more than 120 studies of the relation between school racial composition and the achievement, attitudes, or behavior of children. Twenty-two of these studies, most of them from the 1960s, dealt specifically with school desegregation and the interracial attitudes of black and white students. On the basis of these studies, St. John concludes that "the immediate effect of desegregation on interracial attitudes is sometimes positive but often negative" (p. 119). Another nineteen studies dealt with social relations and friendship choice in desegregated schools and classrooms. These studies, too, suggest no clear conclusion.

> In sum, comparative studies of the racial attitudes of segregated and desegregated school children are inconclusive. Findings are inconsistent and mixed regardless of whether students' racial attitudes or friendship choice was the object of study, regardless of whether desegregation was by neighborhood or busing, voluntary or mandatory, and regardless of whether the study design was cross-sectional or longitudinal. There is some indication, however, that for black children desegregation appears more beneficial if attitudes rather than friendship behavior is the criterion and that experimental design reveals more deterioration in white attitudes than do other designs. (pp. 80–81)

Thus, despite the methodological weaknesses of many of the studies, one broad generalization could be made: "School desegregation per se has no unitary or invariable effect on children. . . . [D]esegregation is a multifaceted phenomenon which can be simultaneously beneficial in some respects and harmful in others" (p. 121). Overall, desegregated schooling is judged "neither a demonstrated success nor a demonstrated failure" (p. 119).

Cohen (1975), which seems to have been published simultaneously with or even before the review just summarized, is nonetheless really a commentary on it rather than an entirely separate review. Cohen includes some recent studies not discussed by St. John, but her substantive conclusions are essentially the same as the ones just stated (see p. 282). The main contribution of the review is its sharper, more focused argument that attention should shift from research on the effects of desegregation to research on the effects of different kinds of desegregation. In other words, assuming that there is going to be desegregation of some kind, how exactly should it be implemented in order to maximize its benefits and minimize its costs? According to Cohen, the need is for research that will help decision makers "in determining which schools need further expert assistance and resources to enhance the effectiveness of the desegregation process" and also for research that will help the experts to understand "the conditions under which interracial contact might be expected to result in desirable interracial attitudes and behavior" (p. 276).

Weinberg (1977) is the most difficult review to discuss because it comes to conclusions different from those of all the other reviews and because its conclusions are unsupported by the evidence it presents. In addition, its length alone (398 pages) poses a formidable problem. As Karl E. Taeuber, the sociologist who wrote its foreword, states, "like most knowledgeable guides, Professor Weinberg is enchanted with side channels, eddies, and shoals as well as the main current, and the journey he takes us on is long and often intricate" (p. iii). Taeuber advises readers, "before taking Professor Weinberg's complete tour," to consult the final chapter, where the conclusions of the review are reported. Following this advice, one finds that "positive racial attitudes by black and white students develop as they attend school together" (p. 327). But those who subsequently take the complete tour through the shoals and eddies (the approximately eighty-five studies of the attitudinal effects of desegregation discussed in chapter 8), will not find the basis for this conclusion, unless *develop* simply means "change."

Three of the best reviews of the burgeoning literature on desegregation appeared the following year. McConahay (1978) emphasizes the severe methodological weaknesses of practically all the existing research. Unpublished studies are dismissed as "methodologically worthless": "The unpublished studies were (with some noted exceptions) unpublished because they indeed deserved that fate" (p. 80). Studies published before 1960 are similarly put aside on the ground that too much has happened since then for their findings to be worth considering any longer. After weeding out these and many other distracting studies, McConahay concludes that one should be impressed "with how little is known and how much additional research--especially experimental research—is needed" (p. 100). He faults other writers for exaggerating the likely effects of desegregation. "In order to sell or discredit desegregation policy, old-line integrationists and old-line segregationists, as well as their contemporary counterparts in the busing debate, have exaggerated the changes in attitude and behavior we may expect from desegregation" (p. 102). Basic research on interpersonal attraction as well as on the socialization of racial attitudes, properly interpreted, "suggests that we should not expect any positive change in attitudes or behavior from merely putting people together in the same building or room. In fact, we should more likely expect that a poorly planned and executed mixing of racial and ethnic groups would produce negative change" (p. 102).

Stephan (1978) is almost as selective as McConahay: he reviews in detail only ten published and eight unpublished studies of attitudes. But he is not quite so dismissive of earlier work, and he comes to more controversial conclusions. The review is organized as a discussion of four hypotheses abstracted from the social science statement and the other testimony of social scientists in the cases leading up to the *Brown* decision. The first two hypotheses are versions of the contact hypothesis: (1) "for whites, desegregation will lead to more positive attitudes toward blacks," and (2) "for blacks, desegregation will lead to more positive attitudes toward whites" (p. 221). Like McConahay, Stephan emphasizes the difficulty of drawing firm conclusions about these hypotheses, but regarding the first hypothesis, he concludes that "there is little evidence indicating that desegregation reduces prejudice, at least during the first year of desegregation" (p. 233). Eight of the studies whose results he tabulates showed increases in prejudice following desegregation; five showed no change; and only two showed decreases.

As regards the second hypothesis, "considering that white prejudice was often found to be high in desegregated schools and that black self-esteem and achievement were usually unaffected by desegregation, it is consistent to find that the prejudice of blacks toward whites increased in almost as many cases as it decreased" (p. 233). Five studies showed increases; six showed decreases; and one showed no change. In short, it seemed quite clear after twenty-five years that the social scientists of an earlier day had had unrealistic expectations about the attitudinal effects of desegregation (compare Clark, 1979; Cook, 1979, 1984; Gerard, 1983).

Schofield (1978) provides the most detailed discussion of the literature on the attitudinal effects of desegregation from the perspective of the contact hypothesis. She concludes with the following rather sobering statements: "The utter inconclusiveness of the research on the effect of desegregation on intergroup relations is clearly disappointing to those who had hoped to find a simple, straightforward answer to the question, What effect does desegregation have on intergroup attitudes and behavior? These results are doubly disappointing to those whose interest stems from a desire to gain clear support for their position in the heated national debate about desegregation" (p. 357). But according to Schofield, these results suggest that different situations of contact must have different effects on intergroup relations and that research should henceforth focus on a new question: What types of factors influence how interracial schooling will affect children?

> The inconclusiveness of the research suggests that people need to stop thinking about desegregation as a well-defined program with predictable effects that are "good" or "bad" depending on one's value system. Rather, they need to recognize that racial mixing is just one aspect of the schooling children receive in desegregated schools, and that other aspects of that schooling may be far more crucial in determining how children's attitudes and behavior develop. This shift from seeing desegregation as a variable that in and of itself will have clear positive or negative consequences is entirely proper given that the policy of desegregation stems from constitutional considerations rather than from any positive or negative psychological effects that might be attributed to desegregation. (p. 358)

Whatever the sources of desegregation, Schofield was clear about the theoretical as well as the practical advantages of the suggested reorientation. "First, it should lead to a richer development and fuller application of theory relevant to understanding the social and cognitive processes that account for students' reactions to desegregated schooling. Second, theory and research on these processes should be of considerable utility to policymakers and practitioners who are faced with the challenge of structuring desegregated schools so that the impact they have on students is desirable from both a personal and a societal perspective" (p. 358).

The mixture of disappointed expectations and renewed hope evident in these remarks is echoed in Schofield's more recent reviews (Schofield, 1986, 1991; Schofield and Sagar, 1983). Their main point is perhaps best stated in the following passage from the earliest: "There is a growing awareness of the societal costs of intergroup hostility and stereotyping. It is clear that under many conditions interracial contact can lead to increased intergroup hostility. Hence, unless interracial schools are carefully planned there is a real possibility that they will exacerbate the very social tensions and hostilities that many initially hoped they would diminish" (Schofield and Sagar, 1983, p. 59; compare Schofield, 1991, p. 339). Schofield (1986) reiterates the importance of the various conditions and qualifications that distinguish contact theory from the layman's contact hypothesis: "Contact between two previously separate and even hostile groups does not automatically have salutary effects. *The precise conditions of contact are crucial in determining what the outcome of the contact will be"* (p. 80). Schofield (1991), the longest and most thorough recent review of the literature on school desegregation and intergroup relations, echoes earlier reviews in lamenting the state of theory in this field of research: "Because they bring no theoretical framework that would suggest what characteristics of the desegregated setting might relate to those changes, most researchers have paid little attention to what the desegregated setting was actually like. Because desegregated schools differ so dramatically, contradictory outcomes are found. Without a theoretical perspective, one has little idea of what patterns to look for in the data, and confusion abounds" (p. 359). This review points to a variety of important factors that tend to be neglected in studies of school desegregation, such as cultural differences, numerical ratios, and "the social processes that lead to various kinds of intergroup outcomes" (p. 382). But in the end Schofield concludes her "pessimistic" review on a hopeful note: "The theoretical ferment in recent years, both inside the field and in more generic social identity and social categorization approaches to intergroup relations, provides a rich source of ideas for future work" (p. 388).

Stephan's more recent reviews (Stephan, 1986, 1991; Stephan and Stephan, 1996) likewise stress the importance of recent theoretical developments, particularly the growing linkage between contact theory and cognitive psychology, but their main contribution is to distinguish clearly between short- and long-term effects of desegregation. Regarding short-term effects on racial attitudes, Stephan (1986) adds eleven more recent studies to the eighteen discussed in his first review but comes to the same conclusion: "Although it is impossible to conclude anything with confidence, these studies indicate that the short-term effects of desegregation on race relations are positive in about one-quarter of the cases that have been studied" (p. 187). For whites, desegregation apparently increased prejudice in eleven of the twenty-four relevant studies and decreased it in only four of them. Stephan and Stephan (1996, p. 79) conclude simply that "in the short run, desegregation does not produce the anticipated positive effects on race relations."

For testing the contact hypothesis, short-term effects on attitudes are the most important effects, but for evaluating the policy of desegregation, longer-term effects, both direct (for example, the effects of attending a desegregated school on the probability of attending college or living in an integrated neighborhood) and indirect (the effect of the policy itself on social norms and expectations), must also be taken into account. Stephan (1986) points out that there has been a "revolution in intergroup relations

. . . since World War II," and "in most respects, blacks and whites are less separate and less unequal now than they were 40 years ago" (pp. 196–97). The Supreme Court's decision in *Brown* was "the spark that ignited the civil rights movement" (p. 197). It was "particularly important as a lesson in how the courts could be used [by minority groups] as a tool to forge [*sic*] social change from a reluctant society" (Stephan, 1991, p. 111). And although it may have increased the salience of the race issue in public consciousness, causing an apparent reduction in racism that may be little more than a shift from overt to symbolic or aversive forms of racism, it has probably also accelerated the acculturation of minority-group students: "Desegregation provides minority students with first-hand opportunities to observe the language usage, norms, and behaviors of members of the majority group. This knowledge may enable them to interact more effectively with majority-group members, although it may do so at the cost of highlighting the differences between the groups. Desegregation may also contribute to the accommodation of majority students to minority students by increasing opportunities for them to learn about one another" (Stephan, 1986, p. 198). Overall, "desegregation has contributed to narrowing the gap [in status between blacks and whites] and has brought us closer to being the kind of society many Americans want to live in, one in which the different racial and ethnic groups in our society have a mutual respect for one another that enables them to live and work together productively" (Stephan, 1991, pp. 117–18).

Research Elsewhere.

Nowhere have the processes of school desegregation and its effects been studied as intensively, over as long a period of time, as in the United States. A few roughly comparable studies of contact and attitudes have been conducted in other countries (for example, James, 1955; Kawwa, 1968; Reich and Purbhoo, 1975; Wagner and Schonbach, 1984), but their findings are difficult to summarize and to compare with the American findings, since the studies do not involve the element of change from segregated to desegregated education that is crucial in the American studies. The only directly comparable literature that can be cited here is a volume containing reports of research on desegregation in Israel (Amir and Sharan, 1984).

In Israel, the relevant groups are European Jews and Middle Eastern or North African Jews. For many years there has been a gap in their educational achievement like the gap between that of blacks and whites in the United States. Because of residential segregation, the children of the two groups do not normally go to school together. Out of concern for equalizing educational opportunities and strengthening national unity, Israeli officials in the late 1960s adopted a policy of deliberate integration of the two groups at the junior high school level (grades 7 through 9). The implementation of this policy did not produce negative reactions at all comparable to those sometimes observed in the United States. (In Israel, Western and non-Western Jews are roughly equal in numbers, are often not distinct in physical appearance, and are bound together by common national aspirations and a common fear of internal and external enemies.) Nonetheless, the studies of the effects of desegregation on intergroup attitudes and interactions seem to have produced results roughly comparable to the results of American research.

> In general, our review indicates that despite the readiness, or at least the lack of objection, on the part of both groups to come into contact with each other and participate in joint activities positive changes in intergroup relations do not necessarily occur. Even in those studies where the overall results indicate a positive change, these changes are quite small or are found in special social settings (such as boarding schools and summer camps). It is possible that at present the major social contribution of desegregation in Israel is in preventing a possible deterioration of interethnic attitudes that might otherwise have developed. (Bizman and Amir, 1984, p. 180)

As another writer states, in the concluding chapter of the volume, "Researchers both in the United States and Israel seem to be increasingly aware that the contact provided by desegregated schooling will not consistently produce intergroup acceptance" (Miller, 1984, p. 245).

Conclusions

In 1953 many leading social scientists encouraged American policy makers to embark upon a great social experiment. They expected it to have good effects within a very short time. They were genuinely surprised and perplexed when more or less rigorous quantitative research began to reveal that racial attitudes do not consistently improve after desegregation. The process of desegregation, it seemed, can aggravate racial tensions and can lead to the development of new and more subtle forms of racism.

Social scientists have always recognized, of course, that contact is a condition for conflict as well as for cooperation. Two groups must be in contact before they can fight or compete. But there are good reasons for expecting that the simple, familiar contact hypothesis, with no fancy restrictions, would describe schoolchildren better than adults. Children have minds that are almost blank slates, lacking historical lore or knowledge. Their thinking, unlike that of adults, is not tangled up with complicated ethnic mythologies. In addition, children do not meet as superiors and inferiors, in relations of authority and subordination, for they are all subject to the common authority of parents and teachers. Children thrown together in desegregated schools, it seemed reasonable to suppose, would naturally form interracial friendships, and these friendships would inoculate them against the groundless stereotypes and racist superstitions of their elders. The vicious cycle of prejudice and discrimination could be broken in a generation. A generation ago, as David Armor has recently written, "school desegregation promised not only improvements in black self-esteem and academic achievement, in effect remedying the damages inflicted by past discrimination and segregation, but also a reduction in one of the root causes of racial discrimination and segregation—white prejudice. Thus school desegregation was supposed to relieve the psychological harms of segregation and at the same time eradicate or at least diminish its source" (Armor, 1995, p. 102).

Generally speaking, empirical research since the 1950s has not justified these expectations. Thus the keynotes of more recent writing about desegregation and the contact hypothesis have been caution and qualification. For more than a generation the basic hypothesis with no limiting conditions has been tested in a situation where it was clearly expected to apply. As a result of these tests, the latent qualifications, which used to be given very little attention, have risen to the surface of discussion, and the hypothesis itself has sunk from view. "If there is one thing that social psychological theory and research have taught us about racially and ethnically diverse schools during the last 40 years, it is that simply putting students from different backgrounds together is not enough to ensure positive social outcomes" (Schofield, 1993, p. 303; see also Schofield, 1995, p. 264). But the author of this statement is typical in moving from the fact of predominantly negative or discouraging results to a stronger insistence on the merits of contact *theory*. As Armor (1995, p. 106) observes, "Many researchers have acknowledged that desegregation has not brought about the expected benefits in race relations and attitude changes, but the reason is not the fault of social science theory. Rather, the fault lies with the designers of desegregation plans—including, presumably, courts that order their adoption—who did not create the conditions necessary for successful racial contact."

During the past generation, the attention of social scientists has shifted from the overall effects of desegregation to the precise interventions necessary to produce positive changes in the verbal attitudes and behavior of children. Recent literature features a distinction drawn more than twenty years ago between mere desegregation and true integration (Pettigrew, 1971, pp. xvii, 312–14). Mere desegregation means simply mixing two races in the same schools. Such mixing may be a necessary condition for genuine interpersonal relations, but it may not alone produce the kinds of contacts between different groups that have positive effects. More deliberate interventions by those in authority may be needed to create the kinds of social climates and interpersonal interactions that produce the kinds of respect for others and the genuinely democratic attitudes that the authorities should be trying to inculcate. These points have been frequently repeated (for example, Amir, 1992, pp. 34–36; Cohen, 1975, p. 292; McConahay, 1978, pp. 105–7; St. John, 1975, pp. 97–99, 107–9, 124–27; Schofield, 1986, pp. 90–92; and Stephan, 1991, pp. 113–15), and many researchers have turned to contact theory for guidance regarding appropriate interventions (for example, Cook, 1984; Johnson, Johnson, and Maruyama, 1984; Rogers et al., 1984; Schofield, 1993, 1995; and Slavin, 1985, 1995).

Researchers now also emphasize how difficult it is to do theoretically relevant empirical research in schools. It is easy enough to get children to play with dolls or to fill out simple questionnaires. But the attitudes of children undergoing various interventions can be easily contaminated by influences emanating from their parents and teachers. As a result, it is often hard to distinguish between the effects of a particular experimental manipulation and the contaminating effects of parents and teachers. The relevant behaviors of parents and teachers are hard to observe, particularly if they are reluctant to cooperate in academic research, as they often are, and therefore hard to control statistically. Much of the literature on the effects of desegregation, and of various kinds of desegregation, must be heavily discounted, as we have seen, because of the methodological shortcomings from which these studies typically suffer.

Finally, it should hardly be necessary to emphasize that the legitimacy of the decisions made by the Supreme Court of the United States in no way depends upon the inherently uncertain and debatable findings of social science. As eminent legal scholars have pointed out, the justices, in their opinions, were pronouncing on the meaning of the Constitution; they were not offering conjectures about controversial scientific hypotheses. Their decisions had to do with constitutional law, not the somewhat exaggerated hopes that some social scientists may have entertained a generation or two ago for a relatively quick and painless resolution of the American racial dilemma.

Looking back over the past forty years, however, one cannot help but be impressed by the steady accumulation of evidence that clashes with the dominant opinions among social scientists at the time of *Brown v. Board of Education*. The effects of desegregation have not been as positive with respect to racial attitudes as many social scientists were once confident they would be. One must not of course oversimplify a complex reality. But if any simple conclusion can be drawn from more than a generation of social science research on the attitudinal effects of desegregation, it is that no simple conclusion about its effects is possible. In this limited sense, the great social experiment of desegregation has been a failure, and we must look elsewhere for evidence with which to judge the contact hypothesis.

3 Two Simple Correlations

This chapter reviews the bulk of the quantitative literature on the contact hypothesis. Relevant studies have steadily accumulated, and the literature is now extensive, even without the studies of school desegregation discussed in Chapter 2 or the closely related studies of primary and secondary school students. The aim of this chapter is simply to clarify the most important lines of evidence that must be taken into account in any theory about contact and ethnic attitudes.[1] It uses two main criteria for classifying studies: research design (observational studies are distinguished from experimental and quasi-experimental studies) and the nature of the independent variable (studies of actual interaction are distinguished from studies of opportunities for interaction). Readers interested only in the main point of the chapter may wish to skip its middle part, from pages 73 to 97. A summary of the whole chapter begins on page 111.

Classifying Studies

Differences in research design provide one important basis for classifying studies. Observational studies correlate naturally occurring differences in contact with differences in ethnic attitudes or behavior. They try to describe people in their natural setting, making it relatively easy to generalize from the situations studied to other situations of interest. Such studies typically have few problems of "external validity," but they cannot (strictly speaking) distinguish correlation from causation. One cannot infer, from the mere fact of a correlation, which variable is cause and which is effect, nor can one dismiss the possibility that both are the effects of some unexamined third variable. Observational studies typically lack "internal validity" (Campbell and Stanley, 1966). Experimental studies, by contrast, typically have the opposite strengths and weaknesses. Randomization and the deliberate manipulation of independent variables ensure that any correlation discovered in such studies can be given a causal interpretation: their strength is internal validity. Their weakness, generally speaking, is their lack of external validity: the causal mechanisms manipulated in the social or psychological laboratory, under the watchful eyes of psychologists and sociologists, often differ from those that matter in the real world. It should not be surprising, then, that some of the most influential studies of the contact hypothesis have been, as we shall see, "quasi-experimental" studies employing a mix of observational and experimental methods to achieve a good balance of internal and external validity.

An even more important basis for classifying studies is the nature of their independent variable. Contact is a broad concept that can be operationalized in a number of ways. Studies of the effects of *interaction* can be distinguished from studies of the effects of *proximity,* and both can be distinguished from studies of the effects of different *proportions* of an ethnic minority in given social units or territorially defined populations. Sometimes these distinctions are hard to apply in practice—a particular study may fit in more than one category—but they are clear enough in principle. Studies of the effects of direct, interpersonal interaction with members of an out-group must not be confused with studies of the effects of population movements or changes in public policy that increase (or decrease) the opportunities for such direct interaction (compare Pettigrew, 1986, p. 189).

Some attention must also be paid, of course, to the dependent variables in the studies reviewed here. Attitudes are not the same as behavior, although they are inferred from behavior; cognitions are not the same as affects or evaluations; and opinions about government policies may have to be distinguished from opinions about groups of people. Measures of social distance may behave one way, measures of stereotyping another, and people themselves a third way, their real-life behavior having little to do with their questionnaire behavior. Not all distinctions can be given equal attention simultaneously, however. The problem of defining the main dependent variable in studies of intergroup contact is discussed in Chapter 5.[2]

Studies of Interaction

Observational Studies.

Among all the studies in this category, one deserves special attention because of its early date, its simple design, its clear results, and its historical importance. Allport and Kramer (1946) surveyed the opinions about minorities of 437 undergraduates enrolled in elementary courses in psychology at Dartmouth, Harvard University, and Radcliffe. The respondents were asked to agree or disagree with a series of twenty-one broad evaluative statements about minorities. Nine of these statements concerned Negroes (for example, "In general, Negroes are shiftless"); eight concerned Jews (for example, "American Jews are as loyal to their country as any other American"); and four concerned Catholics (for example, "Though there are some exceptions, in general Catholics are fascists at heart"). The questionnaires also contained two sets of questions about contact. The students were asked to indicate the degree to which they had "lived with, worked with, played with, or, in general, had contact with members of various groups." Negroes, Jews, and Catholics were listed. Four different responses were possible for each group (none, very little, average, and considerable). This set of questions yielded two measures of "overall contact," one for contact with Negroes, the other for contact with Jews. Then the students were asked to indicate whether they had gone to school with, worked with, played with, had as neighbors, or had as friends individuals from each of seven groups (Jews, Catholics, Negroes, Italians, Irish, Mexicans, and Orientals). By adding up the number of positive responses to these five questions for Jews and for Negroes, the researchers derived two measures of "equal-status contact."

When the four measures of contact were correlated with the two relevant measures of prejudice, all the correlations were statistically significant, and all were in the expected direction (the more the contact, the less the prejudice), but the correlations were stronger for equal-status contact than for overall contact.

From these results the authors drew a broad conclusion—that more contact is a good thing, but that merely casual contact is less beneficial than equal-status contact: "Casual contact with minority groups does not diminish prejudice as markedly as does intimate (equal-status) contact. Only a fairly close knowledge of a minority group reduces one's susceptibility to second-hand stereotypes and epithets concerning it" (p. 37).

Two damaging objections can be leveled at these broad statements. First, the observational method of the Allport-Kramer study does not provide any real evidence for the causal interpretation implied by saying that contact "diminishes" prejudice or "reduces one's susceptibility" to it or, equivalently, that contact has good *effects* on attitudes. The observed correlations may show only that prejudiced people tend to avoid ethnic minorities, whereas more tolerant people are more willing to interact with them (or to say that they do so). The correlation could be due to the effects of prejudice on contact, not those of contact on prejudice. Thus two quite different stories could be written around the same statistics. With no experimental manipulation of the "independent" variable, contact, there is no solid scientific reason for interpreting the correlation one way rather than another (compare Allport, 1954, p. 254).

Second, there is little reason to believe that the set of questions about "equal-status contact" (or "intimate contact") measured anything very different from the questions about "overall contact" (or "casual contact"). Equal-status contact may have more beneficial effects on prejudice than contact that is not equal status (a widely accepted hypothesis that will be discussed at length in Chapter 4), but the questions used by Allport and Kramer failed to make the distinction needed to test this hypothesis. It is certainly reasonable to assume that the second series of questions, being more specific, provided better measures of overall contact than did the simple ratings the respondents checked first. But there is no reason to believe that the two sets of questions measured different kinds of contact.

The correlation Allport and Kramer discovered certainly exists, however. Williams (1964), who conducted opinion surveys in four medium-sized American cities, one in upstate New York, another in the Midwest, the third in California, and the fourth in Georgia, provides the most impressive supporting evidence. He interviewed both majority and minority individuals, clearly separating opportunity for interaction with out-group members from the frequency of actual interaction and relating both to various measures of prejudice (having to do with acceptance of derogatory stereotypes, insistence upon social distance, and approval of public discrimination) as well as to a variety of background variables. The main finding of his research is summed up in the following statement: "Out of hundreds of tabulations, there emerges the major finding that *in all the surveys in all communities and for all groups, majority and minorities, the greater the frequency of interaction, the lower the prevalence of ethnic prejudice*" (pp. 167–68).

Many other studies have reported this same basic correlation. Rosenblith (1949) simply replicated the study by Allport and Kramer and came to identical conclusions. Gray and Thompson (1953) studied social distance attitudes among a sample of Georgia undergraduates toward a variety of out-groups (Belgians, Chinese, and so on) and found that those who claimed to be acquainted with at least five individuals from a given group were more willing to associate with members of that group than those who claimed four or fewer acquaintances. Rose, Atelsek, and McDonald (1953) investigated the effects of black neighbors on whites living in almost exclusively white neighborhoods of Minneapolis. They found more favorable attitudes toward interracial association among those whites who spoke with their black neighbors than among those who did

not. Kelly, Ferson, and Holtzman (1958), in a study of white undergraduates at the University of Texas, found more favorable attitudes toward
blacks among those who had experienced relatively close personal contacts
with them. Similarly, Segal (1965) found cross-group friendship ties associated with lower social distance scores among both Jewish and non-
Jewish students at a northeastern liberal arts college for men. Hamilton
and Bishop (1976) analyzed the reactions of white homeowners in the suburbs of New Haven to a new black neighbor and found that those who
established personal relations with their new neighbor got lower scores on
a measure of "symbolic racism" than those who did not. Smith (1994)
found a clear association between interracial interaction and relatively low
social distance among white housewives living in biracial neighborhoods
in South Bend, Indiana, in 1974 and again in 1984. Similar studies with
similar findings include Butler and Wilson (1978); Harlan (1942); Hunt
(1959); Jeffries and Ransford (1969); Morris and Jeffries (1968); and Riordan (1987).

One of the most careful and detailed studies of naturally occurring interracial contact, Jackman and Crane (1986), sometimes cited as evidence
against the contact hypothesis, can be used to support it. The study examined conservative racial attitudes among a national sample of white
Americans and found that such attitudes varied among whites depending
upon the quantity and quality of their personal relations with blacks. The
minority of white respondents who numbered one or more blacks among
their good friends, and especially those who had both friends and acquaintances among blacks, were less likely to express a variety of conservative
or reactionary sentiments and opinions. Although difficult to distinguish
conceptually as well as statistically, the two independent variables, friendship and acquaintance, seemed to have had a strong effect only in combination. "In general, whites must have both friend(s) *and* acquaintance(s)
who are black before there is any appreciable impact on their attitudes
toward blacks. It seems more important to escape tokenism by establishing
multiple contacts with blacks than to attain a high degree of personal intimacy with one's black contacts" (p. 470). The findings of this study with
respect to *proximity*, which point in a different direction, will be discussed
below.

Social categories other than ethnic or racial ones are often stereotyped
(a category is in a sense a stereotype), and even if these stereotypes are not
thought to illustrate prejudice, variations in them may still be connected
statistically with contact. Thus Biernat and Crandall (1994) investigated
"the contact hypothesis" in a study of stereotyping of three groups on the
University of Michigan campus—"football players, sorority women and
students in the Residential College." In a sample of undergraduates, mostly

freshpersons, they found strong correlations between reported contact with and liking for these groups. Similarly, in an intriguing study of the attitudes of heterosexuals toward gay men, Herek and Glunt (1993) found a strong correlation between contact (having a close acquaintance who is a homosexual) and favorable attitudes in a large sample of English-speaking American adults. Among all the variables included in the study, personal contact with a gay man or a lesbian was the most powerful predictor of positive attitudes (see also Gentry, 1987, and Herek, 1988).

Most studies of contact as *interaction* have investigated the effects of contact on the attitudes of individuals belonging to a majority group: the question has been whether contact with minorities improves the attitudes of majorities. Few studies have focused on the attitudes of minorities, even though the contact hypothesis, as usually stated, covers both majorities and minorities. The situation of minorities with respect to contact may be quite different from that of majorities, however, and its effects on the contact-prejudice relationship deserve attention.

The importance of separately examining the attitudes of minorities is made clear by Sigelman and Welch (1991). Their book focuses on the opinions of black Americans about racial inequality in the United States, using data from several national surveys from the 1980s. Two of these surveys included a question about interracial friendship: "Do you yourself know any white/black person whom you consider a fairly close personal friend?" Among blacks, contact in this sense was unrelated to all the main dependent variables in the study—perceived discrimination against oneself or against blacks generally, the perceived trend in antiblack feelings among whites, opinions about the sources of racial inequality, and support for or opposition to busing, affirmative action, and welfare programs. Almost the same negative results were found in parallel analyses of the attitudes of white respondents.

How are these unusual results—so much at odds, it seems, with the results of the studies cited so far—to be explained? Perhaps the crucial difference was the dependent variables in the study. In most studies of the contact hypothesis, the dependent variables have been quite crude indicators of hostility and stereotyping (for example, white agreement or disagreement with statements like "in general, Negroes can't be trusted"). In Sigelman and Welch (1991), by contrast, the dependent variables are controversial opinions about the causes of racial inequality and its possible cures.[3] To test the contact hypothesis (as conventionally understood) among blacks, it would be necessary to focus more clearly on variations among blacks in their tendency to stereotype whites and to avoid contact with them.

In a follow-up study, Sigelman and Welch (1993) found that contact in the sense of interracial friendship was clearly associated with commitment to black-white social interaction among whites but not among blacks. Among blacks, however, contact was associated with a tendency to minimize Klan-like attitudes among whites, whereas among whites it was weakly associated with greater perception of such attitudes. Among both blacks and whites, contact or interracial friendship was associated with a tendency to minimize the growth of antiblack feelings.

Brigham (1993) carefully developed new scales to measure contemporary racial attitudes and then related the differences they measured to differences in self-reported contact among both black and white students at two southern universities, one predominantly white, the other predominantly black. For both blacks and whites, the new scales, which emphasized affect and social distance, correlated in the expected way with various measures of contact. The questionnaires for the white students included scales designed to measure "modern racism" (McConahay, 1986) and "symbolic racism" (Kinder and Sears, 1981), but differences on these dimensions showed no connection with differences in contact.

Ellison and Powers (1994), in a study of a national sample of black Americans, found strong correlations between personal contact (knowing a white person who is a good friend) and various racial attitudes (see also Powers and Ellison, 1995). Blacks reporting one or more white friends were significantly less likely to oppose interracial dating, more likely to believe that whites want to facilitate black progress, and more likely to perceive a decline in racial discrimination since the 1950s. The authors summarized their main findings as follows: "Blacks who report having close white friends express more favorable views of whites and race relations than those who lack such friends" (p. 395).

Bledsoe et al. (1995) studied "racial solidarity" (a sense of union or community of interests with other blacks, deeper than mere identification or consciousness, expressed in endorsement of various "nationalistic" norms and opposition to intermarriage) among black respondents to a 1992 survey of residents of the Detroit metropolitan area. They found a statistically significant negative correlation between interracial contact (number of white friends, frequency of more casual contact with whites on the job, and so on) and racial solidarity. In other words, those with more contact tended to have more favorable attitudes toward whites. They were less inclined to say that blacks should always vote for black candidates, shop in black-owned stores, give their children African names, and the like. Conversely, "those whose personal interactions are more focused on blacks express greater solidarity with their fellow blacks" (p. 451).

The studies cited so far bring out the main parallels between majorities and minorities with respect to contact and attitudes, but they do not focus on the specific difficulties that minorities may have in dealing with majorities. In the study of interracial visiting and social distance among housewives in South Bend, Indiana, mentioned above, Smith (1994) found strikingly different results for the black housewives in 1984 than ten years earlier. The results of the first study supported the standard contact hypothesis, but those of the second study did not: more contact was associated with more social distance. This puzzling result may have something to do with changes in perceived "belief similarity" between 1974 and 1984 (see p. 447).

A new and potentially important line of research has been opened up by the concept of "intergroup anxiety" (Stephan and Stephan, 1984, 1985). This concept implicitly shifts attention from cultural similarities to cultural differences (compare Stephan, 1987, pp. 30–31). Is the basic problem of intergroup contact one of overcoming false beliefs about imaginary differences among groups or one of learning to cope with real differences? In a study of Asian-American and Hispanic college students, Stephan and Stephan (1989) found that more contact was associated with less "intergroup anxiety" in relations with Caucasians (or Anglos). In addition, more contact was associated with more positive attitudes toward Caucasians but not with any less stereotyping of them.

Finally, one of the most important studies of interaction and ethnic attitudes from a theoretical standpoint focused on two minorities, blacks and Jews. Tsukashima and Montero (1976) used black female interviewers to collect data on attitudes toward Jews among a diverse sample of blacks in two areas of Los Angeles. They found weak negative correlations between contact and anti-Semitism when the contact was with Jews as neighbors or fellow workers. There was a stronger negative correlation when the contact involved "doing something social with them like going to the movies, to a sports event, or visiting each other's houses." There was a much stronger *positive* correlation between contact and anti-Semitism, however, when the contact was shopping in stores owned or run by Jews, renting from a Jewish landlord, or working for a Jewish employer. This study comes closer than any other in the literature to demonstrating that contact has opposite effects depending upon the status relations of those in contact. Its findings will be discussed in more detail in Chapter 4.

Most of the literature on interaction and ethnic attitudes is American, but some comparable studies have been conducted elsewhere and have produced similar results. Rabushka (1969) used "feeling thermometers" to investigate the attitudes and behavior of students from three ethnic backgrounds at the University of Malaya. The students whose social interactions included members of other ethnic groups (for example, Malays who "spent time" with Chinese) were less likely to be ethnocentric and more willing to accept intermarriage. Schaefer (1973) analyzed data from a large survey conducted in areas of England with relatively high proportions of recent Caribbean and Asian immigrants and found that social interaction was associated with more tolerant attitudes. The native white respondents who were acquainted with nonwhite immigrants (as neighbors, as co-workers, or even just as passengers on a bus with an immigrant bus conductor) tended to get lower scores on a measure of prejudice than did their more isolated or aloof compatriots (see also Elkin and Panning, 1975, p. 173). Ray (1983) interviewed two hundred Australians living in Sydney and found a positive but not statistically significant association between having "met and talked to an Aborigine" and approval of Aborigines. (Other questions in his survey revealed a stronger connection between contact and favorable attitudes toward divorcees and nude sunbathers.) Several studies in Germany have apparently shown connections between contact and relatively tolerant attitudes (see Wagner and Machleit, 1986). In Israel, Goldberg and Kirschenbaum (1989) interviewed 422 residents of Haifa about their contacts with Ethiopian Jews, who had recently migrated to Israel, and their attitudes toward them. Various forms of contact were associated with relatively low scores on a social distance index. Bornman and Mynhardt (1991) asked probability samples of Afrikaners and Coloureds in the Cape metropolitan area (more than eight hundred from each group) about their attitudes toward their own and the other group as well as about the quantity and quality of their contacts with each other in a variety of situations. Stepwise multiple regression was used to analyze the dependence of the main attitude variable on the contact variables as well as on ethnic identity, perceptions of intergroup relations, and a variety of background variables. Quantity of contact with Coloureds in the respondent's own home and in other people's homes significantly predicted attitudes toward Coloureds among the Afrikaner respondents. Finally, Pettigrew and Meertens (1995) report comparable results from an unusually thorough study of "subtle" as well as "blatant" prejudice in Western Europe. Using seven independent probability surveys conducted in 1988 in four European countries, with a great variety of scales, they found that respondents who reported having friends from the relevant out-groups (West Indians, Asians, Turks, North Africans, and so on) scored significantly lower than others on both forms of prejudice, in all four countries.

The studies summarized so far illustrate one of the simplest possible designs for testing the contact hypothesis. In all of them individual differences in attitudes toward some out-group are correlated with naturally occurring, essentially voluntary differences in social interaction with members of that out-group. The in-group and the out-group are typically a majority and a minority within a single society—for example, white Americans and black Americans, or Germans and Turks in Germany. The individuals studied are observed in their normal social setting, "at home" so to speak, rather than as tourists or as foreign students. And whatever the sampling methods used, the respondents are treated as random samples of some relevant population (country, city, ethnic group, university student body). These simple studies will be contrasted below with other studies employing fundamentally different designs. First, however, it will be helpful to contrast them with seven studies that employed the same basic design but in which "contact" involved more physical displacement or crossing of geographical boundaries with national or cultural significance.

Reigrotski and Anderson (1959), using standard survey techniques, investigated the impact of contact on the attitudes of French people toward Germans and of Germans toward the French. (The study also gathered data from and about Belgians and Dutch, but the analysis focused on the French and the Germans.) The measure of contact was a sum of positive responses to questions about (a) visiting the other country, (b) speaking its language, and (c) having friends or relatives in the other country. The greater the contact between French and Germans measured in this way, the more positive the stereotype each held of the other and the more likely they were to rate each other as easy to get along with.

In a wide-ranging study of the favorableness of the stereotypes that Greeks and Americans held of themselves and of each other, Triandis and Vassiliou (1967) compared Greeks in Greece with Greeks in the United States and Americans in Greece with Americans in the United States. They found that increased contact between Greeks and Americans was associated with a more favorable Greek stereotype of Americans (essentially as "well-oiled work horses") but a less favorable American stereotype of Greeks (as "inefficient" and "rigid"). They concluded that "when (a) two cultures have similar goals [in this case, material success and a high standard of living], and (b) one is more successful in reaching these goals than the other, *and* (c) members of the two cultures meet, then the successful culture's members become less favorable and the unsuccessful culture's members become more favorable" (p. 327).

In a study of the attitudes of white southerners toward northerners in the United States, Reed (1980) found that southerners who had traveled or lived in the north tended to be more accepting of northerners than those who had not, but they were also more likely to stereotype them. As a result of contact, it seemed, southerners became more definite in their judgments of northerners but also more favorably inclined toward them (compare Biernat, 1990).

For a national sample of Canadians, Kalin and Berry (1980) report significant correlations between geographic mobility, both within Canada and outside it, and various measures of tolerance of ethnic diversity. Those who had traveled widely were less authoritarian, less ethnocentric, more inclined to expect positive consequences from immigration, and more supportive of multicultural ideology than those who had not. But Hewstone (1986), in a study of university students from four European countries, found no statistically significant correlations between time spent in other European countries and overall attitude toward the European Community.

In a study of Qatari students in the United States, Kamal and Maruyama (1990) found that those who reported "direct" contacts with Americans (spending time with Americans, having American friends) had a more favorable attitude toward the American people than those without such contacts or with only "indirect" contacts. The attitude variable was unrelated to length of stay in the United States and to previous contact with other cultures. A similar finding is reported by Ibrahim (1970): Arab students who had American friends tended to be more friendly toward Americans.

One must, of course, be cautious in interpreting the results of observational studies of contact. Differences in attitudes can be confidently attributed to differences in contact only if the high- and low-contact groups were initially similar in all relevant respects except contact. This condition is sometimes—perhaps often—not satisfied. In the study by Triandis and Vassiliou (1967) the thirty "maximum contact" Americans were businessmen, military officers, and professionals working for philanthropic organizations or advising the Greek government. Their "minimum contact" counterparts were twenty-eight University of Illinois students who had said in a questionnaire that they had no personal contact with or knowledge of Greeks or acquaintances among Greeks. Plainly the two groups differed in age, education, experience, and responsibilities as well as in contact. On the Greek side of the study, the maximum contact sample consisted of twelve Greek nationals studying at the University of Illinois. It was compared with a minimum contact sample consisting of fifty-two Greeks studying at the University of Athens. Favorable attitudes toward Americans prior to contact may have played a part in the decisions of the first group to study in the United States. Differences in contact may have been not the cause, but rather the effect, of the attitude differences later observed.

Essentially the same problem appears in a somewhat different form in the study by Herek and Glunt (1993) summarized above. The heterosexual respondents were said to have or not to have contact with homosexuals depending upon how they answered the question "Have any of your female or male friends, relatives, or close acquaintances let you know that they were homosexual?" As the authors point out in their discussion of their results, their independent variable—contact—may in fact have been dependent upon their nominally dependent variable—attitudes toward gay men—since lesbians and gay men are likely to be selective about the heterosexuals to whom they disclose their sexuality. "Heterosexuals who express positive attitudes toward gay people . . . are more likely than others to be the recipients of self-disclosure by gay men and lesbians" (p. 244).

Experimental Studies.

Experimental studies are necessary to determine whether contact has an effect on ethnic attitudes, but such studies are hard to conduct, as will be shown by the following summaries of Cook (1969), Wilder (1984), Barnard and Benn (1988), and Desforges et al. (1991). Readers impatient with the details of empirical social research may wish to skip at this point to page 97, where the discussion of a significantly different correlation begins.

Cook, one of the pioneers of research on contact and ethnic attitudes, designed an experiment to demonstrate the effects of unintended, or involuntary, black-white contact on the attitudes of whites toward blacks and to throw light on the importance of five different conditions for a favorable outcome of such contact (equal status in the situation, cooperative interdependence, positive social norms, violation of stereotypes, and intimacy of association). He seems to have carried out only one part of the experiment he designed, however, because its results were discouraging. Nonetheless, his work illustrates what it would mean to test the contact hypothesis by studying the effects of social interaction experimentally.

The planned experiment was simple in design but complicated and time-consuming in execution because of the deceptions necessary to keep the experimental subjects ignorant of the connection between the testing of their attitudes (before and after their contact experience) and their exposure to that experience. The subjects were white female undergraduates at a number of neighboring colleges and universities in a "border" state (see Cook, 1969, pp. 187–97 for details). They were paid to take a large battery of paper-and-pencil tests of attitudes, interests, and abilities (about twelve hours of testing spread over ten days) twice, at the beginning of the experiment and again at the end, three or four months later. Buried in all these tests were a few (about two hours' worth each time) that had to do with attitudes toward blacks. The testing was conducted at "Biltmore University," and its purpose, the students were told, was to help the "Educational Testing Institute" to evaluate its tests.

A few weeks after the first round of testing, some of the students with strong antiblack attitudes were recruited, apparently independently, by a faculty member at "St. George College" to work part-time on a simulated management task, the purpose of which, they were told, was to develop ways of selecting and training small units to work together under conditions of isolation such as those at early-warning radar outposts. The management game involved running an imaginary railroad. The students worked in teams of three, one student and two trained confederates of the experimenter (one black, the other white) whom the students being tested thought were just other students from the area. The students together managed the railroad for twenty hours spread over as many days. Their success was measured by an imaginary profit that would become bonus money for the students if their performance excelled that of other teams. By varying the characteristics and the roles of the two confederates, the contact situation could in principle be varied with respect to the five conditions noted above. In fact the experiment seems to have been run only with all conditions (equality of status, cooperative interdependence, and so on) favorable.

The key question was whether contact had a positive effect on the attitudes of the experimental subjects as shown by a change in their scores on the relevant tests before and after playing the management game (that is, a change significantly greater than whatever trend there was in the scores of a similar group of extremely prejudiced students due to regression, the effects of testing, or events other than the experimental manipulation). Statistical analysis of the scores revealed that such a change had taken place, but by no means did all the experimental subjects change significantly in the direction expected. In fact, only eight of the twenty-three subjects (or 35 percent) seem to have done so. Given the time and resources needed for the experiment, it appeared to Cook (or to the Department of Health, Education, and Welfare, which was funding his research) that a higher base rate of change (75 to 80 percent) had to be achieved before beginning the experimental variations that would show whether unintended contact under less than optimal conditions had positive effects on attitudes. The experiment was repeated once, apparently with no more encouraging results (Cook, 1978, 1984, 1990). In this limited sense the experiment was a failure, but it nonetheless illustrates good experimental design.

Wilder (1984) reports a much less relevant series of experiments on "intergroup contact." The groups he studied were not blacks and whites but white female undergraduates from Douglass College and Rutgers College, two independent undergraduate colleges within Rutgers University. The women at these colleges apparently hold complementary stereotypes about each other. Douglass women are perceived by Rutgers women to be rather conservative and overly concerned with their appearance and with getting good grades. Conversely, Rutgers women are perceived by Douglass women to be liberals more interested in having a good time than in academic achievement (Wilder and Thompson, 1980).

Wilder reasoned that positive interaction with an out-group member (that is, interaction with a pleasant member of the out-group) would have a favorable effect on evaluation of the out-group provided that the member was perceived to be highly typical of the out-group. Positive interaction with a pleasant out-group member might have little impact on evaluation of the group, however, if the member was thought to be atypical. And given most people's propensity to stereotype out-groups, he hypothesized, *negative* interaction with an out-group member (an interaction with an unpleasant member of the out-group) would have an unfavorable impact on evaluation of the group regardless of whether the member was typical or atypical.

Three experiments were conducted in order to test these hypotheses. The student subjects were told that the experiments were meant to compare the problem-solving abilities of groups of different sizes. Each subject worked with another young woman on short essays, anagrams, riddles, and so on. If a particular subject was from Douglass, the other young woman was said to be from Rutgers, but if the subject was from Rutgers, she was said to be from Douglass. In fact, this second young woman was a confederate of the experimenter. In half of the sessions—including half of those in which she was said to be from Rutgers—this confederate presented herself in such a way as to fit the stereotype of a Douglass student (wearing a skirt and blouse and a moderate amount of makeup, saying that she was a home economics major, and claiming membership in a conservative political club and concern about studying). In the other half of the sessions—including half of her sessions as a Douglass student—she fit the stereotype of a Rutgers student (wearing faded jeans with a plaid shirt and no makeup, saying that she was an economics major who belonged to a liberal political club, and claiming to have plans to party). This confederate also varied systematically in pleasantness. In half of the sessions (and half of all the halves) she regularly praised the naive subject's performance on the various tasks, and in the other half she regularly denigrated it. Finally, a number of the participating students were assigned to a control group and worked on the same tasks alone.

Two principal findings emerged from the statistical analysis of the resulting data. First, experimental subjects who had had pleasant contact with the confederate made more positive evaluations of the rival college, whether Douglass or Rutgers, provided the confederate posed as a typical member of that college. But second, no improvement in attitudes occurred, even after pleasant contact with an apparently typical student, if she illustrated "relevant" stereotypes (that is, made disparaging, elitist remarks about the college attended by the experimental subject).

These experiments nicely illustrate the ingenuity and rigor of experimental social psychology, but they also reveal some of the barriers to experimental testing of the contact hypothesis. Experiments can be designed and carried out to manipulate attitudes toward rival colleges or other groups that elicit only tepid loyalties, but similar experiments to study the rivalries of racial and religious groups would probably evoke protests. There would be difficulties, for example, in getting black and white undergraduate confederates to mimic the types of interest to the experimenters and then to behave pleasantly or unpleasantly to members of the other racial group. Similarly, there would be problems developing operational definitions of typical and atypical Protestant, Catholic, or Jewish behavior. Even naive undergraduates participating in experiments with "typical" blacks or Jews might suspect that their ethnic attitudes were being tested, not their problem-solving ability in groups of different sizes. And if a white Protestant confederate made disparaging remarks about blacks or Jews such as those the "Douglass" woman made about Rutgers women, there might be derisive laughter or angry retorts followed by complaints to the university authorities. Wilder rightly understood that racial and religious sensitivities dictate a more indirect test of the contact hypothesis, but the experiments he conducted are rather remote from the questions of real interest—in other words, they illustrate the problem of "external validity."

The experiment reported by Barnard and Benn (1988) investigated racial attitudes more directly, but by doing so it probably evoked the common tendency to hide disreputable prejudices. The experiment was designed to test the hypothesis that dissimilar beliefs, real or imagined, are a cause of racial prejudice. White male students at a small rural community college, many of whom had had almost no previous contact with blacks, were recruited to participate in a study of "college students' attitudes in the 1980s." After completing a questionnaire designed to measure their attitudes toward blacks (the Otis Stereotyped Attitude Scale—twenty agree-disagree statements "regarding the general nature of Blacks on a number of topics")—they were randomly assigned to six-man discussion groups. Each subject participated in two such groups. Each group met for about an hour and discussed six topics. Three of the topics related to race (for example, "Do you think that white families should adopt racially different children?") and three to other current issues (for example, "Do you think there is too much emphasis on sports in school?"). The experimental subjects were assigned to groups consisting of themselves and five confederates (posing, of course, as naive subjects), two white and three black. The subjects were required to lead the discussions in their groups by stating their opinions on each of the assigned topics before the others in the group stated theirs. The others (the ten confederates) were instructed either to agree or to disagree with the subject's opinions (the belief manipulation). Control groups consisting of six white subjects, with leaders chosen at random, discussed the same twelve issues but with no manipulation of agreement. Following these discussions, all the subjects again completed the Otis Stereotyped Attitude Scale as well as two other questionnaires.

The study found a slight decrease in "stereotyped attitudes" for *all* the experimental groups, by contrast with no change in the attitudes of the control groups. There were no significant differences in attitudes attributable to different experimental manipulations (that is, exposure to "similar" or "different" blacks). The experiment thus failed to support the original hypothesis, since "prejudice reduction was evident for all interracial discussion groups, regardless of the degree of agreement with outgroup members on a series of discussion topics" (p. 132). But the brief interracial contact itself, it seemed, was sufficient to reduce prejudice. The authors concluded that their results "clearly support prejudice reduction programs employing small group discussion procedures within the conditions prescribed by the interracial contact literature" (p. 133).

The unanswered question is how to specify these conditions. According to Barnard and Benn, there need only be "the opportunity for oppositional groups to interact and exchange ideas in a safe and cooperative social context" (p. 125). But the design of their experiment leaves open the possibility that the stereotyped attitudes of their experimental subjects changed not because of a brief contact with blacks but because of the "normative influence" of the experimenters, Barnard and Benn. Attitudes sometimes change when higher authorities make rewards or punishments contingent upon a change in attitudes. It seems that even very subtle rewards and punishments, like the good feeling that undergraduates sometimes get from helping their professors to prove their hypotheses, can have an effect (Rosenthal, 1966).

Some simple experimental studies of contact and homophobia by Lance (1987, 1992, 1994) may illustrate this possibility. An experimental approach easily overcomes the methodological problem noted earlier in observational studies of attitudes toward gay men and lesbians. The independent variable—contact—can be directly manipulated and need no longer depend upon self-disclosure, itself evidently dependent upon attitudes toward homosexuals (Wells and Kline, 1987). But the effects of the manipulator may be hard to separate from the effects of the contact that is manipulated. Lance provided his classes in human sexuality with three hours of contact with homosexuals (four lesbians and four gay males from local gay organizations). Some of his classes filled out a questionnaire about homophobic attitudes before meeting with the gays and lesbians, whereas others completed it only after the experimental treatment. Students in the second set of classes showed lower levels of homophobia on the average than did those in the first set. The effect was quite pronounced, and although it seemed to wear off after about a month, Lance concluded that "intergroup contact can break down people's prejudices and tensions by showing them that their stereotypes and fears are unfounded" (1992, p. 298; 1994, p. 432). The difficulty is, good teaching can have the same effects.

Finally, Desforges et al. (1991) report an experiment in which the "stigmatized outgroup" was former mental patients. Attitudes toward this group were measured before and after a brief interaction with another student who the subjects were told was a former mental patient but who in fact was a confederate of the experimenter and who did not behave strangely. A subject and the confederate worked in pairs for fifty minutes on what the subject was told was a learning experiment involving intravenous therapy. They worked under three different conditions of contact: scripted cooperative learning, jigsaw cooperative learning, and individual study. The purpose of the experiment was to determine the interaction between contact and cooperative interdependence as determinants of attitudes toward stigmatized out-groups.

After some unusually complicated statistical analyses, the authors conclude that "a structured cooperative contact experience, whether using the scripted cooperative contact or the jigsaw cooperative contact technique, convinced students with negative attitudes that former mental patients are not so bad after all" (p. 539). Attitudes were apparently unaffected by the presence or the absence of a material incentive to cooperate: it made no difference whether or not the students had been told that they would get a prize for effective cooperation in learning the material (p. 534). The important contrast was not between subjects who did and those who did not have contact with (real) former mental patients (a rather shadowy and elusive "group"), but only between those in the two "cooperative contact" situations and those in the "individual study" situation (those who sat quietly in a room with a "former mental patient" studying material about intravenous therapy).

The studies just summarized suggest how difficult it is to test contact theory experimentally. Experimental manipulation of variables can in principle untangle cause and effect in social relations just as it does in agriculture, medicine, and engineering, but the variables studied must be the variables of interest, and the experiments must not introduce disturbing new variables such as the influence of the experimenters. These conditions are very hard to satisfy in experimental studies of the contact hypothesis, and there are no such studies that clearly demonstrate a strong effect of interaction on *ethnic* attitudes. Academic psychologists evidently have difficulty manipulating the crucial independent variable: the amount of personal interaction with out-group members. As the studies just summarized show, very superficial interaction can be manipulated by assigning some subjects to a contact condition in which they are required to cooperate with members of an ethnic or other out-group for a very short time on a common task while assigning other subjects to a control group of no contact. But it is impossible in the psychological laboratory to create the distinctions made by survey questions about prolonged association as friends, neighbors or coworkers, and it is surprisingly hard to separate the potentially significant "experimenter effects" from the generally slight effects of limited and superficial contact. Nonetheless, well-designed experimental studies of personal interaction represent a potentially important line of evidence regarding the contact hypothesis.

Quasi-Experimental Studies.

Studies in this category attempt to break the link between prior attitudes and subsequent interaction by measuring attitudes before and after a fortuitous increase in contact or by deliberately manipulating contact, but without the random assignment of individuals to experimental and control groups that is the hallmark of a true experiment. Without the need to create two equivalent groups by randomization, researchers are free to conduct (or analyze) far more realistic experiments than the ones just summarized. The quasi-experimental approach does not eliminate all problems, however.

Mann (1959) investigated the impact on friendship choices and ethnocentrism of mixing blacks and whites in leaderless discussion groups meeting for about an hour, four times a week, for a period of three weeks. These meetings were an integral part of a short, intersession graduate course at Teachers College, Columbia University, in which all the subjects were enrolled. The ratio of whites to blacks in the course was 3:2, and individuals were assigned randomly to six-person groups. A sociometric perception questionnaire (essentially a request that each of the students rank the other members of his or her group according to which he or she would "most like to continue to be friends with after the end of the Summer Session") and a short version of the California ethnocentrism scale (the "patriotism" subscale) were completed by all the students at the third and the eleventh general class sessions. Various hypotheses were tested by comparing "before" and "after" scores derived from these questionnaires. Statistically significant declines in both "racial favoritism" (the tendency to prefer members of one's own race as friends) and ethnocentrism (that is, "patriotism") were found. These results were consistent with the working hypothesis that intergroup contact reduces prejudice.

Similarly, Robinson and Preston (1976) report reductions in prejudiced attitudes among black and white teachers in Texas who had voluntarily participated in a racially integrated in-service training institute on problems of school desegregation (see also Preston and Robinson, 1974). The teachers were interviewed and their prejudices measured both before and after participating in the institute. Control groups of teachers from the participants' schools who had not been involved in the institute were also interviewed. Statistical analysis of the prejudice scores showed that although the institute experience had reduced prejudice, it had had more effect on white prejudice toward blacks than on black prejudice toward whites. Robinson and Preston explained this discrepancy by saying that equal-status contact reduces prejudice but that many interracial contacts that are perceived as being between equals by whites are still perceived as situations of subordination by blacks because they have internalized the belief that whites are more competent (compare Cohen and Roper, 1972).

A less encouraging note is struck by Teahan (1975a, 1975b), who studied the attitudes of black and white police officers when entering a racially integrated police academy, at graduation thirteen weeks later, and after a year and a half together on the force. The results showed sharp increases in white officers' prejudice toward blacks and in black officers' dislike for whites. Both groups harbored resentment that the other group received preferential treatment in the police department. Both expressed an increasing desire for two separate police associations, one for each race, and both showed growing interest in segregated scout car duty.

Riordan (1978) studied the effects of black-white contact among teenagers (aged sixteen to nineteen) in two Encampments for Citizenship during the summer of 1972. The purpose of the six-week encampments was "community leadership training and education in democratic political process" (p. 321). The participants were exposed to "speakers, films, role-playing, discussions, workshops, community service work, field trips, and recreational and cultural activities" (p. 312) designed to increase their tolerance not just of racial and ethnic groups but also of homosexuals and ex-convicts. Their attitudes were tested on the first day of camp and immediately after their return home. Changes in the black and the white experimental or contact groups were compared with those observed in control groups chosen to be as similar as possible to the experimental groups. Analysis of the results showed a statistically insignificant deterioration in the interracial attitudes of the black contact group and a statistically significant deterioration among the whites. "There is no consistent evidence that either Blacks or whites in contact with one another became [more] tolerant or less ethnocentric in this study. Rather, it appears that whites may have actually become less tolerant of Blacks, and that Blacks may have become more ethnocentric with respect to themselves" (p. 324).

Two of these studies employ control groups, but two (the studies by Mann and Teahan) do not. More important, the first two studies are unable to distinguish the effects of contact from the effects of authoritative suggestion, inviting an interpretation of their results in terms of "experimenter effects" (Rosenthal, 1966). In these studies the subjects were students who may have wished to please their teachers, the experimenters, who were seeking to demonstrate the beneficial effects of contact with members of an out-group. As Amir (1976, p. 286) has remarked, "Studies in which prestigious persons such as teachers have led subjects through a series of experiments with blacks have the problem that the research subjects simply cooperated by providing their leader with the changes they knew he was looking for." This interpretation is tempting in the case of Mann (1959) because the student subjects were taking a course that "emphasized the importance of the democratic sharing of ideas, feelings, and experiences," and the groups to which subjects were assigned "were designed to provide an opportunity for such democratic sharing" (p. 145).

This interpretation is even more tempting in the case of Robinson and Preston (1976) because, as they explain in their report, the training offered by the "institute" in question had been carefully designed "to promote favorable attitude change": "These in-service training sessions for teachers included lectures by nationally known consultants and local college professors. Seminars, films, group discussions, field observations, trips, reports, and small group sensitivity sessions were included in the institute program format. The program dealt with the social, psychological, economic, and political foundations of racial discrimination and prejudice. The role of the teacher in the desegregation process was especially emphasized" (p. 914). The authors correctly conclude from their quasi-experiment that "equal-status interracial interaction which is intimate, intense, of some duration, and specifically directed toward modifying attitudes of *both* black and white subjects can be highly successful in reducing prejudice" (p. 922). But their data throw no light on the crucial question whether it was the contact itself or the efforts made by the institute's organizers to modify attitudes that should get the credit for the changes observed.[4]

Quasi-experimental before-and-after comparisons are possible when the relevant increase in contact is not imposed by an experimenter but arises accidentally or from individual choice. Thus Williams (1964) collected panel data (repeated measurements of the same respondents separated by a period of time) in "Hometown," the city in upstate New York that he studied. By examining the relations over time between changes in contact and changes in prejudice, one can in principle determine the relative importance of the two relevant processes, contact tending to reduce prejudice and prejudice to reduce contact. Williams concluded that "both do happen and are probably of roughly equivalent importance" (p. 174; also pp. 214–15).

Zeul and Humphrey (1971), in an attempt to show the irrelevance of the contact hypothesis for understanding the integration of black residents in predominantly white suburban neighborhoods, found instead the usual correlation between contact (amount of "neighboring") and positive attitudes toward blacks among their white respondents. But a comparison between the attitudes their respondents recalled prior to contact and their attitudes at the time of the study suggested that prior attitudes influenced subsequent contact much more than contact influenced attitudes. "Respondents seemed to be demonstrating their attitudes via their behavior" (p. 472).

Butler and Wilson (1978) used nonrecursive statistical models to analyze the interdependence of contact and attitudes in a large collection of data from American military personnel in 1973 and 1974. Their figures seem to show that interracial contact had a significant negative effect on "separatist attitudes" for both blacks and whites but that these attitudes had very little influence in turn on contact. Unfortunately, this potentially important point is lost in a haze of statistical uncertainty (see Sanders and Bielby, 1980, and the reply by Butler and Wilson; compare Powers and Ellison, 1995).

Rothbart and John (1993), in a careful study of the changes in white college students' stereotypes of blacks and Asians over a period of four years, found that those with more intergroup contact tended to have more *stable* stereotypes. In addition, it seems that they found no overall relation between contact and favorable attitudes. "Increases in the total amount of contact and in personal closeness to members of the groups were unrelated to increases in the favorability of the final stereotype" (p. 55).

Studies of the effects of tourism and of student exchanges on attitudes can also employ a longitudinal, quasi-experimental design, with measures of attitudes taken before and after a stay in the host country. Any change observed can be treated as an effect of interaction with a variety of the host country's citizens.

Studies of tourism along these lines suggest that it has more negative than positive effects on attitudes. In a study of American students traveling in Europe for a summer, Smith (1955, 1957) found few changes of any kind in attitudes (ethnocentrism, fascism, and conservatism, as measured by standard scales) that could be attributed to contact with Europeans. Hofman and Zak (1969) report no overall change in attitudes among Canadian and American teenagers attending a six-week summer camp in Israel. Pearce (1982) found that British tourists visiting Greece or Morocco became more confident in judging these nations but no more favorable in their judgements; most of the changes observed on a measure of stereotyping were negative. Ben-Ari and Amir (1988) studied Israeli tourists before and after a visit to Egypt and found positive changes on the "social" dimension of evaluation (Egyptians were perceived as more polite, friendly, honest, and so on than expected) but negative changes on the "intellectual" dimension. Similarly, Milman, Reichel, and Pizam (1990) found that the attitudes of Israeli tourists visiting Egypt either remained unchanged or became more negative as a result of their visit. Pizam, Milman, and Jafari (1991) found only slight improvements in the attitudes of American students after a visit to the former USSR. Anastasopoulos (1992) studied Greek tourists before and after a visit to Turkey. Contact with Turks sharply reduced the Greeks' initially favorable attitude toward them: after the trip, the Greeks were more likely to describe the Turks as dishonest, cruel, unreliable, slow, lazy, boastful, illiterate, and sexist; they attributed more hostility to the Turks; and they had a lower opinion generally of Turkish institutions. Finally, Stephan and Stephan (1992) report a decrease in "intercultural anxiety" among American college students following a four-day visit to Morocco but no correlation between changes in anxiety and students' overall amounts of contact with Moroccans.

Studies of university students, academics, and professionals involved in exchange programs are much more common than studies of tourists. This is hardly surprising, given the involvement of governments and foundations in sponsoring exchanges and their legitimate interest in knowing whether the programs they support are having good effects. But the result is a surfeit of studies, only a few of which test the contact hypothesis, although many throw some light on it. To review all the studies of adjustment and performance of students and others involved in exchange programs would be a task comparable to that of reviewing all the literature on contact as a result of school desegregation. Generally speaking, however, the studies concerned with attitude change have produced disappointing results (see the reviews by Bochner, 1982; Brein and David, 1971;

Sell, 1983; and Spaulding and Flack, 1976). A generation ago an authoritative review of the relevant literature included the following remarks: "It is a common assumption that getting to know the people of another country will lead to liking them; this assumption underlies the expectation that exchange-of-person programs will increase international good will. In its simplest form, this hypothesis would lead one to expect that, on the whole, visitors to a country will leave with more favorable views than they held before their arrival, and that their views after the trip will be more favorable than those of their compatriots who have not visited the country in question. The entire body of research on cross-cultural education, however, suggests that this expectation is oversimplified and overly optimistic" (Selltiz and Cook, 1962, p. 10).

A recent review concludes that "the majority of studies on the impact of foreign exchange on stereotypes of, and liking for, the host nation seem to challenge the expectation that meeting and 'getting to know' people of another country will increase attraction toward them" (Stroebe, Lenkert, and Jonas, 1988, p. 171). These authors summarize the data from their own study of American students in France and Germany as follows: "Consistent with the findings of research reviewed earlier, there was no evidence of any improvement in these students' attitudes or stereotypes toward their host population. On the contrary, after spending a year in France or Germany, students liked their host nation (whether French or German) less than before, an effect that seems to have been somewhat more marked with regard to the French than the Germans" (p. 180).

Studies of Proximity

Studies of proximity are studies of the *opportunity* for interaction, where having opportunity means living or working relatively close to members of an out-group. Proximity in this sense presumably increases interaction: those who live and work close together should tend to interact with each other more frequently than those who live and work farther apart, but of course they need not do so. Proximity is a necessary but not a sufficient condition for interaction. The difference between proximity and interaction is clear in principle but sometimes hard to apply when classifying research reports. Much of the literature on the contact hypothesis ignores the difference. Some of the studies summarized below may provide evidence of the effects of either proximity or interaction. Other studies, however, incorporate the distinction as part of their research design or analytic strategy.

Observational Studies.

Williams (1964) distinguishes the two variables and provides the simplest and clearest analysis of proximity (or "opportunity") as a variable influencing both interaction and ethnic attitudes. Unfortunately, no simple generalization emerges from his data, partly because of the limitations of the methods of statistical analysis that he used.

As explained earlier, Williams conducted surveys in four widely separated cities with contrasting racial and ethnic mixes, which provided quite different opportunities for interaction. Moreover, individuals within each of the cities had different opportunities depending upon such factors as age, sex, employment, and place of residence. Among those with similar opportunities, some actually interacted with members of out-groups, whereas others did not. Among those who had no opportunities, there could of course be no interaction: the two contact variables are necessarily correlated.

Williams assessed each of his respondents' opportunities for interaction by means of questions such as "Are there any Jewish people living within a block or two of your home?" Actual interaction was defined as having a good or close friend with whom the respondent did something of a social nature, and it was measured by follow-up questions such as "Have you ever done something social with this Jewish person, like going to the movies, or to a sports event, or visiting in each other's homes?" Various indices of opportunity and interaction were constructed by summing responses to questions about neighborhood, work, and voluntary organizations and about blacks as well as Jews. Separate analyses were done for each of the cities.

It is reasonable to expect a stronger connection, generally speaking, between attitudes and interaction (whatever the direction of causation) than between attitudes and the opportunity for interaction. Interaction implies a closer, more voluntary relation than does the physical proximity that largely determines opportunity. Interaction should be more important, therefore, as both an indicator and a determinant of ethnic attitudes.

Williams's findings are in line with this expectation: more interaction always goes with less prejudice, and in three of the cities he also found that greater opportunity for interaction was associated with lower levels of prejudice (p. 158). This is to be expected, of course, given the strong connections between opportunity and interaction on one hand and between interaction and attitudes on the other. Decreased prejudice from increased opportunity need not always be found, however, and in "Southport," the southern city with a large black population, the expected relation between opportunity and attitudes did not hold: the racial attitudes of whites were unrelated to their opportunities for interaction with blacks (p. 158). In the other three cities, both interaction and opportunity for interaction seemed to influence racial and ethnic attitudes, but some of the key statistical tables are unfortunately hard to interpret because of the small numbers of cases underlying some of the percentages (due to the small sample sizes for each city and the strong correlations between opportunity and interaction). The study leaves it unclear, therefore, whether proximity has any *independent* effect on attitudes once the effect mediated by interaction is taken into account.

Other studies of proximity and attitudes are similarly inconclusive. In an unusually thorough analysis of the attitudes of a small sample of whites living in St. Louis, Hamblin (1962) found that those who reported "being around Negroes" at work or in the neighborhood were somewhat less inclined to discriminate against them. But he also found that those with a "feeling" that Negroes were crowding into parks, playgrounds, schools, jobs, and housing in the area were more likely to harbor discriminatory attitudes. Perhaps the only conclusion that should be drawn is that proximity may be hard to measure objectively from subjective reports.

Brown and Albee (1966) found a positive correlation between greater contact with and greater prejudice against blacks in a study of hospitalized white males from rural Ohio and western Pennsylvania. Patients from racially integrated wards in tuberculosis hospitals, who had had prolonged contact with blacks in that setting, were more opposed to desegregation and more inclined to maintain social distance than were similar patients from all-white wards or patients hospitalized for only a short time in general medical and surgical hospitals. The authors speculate that a "total institution" such as a hospital for the chronically ill, by imposing close physical proximity upon groups in some measure alien to each other, might produce a tendency among them to withdraw from any truly effective interaction and to maintain an even greater social distance than they had previously maintained (p. 332).

Robinson (1980) provides an unusually straightforward analysis of an unusually large data set (the six General Social Surveys from 1972 to 1977) and comes to more encouraging conclusions. Six questions having to do with interracial marriage, social visiting, and residential segregation or integration provided insight into the racial attitudes of the white respondents to the surveys. Their proximity to blacks was measured by means of their answers to a simple question: "How many (blocks/miles) away do they (the Negro/Black) families who live closest to you live?" The results clearly supported the contact hypothesis: "Physical distance was indeed associated with negative racial attitudes" (p. 327). The six basic correlations were not very strong, but they were clearly significant, and they held up under various controls, in particular a control for the four main regions of the country.

Jackman and Crane (1986) also investigated neighborhood proximity in the elaborate and theoretically ambitious study whose findings regarding interaction and prejudice have already been presented. They seem to have relied upon their respondents' reports of the racial composition of their neighborhoods to establish high- and low-proximity groups. They found clear connections between proximity and interaction (friendship as well as acquaintance) but not the expected overarching positive correlation between proximity and liberal racial attitudes, apart from friendship. "Sheer proximity to blacks appears to be of little value, unless it is accompanied by personal contact, but proximity does have a direct effect of its own on racial attitudes when personal contact accompanies it, and the more personal contact there is, the greater the effect of proximity" (p. 474).

Similarly complicated results are reported by Kinder and Mendelberg (1995). Using the data from the white respondents to the 1990 General Social Survey, they found no correlation whatever between racial proximity (judged by responses to questions about neighborhood, church, and workplace) and prejudiced beliefs about blacks. They did find, however, a clear *interaction* between proximity, prejudice, and opinions about relevant policies (segregation, busing, affirmative action): racial proximity weakened the correlations between prejudice and policy opinions, whereas isolation increased them. Racially prejudiced whites seemed to rely less on their general beliefs or stereotypes when judging policies under conditions of proximity, whereas racial isolation strengthened the statistical connection between favorable or unfavorable judgments about blacks generally and judgments about relevant policies. "Proximity appears to offer whites the opportunity to become acquainted with the diversity and commonality of their fellow black citizens. Such learning may not overturn conventional stereotypes, but it does seem to supply additional and distinctive grounds for opinion [about policies]" (p. 420).

Wood and Sonleitner (1996) report simpler results from a study of the white respondents to the 1991 Oklahoma City Survey. Childhood interracial contact was measured by means of three questions about proximity to blacks when growing up. More contact in this sense correlated negatively with current antiblack prejudice. In addition, those with more contact in the past were less likely to stereotype blacks. These correlations remained significant even with controls for age and education.

With regard to the attitudes of blacks, Demo and Hughes (1990), in a study based upon data from a 1979–80 national probability sample of black Americans, found *negative* correlations between contact and both black separatism and feelings of closeness to other blacks but a *positive* correlation between contact and black group evaluation, or racial self-esteem. Contact was measured by having respondents report the racial composition of their neighborhoods, churches, and workplaces. "Dissonant racial contexts," the authors concluded, "detract from blacks' feelings of group identification and attachment," but the interracial interaction promoted by such contexts promotes "positive black group evaluation" (pp. 371, 372). Using data from the same survey, Powers and Ellison (1995) found no correlation between proximity to whites and the amount of skepticism that blacks feel toward whites but found a negative correlation between proximity and opposition to interracial dating (those respondents with more opportunities for interaction with whites tended to be less opposed to interracial dating). Harris (1995), also using the same survey, found weak statistical connections between childhood proximity to whites and weaker racial identity (feelings of closeness to other blacks) among adults.

Residential proximity has been investigated in five other American studies that merit brief mention. Irish (1952) compared Caucasian residents of Boulder, Colorado, who had either had or not had Japanese-American neighbors after the United States Navy established a Japanese language school there in 1942. Those who had had such neighbors expressed more willingness to associate with Japanese than those who had not, but there was no difference between the two groups on national policy toward the Japanese. Rose, Atelsek, and McDonald (1953) studied the racial attitudes of whites living in eight overwhelmingly white neighborhoods in Minneapolis when blacks made up only about 1.3 percent of the total population of the city. They found that whites living within a block of black families had slightly more favorable attitudes than those living slightly farther away. The difference was slightly clearer in the four neighborhoods where blacks had been living for a relatively long time (more than ten years) than in the other four neighborhoods (where they had been living for less than two years). Hunt (1959) studied the white neighbors of black families in predominantly white neighborhoods in Kalamazoo, Michigan, a medium-sized city with a small black population. He found no significant differences in attitudes between the next-door neighbors of the black families and whites a block away. A similar study of a middle-class neighborhood in Stockton, California, by Meer and Freedman (1966) found almost no correlation between proximity and attitudes. Finally, Hamilton and Bishop (1976) investigated eighteen neighborhoods in the suburbs of New Haven, Connecticut, using a measure of "symbolic racism" (McConahay, 1986) as the main dependent variable. In eight of these previously all-white neighborhoods, a house had been sold to a black family. In the other ten neighborhoods, all white, a house had been sold to a white family. The attitudes of the residents in adjacent houses were measured before the new families moved in, three months afterward, and a year later. After a year the two groups of whites—those with and those without new black neighbors—diverged on only two items of the symbolic racism scale. These weak correlations do not clearly support any simple generalization about proximity and ethnic attitudes.

David (1971) gave questionnaires to American servicemen on military bases in four Asian countries—Japan, Korea, Okinawa, and Thailand—and found almost no connection between their location and their rating of host country nationals. Thus, servicemen living in Japan, who had had more opportunity for interaction with Japanese, were no more likely to rate the Japanese favorably than were those living in the other three countries. Those living in Korea or Thailand did not rate Koreans or Thais more favorably. The servicemen living in Okinawa, however, gave significantly more *unfavorable* ratings to Okinawans.

One British study discussed earlier deserves attention again at this point because it also reports a significant association between proximity and prejudice. Schaefer (1973) found more prejudice among white English respondents who reported living next door to nonwhite immigrants than among those living farther away. The general rule seemed to be "the nearer the immigrants the greater the respondents' racial prejudice" (p. 362). The opposite rule, however, appears to fit the results reported by Kirchler and Zani (1995) from a study of 222 residents of Bologna, Italy, who were given a twenty-minute questionnaire about black immigrants in 1991. The data in this case show a modest negative correlation between proximity and prejudice: "People living in the neighbourhood of black immigrants have more favourable attitudes towards them than those living in districts without black immigrants" (p. 63).

The difficulty of drawing any simple conclusion from the results of empirical studies of proximity and prejudice is illustrated by a recent study based upon large national samples from twelve European countries in 1988. Using the data from Eurobarometer 30, Quillian (1995) shows clear connections between contact in the sense of neighborhood proximity (respondents reporting that there are people of another race or nationality who live in the neighborhood) and both racial prejudice and anti-immigrant attitudes. Contact in this sense seems to produce prejudice. But proximity to racial minorities or other immigrants at work seems to have the opposite effects: those with more contact show lower levels of racial and anti-immigrant prejudice. Since Quillian's study is an unusually good one, it nicely illustrates the difficulties in the way of any broad generalization about the relation between proximity and prejudice.

Eight other studies worth noting here have examined the attitudinal correlates of proximity in occupational settings. Using an unspecified measure of antiblack prejudice, Brophy (1946) found a strong correlation between contact with blacks (number of voyages with black crew members) and low levels of prejudice in a sample of white merchant seamen, mostly American, interviewed in New York City. Interpretation of this correlation is complicated, however, by the apparent effect of membership in the National Maritime Union, to which most of the seamen belonged and which was forcefully promoting nondiscriminatory ideals: there may have been a relation between number of voyages and length of membership in the union and thus exposure to its educational activities (compare Gundlach, 1956). Harding and Hogrefe (1952) found that clerical and sales workers in two large department stores expressed greater willingness to take a job "in which there were both Negroes and white people doing the same kind of work as you," if they were presently working in departments with blacks doing work similar to their own. Equal-status-work contact was unrelated to a variety of other racial attitudes, however, and as the authors said, "the most plausible explanation of the attitudes of the equal-status contact respondents is that the great majority of them have simply accommodated to a situation in which they found themselves, without any change in their basic orientation toward Negroes" (p. 26). Hamilton (1972) examined the attitudes of nonsouthern white workers in 1964 and found a weak association between living or working in an integrated environment and support for equal employment opportunity legislation.

In South Africa, Spangenberg and Nel (1983) compared (a) the social distance attitudes of white academics working with Coloured colleagues in a university for Coloured students with (b) the attitudes of white academics in another university with no Coloured colleagues and few Coloured students. ("Coloured" is—or was—a distinct category of the South African population. The word is used as I use it here in the articles I am summarizing.) The academics in the first university expressed more willingness to have close social relations with Coloured individuals. Also in South Africa, in a study of nursing students, Finchilescu (1988) showed some association between occupational proximity and positive attitudes. White student nurses in a hospital with a racially integrated training program, by comparison with similar nurses in a hospital with an all-white program, tended to evaluate the personality and work ability of nurses of Indian origin more favorably. But Bornman and Mynhardt (1991), in the large study already described, found no significant correlations between amount of contact in the workplace and relevant attitudes of Afrikaners or Coloureds in the Cape metropolitan area. And Bornman (1992), in a national sample of Coloureds, found no connection between the ethnic composition of the respondents' workplaces and their attitudes toward Afrikaners. Among Afrikaners, however, significantly more negative attitudes toward Coloureds were found among employees of organizations in which the majority of employees were blacks or Asians. In short, the study lends little support to the idea that contact in the workplace generally improves ethnic attitudes. "On the contrary, there were indications that contact could result in more negative attitudes" (pp. 650–51).

Proximity is inherently more difficult to measure than interaction. Are the relevant distances physical or social? How should they be measured? In some of the studies just summarized, the respondents were asked to classify themselves with respect to proximity, whereas in others they were classified by the researchers according to "objective" differences in their distances from relevant out-groups. Some of these studies focused on small differences in distance; others dealt with much larger differences. Close proximity is plainly associated with frequent interaction, and interaction, as we saw earlier, is consistently associated with positive attitudes. But is proximity consistently associated with positive attitudes? It seems not. The explanation may be that changes in proximity are often associated with changes in the "territories" of different groups, and these territorial effects may be quite different from the effects of personal interaction. At any rate, the twenty-five studies summarized in this section make clear how weak the correlations are, generally speaking, between proximity and attitudes and how difficult it would be to defend any simple generalization about the effects of proximity on attitudes.

Experimental Studies.

Rigorous inferences regarding the causal impact of one variable upon another require random assignment of subjects to experimental and control conditions that differ only in the variable whose causal impact is being investigated. The five experimental studies summarized earlier, in the section on contact as interaction, illustrate this methodology in studies of the contact hypothesis. Unfortunately, no genuinely experimental studies of proximity have been published so far.

This gap in the literature is easily explained. A relevant experiment would involve assigning subjects (individuals or families) randomly to conditions (jobs, housing, clubs, churches) that placed half the subjects near individuals or families belonging to a relevant out-group and half far away from them. Ideally, in order to test the relative effects of proximity and social climate or to test for an interaction between them, the subjects should be assigned randomly to integrated and segregated environments—half of each half near and half far away from the relevant out-group—in which features other than proximity clearly and convincingly symbolize the commitment of public authorities to either integrated or segregated norms of intergroup interaction. It would also be helpful if nonreactive or unobtrusive instruments could be developed for measuring the relevant attitudes (Weitz, 1972; Crosby, Bromley, and Saxe, 1980), because experimental subjects given standard questionnaires might guess that they were being assigned to jobs, housing, or churches by social scientists interested only in testing hypotheses about how to improve their ethnic attitudes, and they might react negatively to such a discovery. The biggest hurdle, however, is the random assignment of individuals to the various experimental and control conditions. Social scientists are not licensed to make such assignments. At best they can observe and discuss the effects of the quasi-experiments conducted by others.

Quasi-Experimental Studies.

Broadly speaking, quasi-experimental studies of proximity have provided the most important evidence on the contact hypothesis, for they have thrown light on the effects of the variables that are under the control of policymakers. Most of the studies making up the extensive literature on school desegregation, for example, belong in this category.

Perhaps the most important practical experiment concerning proximity and ethnic attitudes was the one conducted with the help of the Research Branch of the United States Army in 1945 (Stouffer et al., 1949, pp. 589–95). The policy of the army up to that time had been to train few black combat soldiers (blacks were used, for the most part, in support roles) and to group those trained for combat in their own divisions. To the extent possible—consistent with the desire to use black manpower efficiently—the army followed a policy of racial segregation.

Near the end of the war, however, because of severe shortages in the European theater, the army decided to organize black volunteers as separate platoons within several white infantry companies with white officers. Shortly after the end of the war, a survey was conducted by the research branch to determine the effect of this experiment on the soldiers involved in it. The data showed that both the white officers and the white enlisted men thought highly of the fighting ability of the black infantrymen and that they generally approved of the way in which they had been integrated into their companies—as separate platoons. Many noted that the relations between the races had been better in combat than they had been in garrison. But the most important finding emerged only when the responses of the white soldiers in the integrated companies were compared with those of other white soldiers on a question about integration. The soldiers who had fought with blacks were much less likely (7 percent versus 62 percent) to strongly oppose having army divisions with companies including black platoons and white platoons. "The closer men approached to the mixed company organization, the less opposition there was to it. That is, men actually in a company containing a black platoon were most favorable toward it, men in larger units in which there were no mixed companies were least favorable, while men in all-white companies within a regiment or division containing mixed companies held intermediate positions" (p. 594). The researchers concluded that "a revolution in attitudes" had taken place among these men "as a result of enforced contacts" (p. 595). Proximity to black soldiers had improved the attitudes of white soldiers (compare Roberts, 1953).

A much larger study, Project Clear, was conducted in 1951, in the midst of the Korean War and after integration of the army had gone much farther than it had at the end of World War II (Bogart, 1992). The study employed lengthy questionnaires in two large surveys, one of officers and enlisted men in Korea and another of officers and men in ten military installations in the continental United States. In general, the results of this study were similar to those of the earlier study.[5] White soldiers in integrated units favored integration and had relatively positive attitudes toward blacks, whereas those in all-white units were less favorable. In addition, those who reported contact with blacks in civilian life before enlistment tended to have more positive attitudes toward blacks. Among the conclusions of the study, the most interesting from the standpoint of contact theory is the following: "Men learn to accept integration. As it is experienced, attitudes become more favorable. Thus the probable success of any new attempt at integration may be gauged not in terms of what attitudes men hold at present, but in terms of what attitudes they are likely to hold under the impact of their new experience" (p. 141).

In short, integration seemed to have an educational effect: an exercise of authority had produced an overt change in behavior, which seemed to be producing a change of opinion, "bending" opinion to justify the changed behavior. As one of the researchers explained years later, "*Clear* demonstrates that authority excercised firmly and without ambiguity can control behavior and shift opinion in potentially tense situations. . . . Strong hierarchical structures like the Army and the Roman Catholic Church have been able to bring about desegregation far more efficiently than institutions that depend on voluntary action" (pp. xlviii–xlix).

The most frequently cited quasi-experimental studies of the contact hypothesis are two similar studies of interracial public housing by Deutsch and Collins (1951) and by Wilner, Walkley, and Cook (1955). Both studies tested the hypothesis that greater proximity between blacks and whites, resulting from the "color-blind" assignment of families to public housing units, would lead to greater contact between the races, which would in turn lead to friendly social relations and ultimately to the development of more positive intergroup attitudes. Both studies compared the attitudes of whites who lived close to blacks with the attitudes of whites living farther away. In both studies the near group and the far group were analagous to the experimental and the control groups in an experiment, since tenants had been assigned to housing units without regard to their racial attitudes. The groups were treated as having had the same attitudes, on the average, before moving into the housing projects. The demand for public housing was great enough at the time, and the color-blind policy new enough, that white applicants for public housing very rarely turned down an assignment because it would involve living close to blacks.

Deutsch and Collins studied four public housing projects in the New York area. Two were fully integrated interracial projects in New York City (black families and white families living side by side in the same buildings) and two were "area segregated" biracial projects in Newark, New Jersey (black families and white families living in the same projects but assigned to buildings in different areas of the projects). The hypothesis was that integration would lead to more frequent interaction between blacks and whites and that the integrated pattern would also better symbolize the commitment of the political authorities to racial equality, so that the social norms of the integrated projects would be more favorable than the social norms of the segregated projects. For both these reasons, the researchers hypothesized, "white tenants in the integrated projects will have less prejudice toward blacks than their counterparts in segregated projects" (pp. 33–37).

Data were obtained by means of one- to two-hour interviews with random samples of white housewives in the four projects. Analysis of these data showed that "the likelihood of getting to know people of the other race and of having intimate contact with them is considerably greater in the integrated interracial than in the segregated bi-racial project" (p. 62). Further analysis revealed that the housewives in the integrated projects had more positive feelings toward blacks, generally speaking, than did housewives in the segregated projects. They were much more likely to describe their relations with them as friendly, more likely to ascribe positive attributes to them, less likely to describe them negatively, more likely to hold them in esteem, and generally more likely to say that they liked blacks and wanted to be friends with them. Finally, the analysis demonstrated that housewives in the integrated projects were more friendly toward black people generally, less likely to endorse unflattering stereotypes of blacks, less concerned with maintaining social distance between the races, and more likely to support integrated housing as a general policy. From these marked differences in racial attitudes and behavior between the two kinds of projects Deutsch and Collins inferred that contact had reduced the prejudices of a considerable number of tenants in the integrated projects (p. 123). Provided that certain simple conditions can be fulfilled, they concluded, "prejudices are likely to be diminished when prejudiced persons are brought into situations which compel contacts between them and the objects of prejudice" (p. 128).

Wilner, Walkley, and Cook (1955) is a replication of the Deutsch and Collins study that eliminates some of its methodological weaknesses. Four public housing projects, two in medium-sized cities in New England and two in larger cities in the middle Atlantic region, were studied. Like the four projects studied by Deutsch and Collins, two of these projects were fully integrated and two were "building segregated"—one of each type in each region. The proportion of blacks in all the projects was about 10 percent. The respondents were white housewives.

The most interesting refinement of this study is the introducion of proximity as an independent variable distinct from the formal pattern of integration or segregation within each project. In fact, proximity was crucial because of the racial balances and architectural designs of the projects studied. Even in the integrated projects, relatively few white families had blacks as next-door neighbors, and some lived in buildings with no blacks; in the segregated projects, the buildings for blacks and whites were interspersed so that some white families lived relatively close to blacks in adjacent buildings or in buildings on the same court.

As one might expect, the data showed that white housewives living near black tenants were more likely to have relatively intimate interracial contacts (borrowing and lending, helping out, minding children, visiting back and forth) than were white housewives living farther away. These differences in interactions with blacks were associated with differences in attitudes. Generally speaking, the nearby women held more favorable views of blacks than did those who lived at a distance. The results were clearer for "specific attitudes" toward blacks in the projects than for "generalized attitudes" toward blacks as a group and clearer for the projects in New England, on the whole, than for the projects in the middle Atlantic states. Further analysis revealed that the main link between increased proximity and more favorable attitudes was the greater likelihood of developing personal relations with blacks. Tenants equated on proximity but differing in the nature of their contacts with blacks (conversational or neighborly contacts as opposed to no contacts beyond casual greetings) differed markedly in their attitudes. There seemed to be no effect of proximity on attitudes, except through interaction.

These results more clearly support the contact hypothesis than do the results of the earlier study (Deutsch and Collins, 1951), because differences in proximity are not confounded with differences in location or type of project. In the earlier study, the contact variable was confounded with city (New York or Newark) and type of project (fully integrated or area segregated). Strictly speaking, all it shows is that white tenants in the two integrated projects in New York City had more contacts with and more favorable attitudes toward blacks than did the tenants in the segregated projects in Newark. It does not demonstrate an effect of proximity (or interaction) on attitudes because different institutional and community norms could, in principle, explain the attitude differences observed without any reference to contact. As noted in the research report, one of the main differences between the integrated and the segregated projects was "the social norms regarding racial relations implicit in the policy decision of the occupancy pattern by an official public authority" (Deutsch and Collins, 1951, p. 32). The later study, by contrast, found remarkably few differences between the integrated and the segregated projects: attitudes seemed to be unrelated, generally speaking, to different occupancy patterns. Rather, the differences observed were correlated with proximity and neighborly contact. The study suggests that prejudice can be reduced if people are made to live in close proximity to the objects of their prejudice, because doing so promotes friendly interaction with them, and friendly interaction reduces prejudice.

More recent studies suggest that the proximity technique may work better with whites than with blacks. Ford (1972, 1973) examined the attitudes of both black and white housewives in three public housing projects in Lexington, Kentucky. His methods and measures were similar to those used in the earlier studies in the field. For the white housewives, his data supported the contact hypothesis. "The more a white respondent engages in interracial neighboring, the less prejudiced she is likely to be" (pp. 1435–36). This relationship did not hold for black housewives, however. The blacks living in segregated projects showed less prejudice than blacks in integrated projects and, among the latter, the longer they had lived in the integrated projects the greater their antipathy to whites.[6] There was no relationship between the racial attitudes of black housewives and their interracial neighboring.

Works (1961), by contrast, found significant correlations between proximity and positive interracial attitudes among seventy-six black housewives and their husbands living in partially integrated public housing in a medium-sized midwestern city (Youngstown, Ohio). But the groups he compared may not have been equivalent prior to moving into public housing. His two samples, "integrated" and "segregated," came from different parts of a single project with an open-occupancy policy. Despite this policy, the two parts of the project, lying north and south of a major thoroughfare, had very different mixes of blacks and whites. On the north side, representing integrated occupancy, 54 percent of the units were occupied by blacks and 46 percent by whites. On the south side, representing segregation, 94 percent were occupied by blacks and only 6 percent by whites. The housing authorities could not explain this difference in occupancy patterns, but self-selection may have been a factor. The groups north and south of the thoroughfare differed on a number of background variables. For example, the integrated respondents were younger, likely to have lived in the project a shorter time, more likely to have completed high school, and more likely to have had contact with whites before moving into the project, all differences that are generally correlated with racial attitudes and that complicate the interpretation of the results of this quasi-experiment. Such differences would be controlled in any genuinely experimental study of the effects of proximity on intergroup attitudes.

Quasi-experimental studies of the kind just summarized provide the best evidence for the contact hypothesis as commonly understood. Questions can be raised, however, about whether proximity reduces social discrimination and the feeling of separateness among ethnic groups as much as it changes their verbal attitudes (Cagle, 1972). In such experiments it is also difficult to separate the proximity-interaction-attitude connections from the normative effects of the authorities who require proximity and interaction among their subordinates (Riordan, 1978a). The results of these studies need to be considered in light of the pattern revealed by the next major group of studies.

Studies of Proportions

The studies discussed so far—studies of interaction and studies of proximity—group individuals for purposes of comparison and thus end up comparing groups, but these groups are not social networks, and the "units" being compared are individuals, not groups. In the studies of proximity just examined, for example, individuals belonging to a single ethnic group (or collection of groups) were classified according to their distances from members of some contrasting ethnic group with whom they could interact. The closer people are to each other, the hypothesis was, the more they should interact, and the more they interact, the better their attitudes toward each other should be. The distances involved were often only a few yards or a few blocks. The individuals being compared were usually drawn from a single city, firm, neighborhood, company, or public housing project. A great many troublesome sources of variation were thus effectively controlled.

The studies of proportions to be examined in this section group and compare individuals classified according to a "group" property, ethnic heterogeneity. Differences in the ethnic composition of groups such as cities or neighborhoods can be correlated with differences in the ethnic attitudes or behavior of their members in order to test the hypothesis that ethnically heterogeneous groups, which provide more opportunities for contact with relevant out-groups, should, other things being equal, show relatively low average levels of prejudice.

Strictly experimental methods have almost no application in testing this version of the contact hypothesis, however, and simple models of sampling, with their associated tests of significance and confidence intervals, are hard to use given the lack of a clearly defined universe or population the elements of which are independent. The rigorous quantitative literature that deals with differences in proportions from the standpoint of the contact hypothesis is thus relatively limited, but a few studies deserve careful consideration because they illustrate an important line of evidence bearing on the hypothesis. Unfortunately the evidence they provide is difficult to assess, as a simple example will quickly make clear.

In his book-length study of the contact hypothesis, Williams (1964) focuses most of his analysis on individual differences in proximity and interaction, but he also provides detailed discussions of the four main cities in his study. Table 3.1 presents some figures culled from Williams's text. It illustrates a positive correlation between percentage black, a measure of ethnic heterogeneity, on one hand and prejudice on the other. The measure of prejudice is the following social distance question: "Do you think you would ever find it a little distasteful to eat at the same table with a [Negro] [white person]?"

The figures in Table 3.1 are not brought together in this way by Williams and do not represent an adequate summary of all the differences discussed in his chapters on the four cities in question (compare Pinkney, 1963). The particular social distance question used is far from being an ideal measure of prejudice. It is used here because it was almost the only relevant question that blacks as well as whites were asked in all the cities, thus simplifying comparisons. Different questions would obviously produce different figures. For example, the white samples in the four cities were asked the following question: "As you see it, are Negroes today demanding more than they have a right to or not?" This question produced proportions prejudiced, for Hometown, Valley City, Steelville, and Southport whites, of 22

Table 3.1   Racial Prejudice in Four American Cities

City	Percentage Black	Percentage Prejudiced White Respondents	Black Respondents
Hometown	3%	50%	14%
Valley City	8	51	10
Steelville	10	61	12
Southport	40	92	35

Source: R. M. Williams, *Strangers Next Door: Ethnic Relations in American Communities* (Englewood Cliffs: Prentice-Hall, 1964), pp. 52, 226–34.

percent, 39 percent, 41 percent, and 58 percent, respectively (p. 51; compare p. 257).

But can this pattern be generalized? Four cities selected to illustrate the range of minority-majority relations in the United States are hardly a proper basis for generalizing to other American cities or to cities elsewhere. Perhaps all that can safely be inferred from Williams's study is that racial prejudice was more widespread and more intense a generation ago in Savannah, Georgia, than in Elmira, New York, Bakersfield, California, or Steubenville, Ohio. This very limited "finding" falls under the broad generalization, suggested by history and casual observation, that racial prejudice is a larger part of southern culture than of northern or western culture in the United States.[7]

Other "ecological" studies, however, generally produce similar results despite dissimilarities in the groups or territories being compared and, in particular, despite their various relations to broad "cultural" differences. Bradburn, Sudman, and Gockel (1971), for example, analyzed the richest body of data on the attitudinal correlates of residential segregation or integration in the United States as a whole and produced the most important results. Using local definitions of neighborhoods and the advice of local experts (as well as census data) to classify neighborhoods as integrated or segregated, they selected a national probability sample of 311 integrated neighborhoods and matched these with forty-nine white segregated and thirty-two black segregated neighborhoods. About three thousand individuals living in these neighborhoods were then interviewed using standard survey methods. Analysis of the data revealed that interracial "neighboring" (chatting on the street, social visiting, and so on) increased with the proportion of blacks in a neighborhood. But the racial heterogeneity of neighborhoods seemed nonetheless to be *inversely* related overall to positive racial attitudes. The white respondents living in integrated neighborhoods with a low proportion of blacks (under 10 percent) were, generally speaking, the most favorable to blacks, closely followed by those living in white segregated neighborhoods. For the white respondents, the least favorable attitudes were found in the neighborhoods with a high or rapidly growing proportion of blacks. The pattern was less clear for the black respondents, but the authors conclude that "integrated living by itself will not produce positive attitudes toward whites" (p. 133).

The regional and socioeconomic correlates of neighborhood integration must obviously be taken into account in any discussion of these findings. Neighborhoods differ in more than just the opportunities they provide for interaction between the races. Relatively heterogeneous neighborhoods offering many opportunities for personal contact tend to be in the South, where racial prejudice has traditionally been high, or in the poorer areas of northern cities, where integration has often been seen as a brief transitional stage between a white segregated and a black segregated neighborhood and where it is thus associated with fears of "invasion" and a decline of property values. Bradburn, Sudman, and Gockel conjecture that people living where the housing market is stable should be more tolerant than those in unstable markets. "When there is a threat to investment . . . less tolerance, indeed often open hostility, is more likely to prevail" (p. 133).

Some American studies based upon units of analysis smaller than states or regions but larger than neighborhoods show no clear relation between heterogeneity and negative racial attitudes among Americans (Giles, 1977; Giles and Evans, 1985), but Fosset and Kiecolt (1989), in the most thorough investigation so far, show the basic pattern seen in most earlier studies, namely, a clear connection between heterogeneity and prejudice. Drawing upon data from three large national surveys and using multiple regression to control the effects of other relevant variables, they reveal significant correlations between percentage black (in counties or metropolitan areas) and opposition to racial integration, both in the South and in the rest of the country. Their key finding is that "whites' perception of threat from blacks increases, and their support for racial integration decreases, as the relative size of the black population increases" (p. 833).

The studies mentioned so far have all related attitudes (as measured in surveys) to differences in proportions, but it would be possible to focus on other dependent variables having more to do with behavior. For example, in a study of the southwestern United States, Frisbie and Neidert (1977) found a relation between minority percentages, black and Hispanic, and disparities in average incomes, suggesting more discrimination in areas with more blacks and Hispanics (see also Reich, 1981, pp. 147 and 163, and Wilcox and Roof, 1978). In addition, there is a large and complicated literature on residential segregation, which seems to be related to relative numbers so that areas of greater heterogeneity are also areas of greater segregation (see Massey and Denton,1993, pp. 109–12; Massey and Hajnal, 1995, and the literature cited there).

Many studies have focused on the sharp contrasts within the South between the lowland areas with substantial black populations, often exceeding 50 percent, and the hill country, which has few blacks. Key (1949) was not the first to notice the significance of the "black belts" within the eleven states of the old Confederacy, but he made it the main theme of his detailed analysis of southern politics and showed its profound significance for southern culture. His book cannot be reduced to a single correlation coefficient, but in broad terms he found that race consciousness was keenest, racial fears most acute, antipathy to blacks most intense, and resistance to their enfranchisement greatest in those areas of each state where they formed the highest proportion of the population. For more than a century the whites in those areas had struggled to exclude blacks from politics, to isolate them socially, and generally to keep them subordinate to whites: "If any single thread runs through most of the preceding chapters, it is that of the association of a special set of political attitudes or at least attitudes of high intensity with the black-belt counties" (p. 666).

Subsequent studies have amply confirmed Key's thesis. A particularly revealing study by Thomas Pettigrew (1957a, 1959) employed standard public opinion polling techniques in eight towns, four in the South and four in New England. The four southern towns were in Georgia and North Carolina. Two of the four—one from each state—had low black population ratios (10 percent and 18 percent, respectively). The other two had relatively high ratios (38 percent and 45 percent, respectively). A comparison of the high- and low-ratio towns showed significantly more antiblack prejudice, as measured by two different attitude scales, in the high-ratio towns, and also more resistance there to the idea of desegregated public schooling. Pettigrew concluded that "the proportion of Negroes living in a particular community appears to be of crucial significance in desegregation attitudes" (1957a, p. 343). In a later study of school desegregation in five border states, using counties as units of analysis, Pettigrew and Cramer (1959) found significant correlations in each of the states between black percentages of the population and the dates on which schools were desegregated. A high concentration of blacks was associated with late desegregation (see also Pettigrew, 1957b).

At least twenty-one additional quantitative studies support Key's rule about the dependence of white attitudes on the concentration of blacks in the South. Percentage black in southern counties or other comparable areas has been linked to segregationist voting among whites (Black, 1973; Black and Black, 1973; Grunbaum, 1964; Heer, 1959; Knoke and Kyriazis,

1977; Ogburn and Grigg, 1956; Pettigrew and Campbell, 1960; Schoenberger and Segal, 1971; Wright, 1976, 1977; Wrinkle and Polinard, 1973), to low rates of black voter registration (Fenton and Vines, 1957; Matthews and Prothro, 1963), to economic discrimination against blacks (Brown and Fuguitt, 1972), to lynching rates (Corzine, Creech, and Corzine, 1983; Reed, 1972; Tolnay, Beck, and Massey, 1989), to numbers of blacks executed legally (Phillips, 1986; Tolnay, Beck, and Massey, 1992), and even to voting against the union of the northern and southern Presbyterian churches among southern Presbyterians (Dornbusch and Irle, 1959). More recently, Glaser (1994) has shown strong correlations between racial environment and political attitudes among white southerners, using data from five National Election Studies from the 1980s together with census data on the percentage black of southern counties. He concludes by reiterating Key's finding: "Whites from the black belt are still the most racially conservative in the South" (p. 34).

Is the correlation between percentage black and prejudice against blacks that is found in the South and in the United States as a whole found also in the North? The best study of this question compared fifteen large cities, none from the South, in 1968 (Schuman and Gruenberg, 1970). The cities, most of which are in the northeastern and north central parts of the United States, included some that had recently had major race riots (such as Newark and Detroit) and some that had had only minor disturbances or none at all (such as Boston and Brooklyn). Probability samples of approximately 175 black and 175 white respondents were drawn early in 1968 from each of these cities. Averages of the responses of the black and white samples were then used, along with data from the census, to describe and compare the cities.

One of the major attitudes studied was "white racial liberalism," which was measured by means of nine questions about sympathy with black protest, belief that blacks are behind because of discrimination, and support for interracial contact. White respondents were also questioned about their awareness of discrimination against blacks in housing and employment. The study revealed a weak positive correlation ($r = .11$) between white racial liberalism and the proportion of the population that was black, but white perceptions of job and housing discrimination were *negatively* related to the percentage black ($r = -.50$ and $r = -.60$, respectively). "Where the Negro proportion of the City population is large, whites tend to deny the existence of discrimination" (p. 251). And apart from Washington, D.C., as will be clear in a moment, the other fourteen cities in the study showed a negative correlation between proportion black and white racial liberalism.

Schuman and Gruenberg also examined the relation between the characteristics of their fifteen cities, including their percentages black, and black attitudes. They found a moderate negative correlation ($r = -.50$) between percent black and an index of "dissatisfaction with city government" among blacks. The larger the proportion of blacks in a city's population, the more satisfied they were, on the average, with their city government. "We suggest as an important hypothesis that, where Negroes constitute a small proportion of the population, they receive (or at least perceive themselves as receiving) particularly poor treatment from their city government. Simple political considerations make this likely, for under such demographic conditions Negroes lack electoral power to influence city officials and policies" (p. 247).

Bledsoe et al. (1995), in the study of blacks in Detroit and its suburbs described earlier, found less "racial solidarity"—less of a tendency to separate from whites—among blacks who lived in more mixed neighborhoods, that is to say, in neighborhoods with a high proportion of white residents. The relationship, although it was not very strong, suggested "that strategies of black advancement premised on the maintenance of strong bonds of racial solidarity will face new challenges, as more and more blacks leave the central cities and as a new generation of blacks grow up in more racially heterogeneous settings" (p. 453).

Carter (1990) uses the survey data collected by Schuman and Gruenberg to show a puzzling *negative* correlation between "black dissatisfaction" (lower on the average in cities with a high proportion of blacks) and the severity of black rioting across the fifteen cities. The more satisfied blacks were with their city government, it seems, the more they rioted in the 1960s. It is hard to make sense of this finding, but it is probably reasonable to assume that cities with large proportions of blacks do indeed tend to have city governments relatively sensitive to black demands. But cities with a high *proportion* of blacks are also, generally speaking, cities with a large *number* of blacks, and in the turbulence of the 1960s the "resource" effect of numbers may have overridden the political effect of proportions (compare Horowitz, 1983; Rossi, Berk, and Eidson, 1974; Spilerman, 1970, 1971, 1976).

Going back to an earlier time, Susan Olzak, in a series of studies designed to test a competition theory of ethnic conflict, has related collective actions to economic and social conditions including rates of immigration (Olzak, 1992, and the earlier studies cited there). Newspaper reports of ethnic collective actions (confrontations or protests involving two or more ethnic populations) in seventy-seven American cities between 1877 and 1914 provide a rough measure of ethnic conflict. Her analysis relates variation in the number of such actions to other variables describing national conditions over the period of the study. The results show a clear dependence of conflict on the growth of immigration: when the immigration rate increased, so did the rate of ethnic conflict. The causes of ethnic conflict are obviously more complicated than can be summarized in a single correlation coefficient, and Olzak's studies bring out some of the relevant complexities, but they also show that fluctuations in immigration can have powerful effects on the rate of ethnic conflict. "Increases in immigration significantly increase the rates of all types of conflict" (p. 105). Applying the same reasoning and the same methods of analysis in a study of antibusing activity in American cities between 1968 and 1990, Olzak, Shanahan, and West (1994) found that antibusing protests were most frequent in areas where racial segregation was breaking down. Again, the relevant statistical results are not easily summarized, but perhaps it is satisfactory to say, as the authors do, that "increases in interracial exposure in schools and neighborhoods trigger racial and ethnic conflict" (p. 196).

A serious difficulty with all these studies, apart from the difficulty of interpreting their sometimes puzzling results, is that of determining the "population" the various cities represent. The statistical results are bound to be sensitive to the sample of cities chosen, as can be shown a little too clearly by eliminating only one observation from the fifteen available from Schuman and Gruenberg (1970). Washington, D.C., which was included in their sample, is an "outlier" with respect to both percentage black and white racial liberalism. (The District of Columbia represents about one quarter of the Washington metropolitan area.) If it is excluded from the sample, the correlation between white racial liberalism and percentage black is −.63 rather than .11, and the correlation between percentage black and awareness of housing discrimination goes from −.60 to −.78. There is evidently a problem of sampling in ecological studies of this sort and also a related problem of the meaningfulness of the legal boundaries of such cities as Washington, D.C., and Brooklyn, which are parts of larger metropolitan areas. Should Brooklyn and Newark, for example, be treated as two independent observations, or are they really just two different windows on New York City? Cities as defined by law may not be the best units for an ecological study of the contact hypothesis.

Comparable studies conducted in other countries have produced mixed results, but most show an association between contact (in the sense of heterogeneity) and prejudice. The most directly comparable studies examine white attitudes toward "New Commonwealth" (or "colored") immigrants in Britain. In an exceptionally thorough study based upon a large national survey and five smaller surveys in five cities or boroughs with relatively high proportions of recent immigrants, Schaefer (1975) found varying levels of prejudice in the twelve regions of Britain he distinguished, but the differences were small and were only weakly related to the numbers of colored immigrants in each region. "Generally there was little association between levels of prejudice and the amount of white–non-white contact" (p. 5). A closer examination of the five boroughs with relatively high proportions of nonwhites revealed, however, a clear positive relation between percentage nonwhite and the average level of prejudice.

Restricting his attention to England, Studlar (1977) used data from the census and three national surveys to relate individual opinions on immigration to the percentage of New Commonwealth immigrants in the parliamentary constituencies in which the respondents lived. He found weak positive correlations between the presence of immigrants in a constituency and hostile attitudes toward immigration.

Taylor (1979) examined the constituencies in which the National Front, a fringe party voicing strong opposition to colored immigration, ran candidates against the established parties (Conservative, Liberal, and Labour) in the general elections of 1974 and 1979. He found quite strong correlations (about $r = .60$) between the share of the vote won by the National Front and the nonwhite proportion of the population in each constituency. Whitely (1979) examined the National Front vote in the 1977 Greater London Council elections and found a weaker correlation ($r = .31$) across the city's ninety-two constituencies between the front's proportion of the vote and the colored proportion of the population.

A Canadian study (Kalin and Berry, 1982) using survey methods similar to Studlar's, but comparing much smaller geographical areas (census tracts or "area aggregates" with a population median of 5,333), found generally positive relations between the concentration of various ethnic groups in an area and attitudes toward these groups among nonmembers. Thus French Canadians were more likely to evaluate English Canadians positively, and vice versa, the larger the number living in the vicinity. The correlations were weak, but the only clear exception to the rule was in the case of Native Indians, where a higher percentage presence was associated with significantly less favorable attitudes. Kalin and Berry explained their positive results in terms of the contact hypothesis, according to which "positive attitudes toward a particular ethnic group are, in part, the result of relatively equal status contact with members of that group." They explained the one anomalous result (the negative correlation between contact and "positive attitudes" in the case of Native Indians) in terms of the differences between "deculturated Indians" living in cities, with whom whites would have contact, and Indians living on reserves.

Using the same Canadian survey, Schissel, Wanner, and Frideres (1989) examined the dependence of attitudes toward immigrants upon various individual and contextual variables for respondents living in Canada's seventeen largest cities. They found no connection between individual attitudes and the immigrant proportions of the populations of these cities.

White and Curtis (1990) used "feeling thermometer" data from two large Canadian surveys conducted in 1968 and 1984 to examine the effects of living in particular "linguistic zones" (regions of greater or less mixing of anglophones and francophones) on ethnic attitudes. They found more positive attitudes (among anglophones toward "French Canadians" and among francophones toward "English Canadians") in the mixed or "bilingual" regions of the country (see also Curtis and White, 1993).

An Australian study (Mitchell, 1968) apparently reports a very strong (r = .90) correlation between the density of Aboriginal population in an area and the number of no votes cast in a constitutional referendum concerned with giving Aborigines the vote. The more contact white Australians had with Aborigines, it would seem, the more negative they were toward them (see Ray, 1983).

A recent study of ethnic tolerance in Romania and Bulgaria (McIntosh et al., 1995) found greater tolerance among those living in more heterogeneous communities in Romania but less tolerance associated with greater heterogeneity in Bulgaria. The study made use of survey data collected in 1991 and 1992. Tolerance was measured by asking ethnic Romanians and ethnic Bulgarians their opinions about the language rights of ethnic Hungarians and ethnic Turks, respectively. The areal units for the study were the sampling points for the surveys—two or three hundred points in each case, it seems. The measure of community heterogeneity was a rating by Romanian and Bulgarian experts of the homogeneous or heterogeneous character of the populations at each sampling point. The two different correlations seem best explained by the different circumstances of ethnic Romanians and ethnic Bulgarians living in areas with large minority populations. Relative proportions may determine the impact of contact on attitudes, and ethnic Hungarians are a smaller proportion of the "Hungarian" areas of Romania, it seems, than Turks are of the "Turkish" areas of Bulgaria. "Living in a heterogeneous community where the majority group still comprises a solid majority of the community population appears to increase ethnic tolerance (at the individual level), but when members of the country's majority group live in a community dominated by the ethnic minority, they are less likely to express tolerant views" (p. 956).

One of the problems in this literature is obviously the choice of areal units for comparison. Evidently it makes a difference which country is studied and how it is divided up. In any study of geographical areas, the number of observations can be increased or decreased almost at will, and the corresponding correlations (and their apparent statistical significance) can be affected one way or the other by dividing or consolidating areas. But adjacent areas are not really independent: they naturally tend to be more alike than areas separated by greater distances. Where to draw the lines is a perplexing problem, solved in practice by accepting the lines drawn by others for other purposes.

The larger the areas compared, the more important broad national and historical forces seem to be; the smaller the areas, the more closely "proportion" approaches "proximity" and thus "interaction." The aim in any ecological study is presumably to compare relatively independent social units the members of which are subject to similar influences, though these differ from unit to unit. It is not easy to define such units in a modern society with mass media and mechanized transport. Whatever the units compared, the researcher must also deal with other relevant differences between them—their political traditions, economic structures, housing stock, and class composition, for example, as well as their differences in ethnic proportions. The average education level of their residents may be particularly important: many studies show very marked differences in prejudice among individuals and groups as a function of their exposure to formal schooling.[8]

Having noted these difficulties, it is also worth noting briefly the findings of some relevant cross-national studies. Not just areas within countries (census tracts, cities, counties, regions), but countries themselves can be compared and their changes over time studied with a view to testing the contact hypothesis. The boundaries between sovereign states can be used to define units for calculating ethnic proportions and measuring average levels of prejudice and discrimination. The main barrier to systematic research along these lines is the difficulty of collecting relevant data, which is at bottom the problem of defining *general* indices of both heterogeneity and prejudice, or discrimination, given that different ethnic groups and issues are important in the ethnic politics of the countries being compared.

The first problem—measuring ethnic heterogeneity cross-nationally—can be solved in a number of ways, among them compiling a census of ethnic groups in each country and then calculating an overall measure of heterogeneity analogous to the variance of a binomial variable. Thus, if there are two groups in a country, its measure of heterogeneity should be greatest if each makes up half the population, and it should have a lower value to the extent that one group outnumbers the other. Ethnic and linguistic differences are admittedly somewhat obscure, politically sensitive matters, but relevant data and statistics are available from several sources, the best apparently being a Soviet ethnographical atlas of the early 1960s (see Taylor and Hudson, 1972, who note that the index ignores religion, apparently because it lacked importance from a Soviet perspective).

The second problem—finding cross-nationally valid measures of prejudice or discrimination—can also be solved in a number of ways. Ideally, there should be well-designed surveys with questions that are both comparable and locally relevant for every country in the world. There are economic barriers to such surveys (about 150 national surveys conducted more or less simultaneously in at least twice as many languages), but the more interesting problems have to do with choosing appropriate questions and constructing comparable attitude scales. A questionnaire designed for Americans would not work very well in the former Yugoslavia and vice versa, and the data from instruments designed for use in different national contexts can be hard to compare.

Quillian (1995) seems to be the only attempt to relate different national levels of prejudice to the racial and ethnic heterogeneity of national populations using individual-level data from national surveys. This ambitious study, whose findings regarding proximity are discussed above, combines data from probability samples of twelve EEC countries (Eurobarometer Survey 30) with measures of economic conditions and ethnic heterogeneity for the subject countries. The percentage of each country's population that consists of non-EEC immigrants is the index of ethnic heterogeneity. Prejudice is measured by means of cross-nationally comparable scales (with seven items each) of racial and anti-immigrant attitudes. Statistical analysis of the data, controlling for individual-level differences among all respondents, reveals clear positive correlations between non-EEC proportions and negative attitudes across the twelve countries. "The central result of this paper is that the average degree of prejudice in an EEC country is strongly related to the threat perceived by the dominant group resident there. . . . The results here indicate that the relative size of the subordinate group and the economic situation of the particular country can strongly influence the degree of prejudice expressed by dominant group members" (pp. 605–6).

Many researchers, lacking survey data of the kind used by Quillian, have had to make do with such crude indicators of prejudiced attitudes as the number of coups or riots in a country or the number of deaths from communal violence over a period of years. Morrison and Stevenson (1972a), for example, in their study of political instability in Africa, correlated two measures of political instability—one essentially a weighted sum of "elite" events such as coups d'état, the other a weighted sum of "communal" events such as riots and rebellions—with complex measures of both cultural pluralism and linguistic heterogeneity for thirty sub-Saharan African nations between the date of their independence and 1969 (see also Morrison and Stevenson, 1972b). They found consistently positive correlations between their measures of ethnic diversity and political instability, the largest being a correlation of .65 between the number of vernacular languages in a country and its amount of communal instability. They concluded that ethnic diversity "increases the likelihood of conflict between members of communal groups in black African nations, and increases the probability of both communal and elite instability in these nations" (1972a, p. 103).

Barrows (1976) analyzed data of the same kind for thirty-two African countries in an attempt to show that "ethnic diversity is less useful as a concept for understanding political instability in Black Africa than most area specialists have hitherto believed" (p. 161). Using four measures of ethnic diversity and three of political instability, he found a variety of correlations, the clearest being three positive correlations between diversity and "turmoil" (a sum of riots, demonstrations, strikes, and declarations of emergency). These correlations were strengthened and clarified by controlling for the size of government, as indicated by the ratio of civil servants to wage earners in 1966–67, whose positive effects on turmoil (the larger the government, the greater the turmoil) seemed to mask the positive effects of diversity on turmoil. Thus, the analysis, which was intended to undermine the conventional wisdom among area specialists, ended by supporting it: "The greater the ethnic diversity, the greater the political instability, other things being equal" (p. 162).

A similar conclusion is suggested by the most recent statistical analysis of the conditions associated with military coups d'état in Black Africa since 1957. Jenkins and Kposowa (1990), using very complicated statistical techniques of causal modeling, report that ethnic antagonism (a compound of general cultural diversity and the competitive positions of the two largest ethnic groups) underlies military coups, generally speaking. "Ethnic diversity and competition encourage groups to mobilize . . . in a bid for political and economic power. These antagonisms, as well as the size and heterogeneity of states with large populations, lead to more powerful military establishments and a greater likelihood of military coups" (p. 868).

What about the correlation between the ethnic heterogeneity of different countries and their internal conflict or turmoil for the world as a whole? Hibbs (1973), using the best data then available, including the Atlas Narodov Mira (ANM) index of heterogeneity, found a positive correlation overall between heterogeneity and mass political violence. His sophisticated statistical analysis, which involves thirty-eight variables and sixteen basic equations, suggests that the correlation was best understood in terms of a causal process involving "political separatism." Ethnically diverse countries tend to produce separatist movements that are the immediate cause of internal war. This is a very simple summary of a very complicated book, but nothing in it suggests a *negative* relation between contact and conflict cross-nationally.

A recent cross-national study of "communal" mobilization and conflict, Gurr (1993a), is not directly relevant here because it focuses on particular ethnic groups rather than on the mixed populations to which they belong. Nonetheless, its statistical analysis of the background conditions associated with political protest and rebellion by communal groups contains many hints of the importance of ethnic diversity as a cause of conflict. Among the 227 groups studied—"groups whose core members share a distinctive and persistent collective identity based on cultural and ascriptive traits that are important to them and to others with whom they interact" (p. 163)—political mobilization was related to political grievances, and these in turn seemed to reflect economic and political disadvantages connected with ethnic identity. Again, this is a very simple summary of an almost unbelievably complicated statistical analysis. Perhaps it is safe to conclude from the study, however, that a specialist familiar with the details of communal conflicts in almost every corner of the world was not tempted to argue that more diversity would produce less conflict. Rather, he seemed to picture political protests and rebellions as arising out of the mobilization of communal groups in response to the disadvantages they suffer in situations of ethnic contact (see also Gurr, 1993b).

A simpler summary of some relevant data for the world as a whole would help to clarify the main generalization implicit in the studies just summarized. No study I know of, unfortunately, focuses on the correlation between ethnic heterogeneity and overall internal conflict or turmoil for all the nations of the world, so no published source can be cited in this connection. But such a correlation is easily calculated from readily available, if somewhat old, data. The data—the ANM index of ethnic heterogeneity mentioned above and a general measure of conflict, namely, deaths from domestic political violence—are conveniently available in the *World Handbook of Political and Social Indicators* (Taylor and Hudson, 1972). When the two series are correlated for the years 1961 to 1967, the result is .31, a value unaffected by controlling for population.[9] In short, death and diversity seem to go together on a world scale. The contact made possible by intranational ethnic diversity seems to create problems more often than it solves them, generally speaking.

Despite the difficulty of making precise cross-national comparisons, then, some hard quantitative evidence is available, and it suggests that there is no good reason for avoiding the "soft" or "rough" comparisons that come to mind when thinking about contact and conflict in ethnic relations.

It is well known that some of the world's most turbulent countries (South Africa, the former Yugoslavia, the former Soviet Union, Nigeria, and Indonesia, for example) have or had ethnically diverse populations (.88, .75, .67, .87, and .76, respectively, on the ANM index), whereas some of the most peaceful (Japan, Denmark, and Sweden, for example) are also remarkably homogeneous (with scores of .01, .05, and .08 on the index). There are obvious exceptions to the simple rule these examples suggest. Ethnic heterogeneity is by no means the only cause of political violence, and countries such as Canada show that it is possible to combine peace (six deaths between 1961 and 1967) with diversity (.75 on the ANM index). Nonetheless, there is clearly a tendency, even in the literature on the contact hypothesis, to assume that diversity creates problems. As will be explained more fully in the next chapter, it would be hard to make sense of contact theory without assuming an underlying correlation between diversity and conflict while keeping in mind the broad contrast between North and South noted earlier.

Summary and Conclusions

The contact hypothesis brings to mind T. H. Huxley's remark about the tragedy that occurs when "a lovely idea is assaulted by a gang of ugly facts." There are roughly equal numbers of studies showing favorable, unfavorable, and no effects of intergroup contact.

—Rothbart and John (1993)

This has been a long and complicated chapter. Some readers may have skimmed over some crucial points or lost the thread of the argument because of their attention to the details. So let me quickly summarize the most important findings so far.

First, there is undoubtedly a positive correlation, generally speaking, between reported interaction with members of an ethnic out-group and positive or friendly attitudes toward that group. Forty-two observational studies of interaction that were mentioned in the first major section of this chapter can be classified by their results. Two of these studies yielded mixed positive and negative results; two showed no significant correlations between interaction and attitudes; all the rest illustrated the standard pattern, which is consistent with the general principle that liking and association go together (Homans, 1950, 1961).

Second, the causal mechanisms that produce this correlation remain unclear despite more than thirty years' worth of rigorous quantitative research on the contact hypothesis. Increases in interaction no doubt sometimes cause reductions in prejudice, but positive ethnic attitudes also sometimes encourage interaction. The one experimental study that might have demonstrated a positive effect of unintended, involuntary contact on ethnic prejudice (Cook, 1969) was never reported in detail and seems to have been terminated because of its discouraging preliminary results. The other experimental and quasi-experimental studies of interaction have either suffered from grave problems of "external validity," confounded contact with normative influences, or produced unclear or negative results. The quasi-experimental studies of tourism and foreign students show that increased contact may often be associated with increased prejudice, generally speaking, particularly if the relevant contact is short-term or "exploratory."

Third, studies of proximity—including most of the studies of school desegregation discussed in Chapter 2—show no clear and consistent correlation between greater proximity and lower levels of prejudice. The correlations reported in these studies are sometimes positive, sometimes negative, generally weak, and always hard to interpret. They leave open the possibility that any reductions in prejudice caused by interaction, as a result of proximity, are somehow offset, generally speaking, by increases in prejudice among others in the vicinity.

Fourth, the quasi-experimental studies of proximity in public housing, the most frequently cited studies of the contact hypothesis, show connections between proximity and voluntary interaction and between interaction and favorable attitudes, but they also show how difficult it is to isolate these relations from the "normative" effects of the authorities conducting the experiments. Hence they contribute less to our knowledge of the effects of contact than is often thought.

Fifth, studies of proportions show, with few exceptions, negative correlations between contact and positive ethnic attitudes. These studies, like nearly all studies in which areas or social groups are the units of analysis, suffer from a common methodological weakness. They cannot use standard methods of sampling from a defined population and so cannot use standard statistical tests or confidence intervals to weigh the evidence they provide for or against any inductive generalization. Nonetheless, a variety of studies in a variety of countries, using different areal units of analysis, point to a common conclusion, namely, that ethnic rivalry and hostile attitudes are most prevalent or intense in those areas where there is the greatest mixing of ethnic groups. This "negative" correlation is consistent with the possibility (or hypothesis) that greater contact causes greater ethnic conflict.

Sixth, the appearance of inconsistency in the findings of the literature on the contact hypothesis is somewhat deceptive. To be sure, roughly equal numbers of studies show positive, zero, and negative effects of contact, but one group of studies shows mostly positive effects, a second group shows a mixture of weak positive and negative effects, and a third shows mostly negative effects. Most of the apparent inconsistency can thus be explained, at one level, by simply distinguishing studies of interaction from studies of proximity and studies of proportions.

But finally, the discrepancy between (a) the positive correlation almost always found in observational studies of interaction and (b) the negative correlation generally found in studies of proportions is an intellectual puzzle with no obvious solution. Attributes that are correlated among individuals are usually correlated in approximately the same way among groups. For example, if individuals who have more education than others earn more money on the average, then neighborhoods or census tracts with higher average levels of education should have higher average levels of income. If one relationship were positive (more education, more income) and the other negative (more education, less income), this discrepancy would call for some further explanation. Such a puzzling discrepancy seems to be visible through the haze of sampling error and other methodological problems in studies of contact and prejudice or ethnic attitudes. How should it be explained?

4 Situations Versus Levels of Analysis

Theories and Facts

More contact may generally reduce prejudice, but it can sometimes be associated with more prejudice and discrimination. Pondering the situation in the American South and similar situations around the world, where frequent contact has coexisted with high levels of ethnic antagonism and inequality, social scientists have searched for a rule or rules that will distinguish the kinds or circumstances of contact that have good effects from those that have bad or no effects. When does more contact improve intergroup relations, and when does it just worsen relations or leave them unchanged? The contact theory that tries to answer this question is best construed as a set of testable hypotheses about "third variables" that are believed to interact with contact and the relevant dependent variables ("prejudice," for lack of a better comprehensive term). As a statistical term, interaction refers to different correlations in different circumstances: when a particular third variable has one of its values (high, positive, present), then the correlation between contact and prejudice will have one sign (positive or negative), but when this variable has its other value (low, negative, absent), then the correlation will have the opposite sign. More contact can lead either to more prejudice and more rejection or to more respect and acceptance, depending upon the situation in which it occurs, as represented by the values of one or more additional variables.[1]

Different versions of contact theory have highlighted a variety of third

114

variables. (In some versions of the theory, it is really a matter of different thirtieth or fortieth variables.) Most contact theorists seem to agree, however, that three specific conditions primarily determine the effects of intergroup contact. Contact will reduce prejudice, it is now generally said, when (a) there is equality of status among the individuals in contact, (b) they meet in a situation of cooperative interdependence, and (c) they have the approval of relevant authorities or of public opinion—in other words, when there is normative support for friendly intergroup relations. This chapter examines the effects of these conditions on the contact-prejudice correlation.

Construed in this way, contact theory is more than just a list of variables that somehow need to be taken into account. It is at heart an *empirical* theory about mechanisms of attitude change. It aims to clarify the situations that produce positive intergroup attitudes, not to show why such attitudes are a good thing for society or for the souls of individuals. It is not an *ethical* theory about true ethical values or the good life, nor does it offer any teleological arguments about "salvation" or the "goal of history." Its purpose is practical: to show how people can be made to have more positive attitudes, and if positive attitudes were undesirable for some reason—in wartime, for example, regarding enemies—then the theory could be put in reverse, as it were, to produce negative attitudes. The theory must be judged by the standard of practical empirical science: Do its hypotheses in fact isolate the most important cause-effect relations?

Contact theory may seem at first glance to fail this test. It may appear unable to explain the broad historical trends of the past two or three centuries (more equality, larger economic units, more international trade and investment, larger wars, more domestic violence, and perhaps more racial and religious bigotry) or even the detailed findings of the little statistical studies reviewed in Chapters 2 and 3. Far from showing different correlations between contact and prejudice in different situations of contact depending upon the values of one or more of the standard third variables such as equality of status or cooperative interdependence, these studies seem to reveal a broad contrast between a negative individual-level correlation (more contact goes with less prejudice) and a positive aggregate-level correlation. This complicated fact—if indeed it is a fact—appears to have more to do with the individual-group distinction emphasized by the critics of contact theory than with any of the conditions it highlights. Perhaps the most important facts about contact and prejudice can be best explained not by contact theory but by some other theory, such as realistic conflict theory or social identity theory. Before jumping to any conclusions, however, let us examine the most relevant empirical theorizing and research more carefully.[2]

Equality of Status

If two individuals interact in stereotyped roles of superiority and subordination, their interaction will likely reinforce rather than break down their stereotypes of superiority and inferiority. They will follow the script and know each other only as actors. This is the basic idea behind the various stipulations of equality of status as a condition for positive effects of contact. The condition makes intuitive sense and seems to explain the most important facts. Individuals differing greatly in status (as determined by age, income, education, occupation, and so on) rarely become close friends. Regions with high levels of prejudice and discrimination are generally regions where different ethnic groups meet in stereotyped roles of superiority and subordination.[3]

Formal Equality.

The most striking difference between the northern and southern states of the United States, aside from climate, has long been the greater equality of blacks and whites in the North than in the South. In the South before the Civil War, blacks were slaves; in the North, they were free. Long after the Civil War, southern whites struggled to keep blacks subordinate and to confine them to menial occupations. Casual contacts in public places were governed by an elaborate etiquette of race relations in which the two races played roles of superiority and subordination. Some blacks became doctors and lawyers serving the black community, but contact between blacks and whites was minimized and structured so as to avoid situations in which blacks worked side by side with whites in jobs of equal status or in which blacks exercised authority over whites. Blacks could polish whites' shoes or dig their gardens but not fix their teeth or advise them in their legal difficulties. In the North, by contrast, blacks and whites have long enjoyed the same basic rights of citizenship. To be sure, blacks have not always enjoyed perfect equality with whites, but relations between the races have for generations been on a more equal footing in the North than in the South. The conditions have been more favorable in the North for the development of close personal relations across racial lines—assuming that equality of status is a condition for the development of such relations.

So how have the correlations between contact and prejudice been affected by the different conditions in the North and in the South? Remarkably little hard evidence exists, in fact, to support the reasoning of Allport and others about equality of status as a necessary condition for positive effects from contact. Nearly all the relevant studies show the same positive or negative correlations between contact variables and ethnic attitudes (more contact goes with more or less prejudice), regardless of the general circumstances surrounding the contact or even the relative statuses of the individuals involved in it. In particular, there are no studies using similar measures of personal interaction and racial prejudice that show sharply different correlations in the northern and southern states of the United States. The few studies that use the same measures in the two regions show similar correlations. Thus, in the mid-1950s Thomas Pettigrew, working under Allport's direction, conducted an elaborate comparative study of the correlates of racial prejudice in four northern and four southern towns, but neither he nor his thesis supervisor seems to have been struck by any interaction between region and contact as correlates of prejudice. Nothing is said about any such interaction, and none can be detected from inspection of his published tables (Pettigrew, 1957a, 1959). Similarly, Williams's (1964) landmark study of the contact hypothesis, which was based upon surveys conducted in four cities, one of them in the South, gives no support to Allport's reasoning because it reports the same basic (negative) correlation between personal interaction and prejudiced attitudes in all four cities. *"In all the surveys in all communities and for all groups, majorities and minorities, the greater the frequency of interaction, the lower the prevalence of ethnic prejudice"* (pp. 167–68, emphasis in original). This is the main finding of all the other studies of interaction that could be cited. Moreover, the extensive literature of contact in schools has not shown any clear differences in the effects of desegregation in the North and in the South apart from greater opposition to desegregation in the South (compare Pettigrew, 1991).

Equality of Achievement.

Is it a mistake to treat regional differences as *situational* differences in the sense intended by contact theory? Broad regional differences in ethnic attitudes or political culture may have very little effect on styles of personal interaction. A simple question about the number of out-group members a respondent knows personally may have the same basic meaning—the same relation to true acquaintance and unrestricted communication, by contrast with casual contact and autistic thinking—in the North as in the South, regardless of the overall levels of prejudice and discrimination in the two regions (compare Riordan, 1978a). Indeed, unless true acquaintance could take place even in an environment poisoned by prejudice, the contact hypothesis would have little practical value in the struggle against prejudice.

Were casual contact alone possible, it might be unrealistic to expect more contact to produce anything except, as Allport put it, "more trouble." But in fact—putting aside methodological scruples—more personal interaction always seems to produce less prejudice, even in apparently unfavorable circumstances, such as those in the South.

To explain this finding, one might focus more narrowly on the situation of contact. The relative status or ranking of the different *groups* whose members come into contact may be far less important than the statuses of the *individuals* who come into contact. For example, the crucial equality of status may be individual equality of education or income, business and professional achievement, or common subordination to higher authority. Thus, more frequent contact, even very close contact, between a white surgeon and a black butcher might have no effect on the prejudices of the former, but between two surgeons or two butchers it might have positive effects, regardless of the history and traditions of the larger society within which it takes place.

MacKenzie (1948) is the classic study of differences in occupational status as a determinant of the effect of contact on attitudes. She found no overall effect of contact on racial attitudes, but the hypothesis she investigated in detail was "to the effect that the occupational status of Negroes whom the respondents had known, rather than contact per se, is an important factor in determining willingness to associate with Negroes" (p. 417). Her subjects were white federal government employees from one government agency in Washington and white college students from two universities, one in the Northeast, the other in the Midwest. They were classified according to the occupation of the highest-status black they had known. Those who said that they had known one or more black professionals or black college students were compared with those whose acquaintance was limited to blacks of nonprofessional status. The first group held more favorable attitudes toward blacks and was distinctly more willing to have contact with them in a wider range of situations.

MacKenzie's findings raise the interesting question of whether interaction with superior members of an "inferior" group may be even more effective in overcoming prejudice than interaction with same-status members of the group (compare Cohen and Roper, 1972). If a white butcher were to interact with a black surgeon, the discrepancy between vulgar stereotypes and tangible realities might be even greater than in the case of true acquaintance between two butchers. (For the black surgeon, of course, such contact may tend to stir up resentment against whites who act as if they were doing blacks a big favor by treating them as human.)

Jackman and Crane (1986), despite being hampered by the very small sizes of the groups they were comparing (whites with one or more good friends who were black), found a strong relation between the status of these black friends and the racial attitudes of their white respondents. Those whites who had black friends of relatively low socioeconomic status (relative to the other friends of the respondents) had no better attitudes toward blacks than did those who lacked such friends, but those who had black friends of higher status had more positive attitudes. "The differences in racial attitudes between whites with lower- and higher-status black friends are generally as large as or larger than the differences observed . . . between whites with no black friends or acquaintances and whites with both black friends and acquaintances" (p. 478). The authors conclude that "racial attitudes are more positive when black friends have *higher* socioeconomic status than when they have equal status" (p. 480).

No broad generalization is likely to fit all cases, however, as Tsukashima and Montero (1976) show. Their study provides a clear illustration of the kind of three-variable interaction among contact, status, and prejudice that is so often said to explain the coexistence of high levels of contact with high levels of prejudice. It analyzes the attitudes toward Jews of a cross-section of blacks in Los Angeles. Using a conventional measure of anti-Semitism, Tsukashima and Montero found (1) weak negative correlations between anti-Semitic attitudes and "equal-status contact" (contact with Jews as fellow workers or as neighbors) and (2) slightly stronger positive correlations between anti-Semitism and "economic contact" (contact with Jews as merchants, landlords, or employers). They concluded that "intimate, equal-status contact may not provide the basis for as much optimism as past inquiries might indicate," because it is hard to promote equal-status contact without also promoting unequal contacts. (The factors that increase the availability of friends and neighbors from a particular group are likely also to increase their availability as employers and employees, merchants and customers, and so on.) "Researchers working on the premise that egalitarian social contact is related to racial tolerance may have to consider the possibility that other contacts may be correlated with heightened prejudice" (p. 163).

Whatever the merits of this conclusion, Tsukashima and Montero clearly illustrate a statistical interaction among three key variables: amount of contact, relative status, and ethnic attitudes. Using the same sample and the same measure of attitudes, the study shows a positive correlation (that is, a negative effect) for one kind of contact and a negative correlation (or a positive effect) for another kind. The two kinds of contact differed in their effects, one can say, because they involved individuals of different relative statuses. This difference may account for the contrasting correlations observed.

Situational Equal Status.

Finally, what about defining equality of status by the situation of contact itself? Equality in this narrowest sense is arguably even more important than overall equality between groups or equality of educational or occupational status between the individuals in contact. The crucial condition for positive change of attitudes may be simply that the contact situation not place majority and minority individuals in traditional roles of superiority and subordination. The contact between a white mistress and her black domestic is the classic example of the kind of contact that does *not* break stereotypes. But contact between individuals who are all on an equal footing—all students, or all tenants, or all new recruits—may have positive effects.

Even before Allport published his book, one of his students, Bernard Kramer, had drawn attention to the crucial difference between equality of socioeconomic status in the surrounding society and formal equality in the situation of contact (Amir, 1976, p. 255). The practical importance of this distinction has already been suggested. Desegregated schooling would make very little sense as a cure for racial prejudices if the children to be integrated had to come from families of similar economic and social status before positive results could be expected. Given the effects of discrimination on the opportunities and achievements of blacks, very few black children would be eligible to attend school with the offspring of many white families (compare Armor, 1972). Thomas Pettigrew has emphatically rejected any such interpretation of the equality condition, remarking that the requirement that groups "bring equal societal status *to* the situation" would be "a rigorous test indeed in a society where racial discrimination has long been endemic" (Pettigrew et al., 1973, p. 91; compare Pettigrew, 1971, p. 276).

Equal status as defined by the situation of contact ("situational equal status") is a much easier condition to satisfy, and a number of famous quasi-experimental studies suggest that equal-status contact in this sense often has positive effects. Among the most important are the studies of integration in the American army and of integrated public housing summarized in Chapter 3. The only clear exception to the rule suggested by these studies, though admittedly a very big and surprisingly clear exception, is that of public schooling, where many studies have failed to show any clear positive effects of increased contact on the racial attitudes of American children (see Chapter 2).

Even the evidence from the more encouraging studies is hard to interpret, however, because of the confounding of a second potentially important "third variable" in such quasi-experiments. Equality between groups as defined by a new situation of contact, in public housing or public schooling, for example, is usually associated with their subordination to a common authority (army officers, employers, teachers, social workers, city officials). The effects of equality of status in such a situation are thus confounded with the effects of the authoritative suggestion (or "normative support") implicit in there being any such contact in the first place, a point that will be discussed more fully below.

Conclusion.

The literature discussed in this section is only a fraction of the literature than could be cited in connection with the equality condition, but it is enough to justify the following rather striking remarks from an exceptionally thorough review of the literature up to 1976:

> Equal status between the interacting groups has generally been accepted by psychologists involved in this area as a prerequisite for positive change. It has been urged that although equal status [contact] does not necessarily produce better ethnic relations, positive change cannot be anticipated at all in its absence. Research findings are not always in accordance with these beliefs about equal status, however. . . . Positive changes in intergroup relations have been found in many studies . . . where real equal status did not exist, either within or outside the interaction. . . . There is some doubt that equal status of the interacting groups is a completely essential requirement for change. What may be important is the gap between what is expected from the other group and what is actually perceived and experienced in the contact situation. . . . In real-life situations, ethnic contact is generally not in conditions of equal status. In these cases contact can generate negative effects on attitudes as well as on the self-concept of the minority or low-status group member. . . . Finally, positive ethnic changes are more easily achieved when contact occurs with high-status individuals of the minority (or low-status) group. (Amir, 1976, pp. 256, 267)

No studies published since 1976 provide any grounds for disputing the main thrust of this sensible conclusion about the importance of equality of status (compare Riordan, 1978a; Smith, 1994; Stephan and Stephan, 1996).

Despite its intuitive plausibility, then, Allport's equality condition has no clear justification.[4] Research has not yielded positive results (negative correlations) only in situations satisfying the condition (in any of its versions), nor has it consistently yielded negative results in situations that fail to satisfy it. Contact with higher-status individuals may often improve attitudes, but sometimes it seems to worsen them (Tsukashima and Montero,

1976). There may always be some interaction between contact and status as determinants of prejudice, but because of its weakness it may rarely show up in empirical research (Smith, 1994). Ethnic attitudes are evidently complex and depend in complex ways upon contact. Without wishing to impugn the validity or worth of equality as a value or a general principle, empirical research has shown that any attempt to explain different correlations between contact and prejudice (including the broad contrast between levels of contact and prejudice in the northern and southern United States) simply in terms of the equality or inequality of those in contact would be unrealistic.

Cooperative Interdependence

Contact certainly involves different attitudes and behaviors depending upon whether the individuals in contact are cooperating with each other or fighting each other, but does contact itself have different effects depending upon the presence or absence of common goals that make those in contact "cooperatively interdependent"? Many social scientists have said that common interests, or common goals, in the sense of reasons for cooperation, must be present before greater contact can be expected to have positive effects. Others—the proponents of realistic conflict theory—seem convinced that cooperative or competitive interdependence is such a crucial variable that its fundamental importance is obscured if it is called just a condition for positive or negative effects from contact.

What exactly is meant by this condition or variable? Statements of the condition by contact theorists often seem to lean for plausibility on two commonplaces that have little connection with contact theory. The basic idea behind the condition can be stated clearly, however, and it must be distinguished from the two truisms with which it is often mixed up.

First, contact theory does not claim (though of course it also does not deny) that conflict or cooperation between two ethnic groups (**A** and **B** in what follows) may have effects on the ethnic attitudes of their members (**a, a'**, and so on; **b, b'**, and so on). The ethnic attitudes of individuals, who are unavoidably members of particular ethnic groups, are undoubtedly influenced by the relations of cooperation or competition that exist between their groups. If two groups share a common or "superordinate" goal (such as victory in a common struggle) that requires a joint effort for its attainment by both groups, then the relations between their members are likely to be better, and their attitudes toward each other more positive, on the average, than if the two groups are competing for a goal (territory, resources, power, victory) that only one can have. This important principle is familiar from the most casual observation of life, and no doubt could be backed up by content analyses of newspaper coverage of international relations (for instance, Soviet-American relations since 1917). It was demonstrated in the famous experiments presented in Chapter 1 involving children at summer camps. Nothing in what follows is meant to dispute this familiar principle. But can it be used to explain the puzzling results of research on contact and prejudice? If so, how?

Second, contact theory neither claims nor denies that the relations between two individuals in contact are likely to be greatly affected by what these individuals actually do to each other. If they help each other to attain important goals, so that both are better off as a result of their interaction, positive attitudes are more likely to develop between them than if they spend their time insulting, frustrating, or torturing each other (negative activities that tend to be accompanied by negative attitudes). But again it is unclear how this simple, uncontroversial idea can be used to explain the puzzling results of studies of contact and prejudice.

Allport's main condition for a positive effect of contact was that the contact be "equal-status contact between majority and minority groups in the pursuit of common goals." It is unclear whether "groups" here refers to the relevant ethnic groups or to other groupings of individuals defined by different levels or types of contact as well as by ethnicity, but perhaps Allport's overly concise formulation should not be scrutinized too closely. It is unlikely that Allport wanted to insinuate the odious, Machiavellian suggestion that friendly attitudes between, say, blacks and whites be cultivated by getting them to cooperate in subjugating and oppressing a third group, such as reds or yellows. He probably had a much more innocent idea in mind (see Allport, 1954, p. 276). Almost certainly he was thinking along the lines explained by Thomas Pettigrew:

> Not only must groups seek common goals, but the attainment of these goals must be a *mutually dependent* effort involving no competition along strictly racial lines. For instance, if the San Francisco Giants were an all-white baseball team and the Los Angeles Dodgers were all Negro, they could probably play indefinitely and not become more racially tolerant. Though equal status and common goal conditions would prevail, the lines of competition would make race relevant. Fortunately, professional athletic teams are interracial and provide a case of relatively successful desegregation. But the lesson is clear: contact situations which lead to interracial harmony must involve cooperative interdependence. (Pettigrew, 1971, p. 276)

This example implies a hypothesis about the effects of contact on such variables as tolerance and interracial harmony, where contact means participation in groups other than the relevant ethnic majorities and minorities. The claim is that relations between one set of groups (here, races) will improve as a result of the "crosscutting" involvement of their members in another set of groups (here, baseball teams) that are competing with each other. Individuals belonging to the first set of groups, who may see these groups as "competitively interdependent," find themselves, to their surprise, "cooperatively interdependent" as members of the second set of groups, with a consequent amelioration of their ethnic attitudes.

Does research generally support this familiar reasoning about cooperative interdependence (as members of crosscutting groups that are competitively interdependent) as a condition for positive effects from contact? No simple answer can be given. The problem is as much conceptual as empirical. What terms are adequate to describe the fundamental processes by which groups coalesce and divide or disappear, old identities fade away as new ones take hold, and former conflicts are forgotten or suppressed as more urgent ones develop? It is hard to write without implying that one already knows what one is trying to discover. The main point of what follows, not just in this section but in the next chapter, is to suggest that the question be answered only in light of the findings of *all* the relevant studies, not just those that discuss somewhat artificial situations of contact, some labeled cooperative, others competitive.[5]

The problem can be quickly clarified, however, by a brief discussion of the well-known research on "cooperative learning." The basic idea of cooperative learning (or the "jigsaw classroom") is to assign the students in an integrated classroom to racially (and sexually) heterogeneous teams that compete for academic honors (Aronson et al., 1978; Cook, 1984, 1985; Johnson, Johnson, and Maruyama, 1984; Slavin, 1983, 1985, 1995; Weigel, Wiser, and Cook, 1975). The students on a team work together on academic assignments, and the success of each team is judged by the average performance of its members, so that all the members of any one team are cooperatively interdependent. Like the Dodgers and the Giants, the teams compete, and like them they are racially mixed, so the lines of competition tend to make race irrelevant. Studies show more interracial friendships in classroom organized in this way than in classrooms organized in the traditional way, where all students compete individually for grades and the attention of teachers. These results are sometimes said to support contact theory (for example, Slavin, 1985, 1995). But do they really do so?

Let us assume for the sake of argument that cooperative learning has positive effects on sociometric choices (friendship groupings among **a, a',
b, b',** and so on). The crucial questions are (a) do the relevant attitudinal correlates of these choices (the **A-B** attitudes correlated with friendship or its absence) differ in any way, because of cooperative interdependence, from the correlates of sociometric (or "contact") variables found in other

situations that are not called cooperative, and (b) do the situations of co-operative contact that promote intergroup friendships have any overall effect on general intergroup attitudes? Finally, one may wonder whether the overall effects of cooperative learning, whatever they may be, are due to the cooperativeness of the relations it establishes between experimental groupings of students or to some other factor such as the normative influence of the teachers and principals who take the trouble to set up such cooperative relations.

The suggestions implicit in these rhetorical questions may seem more plausible if the situation is examined a little more closely. Notice, first, that whatever the relations between two large ethnic groups, **A** and **B,** these relations are the same for all individuals who belong to the groups, and they are not immediately changed in any significant way when two individuals, **a** and **b,** come into contact or come into contact in some particular way (presidents and prime ministers excepted). Whatever the relations between the groups, they will be the same for **a** and **b** as for (let's say) a' and **b',** two further individuals from the two groups who do *not* come into contact. Any difference (or change) observed when the relevant attitudes of **a** and a' (or **b** and **b'**) are measured and compared cannot be explained by the basic situation of cooperation or competition between **A** and **B,** whatever it may be, for it is (assumed to be) the same for all members of the two groups. The same reasoning applies mutatis mutandis for an a' and **b'** who are in contact but in a different situation (for example, cooperatively in a jigsaw classroom rather than competitively in the same classroom or in a traditional one).

Notice, further, that if **a** and **b** are called a team and made to compete with another team consisting of a' and **b',** then the new cooperative relations between **a** and **b** (and a' and **b'**) are matched by new competitive relations between **a** and **b'** and a' and **b.** So far as crosscutting competition and cooperation are concerned, one cannot, it seems, make friends without also in a sense making enemies.[6]

Notice, finally, the perplexing ambiguity of the terms *competition* and *cooperation.* Why do we call one classroom competitive and another cooperative? The terms can refer to overt behavior, to an underlying structure of interests or incentives, or to some combination of behavior and incentives. It is often unclear what exactly is meant by saying that **A** and **B** (or **a** and **b**) are in a situation of cooperation or one of competition. It is often not easy to see whether a particular situation is cooperative or competitive, and the difficulties increase the more closely we look.

If the reference is to overt behavior (are the individuals in the situation actually helping or hurting each other?), then a connection between situation and attitudes may well exist but (as suggested above) may be a little too close to be of much interest. Contact will undoubtedly be associated with certain negative attitudes when the contact in question consists of **a** and **b** (or all the **a**s and **b**s) frustrating and insulting each other and with certain positive attitudes when they are praising and assisting each other. But if these positive and negative attitudes are those of the individuals toward each other, then the differences observed may have very little to do with intergroup attitudes, and it may be misleading to say that different situations of contact, because of their different degrees of competitiveness or cooperativeness, have different effects on intergroup attitudes (compare Cook, 1978, pp. 105–7).

Traditional contact theory, it should be understood, assumes certain potentially cooperative social situations in which individual members of larger ethnic groups come into contact—as neighbors, classmates, fellow workers—and then it asks how these new social relations tend to affect not friendly neighboring or cooperation in the workplace (which are in a sense just the independent variable) but relations between the larger ethnic groups (tolerance, interracial harmony). The theory focuses on an interesting problem that can be obscured if the meanings of *contact* and *attitudes* are allowed to slip so that the emphasis falls on achieving friendly interpersonal relations in public housing projects, classrooms, and factories.

The terms *competition* and *cooperation* can also refer, of course, to underlying conflicts of interest or incentives for cooperation that are in principle independent of—though they may in fact have effects on—attitudes and overt behavior. The behavior of individuals may be strongly influenced by the underlying structures of interests in the situations in which they find themselves. This is in fact the main theme of realistic conflict theory. Competitive situations, in which individuals are competitively interdependent, produce hostile, competitive attitudes and behavior, according to the theory, whereas situations with strong incentives for cooperation produce friendliness and cooperation. Schools are sometimes said to provide a poor context for intergroup contact because the students are all competing for grades and the attention of teachers, or at least for places on the student council or the cheerleading squad, rather than cooperating in getting an education or having a good time.

The key weakness of this "realistic" reasoning is its tendency to depict situations as either simply competitive or simply cooperative. Given the mixture of motives in most real-life situations, and the importance of social norms in overcoming (or obscuring) underlying conflicts, it may be impossible to determine objectively whether a given situation is competitive or cooperative—assuming that these are our only choices. Whether any two groups, large or small, are really competing or cooperating (assuming again that these are our only choices and putting aside for the moment what all their individual members are actually doing to each other) generally is not obvious but is very much a matter of argument and interpretation.

Situations of contact on the job, for example, are likely to involve complex mixtures of competitive and cooperative motives. Firms such as Ford and General Motors may be in competition for market shares but in league against the Japanese, just as two divisions within General Motors may be both competing and cooperating, and so on. Even the Dodgers and the Giants, after all, cooperate in extracting money from baseball fans and television networks by playing a competitive team sport in an entertaining way, according to well-known rules, while the players on each team, although they share victories and defeats, compete for fans, trophies, and contracts. Situations of purely competitive or purely cooperative interdependence seem to be theoretical fictions. Most situations are like markets in which buyers and sellers (or employers and employees, husbands and wives, friends and neighbors) can all gain from trading but in which different trades are possible, so that they are also divided, at least potentially, by an underlying conflict of interest regarding how the "gains of trade" are to be shared (see almost any elementary economics textbook). It may be possible to measure and compare the amounts of conflict in some simple situations, but generally speaking it is not possible to do so, and our *awareness* of conflict seems to vary inversely with the clarity and general acceptance of relevant norms (such as the laws of property, conventions of pricing and bargaining, sex roles, or the absolute value of grades) for regulating conflict. Surprisingly little seems to depend on the underlying situations, abstractly considered (compare Axelrod, 1970, 1984).

The implications of all this for ethnic contact and conflict are hard to spell out, but two tentative conclusions may be suggested. First, the research on cooperative learning may be more important for school principals than for presidents and prime ministers. Few friendships would develop between black and white students in an integrated school if their teachers spent their time promoting schoolyard brawls between blacks and whites. Many more cross-race friendships would presumably develop if the brawling teams were racially mixed "Dodgers" and "Giants." The real question, however, is what happens not just to friendship choices but to general attitudes when the teachers are not organizing brawls but just teaching their classes.

Second, cooperation and competition, in the sense of underlying incentives, may be important for intergroup attitudes, but it is not clear how differences in these incentives explain the findings of the research on contact and conflict. Does public housing differ significantly from public schooling with respect to the motives associated with contact in each situation? The most important studies of contact in public housing have shown positive changes in attitudes, whereas studies of contact in schools have shown negative changes more often than positive ones. It seems far-fetched to attribute the differences observed to any clear differences in the situations studied as judged from the vantage point offered by vague analogies with business or professional sports.

Even more puzzling from this perspective would be the basic finding that different relations between contact and ethnic attitudes can be found in the same series of situations (amounting to the same overall situation) depending upon how the relevant variables are averaged and compared. The best illustration of this fact is provided by Williams's (1964) study of four American cities. His results show a positive correlation between contact and ethnic prejudice when the cities are compared but a negative correlation in all the cities when individuals are compared. (See above p. 65 and pp. 98–99). Harlan (1942) had showed the same pattern earlier with four colleges rather than four cities. It is nonsense to suppose that the respondents to these studies were competitively interdependent when grouped into four cities or four colleges but cooperatively interdependent when grouped according to their individual contacts with minorities.

The above remarks are in no way meant to challenge the platitude that relations between two groups can often be improved by a realistic, dramatic (violent or potentially violent) conflict with a third. World War II and the Cold War almost certainly encouraged cooperation between blacks and whites in the United States and improved their attitudes toward each other. The effects of Vietnam are less clear. What is being disputed is the claim, often not very clearly stated, that cooperation between ethnically diverse individuals as members of crosscutting "teams" can be counted on to reduce their latent or traditional hostilities as members of rival ethnic groups. This appealing idea may be correct, but there is surprisingly little hard evidence for it and no reason to think that it explains why more contact is sometimes associated with more ethnic prejudice and sometimes with less. For explaining the findings of the research on contact and prejudice, "common goals," as commonly understood, is a red herring.

Normative Support

Human beings tend to imitate each other. Their opinions tend to reflect the social environment in which they live. If "everyone" thinks that members of group **A** would be foolish to treat members of group **B** as social equals, the individual will tend to think so as well. Even social scientists, it is sometimes said, hesitate to ask research questions that might lead them to answers that would elicit disapproval. This chameleon-like tendency of individuals to echo safe opinions and to conform to social norms is frequently emphasized in the literature on racial and ethnic attitudes. Much prejudice, Allport and many others have said, is only skin deep, supported by motives no more complicated than the desire to avoid a scene. "Finding themselves with prejudiced people, they string along. Why be rude? Why challenge the community patterns? Only the headstrong idealists make a nuisance of themselves. Better to parrot a folkway than to be a bore. . . . Such chatter—if indeed there is little behind it—can be called *phatic* discourse—the words meaning nothing excepting as a device to avoid silence and signify social solidarity" (Allport, 1954, pp. 286–87).

A classic textbook in the field of race and ethnic relations has a long chapter titled "The Cultural Factor in Prejudice and Discrimination" in which the "cultural factor" responsible for ethnic prejudice is identified as the "tradition of prejudice" that is sustained by conformity and passed on from generation to generation in the process of socialization (Simpson and Yinger, 1985; see also Aronson, 1984, pp. 254–58).

Human beings, even social scientists, generally tend to follow their leaders and do what they are told, especially when the orders are backed by overwhelming force. It is beyond dispute that the example and instruction of leaders—political, military, judicial, intellectual, and correctional—can have effects on racial and ethnic attitudes.

But when Allport writes that the effect of contact is greatly *enhanced* when it is sanctioned by law, custom, or local atmosphere, he implies an effect of public opinion and leadership on prejudice that is more complicated than the direct dependence just noted. The same implication is found in the remarks of Pettigrew (1971, p. 277) about how "explicit social sanction" leads to "more positive effects" of contact. The clearest explanation of this more complicated dependence is found in the review of the literature previously quoted: "The *effectiveness* of interracial contact is greatly *increased* if the contact is sanctioned by institutional support. The support may come from the law, a custom, a spokesman for the community, or simply from a social atmosphere and a general public agreement. In some cases, governmental policy may be the influential factor. . . . However, in many intergroup situations neither the social atmosphere nor institutions favor intergroup mixing for a variety of reasons. When such a state occurs, it may strongly *hinder the development* of successful intergroup contact and ethnic integration" (Amir, 1976, p. 277, emphasis added). This passage suggests a statistical *interaction* between contact and public opinion or leadership as determinants of prejudiced attitudes: to simplify, the greater the contact, the less the prejudice when there is normative support for equal-status contact, but the greater the contact, the greater the prejudice when law or custom discourages equal-status contact. Something like this relationship must be postulated if normative variables are to explain different correlations between contact and prejudice in different situations. A regression of prejudice on contact and norms must show a significant *multiplicative* effect of the independent variables (contact and norms) and not just significant *additive* effects.

Such a relation may well exist, but the literature on the contact hypothesis has conspicuously failed to demonstrate it. (The only real attempt is Smith, 1994.) Rather, as already noted, a substantial number of studies show positive effects of contact in what must be reckoned, from the standpoint of the theory, inauspicious circumstances. If researchers had invested more resources in demonstrating interaction experimentally, they might have succeeded, but they have not done so.

This conclusion is in no way meant to deny the importance of social norms. On the contrary, studies of the contact hypothesis plainly suffer from too much emphasis on contact and not enough on social norms (or simple authoritative commands). The landmark studies of racial integration in the United States army at the end of World War II provide the best illustration of this point (Stouffer et al., 1949). As usually summarized in the literature, these studies show positive effects of contact, in the sense of interaction, on racial attitudes. But the type of contact in question was proximity and would not have taken place if the army high command had not decided that it should. The orders given ordinary soldiers by their commanding officers illustrate normative support, but their effects may be misunderstood if they are called a condition that enhanced the positive effects of contact rather than the main cause of the attitude changes later observed. It may have been not the *contact* but the *enforcement of it* that had an effect on attitudes. Once the brass had made up their minds and integrated some companies, the ordinary soldiers fell into line. The soldiers who were more aware of the opinions of the authorities because they were closer organizationally to the integrated companies fell into line faster. Contact per se may have had little or nothing to do with the statistical relation actually observed. As the authors of a later study put it, "Authority exercised firmly and without ambiguity can control behavior and shift opinion in potentially tense situations" (Bogart, 1992, p. xlviii).

A similar argument could be made about some of the findings from the most frequently cited studies of public housing. When housing authorities tell black and white tenants to live side by side in the same buildings, or close together in common projects, they communicate their opinion—and the opinion of authorities higher up in the chain of command—that equal-status contact between blacks and whites should be accepted and encouraged. The main differences in the opinions of whites living close to and far from blacks are perhaps best explained by such opinion leadership (compare Riordan, 1978a, pp. 170–71, 178).

The integration of schools may have had less predictable effects because of important breaks in the chain of command. Children are under two potentially conflicting sets of authorities: the family and the state. The commands coming from Supreme Court justices through local courts to children can be countermanded by parents and other family members. In addition, the strong traditions of local autonomy in education in the United States complicate matters. Teachers and school superintendents, submissive though they may be toward local elected officials, may feel little obligation to obey the rules made by federal politicians, even Supreme Court justices. The various observed effects of school desegregation on racial attitudes may be due to factors of this sort.[7]

Underlying these conjectures is a simple theory—much simpler than traditional contact theory—about why normative support is important for the reduction of prejudiced attitudes in situations of contact. This rival theory has to do with the power of governments to control behaviors and the tendency of individuals to bring their opinions into line with their behaviors. If the authorities in a society are firm and united, they can generally control what their inferiors do, and once the latter are engaging in positive intergroup behaviors, positive attitudes usually follow. A leading social psychologist has explained the basic idea: "If I know that you and I will inevitably be in close contact, and I don't like you, I will experience dissonance. In order to reduce dissonance, I will try to convince myself that you are not as bad as I had previously thought. I will set about looking for your positive characteristics, and will try to ignore, or minimize the importance of, your negative characteristics. Accordingly, the mere fact that I know that I must at some point be in *close contact* with you will force me to change my prejudiced attitudes about you, *all other things being equal*" (Aronson, 1984, p. 261). Prejudiced attitudes may change, in other words, not as a result of contact with the objects of prejudice (followed by true acquaintance and the breaking of stereotypes) but as a result of *anticipating* that contact is going to be required by the relevant authorities (compare Ellis et al., 1992).

Aronson stresses the importance of inevitability in this process. The authorities must be strong and united. Their support for integration must be uncompromising. Thomas Pettigrew, too, has stressed the importance of rigorous normative support, observing that "total institutions" (such as "residential assessment centers for young offenders") are "ideal settings for cumulative effects [of contact] to occur" (Pettigrew, 1986, p. 188). Regarding the integration of schools, he has noted that "violence has generally resulted in localities where at least some of the authorities gave prior hints that they would gladly return to segregation if disturbances occurred; peaceful integration has generally followed firm and forceful leadership" (Pettigrew, 1961, p. 105; compare Pettigrew, 1991, pp. 168–69). In short, if society were more "total"—more like a residential assessment center for young offenders or a hospital for the chronically ill—and if the authorities in such a society always stood firmly and forcefully behind integration, then increases in contact might more often be associated with more positive attitudes.

Levels of Analysis

I'll teach you differences.
    —*King Lear*, 1.4

Those who study leaves and twigs may with effort keep the whole tree in view, but they are likely to lose sight of the forest. Similarly, those who focus on the evidence for and against particular hypotheses within contact theory are likely to lose sight of the most important alternatives to it.

Contact theory, according to its most vocal critics, suffers from "individualism"—"the thesis that the individual is the sole psychological reality and that that reality does not include a distinct component corresponding to group behaviour" (Turner and Giles, 1981, p. 31). Contact theorists such as Gordon Allport explain intergroup conflict in terms of individual psychological processes. They try to analyze prejudice and discrimination by analyzing the cognitive and emotional processes of individuals dealing with other individuals. They pass almost unconsciously from discussions of individual psychology to generalizations about groups. This is the wrong approach, according to the advocates of both realistic conflict theory and social identity theory. Attention must shift from the individual to the group, they say, because it has a reality of its own. Individual behavior is profoundly affected by identification with groups and conformity to group norms. In fact, there are two fundamentally different kinds of behavior: interpersonal and intergroup. Explanations of prejudice and discrimination must put the emphasis on conflict between groups (and intergroup behavior) rather than on individual irrationality (and interpersonal behavior). More contact may sometimes have beneficial effects on the attitudes of individuals, they concede, but it does not resolve intergroup conflicts, and conflict or cooperation at the group level is what principally determines individual attitudes. Given the linkages between individuals and groups, individual cognitive and emotional processes may have quite different outcomes depending upon the relations between groups.

A simple analogy may help to clarify this idea. Human respiration, one could say, is essentially the same in all environments: the basic chemical and physiological processes are the same in safe and in polluted environments. But plainly it makes a huge difference for the overall functioning of the human organism whether the lungs are drawing in clean air or the noxious fumes of unregulated industry—or worse still, the lethal molecules of a nerve gas released by terrorists. Similarly, the electrical and chemical processes in the human brain may be essentially the same in all social environments, from the healthiest to the most harmful, but it makes a big difference for the social and political behavior of human beings whether their brains are processing the destructive opinions associated with conflicts among groups or the more wholesome ones associated with intergroup cooperation. The basic cognitive and emotional processes may be the same, but the outcomes can be radically different, depending upon whether the leaders of important groups are cultivating harmony or trying to stir up trouble. If there are intellectual "terrorists" in the cognitive environment who are spreading a kind of "nerve gas," hatred, the effects may be just as bad cognitively as the effects of sarin are physically. Realistic conflict theorists and social identity theorists are surely right to insist on the importance of these environmental or contextual variables as determinants of the outcomes of individual cognitive processes. Indeed, contact theorists themselves may have had such contextual variables in mind when they made cooperative interdependence and normative support conditions for expecting positive effects from contact.[8]

Realistic conflict theory and social identity theory help to shift attention from individuals to groups and thus to bring the context of individual cognitive processes into clearer focus. Realistic conflict theory points to the importance of realistic conflicts: it counters the suggestion implicit in traditional contact theory that important intergroup conflicts are simply due to misperceptions, which can easily be corrected by more contact with outsiders. Social identity theory corrects in turn the tendency of realistic conflict theorists to put too much emphasis on material conflicts and to neglect the importance of pride, psychological identifications with groups, and the desire for a positive group identity.

A shift of attention is not an explanation or even a sketch of one, however. The social scientists who have emphasized groups and the conflicts between them may have been too quick to generalize about the causes of conflict, and they have certainly neglected the specific problem shown by the research on contact and ethnic attitudes.

The aim of a theory of intergroup relations should be to explain the relations between groups, not to take them as givens. To the extent that realistic conflict theorists and social identity theorists have faced this challenge, they have emphasized underlying conflicts of interest that exist equally between *all* groups, no matter how they might be defined, for all groups must be regarded as rivals for goods such as power, wealth, and prestige. In this respect, the two theories represent no advance beyond untutored common sense. Despite appearances, they provide no basis for explaining particular patterns of conflict. Nor do they provide any basis for prediction. When should social scientists expect conflicts to develop between groups **A** and **B** (grouping individuals by race or ethnicity, let us say) rather than between **C** and **D** (dividing them by class or gender)? Perhaps there is no predicting or really explaining such things—social science may be limited to analyzing and interpreting what has already happened—but even this more modest objective requires some attention to what people say about the reasons for their loyalties and antipathies, not facile attributions of conflicting desires for power or prestige.

Consider the so-called realistic conflict between blacks and whites regarding jobs or housing—assuming for the moment a fixed stock of jobs or housing. This conflict is no different from the conflict between, say, the young and the old or between Catholics and Protestants, gays and straights, or Geminis and Libras. The more jobs and houses for one group, the fewer (disregarding possible coalitions against third groups) for the other. The same reasoning applies if the good in question is social status or a positive identity rather than jobs or housing: all possible divisions of the population are in principle equally in conflict. Moreover, with goods such as status or prestige, there is no possibility that the conflict can be alleviated by increasing the stock of goods to be distributed.

A simpler example may make the basic point clearer still: when dividing a pie or cake, those who are to share it are all potentially in conflict, no matter how the lines are finally drawn and the competing teams or coalitions are constituted—whether on the basis of class, race, gender, age, religion, nationality, date of birth, or the side of the table on which individuals happen to be sitting. When the lines have been drawn in a particular way (so as to make classes salient, for example), this may explain why there is a particular kind of conflict (class conflict), but this conflict is not fully explained until the reasons for drawing class (rather than, say, race or gender) lines have been explained. As Horowitz (1985, p. 108) points out, "The fundamental deficiency of the class theory of ethnic conflict is that it credits with conflict-producing power every rationally competitive interest that can conceivably be identified, while ignoring all of the forces that work against the emergence of such competitive interests."

Underlying conflicts of interest may indeed explain overt hostile behavior, but before the one kind of conflict can explain the other, it must somehow be restricted to the relevant groups. To say that a latent conflict of interest becomes an actual "behavioral" clash when individuals identify with the relevant groupings may be correct but it does not go far enough: it leaves unexplained why individuals identify with some groups rather than others. To cite identifications as the explanation for conflicts and negative attitudes, after the fashion of social identity theory, is simply to beg the question.

Neither does realistic conflict theory or social identity theory seem able to throw any light on the puzzling discrepancy revealed by the empirical studies of the contact hypothesis summarized earlier. To simplify, the review of the literature in Chapter 3 shows two apparently contradictory correlations: a negative correlation between contact and prejudice at the individual level (in studies of interaction) and a positive correlation at the aggregate level (in studies of proportions). None of the theories discussed so far appears to be able to explain this puzzling "change of sign" of the contact-prejudice correlation depending upon level of analysis. It must have something to do with individual psychological processes and the relations among groups, but what exactly? The critics of contact theory have shown little interest in or even awareness of the problem. One looks in vain for any clear discussion of it in their various publications.

Some readers may be tempted to resolve the discrepancy by dismissing one of the correlations—the negative correlation at the individual level—as merely a methodological artifact. The weaker the studies, they may notice, and the more they treat contact as an attitude (not something observed but something elicited by broad questions in a questionnaire) or the more they leave experimenter effects uncontrolled, the more clearly they seem to show the negative correlation in question (see note 2 above). The line of thought suggested by these observations is tempting, but can it be right to dismiss so many careful empirical studies so quickly? Their methodological weaknesses are hard to evaluate and easy to exaggerate. Voluntary behavior often expresses attitudes, no doubt, but attitudes are sometimes changed by the effects of voluntary behavior—one of the great principles of learning theory. To dismiss the negative correlation in question would be to dismiss the intuitively sound reasoning about contact, friendship, knowledge, and attitudes that underlies the conventional contact hypothesis. Can it really be true that familiarity generally breeds contempt?

A better solution will be found along a second line of thought. Briefly, there is one real ("causal") correlation at the individual level and a different one at the aggregate level, and the difference is explained by social processes. Before pursuing an investigation along these lines, however, let me try to make clearer what may underlie our little, puzzling, but somewhat complicated "fact."

Correlation and Aggregation

The various social sciences tend to treat the individual-group problem in diverse ways. In social psychology there is a tendency to speak of different kinds of behavior at different levels of analysis. People who treat each other as individuals are said to behave in an interpersonal way, but they are said to engage in intergroup behavior when they treat others, and think of themselves, as group members. According to some contemporary social psychologists, this is a crucial distinction. It is vital to specify the conditions that elicit these two very different kinds of behavior. In economics, political science, and sociology, by contrast, the emphasis tends to fall on the distinction between individual-level and aggregate-level correlations.

Economists encounter the problem of abstracting from more detailed relations in order to make broader generalizations in a variety of settings—for example, when constructing index numbers, analyzing demand, defining social welfare functions, and relating the performance of the economy as a whole to the behavior of its individual units. For about sixty years—roughly since the publication of J. M. Keynes's *General Theory of Employment, Interest, and Money* in 1936—economists have distinguished two main branches of their subject: microeconomics (the study of the behavior of households and firms) and macroeconomics (the study of such economic aggregates as savings, interest, employment, and gross national product). The distinction gained sudden prominence because of Keynes's persuasive demonstration that the behavior of the economy as a whole, as reflected in such measures as the unemployment rate, could not be understood simply by extrapolating from models of the behavior of individuals or other small units within the economy. (A reduction in wage rates, for example, might encourage every employer, considered in isolation, to hire additional labor, but in the economy as a whole a drop in wages, by reducing aggregate demand, might tend to produce a rise in unemployment.) Working with simple theories and quantitatively measurable variables, economists easily saw that the underlying problem—the aggregation problem—is a very general one having to do with the effects of aggregation on the relations among variables.

In political science and sociology the aggregation problem is usually presented as a difficulty in making inferences about the behavior of indi-

Table 4.1   Heterogeneity, Prejudice, and Contact in Four Towns

Town	Minority Percentage	Prejudiced Percentage	Percentage in Contact
A (Amityville)	10%	15%	18%
B (Beaconsville)	20	20	32
C (Centerville)	30	25	42
D (Downsville)	40	30	48

viduals from statistical analyses of census data or election returns. It is a topic in quantitative methods rather than in theory or model building. Since Robinson (1950) it has generally been known as "the problem of ecological correlations."

A picture, they say, is worth a thousand words. Imagine four widely separated towns or cities with different majority-minority proportions in their populations and with different average levels of prejudice among the majority. Table 4.1 shows one possible set of proportions and levels for the four imaginary towns (compare Table 3.1, p. 99). Town A combines a low minority percentage with a low average level of prejudice (the percentage of the majority group that get high scores on some measure of prejudice). Town D illustrates the opposite combination: a relatively large minority presence and a higher-than-average level of prejudice. Towns B and C fall between these extremes. In fact, the numbers have been chosen to fit a simple linear relation between prejudice level and minority proportion: $P = 10 + \frac{1}{2} M$. The correlation between them is thus perfect ($r = 1.00$).

There is no need to consider at this point why such a relation might exist between minority percentages and average levels of prejudice. It could be due to competition for jobs or housing or a result of ancient political grudges; it could be a residue of religious conflicts or a product of irrational fears about "invasion" and "race mixing"; or it could be nothing more than a Klee-Kandinsky fight based upon make-believe differences. The only important point, for the moment, is that such a positive relation between the two variables is assumed to exist.

Imagine, further, that the likelihood of personal relations between the two groups depends upon their relative numbers in each town. Members of the majority group are more likely to encounter members of the minority group and to develop personal relations with them in Town D, where they make up 40 percent of the population, than in Town A, where they make up only 10 percent. The chance that two individuals chosen at random from the population of Town A will belong to different groups is only .18;

the comparable probabilities for Towns B, C, and D are .32, .42, and .48, respectively. Let us assume that these probabilities represent rates of contact between majority and minority individuals in the four towns from the standpoint of the majority (the third column of Table 4.1). In the real world, of course, prejudice would be associated with segregation and discrimination, so the real rates of interaction across the group boundary would presumably be lower than these figures imply, and the dampening effect of prejudice would presumably be greater at higher average levels of prejudice, so it would be greater in Town D than in Town A. But for present purposes, the simplest assumption, random mixing, yields a reasonable gradient in rates of interaction for the four towns. The trend in the imagined rates is not misleading: in the real world, despite differences in prejudice, there is undoubtedly more contact in relatively heterogeneous populations than in relatively homogeneous ones. In our example, consequently, there is a positive correlation between overall rates of interaction and average levels of prejudice: more contact goes with a *higher* level of prejudice.

What effect does this contact have on the prejudices of the individuals in contact? Let us imagine, finally, that it reduces prejudice: in all four towns, majority individuals who interact personally with members of the minority group are less likely to score high on prejudice, whereas those who have no personal contacts with the minority group are more likely to be highly prejudiced. Table 4.2 provides some figures chosen to illustrate this "contact hypothesis."

The purpose of presenting all these imaginary numbers is to clarify an important principle, namely, that the correlation between two variables in a given population can be very different at the individual and at the aggregate levels. Here the relation between contact and prejudice is positive at the aggregate level (Table 4.1) but negative at the individual level (Table 4.2). The discrepancy arises from the way the major variables of interest, individual contact and prejudice, are related to the "grouping" variable that defines the aggregate units (place of residence). Broadly speaking, whenever there are differences among aggregate units such as to create a correlation between two variables across these units, the comparable individual-level correlations within the units can differ sharply, in sign as well as in magnitude, from the "ecological" correlation across them. An exact relation holds among all these correlations and the overall correlation among all the individuals in question, but not one that can be stated clearly in a few words.[9] The main result so far is plain enough: negative correlations between contact and prejudice at the individual level are consistent with positive correlations at the aggregate level. No more than simple arithmetic is needed to demonstrate this possibility.

Table 4.2   Prejudice and Contact in Four Towns

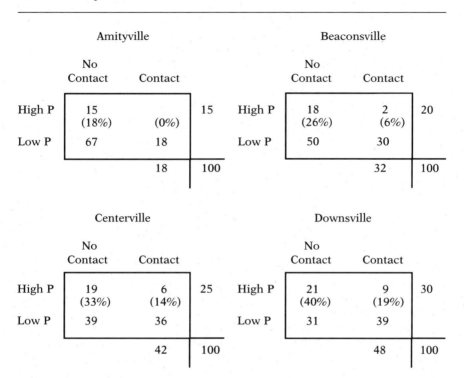

	Amityville					Beaconsville		
	No Contact	Contact				No Contact	Contact	
High P	15 (18%)	(0%)	15		High P	18 (26%)	2 (6%)	20
Low P	67	18			Low P	50	30	
		18	100				32	100

	Centerville					Downsville		
	No Contact	Contact				No Contact	Contact	
High P	19 (33%)	6 (14%)	25		High P	21 (40%)	9 (19%)	30
Low P	39	36			Low P	31	39	
		42	100				48	100

Note: The cell entries are the percentages of each town's majority population that either does or does not have contact with the minority and that scores either high or low on the measure of prejudice. The marginal figures (15 and 18 for Amityville) are the percentages from the second and third columns of Table 4.1. The percentages in parentheses are the proportions scoring high on prejudice among those with and without contact. The numbers inside each subtable have been chosen to make the differences between these percentages—the simplest measure of correlation for tables like these—all about 20 percent. In each town, in other words, the prejudiced proportion is about 20 points *lower* among those with contact than among those with no contact with the minority.

A New Approach

Traditional contact theory rests upon assumptions about the nature of prejudice that deny or at least greatly downplay its "collective" aspects. There are as many variations on this critical theme as there are writers who have contributed to the relevant critical literature. The most influential formulations, those by Herbert Blumer, Muzafer Sherif, and Henri Tajfel, were examined in some detail in Chapter 1. Here only a quick reminder of their basic objection is needed.

Allport and his forerunners and successors all separate ethnic prejudice from realistic group conflict. They find the roots of prejudice and discrimination not in real conflicts of interest between groups but in the moral and intellectual shortcomings of individuals. Their critics, by contrast, reject this "individualistic" way of thinking about prejudice. They say that it tends to personalize prejudice too much and thus to encourage reliance upon inefficient psychotherapeutic manipulations to deal with it. According to these theorists, the variables that determine levels of prejudice and discrimination have little to do with contact among individuals and much to do with the relations among groups. Are the relevant groups divided by important conflicting interests, they ask, or are they united by the pursuit of superordinate goals?

The social scientists who have objected to the excessive individualism of traditional contact theory and of the older literature on prejudice and discrimination generally have clearly sensed the danger of cross-level generalizations. Correlations that hold for interpersonal behavior, at the individual level, cannot be simply extrapolated to intergroup relations, at the aggregate level. Yet these critics may have been too quick to dismiss contact as an important variable. Does it have *no* important effects? Might it not be better to try to work out an aggregate-level account of contact and its consequences, in order to offset the individualism of traditional contact theory? Such an account need not involve complicated distinctions verging on the metaphysical between interpersonal behavior and intergroup behavior. All that would really be needed would be a bit of arithmetic. When individuals come into contact, so do the groups to which they belong, but the effects may look quite different, as we have just seen, at different levels of aggregation. The relevant differences may become clearer if we try to abstract from personal and institutional details in order to understand the basic logic or nature of ethnic conflict.

Chapter 5 outlines a "linguistic" theory of ethnic conflict. Unlike the three well-known theories considered so far, it does not draw attention away from ethnic differences as a cause of conflict. Rather, it uses conflict between languages to illustrate social processes that may be of more general relevance.

Casual observation suffices to establish that greater contact is not always associated with more favorable ethnic attitudes and behavior. Indeed, a generalization frequently found in the relevant literature is that prejudice and discrimination increase with the relative size of a minority group (Blalock, 1967, p. 143). And Van Evera (1994, p. 8) offers the admittedly untested but plausible hypothesis that a denser intermingling of nationalities produces a greater risk of war. Any satisfactory contact theory must evidently explain positive as well as negative correlations between contact and prejudice. But traditional contact theory fails to explain these correlations satisfactorily. Its three standard "situational" variables seem to have almost no explanatory power. And so far as individuals and their prejudices are concerned, one could argue that Allport's basic distinction between casual contact and true acquaintance is simply fanciful. Other things being equal, the greater the casual contact between two groups, the more frequently their members will become personally acquainted with each other, generally speaking, and consequently, perhaps, the more positive the intergroup attitudes of these individuals will become on the average, regardless of their status relations, individual incentives for competition or cooperation, the conflict or cooperation between their groups, or even what their political and intellectual superiors think. Why, despite this general rule of individual psychology (amply illustrated if not demonstrated by the literature on the contact hypothesis), some positive correlations can nonetheless be found at the aggregate level between greater contact and greater ethnic prejudice is a mystery that traditional contact theory just makes more mysterious.

5 A Model of Ethnic Conflict

Modern social science aims to combine far-reaching predictive theories with careful investigations of their factual accuracy. It eschews unverifiable normative or metaphysical generalizations and scorns primitive, "barefoot" empiricism. The desired combination of theory and research is perhaps best illustrated by contemporary "positive" economics, with its abstract mathematical models and its sophisticated statistical methods for their testing and estimation. Elsewhere, in the other branches of social science, theory and research have been harder to join and hold in balance. Theories tend to grow grander and vaguer. Metaphors and ambiguous expressions abound; relevant data are scarce; empirical research sometimes seems to lack any clear purpose beyond itself.

The present investigation of ethnic conflict has featured a profusion of simple facts about contact and ethnic attitudes while giving some attention as well to the reasoning commonly associated with these facts. Now, having made our way through these thickets of theory and research, and having attained a standpoint from which the simple facts begin to form a larger pattern, we may look toward the development of a broader theory about contact and its consequences.

This chapter develops a model of ethnic conflict similar to a model of nationalism found in the work of Karl Deutsch.[1] The main features of Deutsch's definition of nationalism and some limitations of his analysis of its causes are explained in the Appendix. My model, like his, is essentially a quantitative analysis of the effects of contact. It relies on language to provide a pattern for ethnicity. It assumes that ethnic conflict, like nationalism, is ultimately about control of a state. And the result is a simple linguistic model of ethnic conflict highlighting relative rates of change. The working hypothesis on which this modeling exercise rests is that some important "group processes" and "intergroup relations"—in particular, connections between contact and its various hypothesized effects (reductions in prejudice, conflict, and so on)—may become clearer if we restrict our attention, at least initially, to relations among groups distinguished by ethnic or cultural differences, particularly language.

Contact and Its Consequences

Consider two adults who have grown up in different tribes or nations and who have reason to associate with one another. They may wish to cooperate in securing food and shelter, in trading for profit, or in sharing experiences and learning from each other's successes and failures; they may be influenced by loneliness, by sexual attraction, or by a variety of other motives. Let us simply assume that each finds some important rewards contingent upon prolonged association and cooperation with the other. For the moment, it is the consequences of their association, not its causes, that concern us. What are these consequences likely to be?

At first there is likely to be some misunderstanding, frustration, and mutual irritation, especially if the two individuals speak different languages. But after a time, and assuming that the reasons for association persist, each of them is likely to learn new ways of behaving that make him or her a more agreeable partner for the other. To be sure, one of them may be more flexible and accommodating than the other, and one of them may change more than the other. But there will be incentives for both to change, and both will probably do so. Can we reasonably doubt that they will tend to learn each other's languages, perhaps developing some private mélange of the two? Will they not also tend to modify or hide their opinions to lessen their conflicts? Perhaps they will even adopt some of each other's beliefs, tastes, and moral standards, learn to enjoy each other's foods, and perhaps even confer some existence on each other's gods.[2]

If many individuals from two ethnic or cultural groups frequently find themselves in the situation just described, then we say that there is contact between these two groups. Contact in this sense must be distinguished from physical proximity: two groups can live in close proximity, and yet their members may never associate with one another and may not be at all interdependent. Or two groups can be economically interdependent, whether in proximity or at a distance, in ways that require very little contact between their members—perhaps only occasional contact between a few people who arrange the exchange of finished goods. These situations are ones of little or no contact between the two groups. By contrast, the groups can become interdependent in ways that require or encourage frequent association across ethnic boundaries. They can find themselves in situations where large numbers of their members have strong incentives to associate frequently with members of the other group, and they can develop habits of associating with each other. Then we say that there is considerable contact between the groups.

Increasing contact between diverse ethnic or cultural groups has been an important concomitant of economic development or modernization. Economic progress involves increased specialization, not just among individual workers but also among regions and countries. People are brought together to work in large factories. Great networks of trade and communication develop to link up the specialized activities of different individuals and localities. Complex structures of coordination and control—modern states and corporations—slowly come into being. There is a vast migration to cities and industrial towns, sometimes from thousands of miles away, to find better-paying jobs in industry and government. Enormous investments are made in transportation facilities to move goods and people quickly and cheaply over long distances.

The process of economic and social change just sketched brings huge rewards; the productivity of human labor is wondrously increased; the necessities of life become abundant and the conveniences multiply. But these enticing changes are inseparably linked, both as cause and as effect, with other changes whose appeal is more questionable.

The more frequent and the more intimate the contacts among individuals belonging to different tribes or nations, the more these groups will come to resemble each other culturally or linguistically, other things being equal. Different languages, religions, customs, laws, and moralities—in short, different cultures—impede economic integration, with all its benefits. A certain similarity of culture is necessary before people can work together effectively. Economic progress provides both the incentives and the opportunities for the homogenization of diverse cultures.

Many social scientists have regarded complete assimilation and harmonious cooperation, at least among ethnic or cultural groups, as the inevitable result of prolonged contact. Robert Park provided a classic statement of this expectation when he stated that "race relations" (within which he included relations among national and ethnic groups) would have a "natural history," which he summed up in his famous "race relations cycle." This cycle was a series of stages through which groups in contact were expected to move, the last stage being complete assimilation. "The race relations cycle, which takes the form, to state it abstractly, of contacts, competition, accommodation, and eventual assimilation, is apparently progressive and irreversible. Customs regulations, immigration restrictions, and racial barriers may slacken the tempo of the movement; may perhaps halt it altogether for a time; but cannot change its direction; cannot at any rate reverse it" (Park, 1950, p. 150; compare Allport, 1954, p. 261).

Why can the direction not be changed? Park did not say very much about the inexorable forces driving the processes of contact, competition, accommodation, and assimilation, but he seems to have regarded mankind's long struggle to master nature and to extract a comfortable subsistence from it as more fundamental than any inherited ethnic loyalties or prejudices. Increasing productivity, he seems to have thought, is inseparable from an increasing scale of economic life and from the diffusion of the universal culture associated with popular scientific education. He presented his "natural history of race relations" as an aspect of the transition from traditional to modern society. The forces of modernization, he implied, must ultimately triumph over tradition.

The view represented by Park, though often advanced by social scientists in the past, is now more likely to be criticized and rejected, or at least advanced with expressions of puzzlement about the "paradoxical" persistence of ethnic conflict. Ethnic loyalties and differences are generally more durable and more highly valued than they were often thought to be just a few decades ago. The contemporary authorities stress the power of nationalism and the survival of ethnicity even in modern urban industrial societies. Karl Deutsch provides a particularly interesting formulation of the contemporary emphasis on the modernity, so to speak, of traditional loyalties and prejudices (see the Appendix). For the present, however, let me continue to outline some basic ideas without becoming entangled in technical or scholarly details.

Ethnic or cultural differences would not persist if some people did not attach some value to them. In some circumstances, to be sure, people or their leaders may favor assimilation—for example, when dealing with a troublesome minority. But many people today recognize the value of diversity. Few loudly proclaim their belief in "one world" that would have only one language, one code of laws, one status hierarchy, one literature, one world-wide entertainment industry, and one basic menu in every restaurant. Some may still look forward to the day when only one god will be worshipped in every temple, but others fear that mankind's spirituality suffers when indigenous or autochthonous gods die off or are killed. In some circles there is considerable uneasiness about the "new world order," with its suggestion of universal domination under one, cold, abstract, corporate, bureaucratic rationality. At the very least, the travel industry can testify that people like to learn new cultures. Homogenized humanity would provide less interesting vacations than does a world made up of different nations with their different customs, cuisines, and values.

Those who stand to be absorbed in any process of assimilation defend diversity with special fervor. Threatened by the loss of their identity, they may make serious efforts to preserve their own distinctiveness, sometimes by trying to obliterate that of others. These efforts can be effective, at least in the short run. Whatever the ultimate result of all the factors influencing the evolution of cultures, well-designed "customs regulations, immigration restrictions, and racial barriers," along with related policies of cultural stimulation and defense, seem able to halt and may even reverse the process of assimilation. New nations can be formed; old languages can be revived; and the threat of a simpler, plainer world can be staved off.

But staving off that world often brings ethnic or cultural groups into conflict. In the "global village," measures that preserve one culture may disrupt or undermine another. The policies one group adopts to defend its homeland and to protect its cultural distinctiveness, even if they do not directly threaten other groups, may offend their pride or harm their material interests. One group's defensive immigration restrictions may be another group's odious racism. One group's commitment to its distinctive customs and values may be another group's neurotic and reactionary adhesion to repulsive superstitions. One culture's meat may be another's poison.

There is no contradiction between saying (a) that contact tends to reduce the cultural differences among ethnic groups and (b) that contact also tends to stimulate efforts to preserve or increase these differences. The analysis so far has involved three distinct variables or dimensions of change; more than one relation can hold among them. Contact (variable 1) seems to reduce cultural differences (variable 2) or, in other words, to increase assimilation or homogenization. But this homogenizing effect seems to depend upon another, more subjective factor (variable 3) having to do with cultural identity and deliberate efforts to preserve familiar ways. Such deliberate efforts are one of the things people have in mind when they speak of conflict among ethnic or cultural groups. Much more will be said below about the policies and opinions associated with these deliberate efforts, but for the moment it suffices to state a broad hypothesis: such efforts (that is, ethnic conflict) will be more frequent and more intense when there is a high level of contact between relevant groups than when there is little contact.

Contact seems to be a cause of conflict precisely because it is also a cause of assimilation. In a shrinking world, humanity could converge on many different cultural patterns, and each group wants to preserve as much as possible of its own way of life. To be sure, there is not unlimited freedom of choice (technology is itself a way of life), nor is there any need for total uniformity. But generally speaking, when two ethnic or cultural groups find themselves with economic incentives to cooperate in a wider division of labor, as they do increasingly in the modern world, they also inescapably find themselves in a conflict of interest regarding the modalities of their cooperation. Who is going to imitate whom? Generally speaking, each group would prefer to be imitated and not to imitate.

The interrelations among the three major concepts here—contact, conflict, and assimilation, or the reduction of cultural differences—are particularly clear in the case of language groups. These groups, like other ethnic groups, frequently come into contact because there are benefits to be gained from a wider division of labor. To secure these benefits, some members of each group must be able to communicate easily with the members of the other groups, that is to say, some must share a common language. The incentives for contact are thus at the same time incentives for linguistic assimilation, or linguistic homogenization.

The incentives for linguistic change are such that it often does not matter, in the end, which group adopts which language so long as the net effect is greater similarity between the groups. It does not matter, in other words, whether the languages of the different groups "melt" to form some new alloy or whether most groups simply adopt the language of one of the groups, and if so, which one. The long-term benefits of change are contingent only upon increasing mutual intelligibility and do not depend upon how this is achieved.

The situation is of course radically different in the short run from the perspective of any particular group, because most adults have difficulty learning a new language. Thus it makes a great deal of difference to each individual in the situation we are envisaging whether he or she or someone else is required to learn a new language. While the process of homogenization is taking place, therefore, the net advantage to any group of greater mutual intelligibility will partly depend upon whether they are making the necessary adaptations or whether some other group (or groups) are bearing these costs. Because of the costs of change, any linguistic group in contact with a group speaking a different language will benefit if it can somehow induce members of the other group to adopt its language while at the same time preventing its own members from learning the alien language. Each group has an interest not just in encouraging members of the other linguistic group to become bilingual but also in stiffening the resistance of their own members to assimilation. Each defection adds to the pressure on the remaining "loyalists" to defect. Conversely, the stiffer the resistance, the more likely the group will succeed in making the other group bear the costs of assimilation (compare Breton, 1978; Laitin, 1993; Laponce, 1987; Lieberson, 1970, 1981).

To extend this reasoning beyond the issue of language, one need only assume cultural differences among relevant groups comparable to differences in language. Groups in contact can have conflicting interests because of "culture" if their cultures (customs, values, beliefs) are different and if there are reasons (from the standpoint of each group) for not adopting the customs, values, and beliefs of the other group or groups.

Increased contact can of course reduce cultural differences only if there are such differences to begin with. In fact, one may suppose, the greater these cultural differences, the greater the tendency of contact to stimulate conflict. Admittedly, it is difficult to measure cultural differences, but the functional dependence of ethnic consciousness and conflict upon such differences is a familiar idea. It can be illustrated by the studies of social distance going back to Bogardus (1929) that show that Americans, generally speaking, are more inclined to maintain their distance from such groups as Turks and Hindus than from Canadians. Gordon Allport stated the basic idea in connection with his discussion of the "sociocultural law" that prejudice increases with the size and density of a minority group: "Like all of the other sociocultural laws we are here considering, the principles of relative size and gradient of density cannot stand alone. Let us suppose that a rapid influx of Nova Scotians occurred into a New England city. The resulting prejudice would certainly be less than if an equal number of Negroes should arrive. Some ethnic groups seem more menacing than others—either because they have more points of difference or a higher visibility. Growing density, therefore, is not in itself a sufficient principle to explain prejudice" (Allport, 1954, p. 229).

Michael Hechter has stated the same basic idea in his well-known analysis of "internal colonialism": "The greater the intergroup differences of culture, particularly in so far as identifiability is concerned, the greater the probability that the culturally distinct peripheral collectivity will be status solidary. Identifiable cultural differences include: language (accent), distinctive religious practices, and life-style" (Hechter, 1975, p. 43). And Ted Robert Gurr includes "cultural differences"—"a checklist of six cultural traits that differentiate the group from others; ethnicity or nationality, language, religion, social customs, historical origins, and urban vs. rural residence"—among the independent variables in his very complicated model of the causes of communal mobilization (Gurr, 1993, p. 171). The relevant hypothesis—"the greater the cultural and social differences between a communal group and others with which it interacts, the greater will be the strength of group identity" (p. 174)—seems to have been supported by his analysis of data from 227 communal groups.

Intergroup conflict, in short, may be a function not just of the level of contact between two ethnic or cultural groups but also of their cultural differences.[3] No such conflict will develop if there are either no contacts between the groups or no differences between their cultures. There will be more conflict, at any given level of contact, where the cultural differences are greater. A level of mutual interaction that ethnic English Canadians and Americans could easily tolerate might put considerable strain on Japanese and Jamaicans.

To extend this reasoning beyond two groups to a world of many groups, one would have to reckon with the fluidity of ethnic boundaries and the possibility of ethnic fissions and fusions (Barth, 1969). Groups coalesce and divide in their struggles with other groups. The enemies of one's enemies tend to be one's friends, and necessity is the mother of invention. Cultural affinities, or at least pleasing complementarities, are sometimes discovered where previously only differences had been seen. In a world of radios and jet aircraft, not to mention rockets and satellite communications, the resulting alliances can stretch over long distances. (Even Cuba has had a foreign legion.) Coalitions form that reflect, among other considerations, real cultural similarities and differences, but particular cultural traits are emphasized or neglected as a result of what Horowitz (1985) has called accidents of context and contact. "The differentiating characteristics that become prominent [in the process of coalition building] will be defined in terms of what traits an emerging group has in common as against other groups with whom it finds itself in a single environment. It is, in the end, ascriptive affinity and disparity, and not some particular inventory of cultural attributes, that found the group" (p. 69).

The level of contact has been treated so far as simply an independent or exogenous variable—one determined only by such external factors as technology and economic development. These are certainly relevant factors, and they may determine most of the variation in average levels of contact over long periods of time. But in the short run, technology and the economy can be considered fixed factors, and variations in contact may be more strongly affected by the conflicts among groups and the policies they adopt to preserve their cultural distinctiveness. It seems reasonable to assume that conflict among groups impedes contact among their members. The greater the conflict between two groups, generally speaking, the less friendly or cooperative their members are likely to be toward each other. This relationship will be examined in more detail below.

The correlations (or behavioral relations) just outlined can be seen as a model of ethnic conflict that provides an alternative to traditional contact theory. The model shifts attention from the individual to the group level (as some prominent social psychologists have insisted is necessary), and it draws attention to ethnicity (or cultural differences) as a cause of ethnic conflict. The remaining sections of this chapter explain the model more fully and discuss the perspective it provides on the contact hypothesis.

The Form of Linguistic Conflict

When thinking of ethnic conflict, one does tend to fix one's attention on gore and destruction. The quieter, more benign varieties of ethnic conflict can quickly turn malignant, becoming a matter of killing or being killed (Posen, 1993). The outstanding examples of ethnic conflict in recent times have involved mass murder, genocide, or civil war. Even in countries with a history of relatively peaceful interethnic relations, such as Canada and the United States, there is a tendency to equate ethnic conflict with bigotry and xenophobia. Prejudice brings to mind foolish, mean-spirited opinions, rigidly held. Similarly, ethnocentrism is generally understood to be a dangerous intellectual failing closely related to a fundamental defect in character (Adorno et al., 1950). But in order to understand ethnic conflict, it may help to put many of these associations aside so that we can see more clearly something more familiar and low-key that is normally much less violent, bloody, passionate, dramatic, and irrational than the term *ethnic conflict* may at first suggest. In order to overcome some of the distracting associations built into our language, it may help to focus first on linguistic conflict and only later examine the general problem of ethnic or cultural conflict, for as Horowitz (1985, p. 220) has pointed out, "language is the quintessential entitlement issue."

Isolation and subordination, not gore and destruction, seem to be the main themes in linguistic conflict. Although every such conflict presumably develops in its own way, the conflict between proponents of French and English in Canada may illustrate the basic pattern.[4] The contending parties seem to be trying to modify the incentives and opportunities for linguistic assimilation so as to strike the most favorable possible balance between the economic benefits of contact and the costs of assimilation. For each group, the aim is not to destroy or even to coerce the opposing group, but rather to induce it to learn a new language while minimizing the chances that its own members will do the same. The basic reaction to contact, and to the conflict of interest inherent in contact, is compounded of (a) avoidance of unnecessary association and (b) competition for dominant status in the settings in which association occurs.

A common pattern in situations of contact between language groups is to combine association on the job with isolation in other activities. Isolation is a natural and virtually unconscious result of linguistic differences. Why try to socialize with people you have trouble understanding? By itself, isolation limits both the incentives and the opportunities for learning the language of the out-group. Living in a linguistic enclave minimizes awkward encounters, facilitates the provision of local services (education, church, entertainment, shopping) in the mother tongue, and insulates youngsters from contact with children from the linguistic out-group. The total pattern—isolation in most activities combined with association on the job—can be called residential segregation or simply segregation.

The long-term effects of association on the job will depend greatly on the relative statuses of the groups in contact. Social status is in part a matter of who imitates whom; it has to do with leadership and followership. Superiors lead: they behave as they think right or advantageous, without being constrained by any necessity to please subordinates, at least in the short run. Subordinates follow: for one reason or another they find important rewards contingent upon pleasing their superiors. They tend to be docile, deferential, accommodating, and ingratiating. They try hard to learn the language of their superiors and to imitate their manners.

Superior strength, resulting from superiority of numbers, organization, or fighting ability, is probably the oldest and perhaps the fundamental way for one group to establish dominance over another and to win its respect. A group's willingness and ability to use brute force against its rivals is perhaps the essential condition for its maintaining a dominant position. The possession of power in this sense makes it possible to punish behavior that is not properly respectful of the superior group's practices (grammar, accent, vocabulary) and that implicitly claims for the inferior group the privileges and status of the superior.

Clearly, however, violent conflict is the exception rather than the rule in the continuous competition between linguistic groups in contact. More important from day to day are the quieter forms of jockeying for wealth and status and for the knowledge that serves these ends.

If one group is or becomes much wealthier than another, it may, deliberately or unconsciously, use bribery to induce assimilation: it is likely to make material rewards for the poorer group contingent upon learning its language. Reliance upon wealth as a basis for influence implies, of course, a certain fundamental equality between the groups in contact, because a group bribed to be deferential is a group whose freedom not to be deferential is implicitly recognized. Moreover, bribery represents a real transfer of resources from the bribers to the bribed, and thus it tends to undermine the dominance of the former and to increase the power of the latter, perhaps eventually leading to their practical as well as purely formal equality. Nonetheless, superior wealth is obviously an extremely important source of influence over linguistic practices. It provides a steady, persistent, complex network of subtle incentives for change; it works quietly beneath the surface, seducing rather than compelling.

Modern urban industrial societies are characterized by the presence of enormous corporate and governmental bureaucracies. The wealth and power of individuals is roughly correlated with their rank in such bureaucracies, and the status of groups is determined by their members' access to positions of bureaucratic authority and by the use they can make of the budgets, security forces, and specialized information controlled bureaucratically.

The increasing scale of organization accentuates the importance of discrimination in linguistic conflict. Leading members of the dominant group pay attention to the origins and linguistic skills of their subordinates; they favor the training and advancement of their linguistic compatriots and of assimilated members of other groups; they block the advancement of those who cannot speak their language or who do not want to do so. The result is the establishment or preservation of a monopoly on positions of authority by members of one linguistic group and assimilated members of other groups.

The response of a subordinate group wishing to preserve its language must be essentially a response to discrimination. What it can do to remove restrictions upon the advancement of its members—and eventually to make itself a dominant group able to discriminate against its former masters—will depend upon circumstances, particularly the relative numbers and territorial concentration of the different groups.

If the subordinate group is a majority of the population distributed over some fairly extensive territory, then it is likely to look for remedies that involve controlling the political institutions governing the territory. It may demand that the government of the territory be democratized, with the leaders chosen by popular vote, so that the leaders of the majority group can displace the dominant linguistic minority. Or it may demand the division of an existing state, even one that is democratic, so that its members will no longer be a minority of the total population but rather a majority within their own state. Nationalism of various sorts (liberal, democratic, separatist, federalist) can be an expression of linguistic conflict. A linguistic group that is a majority of a population in control of a democratic state but subordinate in other institutions (economic or religious) may demand that the functions of the state be expanded: socialism, too, can be an expression of linguistic conflict.

If the subordinate group is a minority not sufficiently numerous or geographically concentrated to entertain any realistic hope of independent political existence, then both popular rule and the principle of nationalities may aggravate the group's problems. In these circumstances, the advancement of the subordinate group depends upon its persuading the dominant group to change its discriminatory practices. Thus the subordinate group may sometimes celebrate linguistic diversity, pointing to its advantages in education (students learn from the great books of other lands) and in foreign trade (they can serve foreign tourists in their own language). The minority group may attack discrimination itself, arguing that people are individuals and should be treated as such (that is, grouped by education level or ability, not language) when selecting leaders for economic and political institutions. It may demand that the dominant group continue to discriminate, but *equitably*, in order to make the representation of different groups in elite positions proportional to their representation in some total population. It may demand that linguistic rights be enshrined in a written constitution and that judges be given the power to enforce these rights, so that the minority group will be protected from the whims of democratic politicians more sensitive to majority sentiment than judges are. Multiculturalism, affirmative action, and advocacy of human rights can all be expressions of linguistic conflict. A group's choice of tactics will again presumably depend upon circumstances. It will tend to favor the tactics that promise to produce the greatest gains in status in the foreseeable future.

Isolation and subordination (or domination) have to do with the regulation of contact between groups—the settings in which contact may take place and the rules according to which it must be conducted. The two terms and their cognates describe the usual *objective* consequences of contact and conflict between linguistic groups, that is, what people actually do to advance their interests in the situation of conflict. In addition there are *subjective* consequences that demand attention—feelings that are stirred up, opinions that circulate, and attitudes that develop as a result of linguistic conflict.

In principle it should be possible to distinguish two sorts of opinions—causal and normative—among the participants in a linguistic conflict. Causal refers here to generalizations about the existence of different languages, the consequences of contact between them, and the value of segregation and discrimination in promoting or retarding assimilation. These generalizations may be implicit in what people say, or they may be explicitly formulated as hypotheses about behavior, but in no situation of linguistic conflict are the participants likely to be totally unaware of what is going on. Their opinions about cause and effect are likely to be mixed up, however, with more normative opinions about the rights and duties of different linguistic groups in the situation. For example, there may be opinions about the rights and duties of majorities and minorities—or about the honor due the language of true culture or world commerce, or that of science or diplomacy. Ancestral rights may be pitted against the rights of conquerors. Particular languages may be said to have important values inherent in them—clarity, perhaps, or humor. Diversity itself may be lauded as the glory of the universe. These normative generalizations may be based upon broader principles such as those of democracy or natural law. They may be derived rigorously from some universal consensus in an imaginary "original position" (Rawls, 1971, 1993). No situation of linguistic conflict can be fully described without analyzing the opinions of the people involved. The difficulty is that the two sorts of opinions just distinguished, causal and normative, are likely to be mixed up in complicated ways that hang together rhetorically and that must be studied in detail in order to be understood.

In examining the subjective side of linguistic conflict close up, scientists may well be struck by the amount of ill will and partisan bickering among those involved. Biased generalizations, aggressive fantasies, humiliating epithets, and offensive jokes may give clear evidence of this ill will. Foolish statements about the natural superiority or inferiority of competing languages—refusal to treat them as arbitrary conventions for communication—may show the importance of crude cognitive processes. Like lawyers citing precedents and commenting on the motives of their clients, most people in situations of linguistic conflict may seem to champion any general principle that tends to support the immediate interests of their side. It may even appear to outside observers that the conclusions the participants want to reach are predetermined by the situations in which they find themselves, so that the reasons they give for their actions are best treated as rationalizations. Thus it may be natural in these situations to speak of hostile feelings and attitudes. It may seem absurd to dignify crude impulses by calling them linguistic philosophies or even ideologies. For good reasons, then, scientists are likely to have little patience with the subjective side of linguistic conflict.

Psychology provides a rich storehouse of methods for investigating hostile feelings and attitudes, as well as many theories about their causes. Feelings are closely related to emotional arousal, and some direct measures of such arousal are available (for example, ways of objectively measuring palmar sweat or tone of voice). Verbal attitudes have been one of the central topics in social psychology since it emerged as a distinct discipline in the 1920s, and there is now an extensive literature on attitude measurement with many carefully developed scales of particular attitudes for use in research.

Measures of social distance and stereotyping have been used in studies of linguistic conflict. The earliest work on social distance (Bogardus, 1929) asked subjects about their willingness to accept members of various groups, some of them distinguished by language, in social relations of various degrees of intimacy (as citizens, neighbors, friends, members of the family). Standard tests of stereotyping measure the willingness of subjects to make broad generalizations, flattering or unflattering, about the members of different groups, including their own. Discussions of such tests sometimes emphasize the complexity of the judgments involved and the need for caution when interpreting their results (Brown, 1986; Rothbart and John, 1993). Nonetheless, measures of both social distance and stereotyping can be used in studies of the subjective side of linguistic conflict (for example, Lambert et al., 1960).

The best single term to describe the irrational subjective manifestations of linguistic conflict is undoubtedly *prejudice,* even though it has lingering overtones of positive as well as negative premature judgments. As defined by social psychologists, it provides a familiar label for both (a) the adverse judgments that are used to justify segregation and discrimination and (b) the hostile feelings evidenced by social distance and negative stereotyping of out-groups. Prejudice is generally measured by having subjects agree or disagree with simple evaluative statements about the relevant groups, for example, "Though there are some exceptions, in general Catholics are fascists at heart."

Language and Ethnicity

Are the manifestations of conflict more or less the same when ethnic groups other than language groups are in contact? Do the same relations hold among contact, assimilation (the reduction of cultural differences), and overt conflict in its various dimensions (avoidance, subordination, antilocution) when the differences between groups are not linguistic but rather racial, religious, ideological, or broadly "ethnic" or "cultural"? In short, does linguistic conflict provide a good model for understanding ethnic conflict generally? This is not a question that can be quickly answered and then put aside.

Linguistic conflict often seems to be strikingly different from other kinds of ethnic conflict because it generates relatively little emotion and few hostile feelings directed against outsiders. As a result, it may be far easier to manage. Belgium provides a convenient example: it exhibits severe linguistic conflict, but the tourists are not fleeing Belgium as they have fled Bosnia and Rwanda. Switzerland illustrates the successful management of linguistic conflict. Clearly such conflict lacks the strange, almost spooky quality of "real" ethnic conflict. It is not so primordial or atavistic, and it does not put so much strain on the bonds that sustain civility. It is generally not so episodic and intense. It is more a matter of pragmatic daily accommodation and less a matter of insane explosions of looting and killing. It has less to do with deep, mysterious feelings of kinship and identity.

The real contrast may be clarified by noting some of the prejudices associated with black-white conflict in the United States and what is often said about their psychological sources. As Elisabeth Young-Bruehl has recently explained, there is a remarkable consensus among informed observers that the way in which contact between blacks and whites was originally structured by slavery—great intimacy combined with great inequality—made blacks the objects of sexual fantasy for generations of white children and adults. Out of this situation evolved a network of fantastic fears and beliefs "subtending all subsequent developments and rising into unmistakable view in sexualized violence against Negroes" (Young-Bruehl, 1996, p. 488).

Two further differences may be added, provisionally, to the ones just noted in order to make them more understandable. First, language generally makes different demands on belief or commitment than does culture (apart from language). Many people are undoubtedly attached to their native tongues and disposed to defend them when threatened, but the attachment is not in principle exclusive. One can be bilingual or multilingual without being at war with oneself. It may be difficult to learn a second or a third language, but it involves no contradiction to one's first language, nor does it cause one to lose one's grip on its grammar. (Indeed, a standard way of learning English grammar used to be the study of Latin.) Commitment to the defense of a particular language may impede the learning of another, but knowledge of one language does not interfere very much with knowledge of another, and sensible people do not argue that one language is inherently superior to another. Language is seen as something conventional, like driving on the right or the left.

It is more difficult to be bicultural or multicultural. (It is like driving down the middle of the road.) Most people—perhaps all people—believe that some ways of life are naturally right and just, whereas others are barbaric and inhuman. Commitment to one culture or set of values generally precludes commitment to another. A good Protestant learning a second or a third religion (Catholicism or Judaism, for example) may suffer a kind of vertigo as the whole framework of life seems to turn and dissolve. Cultures, broadly understood, raises questions of belief and valuation that languages do not. When in Rome, most well-educated people are prepared (if they can) to speak as the Romans speak. Not so many are prepared to adopt Roman intellectual fashions or to participate in Roman forms of worship (although learning to cross oneself and sprinkle a little holy water may be easier in a sense than learning to speak Italian). No sincere or authentic person can simply "do as the Romans do" when it comes to basic beliefs and fundamental values. No sincere or authentic American a generation ago could simply "do as the Russians do" just because he happened to be posted to Moscow.

Second, language and culture generally make different demands on politics. In the absence of contacts with outsiders, a group speaking a particular language will generally continue to speak more or less the same language from one generation to the next, without any conscious, organized effort (by parents, teachers, grammarians, "language police") to make them do so. But other cultural traits, such as laws of property or forms of worship, may not be self-maintaining in this sense: even in the absence of contacts with outsiders, they may endure only if their preservation is supported by the efforts of lawmakers, judges, police, jailers, and executioners. Language may be like a large pile of leaves, culture more like a house of cards: both are affected by winds of change, but differently. Ethnic conflict, broadly understood, is likely to involve not just the "negative" use of state power to insulate a national or an ethnic group against disruptive contacts with outsiders but also its "positive" use: to uphold distinctive and controversial ways of life.

Some of the puzzling emotions associated with ethnic conflict are clearer when these differences are taken into account. Situations of contact between groups distinguished by incompatible ways of life, and not just by language, are likely to create many "marginal men" caught between these ways of life. The greater the contact between the groups, the greater the number of people who will have personal relations straddling an increasingly tense border. Depending upon the cultural traits that separate the groups, their divided loyalties, actual or potential, may stir deep emotions connected with problematic sexual and aggressive impulses. Many individuals may not know how to reconcile their various personal relations and commitments or where their ultimate loyalties lie. Their reactions in particular situations of contact may reflect their internal conflicts—strongly supporting one side on some occasions, the other side on others.

Having noted these differences and potential difficulties and objections, let us return to our main theme: the dependence of ethnic conflict on contact among ethnic or cultural groups. An increase of contact gives rise to various manifestations of an increasing conflict of interest as each group tries to vindicate and defend its own customs and values. These manifestations constitute a syndrome of "ethnocentric" attitudes and behavior like the one described by William Graham Sumner:

> The relation of comradeship and peace in the we-group and that of hostility and war toward other-groups are correlative to each other. The exigencies of war with outsiders are what make peace inside, lest internal discord should weaken the we-group for war. These exigencies also make government and law in the in-group, in order to prevent quarrels and enforce discipline. Thus war and peace have reacted on each other, one within the group, the other in the intergroup relation. The closer the neighbors, and the stronger they are, the intenser is the warfare, and then the intenser is the internal organization and discipline of each.
> Sentiments are produced to correspond. Loyalty to the group, sacrifice for

it, hatred and contempt for outsiders, brotherhood within, warlikeness without—all grow together, common products of the same situation. (Sumner, 1906, pp. 12–13)

The cause of this syndrome is in a sense the tendency of human beings to "scale and rate" outsiders by domestic standards—ethnocentrism in the narrow, technical sense. "Each group nourishes its own pride and vanity, boasts itself superior, exalts its own divinities, and looks with contempt on outsiders" (p. 13). The cause, from another angle, is the human craving for honor or status in the eyes of others—Rousseau's amour propre or the moralist's pride or vanity. Nearly all human beings want to think well of themselves, and their feelings of self-worth are tied to the treatment their groups receive from others. This "vain," or "symbolic," side of ethnic conflict often involves, as Sumner points out, "epithets of contempt and abomination" (see Allen, 1983, for many striking examples). But it may also involve much more "realistic" clashes (for example, regarding official languages) that are made more difficult to resolve by their entanglement with underlying issues of relative status.[5] "For our present purpose the most important fact is that ethnocentrism leads a people to exaggerate and intensify everything in their own folkways which is peculiar and which differentiates them from others. It therefore strengthens the folkways" (Sumner, 1906, p. 13).

Much is questionable about this simple description of ethnocentrism (see Brewer, 1979, 1981; Brewer and Campbell, 1976; LeVine and Campbell, 1972), but it has the great virtue of making all the manifestations of ethnic conflict (avoidance, subordination, antilocution) the expressions of a common underlying conflict of interest—"common products of the same situation."

The conflict found in situations of contact has an effect, in turn, on its own causes: tending to limit and structure the contacts among groups in such a way as to either increase or decrease the assimilation that would otherwise take place. The various tactics that groups can use to achieve this goal have already been discussed. Let me review the possible outcomes.

The offensive and defensive maneuvering of competing groups in contact may result in a particular group's being able to adopt policies that give its way of life a relative stability (by comparison with the changes being induced among other groups) while maintaining a profitable interdependence with other groups. Or the group may, in the interest of cultural stability, cut itself off from contact with the outside group or groups and willingly forgo the advantages that would result from specialization and exchange, as the Japanese once did. Or it may fail in its conflict with a foreign group or groups; it may be small and weak, unable to offer any effective inducements to others to adopt its customs and values and unable even to prevent its own members from being assimilated by the foreigners. If so, then it must gradually disappear. Its members will be subordinates who will imitate their superiors. Its adult members will be employed, supervised, policed, and governed by foreigners; they will tend to learn the language, adopt the opinions, and imitate the manners of their rulers. Its younger members will be taught by teachers who represent the foreign way of life, and they will adopt this way as their own. Before long the distinctiveness of the subordinate group will melt away; it will become part of the dominant group, at least from the standpoint of language and culture.

A Simple Model

For a world of only two ethnic or linguistic groups, the generalizations about contact and conflict discussed so far can be reduced to a few simple rules or formulas. Combine these generalizations to make a small mathematical model and the result may help to clarify what has been said.

But first, some key terms must be defined. Here as earlier *contact* refers to the absolute level of social relations between any two groups. Let the groups in question be **A** and **B,** as before. Consider the amount of contact between their members across the boundary that separates them. This quantity or level of contact (measured perhaps in "social exchanges") may be thought of as a number greater than or equal to zero, and it is the same for both groups, even if they are quite different in size. A second key term is *ethnocentrism,* which I shall use to stand for all the different manifestations or expressions of ethnic conflict (segregation, discrimination, prejudice, and so on) outlined above. The term is familiar, having a deep root in the relevant literature. It draws attention to nationality or ethnicity (*ethnos*) while striking a balance of connotations between dislike of out-groups and identification with in-groups. It avoids the very strong derogatory connotations of *xenophobia*—a tempting alternative, to avoid any imputation of bias—while carrying an unmistakable hint of irrationality or psychopathology.[6] Like *conflict,* unfortunately, the term is ambiguous. It can sometimes refer to an underlying cause (or causes) of behavior and sometimes to an observable pattern of behavior. As an observable pattern it could be operationalized by counting the number of relevant positive and negative events, weighted by their gravity or intensity, over some period of time or by taking a sample of opinions as in an opinion poll or attitude test. Failure to distinguish overt from latent ethnocentrism is sometimes a source of confusion, but it should not be so here because the meaning of the term has just been clearly stipulated and because its two relevant senses will be clearly separated in the following analysis.

The leading idea in the preceding discussion of ethnic conflict was simply that contact produces ethnocentrism, so that there is a positive correlation between the two variables at the aggregate, or societal, level of analysis. The greater the contact (the number of exchanges) between two groups, the higher the levels of their reciprocal ethnocentrisms (measured, let us say, in "eths"). This causal relation may of course be quite different in the two groups, for groups may differ in their tolerance of contact with outsiders or, conversely, their tendency to react ethnocentrically against it. Each group's level of ethnocentrism may be influenced by a host of situational and background factors such as its size, wealth, history, culture, child-rearing practices, political institutions, and religious beliefs, but in all groups, we shall assume, there is a relation between contact and ethnocentrism that everywhere has the same basic form. To state this relation clearly, we must first define the following variables:

E_A = the average level of ethnocentrism among group **A**
E_B = the average level of ethnocentrism among group **B**
C = the amount of contact between the **A**s and the **B**s

The suggested causal relations between the first two of these variables and the third can be represented most simply by the following two equations (and figure 5.1):

(1.1) $E_A = a_1 C$
(1.2) $E_B = b_1 C$

The constants in these equations, a_1 and b_1, are assumed to be positive. They may be thought of as measures of the latent tendency of each group to respond ethnocentrically to the other. They represent all the situational and background factors noted above—differences in size, wealth, history, and so on In short, one group may be more ethnocentric than the other— may have a higher "coefficient of ethnocentrism"—for a variety of reasons that have nothing to do with the level of contact between them, which must be the same for both.

Figure 5.1 also shows that the stated functional relations between contact (C) and ethnocentrism (E) can be examined from more than one angle. Contact and ethnocentrism can exchange their mathematical roles as independent and dependent variables. If each group's ethnocentrism can be described as a simple function of its contact with the other group, then

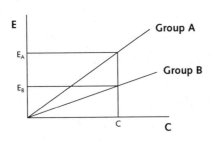

Figure 5.1

contact in turn can be described as a simple function of either level of ethnocentrism:

$$C = \frac{E_A}{a_1} = \frac{E_B}{b_1}$$

In other words, having observed one or both levels of ethnocentrism and knowing the relevant coefficients of ethnocentrism, one could calculate the level of contact between the groups.

These new equations also convey a puzzling suggestion, however, about the causal impact of ethnocentrism on contact. They seem to imply that more ethnocentrism, as defined above, produces more contact. The earlier discussion of ethnic conflict appealed to a quite different and more familiar assumption. The greater the ethnocentrism of a group, it was suggested, the greater should be the reluctance of its members to develop contacts with the members of another group and the greater should be their tendency to break off existing social relations. In short, the earlier discussion did not treat the impact of ethnocentrism on contact as just the mirror image of the impact of contact on ethnocentrism. Rather, it assumed that there was a second causal or productive relation between these variables, the reverse of the mathematical dependence just shown. In figure 5.2, the broken line represents the idea that more ethnocentrism is associated with less contact because all the patterns of behavior covered by the term *ethnocentrism* (segregation, discrimination, prejudice) tend to reduce the level of contact between any two groups. Somehow, other things being equal, more ethnocentrism must mean *less* contact. As Kaufmann (1996, p. 149) has said, "Ethnic war causes ethnic unmixing."

Of course, a simple two-dimensional diagram such as this one cannot properly represent three relations among three distinct variables, and a

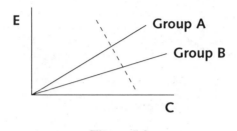

Figure 5.2

fourth variable—time—is becoming relevant. All the interconnections among the three main variables describing our simple world of two groups can be better shown by means of equations. But before presenting some relevant equations, it may be helpful to state the postulates they express more formally:

(1) The average level of ethnocentrism in any group at any time depends upon its situation, traditions, and institutions and upon its level of contact with outsiders at that time: when there is no contact with outsiders, there is no ethnocentrism; when there is more contact, there is more ethnocentrism.

(2) The amount of contact between any two groups depends upon their proximity and the incentives for contact between them (due to factors such as technology or the state of development of the forces of production and hence the possibilities that exist for profitable specialization and trade) and upon the levels of ethnocentrism in the two groups. Higher levels of ethnocentrism, other things remaining the same, tend to reduce or reverse the growth of contact between the groups.

These postulates describe two fundamentally different causal or productive relations between contact and ethnocentrism, and they recognize that their coexistence—how they can be true simultaneously—involves time. At any given time, contact produces ethnocentrism according to the basic rules stated above, but ethnocentrism influences contact only as a force tending to reduce future levels of contact. Higher levels of ethnocentrism reduce the rate of growth of contact or increase its rate of decline. These postulated relations among the three variables discussed so far can be represented by the following three equations:

(1.1) $$E_A = a_1 C_t$$
(1.2) $$E_B = b_1 C_t$$

(2) $$C_{t+1} = C_t \left(\frac{1+g}{1+a_2 E_A + b_2 E_B} \right)$$

The three variables and the constants a_1 and b_1 have the same meanings they had earlier. Equation (2) is one of several possible ways of describing a negative productive relationship over time between ethnocentrism and contact. It uses a constant, g, to represent all the factors that determine the growth or decline of contact other than the repulsive mutual ethnocentrisms of the two groups—factors such as technology or the forces of production. This constant determines a rate of change for contact between the groups if there are no efforts to reduce contact from ethnocentric motives. If g is positive, then according to equation (2), contact will grow indefinitely at an increasing rate, like money invested with compound interest. Higher levels of contact, however, produce higher levels of ethnocentrism—equations (1.1) and (1.2)—which offset and may even override the incentives for contact represented by g. The constants a_2 and b_2 determine how rapidly contact between the groups changes in response to changes in their levels of ethnocentrism. Generally speaking, if either one of the two groups is very ethnocentric, then there will tend to be very little contact between them.

These three equations are the simplest mathematical model that can capture some of the gist of the preceding discussion. The system described by these equations is in no way isolated from outside influences. Moreover, the "constants" of the model represent a variety of factors that in reality are always changing. If these factors are changing relatively slowly, however, then it is legitimate to treat them as a fixed framework for the analysis of the more rapidly changing "variables" of the model. The variables are represented here as having an independent tendency (apart from external influences such as economic changes or political events) to grow or decline depending upon the precise values of the model's parameters. Thus, if the incentives for contact were overwhelmingly strong, or if the ethnocentric reactions against it were exceedingly weak, then both contact and ethnocentrism would tend to grow indefinitely at an increasing rate. If these incentives were relatively weak, however, or if they should decline relative to the strength of the processes represented by a_1, a_2, b_1, and b_2, then both contact and ethnocentrism would grow more slowly or decline, perhaps gradually approaching some very low values. Only when these two tendencies were exactly in balance, $g = a_2E_A + b_2E_B$, would contact and ethnocentrism hold some equilibrium values determined by the constants of the model.[7]

The main limitation of this model as a summary of the earlier discussion has to do with its neglect of the second key variable in the discussion, namely, cultural differences. The model says nothing about the effects of cultural differences on the responsiveness of ethnocentrism to changes in contact, nor does it say anything about assimilation or the effects of contact over time on cultural differences. To make these relations part of the model, one must first define a new variable:

D = the magnitude of the cultural differences between groups **A** and **B**

There is no problem naming the units of this new variable ("diffs" will do), but, as noted earlier, it is harder to imagine these units being counted or the new variable being "measured." Still, one can perhaps entertain the possibility of some kind of weighted average of all the cultural similarities and differences between any two groups, based on ratings by anthropologists or other experts (compare Gurr, 1993a; Morrison and Stevenson, 1972a; Nincic and Russett, 1979; Tims and Miller, 1986). At any rate, the *idea* of such a variable can be incorporated in our reasoning by modifying the first postulate above and by adding a third postulate.

(1') Ethnocentrism depends upon, and increases with, the level of contact and the magnitude of cultural differences, and these two causes of ethnocentrism are multiplicative in their effect. There will be no ethnocentrism in any group if either (a) it has no contacts with outsiders or (b) there are no cultural differences between the group and the outsiders in question.

(3) The cultural differences between any two groups will be influenced by the contact between them and the mutual repulsions generated by this contact. An increase in contact, other things remaining the same, will tend to increase cultural assimilation or, equivalently, reduce the growth of cultural differences due to other factors. Conversely, an increase in ethnocentrism will reduce the rate of assimilation or increase the rate at which cultural differences develop— again assuming that all other things remain unchanged. The adjustment of cultural differences to changes in the levels of contact and ethnocentrism takes a relatively long time to work itself out.

Putting all this together, we now have the following somewhat more complicated model, which exhibits all the key ideas of the earlier discussion:

(1.3) $$E_A = a_1 C_t D_t$$
(1.4) $$E_B = b_1 C_t D_t$$
(2) $$C_{t+1} = C_t \left(\frac{1+g}{1+a_2 E_A + b_2 E_B} \right)$$
(3) $$D_{t+1} = D_t \left(\frac{1+a_3 E_A + b_3 E_B}{1+h C_t} \right)$$

These equations can be regarded as a system that constrains the possible values of its variables, determining a pattern of growth or decay over time. The new constants a_1 and b_1 are similar to the earlier a_1 and b_1; they now represent the sensitivities of the two ethnocentrisms to changes in contact *and* cultural differences.[8] Equation (3), like equation (2), is one of several possible ways of representing a relation that involves changes over time. A critic might well accept the underlying idea (that ethnocentrism and contact tend to have opposite effects on cultural differences) but complain that no good reason has been offered for supposing that the relevant relation has exactly the form shown in equation (3). For present purposes, nothing depends on this equation's being the best one possible. The one shown has at least one merit: it draws attention in a reasonably clear way to the negative dependence of cultural differences on contact (the "homogenizing" effect of contact is represented by positive values of the constant h) while holding open the possibility of an equilibrium of the system at positive values of both C and D. Models or analyses that disregard the dependence of D on E, and that neglect or misstate the dependence of E on C, are likely to be seriously misleading.[9] A more complicated statement, which might express some more plausible assumptions about rates or limits of growth and decline, might have no real superiority, given the lack of any relevant units of measurement for the basic variables C, D, and E.

Indeed, some readers may well wonder whether model-building exercises of this kind, using variables like these, have any value at all. What purpose is served by such extreme and complicated simplifications? Some rather similar models proposed many years ago (Wright, 1942, pp. 1484–92; Simon, 1957, pp. 99–114) seem to have been completely forgotten, and for the good reason, it seems, that little or nothing could be done with them. Variables such as ethnocentrism, contact, and cultural differences, although they may be "measurable" in a loose sense, have no standard units such as feet, pounds, and dollars. It follows that the parameters of models such as these, employing such variables, can have no clear meaning. It makes sense to say that two dollars now buys five pounds of potatoes, whereas six months ago, two dollars bought ten pounds: the numbers have to do with prices, and there may have been inflation, or the real price of potatoes may have gone up. It would not make sense to say that two "exchanges" now yield ten "eths," but in the future, "diffs" having gone down by six, let us say, two "exchanges" will yield only five "eths," for the numbers would no longer refer to anything counted or measured. Their ratios would no longer have any real meaning. Consequently, the equations of the model have not been written with an eye to further mathematical manipulation or even (for reasons that will be explained more fully later) with an eye to statistical fitting.[10] Any further manipulation of the model would likely be pointless, given the inherent vagueness of its three main variables. What exactly would such manipulation be about?

My purpose in writing these equations has only been to clarify the earlier discussion by reducing it to its bare bones. The equations have been chosen to express as straightforwardly as possible a few key ideas, so as to bring out more clearly the logic of the reasoning, in particular the assumptions being made about the interdependence of three distinct causal processes and the relative quickness or slowness of these processes. Thus the model helps to clarify why there is no contradiction between saying, on one hand, that contact increases ethnic prejudice (positive correlation) while saying, on the other, that ethnic prejudice reduces contact (negative correlation), just as earlier there was only an apparent difficulty in finding a negative correlation at the individual level and a positive one at the aggregate level. Finally, the model clearly expresses the basic idea that cultural differences are maintained or increased by ethnocentrism and reduced by contact. It encourages and directs further reflection on the interpretation and validity of the contact hypothesis.

The Contact Hypothesis

Social scientists have always known that high levels of contact can coexist with intense ethnic conflict. But they have often thought that the general rule is just the opposite: increases in contact generally lead to reductions in prejudice. This is the contact hypothesis as commonly understood. The social scientists who have promoted the hypothesis, recognizing that high levels of contact are sometimes associated with high levels of prejudice, have tried to deal with these exceptions to the rule by distinguishing different types, circumstances, or situations of contact. Their goal has been to specify the conditions that determine when increased contact will have its expected positive effects (reductions in prejudice) and when it will tend to have negative effects. Different theorists have advanced different hypotheses, drawing attention to more and more potential conditioning variables, so that contact theory has now lost whatever clarity and simplicity it once had. In recent years, theorists have even edged toward treating the positive situations as the exceptions and the negative ones as the rule, but they still generally adopt a "situational" approach to the problem of contrary correlations. "The basic issue," according to a leading writer in the field, "concerns the types of situations in which contact leads to distrust and those in which it leads to trust" (Pettigrew, 1971, p. 275; compare Pettigrew, 1986, 1991).

A different approach is possible. Two levels of analysis can be distinguished as well as various situations of contact.

Contact has two aspects: the individual aspect and the collective, or social, aspect. When a member of one group begins to interact with a member of a second group, there is an increase in contact both for these two individuals and for the groups to which they belong. This is true regardless of whether the individuals in contact treat each other as individuals or as group members. Moreover, the effects of the increased contact may generally be different for the individuals concerned than they are for the groups.

It is easy to accept, as a very broad generalization, that contact among individuals, particularly voluntary contact, is associated with positive attitudes. What, after all, do we mean by contact when we are talking about individuals? Contact means personal interaction, and one of the great commonsense generalizations (or laws) of social science is that personal interaction generally goes with liking and friendship (compare Homans, 1950, 1961; Kelley, 1968). There are, of course, exceptions to this rule, as the divorce rates show. But the exceptions do not disprove the rule. The rule implies a lower level of prejudice among those in contact, compared to their compatriots who are not, when members of two distinct groups are in contact. If the background level of prejudice remains the same, this implies a reduction in prejudice following an increase in contact—on the average for those who have the contact.

It is not so clear, however, that the effects on groups of increases in contact are simply the sum of the effects on the individuals directly involved. A higher rate or average intensity of contact (and friendship, generally speaking) between individuals may lead to increased conflict and hostility between the groups to which they belong. As Romeo and Juliet knew, when some people become more positive in their attitudes toward each other, other people may become more negative.

The model of ethnic conflict developed in this chapter clarifies this possibility, which tends to be overlooked in the literature on ethnic contact and conflict.[11] If the groups in question differ in language or culture, increasing contact between the groups will mean increasing competition between incompatible ways of life. Friendship with outsiders will generally mean defection from the beliefs and practices of the in-group—or at least a more skeptical conformity with the demands of the group. Those who value the language or way of life of a particular group, and especially those who ardently believe that the group's beliefs are true and that its conventions are the most natural, may find contact with outsiders a threat to the general welfare as they conceive it, and they may react to increasing contact by trying to discourage it. They may foment hostility between the groups and try to keep members of the out-group (or out-groups) in subordinate positions in order to minimize their influence on members of the in-group. These people—the cultural or ideological conservatives—may well become more unfriendly toward outsiders as a result of other people's friendly contacts with them. Their influence on the attitudes and policies of the group may outweigh the influence of those who actually have the contact with outsiders.

There is no contradiction between these apparently incompatible generalizations, one about individuals, the other about groups. As shown in Chapter 4, the correlations between individual attributes (or measurements) can be different in sign as well as in magnitude from the correlations between rates (or averages) of these characteristics for groups of individuals. In general, there can be a perfect positive "ecological" correlation between two attributes, X and Y, within each of the aggregate units (countries, counties, cities, schools), even though these attributes are negatively associated at the individual level. The individual-level correlation between the attributes is a function of the joint distributions of the variables within each group and not of their "marginal" levels across groups.

The findings of the research reviewed in Chapters 2 and 3 are generally consistent with the distinction suggested here between individual-level and aggregate-level correlations. One large group of studies, those of interpersonal *interaction* within a single country, almost without exception support the standard contact hypothesis: more contact is associated with less prejudice and less inclination to become involved (at least in a bigoted way) in racial or ethnic conflict. To be sure, some of these studies fail to provide supporting evidence, and at least two different stories can be written around the significant correlations found in most of these studies. Even the evidence provided by the experimental studies of interpersonal interaction is open to more than one interpretation. But as a general rule, individuals who associate with one another in a friendly way tend to like one another and to have positive attitudes toward one another's groups. Studies of *proximity* involving comparisons within neighborhoods, firms, and other relatively small groups have produced less consistent and less easily interpreted results: many of these studies appear to favor the standard contact hypothesis, but some tend to discredit it, and most provide no real evidence one way or the other. Studies of schools, which are units of intermediate size and independence, have sometimes shown positive effects of contact and sometimes negative effects, but generally speaking, negative effects have been easier to find than positive ones. The studies of *proportions*, in which whole countries, cities, counties, or neighborhoods are compared, have yielded predominantly negative findings. Greater contact is generally associated with greater conflict and hostility.

The analysis of the contact hypothesis developed here differs from traditional contact theory on four main points. First, it suggests that the positive effects of contact are independent of whether prevailing stereotypes are blatantly false (for example, that Jews are plotting to take over the world) or contain a grain of truth (for example, that unilingual English Canadians would prefer Canada to be officially English). Interpersonal interaction will generally be associated with interpersonal liking and the reduction of prejudice in both cases. Second, the analysis suggests that contact leads to conflict between groups in situations of mixed competitive and cooperative incentives, not just in situations of competitive interdependence. Contrary to what some eminent social psychologists have argued, "superordinate goals" seem to be one of the conditions for ethnic conflict, not the cure for it. Third, the analysis suggests that contact, if it tends to reduce intergroup conflict, does so not by breaking stereotypes but by reducing the cultural differences that underlie them, through the process of assimilation it makes possible. At the group level, however, this "positive" effect of contact is a relatively slow one. The main immediate effect is to increase antipathies rather than to reduce differences.

Finally, the analysis suggests that any increase in contact that produces some positive changes in attitudes is also necessarily going to produce some negative changes as a by-product, whether or not this negative effect is large or immediately noticeable. The reason is that contact among individuals is also necessarily contact among groups and ways of life. The contact among individuals that reduces negative attitudes tends to disrupt the languages or cultures of the relevant groups. Thus it leads to efforts to preserve the differences among the groups by reducing the contacts among their members and by arranging those that remain so that the members of the in-group are always clearly superior to the members of out-groups. Social scientists describe these efforts as prejudice, segregation, and discrimination. If one wanted to encourage them for some reason, more flattering terms could undoubtedly be found.

The Linguistic Analogy

The model just presented is a linguistic model of ethnic conflict: it rests upon an analogy between language and culture. Examining the strengths and weaknesses of this analogy is one way of seeing more clearly the strengths and weaknesses of the model.

The analogy is attractive for two reasons. First, it is widely believed that different languages are just different *conventional* instruments for communication, no one inherently superior (or more natural) than any other. ("A rose by any other name would smell as sweet.") Few people now think that Greek and Latin are somehow "better" than Choctaw and Swahili. Greek and Latin would undoubtedly have been more *useful* in the Mediterranean world two thousand years ago, but those who spoke Choctaw or Swahili, even in Rome, were not violating any law of nature or doing anything contrary to genuine moral values.

Second, several important movements in twentieth-century thought—structuralism, hermeneutics, and analytic or "ordinary language" philosophy—have focused attention on language and familiarized academic readers with the idea that different cultures or systems of thought can be regarded as different "languages." Evidently no sharp boundary separates language from other means of human communication and other aspects of human culture. Communication by means of acoustic signals and their written symbols shades off almost imperceptibly into communication by means of gestures, posture, facial expression, and dress. Some aspects of each of these may be purely conventional and thus may vary from group to group. Communication by speech and writing draws not only upon the formal resources of language set out in grammars and dictionaries but also upon a community's stock of proverbs, anecdotes, fictional characters, and historical memories. More loosely, the meaning of any utterance must be understood within a context of shared assumptions about nature, human nature, priorities, values, and tastes. Disagreement on these matters can inhibit communication just as differences in language do, though of course more subtly (compare Hirsch, 1987). Finally, language is only the most striking example of mankind's propensity to engage in complex forms of behavior that can be construed as following rules. Culture itself can be regarded as an enormous set of rules—do's and don'ts and other ideas about what goes with what—all on the model provided by grammar and phonology.

If one accepts language as purely conventional and as a model for culture, one can clarify the nature of ethnic conflict without raising awkward questions about the merits of different cultures. The model shows how contact between different cultures produces conflict even when these cultures cannot be ranked on any scale of superiority and inferiority.

The weak point of the analogy is its neglect of the unconventional and unsystematic aspects of culture. Language, we assume, is immune to judgments of inherent superiority or inferiority. This assumption is obviously plausible if we restrict our attention to such great modern languages as English and French. Yet one of these languages may have to be adopted by a society. People must be able to communicate if they are to work together efficiently, and this normally means having a common language that is taught in school. Most aspects of culture, however, are not so readily treated as immune to evaluation, for they are not so clearly arbitrary and conventional. Moreover, culture as a whole is not as systematic as language is (with its phonetic patterns, sentence structures, and conjugations and declensions). Most aspects of culture can change a bit at a time as a result of piecemeal adaptation to new discoveries or external influences, much as new words are coined or foreign terms are added to a language, without altering its basic structures. A few contrasts between language on one hand and technology and religion on the other will help to clarify these points.

Technology, like language, refers to a vaguely defined network of social practices, but surely not one that most people today are inclined to immunize from judgments of better or worse. The English of Shakespeare's time may have been just as good as the English of our own time (despite some differences), but our technology is clearly superior to that of the sixteenth century. Shakespeare could write poetry about the moon ("by yonder blessed moon I swear"), but now our rockets take us there. Technology—whatever the truth of theories about it as a system (destiny, metaphysics) that a society accepts or rejects as a whole—can also be regarded as a collection of practices or devices to be evaluated piecemeal. Individual elements of the technological system, that is, particular techniques, can be tested pragmatically, and the rational person will presumably adopt the ones that receive the highest grades without regard to their national, ethnic, or racial origins.

Social scientists are thus inclined to say that a rational society, far from wanting to preserve ancient indigenous traditions, should strive to adopt the very best practices or techniques that it can develop or that it can find in all the diversity of the world's cultures. Ethnocentric opinions, from this perspective, are not just mean-spirited and hateful; they are brakes on progress. Traditions are mixtures of good and bad; they should be ransacked, not revered. And there is no good reason why conflict should result from nonlinguistic, broadly technological, differences. Tolerance and the free competition of ideas are clearly the better policies.

The difficulty with any technological concept of culture becomes apparent, however, when its basic values and ethics (or morality) are considered. There are no pragmatic tests for a society's ranking of values, for all such tests presuppose such a ranking. This difficulty gives rise to the practically sound conventions of cultural relativism ("When in Rome do as the Romans do") and to its disturbing intellectual puzzles ("How can it be equally good to do as the Romans do and as the Russians do?"). Is there no nature, but only convention?

An enormous debate, obviously influenced by the "Roman" practices the debaters have in mind, surrounds this question. If the implied reference is to speaking Italian, then the answer (for the purposes of this argument) is that no better reason is available or necessary (for speaking Italian in Rome) than the fact that Italian is the only language most Romans understand. The convention justifies itself, so to speak, just as a convention about driving on the left or the right side of the road needs no justification beyond the fact that it is the convention. But if the reference is to some technological practice, then there are presumably good practical reasons for either doing as the Romans do or doing as some others do, regardless of where one lives. There is no good reason why Romans should not have the best technology available—furnaces, factories, appliances, and gadgets that are as good as the ones available elsewhere. It is no justification for poor mousetraps in Rome to say that Romans have always wasted cheese or to say that most Romans are used to living with traps that hurt their fingers more than they do the mice.

A third possibility comes to light if we think of culture in terms of religion—another hard-to-define network of beliefs and practices. Most people are reluctant to regard religion as simply conventional, but neither are they willing to submit different theologies and liturgies to pragmatic technological tests. (It is a vulgar error to confuse religion with magic, and no one today thinks that prayers can be tested by seeing which ones bring the most rain.) Religion is commonly regarded as something "higher" than mere convention or mere practical ingenuity, but fortunately it can also be regarded as something more private. One can argue that there is no need for any uniform rule or public choice in the realm of private beliefs and rituals. Just as curry can be prepared by one family while cabbage is being boiled by another, Shiva and Kali can be honored in one household, Mary and Joseph in another, provided a reasonably clear distinction can be made between public and private. In this realm, tolerance and sensitivity provide a solution to the problem of ethnic conflict.

The linguistic model of ethnic conflict is inapplicable to the extent that such solutions are available and such attitudes prevail, for the model assumes a direct connection between contact and conflict due to the incentives for cultural uniformity and the resulting tendency to assimilation among individuals or groups in contact. The model will thus be valid if the people to whom it is being applied think of culture as a language (something arbitrary, systematic, and public) rather than as a technology (something testable and improvable piecemeal) or as a religion (something systematic and beyond pragmatic tests but inherently private). People tend to do so because of the many similarities between language and culture already noted. The extent to which they do so is in principle a factual question distinguishable from the normative question of whether it is right to do so. To the extent that they do so, the model will be helpful for understanding their behavior, and its helpfulness will naturally tend to strengthen belief in its assumptions. But a strictly scientific social scientist will not waste time railing at people because of their moral shortcomings: that task belongs to the moralists and the social critics who are responsible for popularizing ideas that have good practical effects (if necessary, by discreetly veiling disturbing realities). Social scientists, many now say, should be the specialists society charges with removing ideological veils. The more penetrating their descriptions, the better. Just as it was no business of Galileo, qua scientist, to worry about the effects of his astronomical theories on religious faith, so is it no business of social scientists today to popularize "good" ideologies by making them seem believable.

Before accepting these conclusions the cautious reader will, of course, want to consider a much wider variety of studies than those discussed earlier. The whole literature on nationalism, for instance, is obviously relevant. So are studies of revolutions, political violence, and war (compare Rule, 1988). Some reflection on the social roles of social scientists might also be helpful before deciding whether it is really true, as the model implies, that increasing contact among diverse groups, one of the most attractive feature of the modern world, is generally associated with increasing ethnic conflict, both within and between nations.

6 Truth in Modeling

Social science has a history almost indistinguishable from that of philosophy, but its specialized disciplines have gradually separated themselves from philosophy, becoming in the process quite practical and, in the twentieth century, resolutely empirical. Where once there were philosophical debates, there now are statistics. Contemporary social scientists are trained to test hypotheses by closely scrutinizing many little facts. Clear thinking about moral or ethical questions is naturally still admired, but its cultivation is thought to belong to others. The social sciences and moral philosophy are now generally thought to have different goals and to use different methods. These developments have understandably been controversial: the advocates of the new empiricism point to its great achievements and practical advantages; its critics emphasize its limitations and even its dangers.

Some thoughtful people now fear a loss of normative direction or secure grounding for our highest political values. We may know more than ever before about human history and the laws of psychology, sociology, and economics, they say, but we are losing our moral bearings. Science threatens to dissolve our binding beliefs. Scientific research may equip us to get what we want, but can it tell us what is worth having? The quest for scientific truth, though powerless to create any new values, may ultimately devaluate all the old ones. The tragic result may be nihilism or a crude hedonism. Modern social science seems in this respect to be just an extension of modern natural science—strong on facts but weak on values.

A somewhat different criticism may be indicated by speaking of forests and trees rather than facts and values. Perhaps we have lost our bearings and now are nervously wondering where we are heading because of our carefully cultivated scientific myopia and not because of any tragic loss of values.

The seed from which this book grew is the model of ethnic conflict presented in Chapter 5. It is essentially a "positive" theory of ethnic conflict that neglects or even obliterates some crucial normative distinctions. For example, it does not clearly distinguish destructive prejudice from legitimate demands for recognition and for a secure ethnic identity. Defensive patriotism is not clearly set apart from aggressive nationalism. A key term in the theory, *discrimination*, covers both good discrimination (invoked for the sake of equality) and bad discrimination (motivated by hatred and fear).

Some readers may object to the model as morally obtuse. They may insist that some moral distinctions be built into the causal analysis in order to reveal the fundamental differences between ethnic offense and defense: they are not just two sides of the same coin. Social scientists, however, are likely to demand that it be evaluated empirically. The crucial objection, from their standpoint, would be that its generalizations do not correspond to reality as determined by objective methods of observation. But what are these methods? Presumably they involve paying close attention to relevant, indisputable facts. But which facts are relevant and indisputable?

Chapters 2 and 3 of this book directly or indirectly summarized more than 250 studies to illustrate a simple rule about the empirical relations between contact and prejudice. Chapters 1 and 4 explained and criticized the theories that social scientists have developed in order to account for the findings of the research on contact and prejudice, showing that these theories do not in fact explain the relevant facts very well. Indeed, the theories seem to obscure the most interesting facts or draw attention away from them. Social scientists have evidently become entangled in some perplexing difficulties in their theorizing and research about the contact hypothesis. The model outlined in Chapter 5 has at least the merit of suggesting a new approach to some of these difficulties.

Only in a very loose way, however, can the empirical materials summarized in Chapters 2, 3, and 4 be considered evidence for or against the model presented in Chapter 5. The model seems to provide a good basis for explaining the puzzling correlations between contact and prejudice, but this hardly settles the larger questions it raises. Indeed, a critic might well say that the preceding four chapters have been a gradual turning away from sound methods for dealing with a clear empirical question (what is the effect of desegregation on racial attitudes?) toward a more speculative investigation of larger patterns. Perhaps we should now turn back, adjust our focus, and carefully scrutinize some directly relevant data. Models are fundamentally empirical hypotheses, he or she could say, and hypotheses need to be tested using the best methods available for weighing empirical evidence.

This chapter will pursue this line of thought in order to clarify what is involved in judging social science models. Some elementary points will be reviewed and some deeper problems indicated.

Theories and Hypotheses

Simple empirical hypotheses are easier to test than more complicated theories. Theories have a way of eluding decisive refutation. Empirical research may show one theory to be clearly more satisfactory than another, but generally speaking, theories cannot be proved or disproved in the same direct way that simple hypotheses can be. The contact hypothesis can be used to illustrate this basic point.

Consider for a minute the simplest possible contact hypothesis, the layman's contact hypothesis: more contact produces less prejudice. Disregarding possible problems arising from the vagueness or ambiguity of the terms *contact* and *prejudice,* and assuming no relevant differences between individuals and groups, one can easily test such a simple generalization. The relevant empirical studies (Chapters 2 and 3), taken at face value, do not support it. Many of the studies may seem to support it, but at least as many seem to support the opposite generalization (the more contact, the more prejudice), and some studies show no clear relation whatever between contact and prejudice. In short, the simplest contact hypothesis has been repeatedly tested and can now be dismissed as false, since no simple generalization will fit even a reasonable portion of the relevant facts, let alone all of them.

Contact *theory* is another matter. Despite its undeniable empirical content, it cannot be so easily tested and dismissed. (When social scientists today refer to the contact hypothesis, what they really have in mind is some version of contact theory.) Contact theory is essentially the hypothesis that different correlations between contact and prejudice can be explained by different situations of contact, for example, whether those in contact are of equal status. Particular hypotheses about relevant "third variables," such as equality of status, can be tested in particular situations, however described, and found to be true or false (for example, Smith, 1994). Surprisingly few relevant studies have been conducted, however, so there is little hard evidence one way or the other regarding the most important empirical hypotheses within contact theory. Moreover, the connection between testing these hypotheses and verifying or falsifying the theory as a whole is exceedingly loose. The theory makes so many suggestions that there is no possibility of using any standard statistical method to weigh the evidence for and against it. In principle, the basic theoretical strategy of distinguishing different situations of contact can handle any case. With thirty or more variables available, auxiliary hypotheses can always be developed to accommodate any pattern of findings.[1] Epicycles can be added to epicycles, a hostile critic might say. At any rate, the theory does not stand or fall by the truth or falsehood of any broad hypothesis that can be tested even in principle. Its popularity must have more to do with its theoretical merits than its empirical strength.

Worth noting in this connection is an apparent consensus among the most relevant specialists. These specialists—contact theorists and experts on race and ethnic relations—express reservations that seem to have more to do with aesthetics than with questions of empirical content or accuracy. As the number of situational variables thought to be important has increased, the complexity of the theory has increased, as well as its invulnerability to empirical testing. The real problem seems to be the complexity, however, not the invulnerability. The complexity deprives the theory of its appeal as an easily understandable model or simplification of more complicated processes.

Walter Stephan has provided an analogy for this problem that sticks in the mind. Contact theory once aspired to "the role of dragon slayer," he has written, but even twenty-five years ago it was more like "a bag lady who is so encumbered with excess baggage she can hardly move" (Stephan, 1987, p. 17). Since then even more conditions, particularly those having to do with the psychological processes that mediate changes in intergroup behaviors and cognitions, have been specified and investigated. "Nothing should be clearer than the fact that, like the bag lady's packages, the list of conditions considered important in creating contact situations that have positive outcomes continues to grow and grow" (p. 31; compare Stephan, 1991, p. 113). Researchers have discriminated more and more different situational variables and examined more and more closely the cognitive processes by which information about groups is derived from association with their members (for example, Rothbart and John, 1985, 1993). By listing so many variables, they may have failed to isolate and clarify the most important conditions that determine the relations between contact and intergroup attitudes. Indeed, Stephan writes, contact theory may have arrived "at that stage in the life of a paradigm where the working assumptions become so complex that the paradigm begins to die" (1987, p. 17). But rather than letting it die under the weight of its own superfluous complexity, he tries to give it new life by tidying it up—grouping its variables (about fifty of them in his presentation) under a few major headings.

Turning now to the linguistic model of ethnic conflict outlined in Chapter 5, we confront a similar problem, even though the theory represented by the model is much tidier and much closer to being a testable statistical hypothesis, at least in principle, since it involves far fewer variables and far more definite links between them. The next step in the discussion of the theory might therefore seem to be a statistical analysis of some hard evidence regarding its validity. Looking like a testable statistical hypothesis, the model seems to demand testing.

Appearances can be deceptive. What if no direct test of the model's validity were possible? Just as the only pertinent tests of the contact hypothesis are much more complicated than may appear at first glance, so also the *theoretical* merits and shortcomings of the linguistic model of ethnic conflict may be more important than simple statistical considerations. When trying to come to a sensible conclusion about its strengths and weaknesses, the most important considerations may have to do with such things as simplicity, elegance, and usefulness rather than with the results of simple (or even more complicated) statistical tests. In order to clarify this important point, let me explain in some detail what would be involved in a direct and systematic test of the model. Then it may be clearer why the model is not as testable (in practice) as it may seem to be. Yet this untestability may not be as important as it may seem, since the model is after all a theory, not an empirical hypothesis.

Testing Quantitative Models

Most readers, I assume, have a clear understanding of hypothesis testing as this is generally understood today in empirical science, but some may find it helpful to have a quick review of the specific problems encountered when trying to test models like the one developed in Chapter 5. Such models are no less testable, in principle, than are simple hypotheses about statistical correlations between two easily measured variables (height and weight, for example, or income and education). Let me begin by reviewing some elementary points about the testing of statistical hypotheses. Of course the simple, familiar statistical techniques have to be extended to deal with more complicated problems. My purpose here is *not* to urge that these more complicated methods be used to test the linguistic model but rather to make clearer how difficult, nay, impossible, it would be to do so, and why, even if these methods were used and the model were to be vindicated "empirically," two more fundamental objections would still remain to be dealt with. It will be best to approach a complicated conclusion slowly, relying on some simple models of the underlying problem to guide our reflections.

In order to fix ideas, consider an extremely simple model of the rather complex social process by which individual income is determined in such countries as Canada and the United States. There is a large pie to be divided, and different individuals get slices of different sizes. Many different factors undoubtedly help to determine the size of each individual's slice, but let us hypothesize that income is determined by success in school. Those who get more formal education ultimately get more money. Doctors and lawyers certainly seem to earn more than high school dropouts, on the average. There are of course a few fabulously rich dropouts and a few impecunious doctors (of philosophy), but these exceptions just prove the rule.

The hypothesized rule can be represented graphically, using a widely accepted convention, as follows:

$$E \longrightarrow I$$

Here E stands for education, I for income, and the arrow for "causes" or "influences." This idea can also be represented mathematically by a simple linear equation:

$$I = a_1 + a_2E$$

This equation says that income is a linear function of education. The parameter or constant a_2 measures the dependence of income on education, and it is assumed to be positive. The model has a moral—stick to your studies if you want to be rich—but it is not an ideal to be imitated or a form to be realized on a different scale or in some other medium, as is a model airplane or an architect's model.[2] The model is simply an attempt to represent compactly and abstractly the social process by which incomes are determined.

Now "true or false?" applies to this simple model in more than one way. Let me distinguish four elementary ways in which this model could be false.

First, there might simply be no statistical relation at all between income and education. Despite all the affluent doctors and lawyers and the impoverished high school dropouts, average income might still be the same, and the variation around that average the same, at all levels of education, from those with absolutely no schooling to those with several advanced degrees. With this possibility in mind, data on the incomes and educations of a population (or some relevant sample of a population) of individuals can be used to test the model using standard statistical methods. That is to say, the "null hypothesis" of no statistical relation between the variables can be tested. If it cannot be rejected (falsified with an acceptable risk of "Type I" error), then the model can be considered false in the sense of "unproved": there is insufficient evidence to support a claim that there is any "statistically significant" linear association between income and education for the population in question. Conversely, if the null hypothesis can be safely rejected, the model (or "alternative hypothesis") can be considered true in a weak sense.

The underlying statistical relation need not be linear, however. The linear model could be false in a second way: by misrepresenting the *form* of the relation between income and education. A little learning might be a valuable thing, but a lot might be a drag. The average income of those with sixteen years of schooling might be considerably higher than the averages of those with either six or twenty-six years. The underlying relation between income and education might be better described by a simple curve (⌒) than by a straight line, even if, because of relative numbers, a straight line (╱) provided a good enough fit to the observations for a "significant correlation" (linear association) to be found between the two variables. Again, there are simple statistical tests (of relative "goodness of fit") that can help to determine whether the linear model is true or false in this more complicated sense (that is, whether it provides a significantly worse summary of the data than would a nonlinear model such as $I = a_1 + a_2E + a_3E^2$).

Third, the connection between income and education, though linear and strong enough to be distinguished from sampling error, might still be too weak to be of any real interest. Those with many years of schooling might earn, on the average, noticeably more than those with little schooling, but the variation around the averages might be enormous at every level of schooling so that very little of the variation in income (say, less than 5 percent) could be explained by differences in education. Conversely, the connection might be a strong one able to explain more than 50 percent, say, of the variation in income. The model can thus be true or false in a third sense: income can be strongly or weakly correlated with schooling, implying that education is either an important or an unimportant variable in income determination.

Correlation is not causation, however, and the fourth major way in which this simple model could be false is by ignoring or obscuring some more basic relation that "explains away" the statistical association between income and number of years in school. The social process in question might be better represented by a model of the following form:

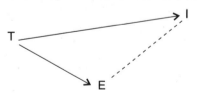

The T here stands for some third variable that, by influencing both income and education, accounts for the "spurious" correlation between them. This third variable could be intelligence, for example, or family fortune. The children of affluent families might stay in school longer (it's more fun than working) and then get better-paying jobs (because of their parents) and thus ultimately earn more money, along with having more degrees, but not *because* they have more degrees. Again, there are standard statistical methods of "partial correlation" for testing this more "critical" (or "Marxist") model of the social process that determines income shares and accordingly for determining whether the simple model with which we began is true or false in this fourth distinct sense.

It is perhaps contrary to good usage to call one linear equation a model of a complex social process. The term usually suggests something more complicated and impressive. The "correlation" between income and education is usually discussed without any explicit reference to models. But one simple equation, with some assumptions about sampling and measurement error, can nonetheless be properly called a "statistical model," and there are evidently several senses in which such a model, or any more complicated model of the same sort, can be true or false.

Turning now to the model of ethnic conflict presented in Chapter 5, we see that it consists of equations resembling the equations of our simple model of income determination. But three serious obstacles block any attempt to test it in any of the four ways so far distinguished: (1) the model involves three mutually interdependent variables; (2) some of the relations among these variables are more complicated than can be represented by simple linear equations; and (3) none of the relevant variables can be easily measured.

Between variables such as income and education there is a clear "causal ordering." Education early in life may determine subsequent earning power, but it does not make sense to say that a person's income at age forty or fifty determines his or her experiences in school thirty years earlier. If there is a direct causal connection between income and education, it must be because education determines income, not the other way around. In the model of ethnic conflict, however, each variable is both cause and effect of the other variables. Contact, for example, is one of the determinants of ethnocentrism (greater contact produces greater ethnocentrism), but ethnocentrism acts as a determinant of contact (greater ethnocentrism tends to reduce contact):

$$C \underset{-}{\overset{+}{\rightleftarrows}} E$$

With such an interdependence assumed from the outset, little may be learned from simply correlating (or fitting a simple linear equation to) the two variables. The causal influence in one direction is expected to offset (and to be offset by) the influence in the other direction, so the net effect may be a positive correlation, a negative one, or no apparent statistical relation whatsoever between the two variables. The hypothesis of mutual interdependence is consistent with *any* observed correlation between the variables. No observed correlation or simple regression equation will properly sum up the relations of interest.

Mutual interdependence between two variables can be modeled by two simultaneous equations, as already suggested (Chapter 5, note 7). Simultaneous equation models can be tested using standard statistical procedures, but these procedures are more complicated than simple correlation and regression and they require more data. Some "exogenous" variables with known connections to the "endogenous" (or mutually interdependent) variables of the model have to be incorporated in it.[3] Suppose, for the sake of the argument, that technology and politics are independent exogenous variables and that technology (operationalized by number of radios, telephones, automobiles, and computers per capita, the circulation of newspapers, consumption of petroleum, miles of railway track, and so on) is known to influence contact but not ethnocentrism, whereas politics (the competitiveness of the party system, the size of police and military budgets, the number of young people studying political science) is known to affect ethnocentrism but not contact. Then the system of equations represented by the following diagram could be a basis for empirical estimation and testing.

The practical problem of finding good quantitative measures of all four variables, cross-nationally or over time, would remain, but by analyzing relevant data within this framework, we could begin to test the hypotheses of interest, determining first of all, presumably, whether there were statistically significant relations in both directions between contact and ethnocentrism.

Similar but more severe problems would impede the testing of the three-variable model of ethnic conflict. The model would first have to be simplified in order to make it suitable for statistical analysis. Then at least three additional variables would have to be incorporated in it, and these three "instruments" would have to be independent determinants of C, D, and E, respectively. Relevant data would have to be found. Data collected at one time or over a short period of time would no longer be satisfactory, since cultural differences are expected to change only very slowly in response to changes in contact and ethnocentrism. Finally, the formidable problem of measurement would have to be tackled and some solutions found. There are no units comparable to dollars and pounds for measuring contact, ethnocentrism, and cultural differences. Serbs and Croats undoubtedly have more contact with one another than do Icelanders and Zambians, but it is hard to state the difference quantitatively. Some counted data exist or could be collected, but they would be hard to reduce to a single index or numerical measure of contact. Similarly, it would be easy to show that there is more ethnocentrism between blacks and whites in South Africa than between Swedes and Norwegians in Canada, but how much more? Twice as much? Four times as much? Or is it exactly one hundred times as much? Such precise comparisons presuppose precise numerical measures of ethnocentrism as a set of dispositions toward particular groups that neither counts of events nor ordinary attitude scales can provide. Finally, Swedes and Norwegians are plainly more similar culturally than Danes and Turks, but how much more similar? Again it is virtually impossible, by any rigorous method, to associate numbers with these differences so that one could say, for example, that the Swedes and the Norwegians differ by only 5 units of culture, whereas the Danes and the Turks differ by, say, five times that many or even 135.642 cultural units. Yet it is necessary to say something like this—necessary to enter this world of make-believe—if we are to talk about a rate of change of cultural differences.

The linguistic model of ethnic conflict is clearly an *empirical* model. It cannot be dismissed as metaphysical (untestable in principle) or normative (an ideal expressing the values of its creator). But an empirical model may be testable in principle without being testable in practice. We may know what to do in order to turn its conjectures into verified laws but be unable to do it. Testing even the simplest empirical models often involves more difficulties (or ambiguities) than one might at first suppose, and these difficulties multiply when the model involves mutually interdependent variables that are hard to measure.

A Thought Experiment

An empirical model for which there are no proper empirical tests puts us in a quandary. How should it be judged? Should debate about its merits be put on hold until some relevant tests can be devised and carried out? Some headway may be made in these difficult circumstances by indulging in a little make-believe.

Let us imagine that the linguistic model has successfully passed a rigorous empirical test. Good measures have somehow been found for at least half a dozen variables, such as history, technology, politics, contact, ethnocentrism, and cultural differences, for a large number of countries over a fairly long period of time. All the interconnections and differences among these countries—Iceland with Zambia as well as with Denmark and the United Kingdom, India (or its components) with Nigeria and Yugoslavia (or their components) as well as with Pakistan and Sri Lanka, Fiji with Finland—all have been reduced to tables of numbers. The model has been simplified for ease of statistical estimation, and the data have been analyzed. It has become clear that the parameters of the model (or averages of them) have approximately the values that were hypothesized. Various other specifications of the model have been tried and found wanting. The relations between its endogenous variables are strong, and together with the exogenous variables they explain most of the variance in ethnocentrism ($R^2 = .89$). Would these remarkable results—surely deserving a Nobel Prize in econometrics—suffice to allay all our doubts about the way of thinking about ethnic conflict represented by the model? Should they?

Two Fundamental Objections.

A social scientist not intimidated by complicated statistics might rise from perusing the imaginary statistical study just described, take a deep breath, and reiterate two fundamental objections to the linguistic model of ethnic conflict. It makes ethnic conflict look too reasonable, he or she might say, and it suggests that nothing can be done to overcome it.

Anyone analyzing ethnic conflict along the lines suggested by the model, we may reflect, has failed to grasp what is meant by saying that hostile ethnic attitudes are prejudices. The point is that they are *not* reasonable reactions to cultural differences reflecting personal experience with ethnic out-groups. Moreover, no one who rationalizes ethnic conflict along these lines has seen the point of saying that ethnic loyalties are primordial: they have a spooky, atavistic quality completely different from the tepid, sensible, pragmatic loyalties that people have to their mother tongues or to other familiar practical conventions. In places such as Bosnia and Rwanda people seem possessed. They act more like zombies than rational utility maximizers. In order to understand their murderous hatreds, we have to probe the murkiest depths of the human soul. The insights of psychiatrists, not the models of statisticians, are needed to unravel the mystery.

Our reservations may be strengthened by seeing that the linguistic model is demonstrably false as a *universal* rule, regardless of any purely statistical merits it may have as a set of averages. No sensible person claims that statisticians can use statistics to prove anything they want to prove, but it is remarkable (and too seldom appreciated) how little statistical analysis can in fact reveal about basic social regularities. A model like the one in question here may seem to explain some important facts, but can it explain the success enjoyed by multiethnic and multiracial societies such as Canada, the United States, and Switzerland? Surely their existence casts doubt on the model's *general* validity regardless of the outcome of any statistical tests. X goes with Y, on the average, other things being equal? Perhaps so, we may say, but other things are never really equal. And these other things may be the most important things.

The model neglects political factors in order to focus on social processes. No complicated statistical calculations are needed to show the importance of the factors it neglects; some simple descriptions of countries such as Canada and the United States suffice. The objection would not be that the model is untestable. We would not say that there is anything wrong with our imaginary statistics (we have imagined that they are perfect), but rather we would say that the basic theory in question is demonstrably false and misleading.

It may require some effort to hold onto such a resolutely negative judgment in the face of the almost overwhelming statistical "proof" we have imagined. Broad rules always have exceptions, we may think, and now we are just highlighting the exceptions (the 11 percent of the variance that the model supposedly does not explain). How important is this small amount of unexplained variance?

Obviously, the model abstracts from a complicated network of social and political processes in order to clarify a few simple relationships. By doing so, it suggests that there are "iron laws" of ethnic conflict that cannot be overcome by individual and social effort. Like so much of positivist (or "naturalistic") social science, we could say, the model encourages confusion about nature and convention. It treats the products of human action—roles, institutions, and other patterns of social behavior—as if they were regularities of nature, like the laws of physics or chemistry. But in fact such countries as Canada and the United States show that quite different patterns of intergroup relations are possible. Something can be done here and now to overcome ethnic prejudice and discrimination. No "iron laws of ethnic conflict" govern all countries. Whatever generalizations a statistical study of the world as a whole might seem to support, such a study cannot "prove" that its "laws" must apply to the internal working of countries such as Canada and the United States.

Critical Thinking.

A very brief excursion into "critical theory" may help to put the basic problem in the right perspective. Contemporary exponents of critical theory often argue that orthodox, positivist social science misunderstands its models when it thinks of them as collections of natural laws.[4] Models define and explain by isolating and simplifying patterns of human behavior that are in principle changeable. By seeming to freeze these patterns, the models fundamentally distort the reality they describe, for new social roles can always be defined, new institutions can be built, and new ways of life can come into being. To treat the patterns of the past as an inescapable necessity is to have a false consciousness of social reality. It is to reify—to treat abstractions as concrete things. It is to lose sight of the fact that human beings themselves produce the social forms that then, in a sense, confront them as external necessities. To treat social forms as thing-like facts separated from their human sources is to deny human freedom. It is the deepest self-delusion and the most serious mystification possible in social science, according to critical theorists.

An example may help to clarify this line of thought. A century ago a French Italian engineer turned economist and sociologist, Vilfredo Pareto, discovered a statistical "law" that seemed to govern the distribution of income in all the societies for which he could easily find relevant data. To simplify, his law of income distribution states that income is distributed unequally and that the inequality is more or less the same everywhere—unaffected, it seems, by the different laws, customs, climates, histories, mythologies, and economic systems of different countries. Pareto was a major figure, one of the founders of mathematical economics, so his provocative claim has stimulated a lot of debate among economists and statisticians. It has often persuaded those who want to be persuaded that progressive taxation must have bad effects, since such taxation aims to change the "natural" distribution of income that the law describes. Any attempt to equalize incomes must be doomed to fail, some have concluded, because it is contrary to a "law of nature." Pareto's critics have not been convinced, however. They have pointed out quite rightly that any society that truly wants to equalize incomes can obviously do so by deliberately changing its laws and customs. Despite the generalizations of social scientists, nature permits different conventions. In most countries people drive on the right, but in some they drive on the left. That a group of countries at some particular time all happen to have essentially the same conventions (with respect to income distribution) does not mean that these conventions are "natural" in the sense of inescapable (compare Cirillo, 1979, pp. 61–87; Tawney, 1931, pp. 56–61).

A similar argument could be made about intergroup relations and the linguistic model of ethnic conflict—to demonstrate its fundamental falseness. Any society that truly wants to overcome its traditions of ethnic prejudice and discrimination can obviously do so by abandoning its prejudiced beliefs and stopping its discriminatory practices. Where there is a will, there must be a way.

Practically speaking, of course, any such exercise of human freedom always has a collective, or political, dimension. Income distributions are not changed overnight just because everyone has a dream of perfect equality. And the relations among ethnic groups cannot very well be improved by waiting for every individual to wake up one morning magically imbued with new, more tolerant beliefs and attitudes. Such changes require leadership. New laws must be adopted and new methods of socializing individuals must be developed. People must be gradually "reprogrammed" so that they are freer and more willing to treat each other with respect.

Various reforms adopted by Canada and the United States during the past fifty years illustrate some of the practical measures that can be used to bring about relevant changes. The practical measures already well known and widely used include human rights policies, equal opportunity policies, official languages policies, affirmative action (or employment equity) policies, general policies to enhance cultural pluralism, larger subsidies for the cultural activities of minority groups, multicultural programs in education and health care, quotas or set-asides for minority firms requesting loans from banks or bidding on government contracts, preferential admissions policies for colleges and universities, minority redistricting policies, new jury selection procedures, new restrictions on freedom of speech and freedom of the press designed to eliminate expressions of hatred against identifiable groups, special penalties for racially or ethnically motivated crimes against minority individuals, special fellowships for graduate students doing research on race and ethnic relations, and generous subventions for research on intercultural understanding and for travel to international conferences on intergroup relations. The point of such policies and programs is precisely to overcome the conflicts associated with increasing contact among different racial and ethnic groups. The point, one might say, is to prove the linguistic model of ethnic conflict wrong. Far from treating greater contact as a cheap cure for ethnic tensions, these policies recognize that it is the source of unwanted behaviors (broadly, segregation, discrimination, and prejudice) that must be dealt with before there can be free and equal relations among different groups (compare Hawley et al., 1995).

It would be foolish to suppose that all the practical devices developed in the past century to deal with ethnic conflict can be reduced to a few quantitative variables suitable for incorporation in a still more complicated statistical model. Nonetheless, the practical measures that experience has suggested may be effective seem to be of two main types. On one hand are the measures designed to eliminate prejudiced and discriminatory behaviors (whatever the underlying attitudes or beliefs such acts may express)by penalizing them. The behaviors to be eliminated are essentially instances of overt disrespect and discrimination that reflect and intensify the inter-group conflict. Speech codes, laws for or against discrimination, and special penalties for ethnically motivated crimes are among the practical measures that can be used to reduce these negative behaviors.

On the other hand are the measures designed to inculcate attitudes and behaviors that are positive—that tend to attenuate the antagonism and to promote friendly cooperation among the groups in question. The practical measures that can be used to these ends include dramatic demonstrations of the falseness of negative stereotypes about groups, simple explanations of the errors involved in applying broad generalizations about groups to their individual members, good illustrations of the unfairness of judging one group by the standards of another, careful instruction in the real differences between groups (so as not to encourage negative stereotyping), attractive presentation of visions of a multicultural society, reassuring explanations of the opportunities it provides for new insights and experiences, and helpful instruction in how to take a modest, constructive pride in being equal citizens of an advanced democracy that is ahead of other countries in mankind's long struggle to overcome ethnocentrism. These demonstrations and explanations can be made part of instructional media, and they can sometimes be worked into commercial advertising, movies, and other entertainment, but they are probably most effective when they are communicated face to face by respected authorities such as business, political, and religious leaders.

It is convenient to have two new technical terms to refer to these two important bundles of practical measures designed either to damp down ethnic conflict or to raise people above it. *Repression* and *education* may serve this purpose as well as any two words can, and they point to the most important factors neglected in the linguistic model of ethnic conflict.

Just as contact, differences, and ethnocentrism can be considered variables for the purpose of constructing a model, so can repression (R) and education (S, for schooling, to avoid confusion with E, for ethnocentrism). In fact, a more adequate model could probably be built using these new variables, although no purpose would be served by trying to give it mathematical precision.[5] A simple diagram using "causal arrows" sufficiently clarifies the relations. Interactions among independent variables cannot be represented very well by causal arrows, and relations that develop over time can be properly represented only by greatly complicating such diagrams, but the first panel of figure 6.1 adequately summarizes the relations postulated in the linguistic model of ethnic conflict. (The broken arrows represent relations over time; the question marks stand for exogenous var-

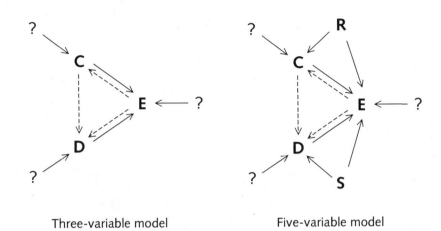

Three-variable model   Five-variable model

Figure 6.1. Two Models of Ethnic Conflict

iables such as history, ideology, and technology.) The second panel of figure 6.1 shows a five-variable model in which repression and education modify the relations that would otherwise exist among contact, differences, and ethnocentrism. It suggests that the right education can break the difference-ethnocentrism link and that good laws can keep order despite the tendency people may have to treat differences as a cause for discrimination. The idea is to use the tools of government to stifle the ethnocentric consequences of contact long enough for assimilation to eliminate the troublesome differences.

It may seem contrary to the spirit of critical theory to counter its objections to naturalistic models of society by proposing another, more complicated model of the same type. The more complicated model may well explain more of the variance (rare indeed is the statistical model that does not do so, when it employs more explanatory variables), but that's not the point, some readers may protest. Practically speaking, they may concede, those who are trying to produce social change have to rely on manipulating variables—or efficient causes—such as repression and education. But social and political processes of change are still being misunderstood, they may insist, if they are understood "scientifically" as the lawful working of some complicated machinery that can in principle be described theoretically by a mathematical (or "mathematistic") model. The point is that no model can properly take into account all that is involved in the repressive and educational activities of governments and other groups, for the details are crucial and cannot be generalized, so no statistical analysis (or empirical model) can provide any theoretical guarantee of a predictable outcome. Theory and practice are too closely related in the nature of things to justify any practical reliance on such theoretical abstractions. Political theories can be tested only in political practice. Theory and practice are not distinct activities, critical theorists insist, even though they may seem to be distinct academic specialties. A good model is one that is good politically and not just statistically or theoretically.

The Politics of Modeling.

Theories or models deliberately simplify the phenomena in their domain. They generalize far beyond, and sometimes against, the available data. They attempt to describe not every little wrinkle in the terrain they cover but only its broad contours. They may even neglect some of the latter. (Contact theory, for example, neglects the continental divide between individual-level and aggregate-level relationships.) The "empirical" weakness of a good model may be its "theoretical" strength. Factual objections can often be countered by adding a few new variables and auxiliary hypotheses. In the cases at hand, both contact theory (with its thirty to fifty variables) and the linguistic model of ethnic conflict (in its expanded five-variable form) seem quite able to handle all the available facts. Neither can be dismissed as simply disproved. How then is one to choose between them?

Scientists and philosophers of science sometimes invoke considerations such as simplicity, breadth, parsimony, and elegance when it is necessary to choose between competing theories or models, all of which are satisfactory (more or less) from the standpoint of agreement with "the facts."[6] Among these vaguer criteria, the most important by far when judging *social* theories is their contribution to political practice, not just as guides to the development of public policy but as aids to the promotion or overcoming of ideological obfuscation.

Critical theory has made an important contribution to understanding the puzzling relation between social theory and social practice. The fundamental weakness of naturalistic social science—whatever the scientific or statistical merits of its positive theories about existing patterns—may be its tendency to reify fluid social realities. According to critical theorists, however, this weakness may be one of the greatest *strengths* of conventional social science from the standpoint of the dominant class in a capitalist society. For them, reification may serve a clear practical purpose, because it may tend to stabilize a class-divided society. If people cannot imagine things being different from what they are, they will not fight for change. Movements for reform or revolution can be nipped in the bud. A "mechanical" interpretation of society, such as the one classical political economy provides, may be a real barrier to social progress, discouraging any attempt to overcome the practices it describes. Models of firms and markets may do on a large scale what Pareto's law of income distribution does on a small scale. The first task of intellectuals committed to social change may be to critique such "science." Like crude generalizations about economic or sexual inequality presented as "universal laws," even complicated models, if misunderstood as natural laws, can undermine support for change.

A model, even a very simple model like the contact hypothesis or the linear hypothesis about income and education discussed earlier, can lead thinking about practical problems in a particular direction, with definite practical consequences, strengthening some political tendencies or positions and weakening others. It can, for example, seem to support the legitimacy of capitalism and to undermine the complaints of socialists. A rival model (for example, the model of spurious correlation discussed earlier) can have the opposite practical effects.

Two consequences follow. First, the acceptance of a model may tend to strengthen or to undermine its empirical credibility. How people behave depends in part on what they think is true. Planets are no more likely to move in ellipses just because human beings think they do, but citizens may get out and vote if they are persuaded (because political scientists tell them) that voting is an effective way to discipline political elites and to make them serve the people's interests and not just their own. Or—to use a more pertinent example—the variable T in the three-variable model of education and income could be acceptance or rejection of the "truth" that more education leads to more income. General acceptance of this "truth" might tend to create a positive correlation between education and income as the more talented and energetic members of the society, imbued with the "truth," successfully pursued both academic qualifications and high incomes. General skepticism about the "truth" might even produce a negative correlation as the bright and energetic stopped wasting their time in school and instead concentrated on making money. This is the familiar problem of the self-fulfilling prophecy: the validity of a model may depend upon its acceptance or popularity (or even upon its *not* being accepted or generally known) in the population it is supposed to describe, because human behavior is affected by the models that are generally held to be true.

The second consequence is that political differences come to be reflected in arguments about the choice of models. Capitalists favor one model, socialists another. Within each camp there is a tendency to debate refinements of its favorite model and to avoid thinking about the rival model or models favored by political opponents. Arguments about trivial refinements may even be deliberately cultivated to draw attention away from the practically more important alternatives that deserve consideration. Thus, if a controversy rages among famous social scientists about whether a straight line or a curve better represents the dependence of income upon education, graduate students and others may never ask themselves the more interesting and important question of whether the relation (linear or curvilinear) is causal or spurious.

The essence of ideology is in a sense distraction: the mind is occupied with false choices and fails to think about the real ones. It's like asking a toddler who would prefer honey-coated sugar crunchies whether he wants his oatmeal in a red bowl or a green bowl. Given a choice of bowls, he is more likely to eat his mush.

Style and Substance

Contact theory and the linguistic model of ethnic conflict are typical products of modern social science, which tends to produce modest "mini-theories" rather than "grand theories" such as Marxism, Freudian psychoanalysis, structuralism, or hermeneutical theory (compare Skinner, 1985). Such broad theories, even if they have been developed only recently, seem to recall an age of miracles in a fabled land, "Europe," where individual geniuses provided obscure explanations of "everything" in terms of a few vast principles without ever being required to provide any hard evidence for their views. Modern social science, by contrast, demands evidence and produces a kind of clarity. It rigorously orders smaller domains for practical purposes. At its best it provides theories like those in economics textbooks (Keynesianism, monetarism, and so on). Its most typical products, such as contact theory, are even more modest. Often they are little more than the elaboration or qualification of a rudimentary hypothesis like the layman's contact hypothesis.

The empiricism of social science helps to explain the clarity and limited scope of its typical theories but also some of the persistent disagreements regarding their relative merits. Testability in principle need not produce consensus in practice. For example, the many investigations inspired and guided by contact theory have involved close attention to a host of petty factual details, but the blizzard of facts in the relevant literature may obscure some basic conceptual problems.

Neither contact theory nor the linguistic model of ethnic conflict is in any straightforward sense testable. Both recognize that there can be positive as well as negative correlations between contact and prejudice. In particular, contact theory protects the simplest "contact hypothesis" from decisive refutation. Different correlations can be found, it seems, in different situations. The theory aims to distinguish those situations. It holds that particular "third variables" or combinations of them may explain the different correlations observed in different situations. Particular hypotheses about these third variables can be strengthened or weakened by the results of empirical research, but the fate of the theory as a whole is not tied to the fate of any particular hypothesis within it. The theory is more like a checklist than an empirical hypothesis. Strictly speaking, it is just the truism that third variables can affect the correlations observed between two other variables. Thus contact theory has only a very loose relation to relevant factual detail. The research and theorizing it has guided and stimulated have been more empirical in style than in substance.

The political element may outweigh the empirical element in a social science theory or model and yet be hardly noticeable—if it is uncontroversial. Contact theory nicely illustrates what is meant by subliminal political content. The theory takes relations between individuals as a model for relations between groups. Two individuals kept apart by an old grudge or conflict (A's father cheated or insulted B's uncle), if they can somehow be brought together in some common enterprise (fighting a fire or raising a barn), frequently discover that nothing much really divides them. They are not the ogres they imagined each other to be but agreeable companions and potential friends. The same is true of groups, according to the theory. Contact tends to promote peaceful, friendly relations among traditionally antagonistic groups divided only by ancient prejudices and superstitions. If they get to know each other better, they will see that they are not separated by anything beyond a pointless piety. Contact between groups may initially have low, commercial origins, even a desire to enslave or exploit others, but in the long run it will have good effects.

A commercial or capitalist society has within itself the cure for its own ills—at least with respect to prejudice and discrimination. To be sure, contact sometimes seems to have bad effects, but this is because the circumstances in which the contact occurs are not ideal. Individuals may not be meeting each other on a footing of equality, as all individuals should, given that all have been born equal. Or they may be divided by conflicts of interest of the sort that create difficulties even among members of the same ethnic or racial group. Or outsiders may be stirring up trouble between them. To the extent possible, circumstances of contact that increase prejudice (those of inequality, conflict, and so on) should be changed. Circumstances in which contact has good effects should be created, and the disruptive activities of outside agitators should be curbed. The literature on the contact hypothesis is thus very practical in orientation. It reflects serious concern for an important practical problem—domestic prejudice and discrimination—and a desire to serve policy makers who are looking for "action programs" to reduce prejudice.

The main intellectual roots of contemporary social science theories are often easy to see. For example, there is an obvious analogy between contact theory and the liberalism epitomized by Montesquieu's claim that "commerce cures destructive prejudices." Commercial societies such as England, Montesquieu thought, would be less oppressive and warlike than earlier societies. The long-term growth of commerce would require and promote a more sensible system of education than was common in the past, and this would produce more peaceful relations between traditionally antagonistic groups. Montesquieu's reasons for these expectations—the main lines of his argument—are a little hard to discern under all his digressions and asides, but he seems to have believed that tolerance would cure denominational religious strife. Destructive religious zeal would give way to more constructive pursuits. By treating all religions equally while fostering the growth of commerce, liberal governments could gradually wean their citizens away from their fanatical antipathies and win them over to a more moderate and peaceful way of life. The United States today is the outstanding example of a society founded on these principles.

Conclusions

Models should be tested, and controversial generalizations should be supported by systematic surveys of hard evidence. In this chapter I have tried to show some difficulties with these commonplaces, but I am not suggesting that they be rejected out of hand. Rigorous statistical methods for estimating a model's parameters are worth employing when the uncertainties they resolve are greater than the uncertainties they create or perpetuate. With regard to the linguistic model of ethnic conflict presented in Chapter 5, no one who insists on treating it as simply a set of statistical hypotheses to be tested and then accepted or rejected is likely to come to any sensible conclusions about its merits and its shortcomings. At heart it is no more than the suggestion that relations among distinct language groups may generally provide a better model for relations among ethnic groups than do relations among quarrelsome individuals. Caricatures sometimes help to reveal family resemblances. The proposed model represents a way of thinking about the phenomenon of ethnic conflict, and it can be false only if an alternative way (such as contact theory) is generally better. The main impediment to its acceptance as a model has more to do with political considerations than with any lack of evidence to illustrate its mechanisms.[7]

One of the most surprising sources of relevant evidence is the empirical literature on the contact hypothesis. The studies reviewed in Chapters 2 and 3 provide indirect support for the linguistic model insofar as they reveal a problem for which it provides a plausible solution. The studies pretty clearly show different correlations between contact and prejudice at dif-

ferent levels of analysis—a negative correlation at the individual level and
a positive one at the aggregate level. Conventional contact theory provides
no satisfactory explanation for this puzzling divergence. Rival theories
such as realistic conflict theory and social identity theory ignore it altogether. Chapter 5 suggested that it can be seen as the working out of the
social and psychological processes of assimilation and resistance to assimilation that are highlighted in the linguistic model. Several other relevant
studies were cited as that model was being explained. Moreover, it bears a
close resemblance to Karl Deutsch's model of national integration or differentiation, which was developed with considerable attention to problems
of empirical testing (see the Appendix).

None of this evidence is of course compelling, and none of it is new.
None of it bears *directly* on the truth or falsehood of the three fundamental
laws or relations that constitute the linguistic model of ethnic conflict. But
is it reasonable to demand more?

In its mathematical dress the linguistic model of ethnic conflict closely
resembles a testable statistical hypothesis. This makes it tempting to demand a statistical test of the model. The demand must be judged in the
light of its possible results. For a variety of reasons, including their own
weaknesses and shortcomings, statistical studies may contribute much less
to resolving theoretical disputes in the social sciences than it often is assumed they should. Critical theorists have identified one additional reason
for their limited value: in some cases the only really decisive tests of a social
science hypothesis or theory are the tests of political practice. The standard
use of this argument is of course to undermine tested generalizations (like
those of orthodox economics) in the interest of radical political experiments. Simple generalizations from past experience are challenged, and
their "ideological" misuse is exposed, by pointing to the fundamental fluidity or diversity of social relations. But the demand for evidence to back
a theory or generalization can also function conservatively, in support of
an existing experiment, by checking theoretical speculation about its
mechanisms and results. The demand may involve questions not just of
scientific rigor but also of political commitment.

Reasonable discussion of the merits and shortcomings of alternative
social science models may require a loosening of political commitments
as well as a more relaxed attitude toward evidence. It may normally require
a deliberate turning away from the most obvious facts in a domain toward
their sources in less visible underlying processes. The patterns of coexistence and succession we wish to explain may become clear only on the
condition that we look away from them toward something simpler and
clearer. Models explain facts by providing intelligible patterns as well as
by accounting for variance. Despite its obvious simplifications and limi-

tations, then, the linguistic model of ethnic conflict may provide real insight into the basic form or essential features of ethnic conflict. The case to be made for it would not be that it fits all the relevant facts perfectly or even than it fits them better than do rival models (what would be the applicable standard?) but rather that it brings more clearly to mind the main ideas that must be kept in mind in order to understand ethnic conflict.

7 Conclusions

Politics uses the rest of the sciences.
—Aristotle, *Ethics*

Ethnic conflict appears in many guises. All the social sciences have had something to say about it. Specialists have brought the distinctive theories, methods, and terminologies of many disciplines to bear on the problem of understanding its causes and overcoming or at least mitigating its ill effects. Their studies have produced a wealth of distinctions, observations, and interpretations but little agreement about principles of classification and explanation. No single theory, model, approach, or conceptual framework seems able to capture all the variety and complexity of the manifestations of ethnic conflict. To paraphrase Donald Horowitz, there may be too little understanding because there is too much knowledge (Horowitz, 1985, p. xi).

This book has avoided a frontal assault on the problem. It has adopted an indirect approach, emphasizing situations close to home that are relatively easy to observe. It has focused attention on a modest theory drawn from one discipline. This theory—Gordon Allport's contact theory—has been compared with two others from the same discipline, social psychology, and with a fourth theory inspired by studies of nationalism by political scientists. The main source of the fourth theory—Karl Deutsch's communications theory of national development—is discussed in the Appendix. Up to this point Deutsch's ideas have been used only to illuminate certain preconceptions that may impede the understanding of ethnic conflict.

Contact has been the leading theme of this book. It provides the link— the obvious link—between the two main theories just mentioned. Both are theories about the effects of contact among ethnic groups. They create different expectations about its effects, however. Do their hypotheses simply neutralize each other, or can they be brought together to provide a more satisfactory account of the causes and effects of ethnic conflict?

The best clue to the right answer to this question can be found, I have tried to show, in the quantitative literature on the contact hypothesis. A fairly clear picture emerges from a review of this literature that distinguishes levels of analysis rather than situations of contact. Allport's theory, simplified, makes sense of one part of that picture. Deutsch's theory, simplified and extended, provides a way of making sense of the rest of it. The familiar contact hypothesis is basically right, it seems, as a summary of social and psychological processes at the individual level, but quite misleading as a theory about processes at the group, or aggregate, level.

The contact hypothesis began to be discussed by American social scientists a little over fifty years ago. The practical problem in the background at the time was "the American dilemma" of unequal relations between blacks and whites in a country "dedicated to the proposition that all men are created equal." Following Reconstruction, the southern states, where most blacks lived, had passed various Jim Crow laws, which had kept blacks separate from whites and formally subordinate to them even though the blacks were no longer the slaves of the whites. The great practical question facing Americans was whether this legacy of prejudice and discrimination could be overcome. The unjust treatment of blacks in the South was a blot on America's image in the eyes of the world (Dudziak, 1995). Would other countries be willing to accept America's leadership in the struggle for freedom if freedom meant white supremacy? More specifically, would the southern pattern of segregation and enforced inequality based upon discrimination develop in the North as well, as blacks migrated from the South to take jobs in the growing industrial centers of the Northeast and the Midwest and to escape the worst effects of the prejudice against them in the South? Or would the growing contact between blacks and whites in the North, with its different circumstances and history, produce a happier result?

A simple comparison of the North and the South fifty years ago suggested a generalization directly opposed to the contact hypothesis as now usually understood. Most blacks lived in the South, where they made up about one-quarter of the total population. In the rest of the United States, blacks made up less than 4 percent of the population. Contact between blacks and whites was far more common in the South than in the North. Relations between blacks and whites were generally peaceful everywhere, but lynchings were far more common in the South than in other parts of the country, and levels of prejudice and discrimination were obviously much higher there than elsewhere. Greater contact seemed to produce greater prejudice and discrimination and a greater potential for violent conflict.

Of course, a simple correlation like this, based on just two "data points," North and South, is of almost no scientific value. A wider comparison of relevant cases might reveal a completely different pattern. In addition, any simple correlation between two variables must be interpreted in light of each variable's connections with other, "third" variables. "Correlation is not causation."

During the 1940s and 1950s social psychologists conducted more detailed investigations using surveys or questionnaires. Their studies revealed that more contact with members of ethnic out-groups is generally associated with more favorable attitudes toward them. "The contact hypothesis," referring to this rule, began to be discussed, and a theory was developed to deal with the exceptions to it. The South was the big exception. The coexistence there of high levels of contact with high levels of prejudice and discrimination could be explained, it seemed, by the special circumstances of that region. To be sure, there was a lot of contact between blacks and whites in the South, but the two groups did not meet as equals in situations likely to make them aware of their common interests and common humanity. Friendly and cooperative relations on a footing of equality were precisely what the Jim Crow laws were designed to prevent. The whole southern institutional network was designed to penalize rather than to encourage equal-status contact. Normative support for such contact was notably lacking. Under more favorable conditions more favorable results could be expected, the studies suggested.

Behind the reasoning about the contact hypothesis by American social scientists lay a long tradition of reflection on politics, ethnicity (or religion), and commerce. The theory, with its encouraging implications, reflected American success in forming a new nation from immigrants drawn from every country of Europe and the Americas. Age-old hatreds had been put aside as different nationalities had met as equal citizens for purposes of practical cooperation. Abstracting from this experience, social scientists put forward conditions for the validity of the contact hypothesis that are very much like the prescriptions of modern liberalism (that of Locke and his successors) for overcoming religious hatreds and divisions. In its broad outlines, contact theory is not very different from the ideas underlying Montesquieu's generalization that "commerce cures destructive prejudices."

The classic statement of the contact hypothesis, by Gordon Allport, links it to the theory that negative opinions about ethnic out-groups are prejudices in the sense of erroneous beliefs, held despite contrary evidence. Ethnic conflict is said to spring from defects of character, as if it were the result of a kind of original sin. People unthinkingly adopt the hostile superstitions of their ancestors. They bolster their own sense of worthiness and fight their own demons by rejecting and maligning outsiders. They confidently generalize about racial and ethnic groups numbering in the millions even before they meet one or two individual members. Contact tends to reduce mistaken opinions and thus to moderate conflict because it provides new experiences that break old stereotypes and make people aware of their common humanity.

This way of thinking about ethnic conflict is the source of some of the current puzzlement about its remarkable persistence and amazing intensity. The ideas epitomized in contact theory create the wrong expectations. Yet contact theory cannot simply be dismissed as wrong: it is too deeply rooted, and too much evidence can be marshaled in its favor. Moreover, the basic hypothesis has been developed by social scientists in a way that makes it more or less invulnerable to direct empirical disproof.

The contact hypothesis is a *statistical* generalization, even when fully qualified by a long list of conditions. No social scientist has ever claimed that the attitudes of absolutely every individual must improve as a result of greater intergroup contact, even in the most favorable circumstances. The relevant specialists have argued only that it should be possible to distinguish different kinds or circumstances of contact with different attitudinal effects *on the average*. Since the 1940s a great many empirical studies have tried to clarify the conditions for positive effects of contact.

Practical people may have little patience for the picky details of such studies or for any lengthy discussion of the contact hypothesis. Surely it is clear, they may say, that individuals who get to know each other better generally get to like each other better. People who learn more about alien cultures feel less threatened by them. Don't segregation and discrimination breed irrational suspicions and unfounded antipathies? The relations between different groups are bound to improve if their members cooperate on common endeavors and get to know each other better. Intergroup cooperation obviously improves intergroup relations. The social scientists who study the details of these processes are just wasting their own time and the taxpayers' money proving the obvious.

Those who examine the literature reviewed in Chapters 2 and 3 will see that the contact hypothesis may be true as a broad generalization about the effects of voluntary interaction among individuals but false as a generalization about groups. If two individuals representing antagonistic social categories come into contact or begin to interact more frequently, without being overtly compelled to do so, they are likely to develop more positive attitudes toward each other's groups than they held before their interaction or than most of their compatriots hold. Interaction tends to go

with friendliness just as friendliness goes with interaction. Simple proximity, however, apart from personal interaction, does not seem to have any
clear effects on attitudes, and the mixing of ethnic groups appears to produce conflict and hostility. The higher the proportion of an ethnic minority
in any population, the more common and the more intense the negative
attitudes among the majority, generally speaking. As Allport himself said,
"the more contact the more trouble."

Contact theory draws attention away from these simple rules (which
obviously have many exceptions) by emphasizing others. Thus, it distinguishes situations in which the relevant groups meet as equals from those
in which some lord it over others. It distinguishes situations of conflicting
interests from situations in which common interests predominate. And it
distinguishes situations in which public opinion or important authorities
encourage friendly contact from situations in which they frown on it. Abstractly considered, contact theory has the form of suggestions for developing ancillary hypotheses about the effects of third variables on the
correlations observed between contact and prejudice or conflict. Most of
the suggestions have to do with the situation of contact. Indeed, contact
theory might well be called *situation* theory, since it is concerned above all
with distinguishing situations of contact on the assumption that contact
has different effects in different situations.

The most influential critics of contact theory have called attention to
the differences between individuals and groups. In *The Nature of Prejudice*,
Allport tended simply to extrapolate from the interpersonal level to the
intergroup level, as if intergroup relations consisted of nothing more than
interpersonal relations writ large. He traced prejudice and discrimination
to the moral and intellectual shortcomings of individuals, and he looked
to individual therapy in one form or another—including "genuine acquaintances" among individuals from different groups—to cure the conflicts between groups. This "individualism" has been rejected by such critics as
Herbert Blumer, Muzafer Sherif, and Henri Tajfel as one-sided. Without
simply rejecting Allport's analysis of prejudice, they have denied that it
provides a sound basis for understanding the conflicts between ethnic
groups. Individuals may well have mistaken opinions about ethnic out-
groups, and new experiences may well correct some of their prejudiced
opinions, but the intergroup conflicts may be unaffected because these
conflicts grow out of their real clashes of interest, together with the tendency of individuals to identify with groups. The leading critics and their
followers have tried to join a sound *methodological* individualism—denying
any such thing as group cognitions or group emotions that are not the

cognitions or emotions of individuals—with an equally necessary recognition that groups are more than simply aggregates of isolated individuals.

One might express their basic criticism more pointedly by saying that Allport's individualism is the old anthropomorphism in a new guise—the very anthropomorphism that Allport himself ridiculed: ultimately a god created the universe and benevolent spirits keep it running well. Devils bring evil and disorder. Presidents and prime ministers cause wars and depressions or save the people from these misfortunes. Bankers are responsible for stock market crashes. Monopolists cause inflation. Communists are responsible for fires, explosions, and flying saucers. And bigots can be blamed for prejudice and discrimination (compare Allport, 1954, p. 170).

Continuing in this vein, one might say that it is an unfortunate quirk of human nature to see human agency everywhere. Further, this tendency must be severely disciplined if we are ever going to deal efficiently with the problem of prejudice, for it has much more to do with impersonal causes—the tides of history—than with the sins of individuals. Besides, why must Allport, who treats dichotomizing as a sign of a weak ego, always dichotomize things himself (see Chapter 1, pp. 15–22, 25–27)? Why does he not recognize more gray areas and complexity, instead of drawing simplistic, black-and-white distinctions between two kinds of contact (casual contact and true acquaintance), two kinds of thinking (realistic and autistic), two kinds of conflict (realistic and imaginary) and in effect, two kinds of people—the tolerant sheep and the authoritarian goats? One of the least attractive traits of human beings is their tendency to blame the victims of social ills for their own misfortunes. Did Allport really think that bigots perversely choose to live in discomfort, facing the world as cowards, fearing their own impulses, and repressing their most basic desires? It is morally offensive for smug social scientists comfortably ensconced in elite academies to load society's ills onto the shoulders of weak, emotionally crippled people who cannot think straight. He should have had more compassion for his more muddled compatriots.

Even those inclined to chuckle and brush aside such criticisms must take the empirical weaknesses of conventional contact theory seriously. The studies summarized in Chapter 4 provide virtually no support for the more complicated hypotheses of contact theorists. They give too much attention to the situation of contact when trying to explain different correlations involving contact. The situational factors they highlight seem to have no relevant effects. (Obsessive insistence upon their importance may be evidence of a tendency to think autistically rather than realistically.) The whole approach may be far less efficient as a way of dealing with the reality of different correlations than an approach that emphasizes either methodological differences or two levels of analysis.

The rival social psychological theories outlined earlier—realistic conflict theory and social identity theory—shift attention from individuals and their shortcomings to groups and group processes and from mistaken stereotypes to clashing interests. They rightly suggest that the laws governing intergroup relations may differ from those that govern the relations among individuals. Chapter 4 provided a simple illustration of the basic point that different statistical relations can hold simultaneously among the same variables at different levels of analysis. Contact may have beneficial effects on the attitudes of individuals and yet have no similar effects on the relations among groups. Most people's attitudes toward out-groups may be a function of in-group norms. If there are real conflicts of interest among groups—for power, status, territory, jobs, housing, or even marriage partners—it may be quite unrealistic to try to reduce overall hostility and the potential for violence simply by promoting more contact among individuals. The proposed remedy may have no effect—or the wrong effect—on the disease.

The main novelty of the theory presented in Chapter 5 is the emphasis it places on ethnic differences as a cause of ethnic conflicts. It provides a "realistic" understanding of ethnic conflict by focusing on the group level of analysis, but unlike other realistic theories it shows why there could still be conflicts among ethnic groups even if all were on a footing of equality and if all shared the same strictly economic interests. In other words, it shows why cooperation with out-groups on common projects in order to attain superordinate goals cannot be counted on to cure people of their bigoted or crudely expressed antipathies. Conflict may be a natural and unavoidable consequence of the cooperation among culturally distinct groups that is motivated by common economic and political interests.

Like contact theory, the model emphasizes the importance of the experiences that ordinary individuals have with members of ethnic out-groups and not just the relations among their leaders. It accepts that most people tend to judge out-groups "ethnocentrically"—by the familiar standards of the ethnic in-group—and thus to find them wanting. Ethnocentric judgments naturally strike most outsiders as prejudiced. Descriptions are mixed up with evaluations. But it may be an illusion to suppose that ethnocentrism can be overcome by having more individuals make more accurate and more sympathetic judgments of outsiders as a result of having more contact with them. Improvements in the attitudes of some "insiders" may only make others more hostile. In short, the model highlights real ethnic or cultural differences as a cause of intergroup conflict. Its basic rule is that the greater the contact between groups and the greater the differences between them, the greater the conflict.

The model abstracts from the very complicated social processes involved in the many different conflicts that can be called ethnic or that can be said to involve ethnicity or ethnic differences. It is built upon some drastic simplifications—for example, that all the cultural similarities and differences between ethnic groups can be reduced to a single quantitative dimension of greater or less difference. Moreover, the model abstracts from two very important sets of influences on ethnic conflict: those of the laws and those of the system of education, broadly understood. This is plainly unrealistic. *Within* states, the laws always put some restraints on the expression of negative attitudes and opinions among individuals and groups. The more effective these restraints, generally speaking, the less evidence of conflict there will be, and the less the evidence, the less there will really be, since conflict to some extent feeds on itself. It is the absence of the restraints represented by clear laws consistently applied and backed by effective force that makes ethnic conflict so explosive and so destructive *between* states or even within them when a system of restraint suddenly breaks down. Similarly, the climate of opinion and the understanding of the purposes of society implicit in its *moeurs* (maxims and customary ways of behaving) may tend either to promote or to damp down ethnic conflict. A host of influences may have to be taken into account under this head— not just the enlightenment provided by formal schooling but also the instruction and guidance provided by political and religious authorities, the good and bad examples offered by other role models and even by fictional characters or their creators, the information and good citizenship campaigns of service organizations, the posters in schools and buses, the pamphlets in doctors' offices, the images of different groups found in the media, the stereotypes used in commercial advertising, popular music, sitcoms and other mass entertainment, and other similar influences. The more these influences promote "diversity," the less should any given set of cultural differences produce conflict. None of these profoundly important influences are taken into account in the simple model of ethnic conflict presented in Chapter 5.

As a simplification, the model, like any model, is false. Yet it may also be true in the sense that it may help to clarify the connections among some important variables. By neglecting the confusing or distracting influences of the more conventional variables just noted (repression and education, to use the terminology introduced in Chapter 6), the model may clarify some underlying structural realities. For some purposes, repression and education may be the most important variables, but from a theoretical standpoint they may be less important than contact and cultural differences. By abstracting from the twigs and leaves, one could say, the model reveals the main branches of the tree and may even limn the outlines of the forest.

Some readers will undoubtedly protest that only a statistical analysis of relevant data along the lines explained in Chapter 5 (notes 7 and 8) and Chapter 6 could possibly show whether the model does what has just been claimed or whether it merely magnifies a few distracting twigs. Do the model's parameters in fact have roughly the values hypothesized? Do its equations in fact explain a lot or only a little of the relevant variance? Do other variables better explain the correlations observed? Are some of these correlations entirely spurious, or do they depend on conditions such as unequal relations between groups? Questions of this kind can be answered only through empirical research, some will argue, and no one should rely upon the model until it has undergone some rigorous empirical testing.

This orthodox objection has some merit, but here it amounts to a prescription for inaction. Perhaps the barrier it puts in the way of argument can be surmounted by the thought experiment explained in Chapter 6. Imagine that a thorough, methodologically unimpeachable statistical study has been carried out and that it has produced strong supporting evidence. The linguistic model of ethnic conflict is no longer just a conjecture: it has escaped a threatening refutation with flying colors. But some powerful objections remain. Are the most sophisticated critics cowed by a few statistics? Are they any less likely than before to insist that the model distorts and reifies a fluid reality full of potential for change? The quality of the statistics is not the issue. Can examples not be cited of simple generalizations that are known to be misleading despite the strong empirical backing they have? Does the very idea of natural laws of human behavior not itself provoke fundamental objections that cannot be overcome by even the most amazing statistics? Other generalizations, such as those of contact theory, are widely accepted despite their lack of clear statistical support. Evidently there are broader considerations, beyond mere goodness of fit, that come into play when judging social science theories. The fundamental considerations may always be as much political as statistical. At any rate, if even such a remarkable statistical study as the one imagined earlier would not dispel all the reasonable doubts about the linguistic model or silence all the objections to it, there may be no reason to put discussion of it on hold pending completion of some poor approximation of the study imagined.

It might be unwise to draw any firm conclusions in these difficult circumstances, but perhaps some tentative conclusions can help to bring the most important underlying considerations into clearer focus. The background alternative to the model is, of course, some version of contact theory. Let me suggest four points that anyone leaning toward the model is likely to think justified by the evidence and reasoning presented earlier.

First, the model would point to a plausible explanation for the conflicting findings of empirical research on contact and ethnic attitudes—an inverse correlation between contact and prejudice at the individual level but a direct correlation at the aggregate level. These apparently incompatible correlations could be methodological artifacts, but they could also be an instance of "the aggregation problem"—different correlations can exist simultaneously in the same situation or series of situations at different levels of analysis. The linguistic model of ethnic conflict combines both the individual-level and the aggregate-level relations as parts of a single process. It recognizes the truth of the contact hypothesis as a generalization about individuals but shows why the hypothesis is fundamentally misleading as a generalization about groups.

A simple mistake, it suggests, underlies the contact hypothesis and contact theory as well as the whole "psychological" study of intergroup relations. Fifty years ago social psychologists such as Gordon Allport were evidently struck by the apparently incompatible correlations just noted. Prejudice is relatively low among individuals who have friends or acquaintances from a particular out-group, but it is often high in areas of the world where that out-group is a relatively large part of the population and thus where there are many opportunities for interpersonal contact. Allport and others interpreted the first correlation "cognitively"—in terms of the making and breaking of stereotypes. Then they overcame their puzzlement about the second correlation by distinguishing a multiplicity of different situations in which contact may have different psychological effects. It seems that they should instead have understood the first correlation "sociologically"—in terms of assimilation—and then distinguished two levels of analysis. The mistake they made was, in a sense, to assume that the same correlations must hold across different levels of analysis. They did not consider the possibility that social processes override the patterns found in psychological studies of individuals.

Second, the model offers an explanation for the growth or persistence of ethnic conflict in parts of the world where economic development and political modernization were expected to reduce it, for example, in Yugoslavia. Much of the perplexity about contemporary ethnic conflict seems to arise from a tendency to abstract the individual-level processes of ethnic contact and accommodation from their aggregate-level effects. Contact may well undermine the prejudices of those in contact and thus (other things being equal) improve relations among groups. And by reducing the cultural differences among groups, contact may reduce the potential for conflict among them. But these changes take time, and by raising the specter of assimilation and the disappearance or devaluation of historic "identities" they can give rise to conflict. In fact, judging from recent events, the dominant effect of increasing contact seems to be increasing conflict, despite (really because of) the gradual homogenization of diverse cultures. The members of different groups are presumably becoming better acquainted with each other and more similar to each other year after year, but at the aggregate level these encouraging trends may always lag behind the deterioration of relations among the groups owing to the increasing conflict between them. The growth of global commerce, although it tends to cure some destructive prejudices, seems to foster others more rapidly.

Third, the model helps to clarify a distinct form of social conflict. Indeed, it helps to fill a void. Many social scientists seem to have no clear concept of ethnic conflict at all. Focusing on its most striking effects—hateful attitudes and violent behavior—they tend to mix up ethnic conflict with other types of hatred and violence, paying little attention to its specific causes. Using one word to mean both underlying clashes of interest and overt hostilities—scrambling incentives and actions—they confuse matters further. When social scientists abstract from the details of particular struggles in an attempt to understand how the behavior of those involved can be related to underlying conflicts of interest, they tend to focus on incompatible material interests of the sort that are naturally represented by the payoff matrices of game theory. This locates the major causes of most ethnic conflicts outside the resulting theories. Their artificiality is analogous to that of Muzafer Sherif's experiments with American children at summer camps in the 1950s. By abstracting from communism and capitalism, and from armies and air forces, he was able to use youngsters on vacation to illustrate how conflicting group goals produce hostility and violence whereas "superordinate" goals produce friendship and peace.

The model of ethnic conflict abstracts from the details of different ethnic conflicts to show how superordinate goals and the contact they motivate can produce specifically "ethnic" conflicts of interest. These conflicts sometimes result in violence, and a lot of it, but violence may not be their most characteristic or most revealing expression. The underlying conflict of interest may provide incentives for ethnocentric kinds of behavior (segregation, discrimination, and prejudice) that normally are directed, not essentially to punishing or eliminating the opposing group, but more precisely to getting its individual members to assimilate (and thus to recognize the superiority of the dominant group) by keeping the opposing group as a whole subordinate.

Finally, and perhaps most controversially, the model draws attention to ethnic or cultural differences as causes of ethnic conflicts. These have been downplayed in almost all social scientific theories about ethnic conflict, not just in the three social psychological theories discussed earlier in detail. This neglect seems to be more than just a careless oversight, however; it is more like adherence to a cultural norm. Behind it seems to be the idea that cultural differences are essentially matters of private beliefs and practices, like religious differences, and that their practical importance must not be exaggerated. If only individuals would relax and refrain from trying to convert their neighbors, different groups could live peacefully together, side by side, just as Episcopalians and Presbyterians do, generally speaking. Some quarrelsome individuals will always be finding fault with others because of their private customs and opinions. The deep insecurities of some Episcopalians may lead them to fight their doubts by fighting the Presbyterians next door. But most individuals can learn to resist such evangelical impulses, and all are encouraged to do so when the zealots are called bigots. In a liberal society, ethnic conflict can be traced ultimately to the moral and intellectual shortcomings of these zealots (or bigots). They fail to understand how pointless their bigoted zeal is (no one is ever converted) and how easily it can be avoided (they just need to relax and learn to live with their doubts).

Firmly believing that the liberal state-society or public-private distinction offers a reliable remedy for ethnic or cultural clashes generally, and not just for denominational religious strife, modern societies such as Canada and the United States have opened their doors to migrants from every land. They have sent some of their own citizens to foreign lands to help them to modernize and to find better ways to manage their ethnic conflicts. Their most far-sighted political leaders have laid the foundations in global commerce and international organization for a worldwide free and democratic state. The questions arising from any attempt to judge these policies and activities or ambitions would carry us far beyond the arguments for and against contact theory or the linguistic model of ethnic conflict. The basic question would be, How much assimilation is required and how much can be produced in a modern society that values and promotes tolerance and equality? Against this background, the linguistic model clarifies an important possibility, namely, that as the world shrinks and contact increases, assimilation will always lag behind the development of conflict, so that more and more resources will have to be devoted to repression and education.

Contact theory and the linguistic model of ethnic conflict can be properly understood, it seems, only in their broad political context. Outside the cramped confines of purely methodological or statistical debate, the real issues can be addressed. The most important considerations have at least as much to do with politics as with the always inconclusive results of statistical studies. Let me pursue this line of thought a little further, for it reveals an interesting tension. The trend of events, as it adds to the weight of evidence against contact theory, may be making it ever more important practically. The theory may be needed to help societies to overcome the growing ethnic conflict it leads them not to expect. This strange possibility deserves a little closer attention.

Let us assume provisionally that we are in fact leaving behind the irrational ethnic, national, and religious cleavages of the past and moving toward a condition of ethnic harmony in which different cultural identities will be maintained privately (just as different religions now are) but in which only rational, or "realistic," differences will be important publicly or politically. Individuals in the future will continue to fight for economic and social equality but not for cultural superiority. We are *not* witnessing an intensification of national and religious conflict that we should assume will grow indefinitely. Unfortunately, however, there remain a few conflicts between antagonists who seem to be striving for superiority (Islamic fundamentalists provide the orthodox example). These struggles must be suffocated in order to build a free and equal society. People must learn to concentrate on their common economic interests, not their divisive cultural ones. How can they best be taught to do so?

Individuals steeped in contact theory may be good instructors for those on the front lines of the struggle to overcome ethnic conflict. These frontline troops (teachers, preachers, social workers, personnel managers, media specialists, human rights workers, police officers) may fight better if they keep their attention focused on limited objectives and if those around them exude confidence that the battle can be won. They must learn to see racism, nationalism, bigotry, and hatred (that is, racists, nationalists, bigots, and people full of hate), not contact, as the causes of ethnic conflict. Contact must rather be seen as a cure for prejudice. If they have any doubts about the war as a whole, they must look within themselves for the sources of these doubts, concentrating on their own irrational fears, envy, and inauthenticity. Then they will be more cautious about expressing unorthodox opinions, and morale will improve. A simplified version of the linguistic model of ethnic conflict, disseminated among the troops, might cause dissension in their ranks and a loss of confidence.

According to one of the most basic principles of social science, however, different individuals play different roles in the drama of history. We have not yet attained that condition, beyond the division of labor, of which Marx and Engels dreamed, when a man could be a hunter (a hunter!) in the morning, a fisherman in the afternoon, and a critical critic in the evening (while tending the cattle). And in the struggle against ethnic conflict, generals—to maintain the military metaphor—need to see the larger picture.

They need good maps and realistic intelligence reports. They may be helped to play their roles better if they are shown why contact can be a fundamental cause of ethnic conflict, not just its cure.

What role should social scientists play in this complicated situation? The tendency of mainstream social science, some of its most sharp-eyed critics say, is to do what the powers that be want done—not by spreading falsehoods, exactly, but by emphasizing the importance of limited objectives and neglecting the larger picture. According to these critics, the real function of "social science" is to generate false consciousness. Given the current prestige of both science and democracy, social scientists play their roles as propagandists best if they dress in white lab coats and carry bundles of questionnaires under their arms. Critical theory prides itself on its ability to unmask the charades of social scientists by always showing the larger picture. Its criticisms of ideology and false consciousness are valuable, one can say, not because they sometimes sow dissension in the ranks but because the generals must not be confused by maps designed to sustain morale lower down. *Their* maps must put the mountains, the rivers, and the enemy formations where they really are, not where it is most encouraging to think they are.

Practically speaking, then, different theories are needed for different audiences. Certain regularities must be known by some, others by others. Trouble may develop if maps intended for the generals fall into the hands of the troops or vice versa. Social scientists loudly proclaiming their critical, enlightening mission must sometimes recognize that the goal of a fully enlightened society may be reachable only by a roundabout route, with some detours around rough patches. They must learn to speak quietly to the generals while haranguing the troops. The task of a truly critical social science is to make suppressed knowledge available, but cautiously, with an eye to practical circumstances and attention to details.

Too much attention to details, however, can put an audience to sleep even as it induces a kind of numbness or paralysis among the instructors. Empirical testing of models may always be desirable without always being possible. Some empirical models may be valuable not because they accurately and demonstrably summarize vast numbers of elementary facts in a few simple formulas, or because they lead to the discovery of previously unknown facts, but simply because they highlight a few familiar facts so that they can be surveyed at a glance.

This book has used some simple quantitative models to expose and examine some common intuitions about the effects of increasing contact on the relations among different ethnic groups. The most common intuition today is undoubtedly that contact, when it has any effects at all, has good effects. It destroys prejudices and stereotypes. This layman's contact hypothesis clashes with the vague but widespread suspicion that increasing contact must be counted among the causes of contemporary ethnic violence. The clash of intuitions is entangled with larger networks of conflicting opinions about history, politics, and human nature. What are the causes and cures of war and violence? Should nationalism be blamed for these evils? Can they really be overcome by building a democratic world state in which a wide range of human rights would be upheld by a world court and in which all individuals would meet and mingle on a footing of equality? Very little clarification of these difficult questions can be achieved by pitting one social science mini-theory against another, as I have done here. The theories have had to be isolated from their disciplinary contexts, and their broader political implications have had to be put aside, so that their empirical claims could be examined more closely. Any further investigation would involve a more direct confrontation with the principal arguments for and against the political project summed up in words such as *multiculturalism, openness,* and *diversity*. This book may perhaps serve as a preparation for such a confrontation. It has certainly not been my intention simply to substitute for the orthodox emphasis on the good effects of contact an equally one-sided emphasis on its bad effects. Rather, my purpose has been to break a social science stereotype: when certain facts about contact and prejudice or conflict are examined with a minimum of theoretical preconceptions, they lead to a clearer understanding of something that was already in plain view but difficult to see.

Appendix: Nationalism

Nationalism—or what LeVine and Campbell (1972, p. 112) call "ethnocentrism in its most evolved, or perhaps only pure, form"—can be examined as an expression of ethnic conflict. Like ethnocentrism, it can be understood as a force tending to isolate culturally distinct groups and to reinforce their distinctiveness. But in the standard literature on nationalism, ethnic conflict gets surprisingly little attention. Its simple mechanisms seem to be overshadowed by the need to discuss a wide range of more complicated problems. Nationalism, it becomes clear, is intricately related to social and economic modernization, the development of democracy, the principles of modern political thought, and the problems of militarism, imperialism, colonialism, and war. Nationalism is also, some suggest, a solution to all these problems, including that of ethnic conflict, but others heatedly dispute this suggestion, and the resulting debate is at the heart of the literature on nationalism.[1]

This Appendix briefly discusses some of the questions raised by linking nationalism to ethnic conflict. Its first purpose is to justify such a linkage by explaining the source of the model of ethnic conflict presented earlier and by pointing to some basic similarities between nations and ethnic groups. Contrary to the impression that may have been created by Chapters 1 to 4, the model presented in Chapter 5 did not develop out of an investigation of the contact hypothesis, but rather out of a study of the literature on nationalism. Karl Deutsch's communications theory of national development (Deutsch, 1953, 1954, 1966, 1969, 1979) was its most important source. A brief explanation of the principal similarities and differences between Deutsch's theory and my own may help to clarify both, and by locating the discussion of ethnic conflict within the wider territory covered by the literature on nationalism, it may help to clarify the difficult issues that must be faced when the individualism of traditional contact theory gives way to a more adequate collectivism than the kind promoted by current theories of intergroup relations. And finally, by annexing, as it were, the whole literature on nationalism to the discussion of ethnic conflict, this Appendix may broaden the empirical base for the empirical generalizations suggested earlier.

Deutsch's writings belong to the large literature on nationalism that has tried to answer the question, what is a nation? Is membership in a nation something objective or something subjective? Are nations groups of individuals with common objective characteristics such as language, religion, or historical traditions, and is nationalism an effect of objective differences between nations? Or are nations better understood in terms of subjective states of mind? Are nations simply groups of people who think—for whatever reasons—that they belong together politically? Are nations ultimately the result of willful decisions or commitments rather than facts? Do they perhaps come into being only when the differences used to define them somehow become salient or when people generally begin to identify with them? For political as well as strictly intellectual reasons, these questions have been hotly debated by academics for more than a century.[2]

In his analysis of national consciousness, Deutsch gives priority to the objective facts of which nationalists become conscious, but he does not reduce nationality to objective similarities and differences. He shifts attention from questions about the ethnic characteristics of nations to questions about the processes by which ethnic or national groups come to demand power. His main theme is "the growth of nations," or "recurrent patterns of political and social integration" (Deutsch, 1953). How is it, he asks, that yesterday's ethnic group becomes today's nation-state? His detailed discussions of four main examples of national assimilation or differentiation (Finland, Bohemia, India, and Scotland) show how quantitative differences having to do with modernization (in the sense of economic development, or "social mobilization") and inherited ethnic differences ("habits of communication") may be important in the creation of a modern national consciousness.

At the heart of Deutsch's theory is a distinction between *society* and *community*. He defines a society as "a group of individuals made interdependent by the division of labor, the production and distribution of goods and services. . . . A society in this sense is a group of individuals connected by an intense division of labor, and separated from other societies by a marked drop in this intensity" (Deutsch, 1966, p. 87). The development of society is very largely determined by the development of science and technology—the fundamental forces of production and relations of production of Marxist theory. By contrast, Deutsch links community to culture, defining a community as a group of individuals "who have learned to communicate with each other and to understand each other well beyond the mere interchange of goods and services" (p. 91). The basis for such a broad ability to communicate is the possession of a common culture—a "set of stable, habitual preferences and priorities in men's attention, and behavior, as well as in their thoughts and feelings" (p. 88). And just as different degrees of economic interdependence define distinct societies, different degrees of cultural complementarity define distinct cultures or communities. "Peoples are marked off from each other by communicative barriers, by 'marked gaps' in the efficiency of communication" (p. 100).

Society and community, so defined, can have different boundaries and can grow or contract at different rates. The key to understanding susceptibility to nationalist ideas, Deutsch argues, is the relation between changes in society and changes in community. "It is the complex interplay between society and community which is at the root of many of the baffling problems of nationality" (p. 95).

Deutsch analyzes the rise of nationalistic demands for power as a function of the relative speeds of two social processes—assimilation and mobilization. Assimilation is the process by which individuals belonging to culturally distinct groups come to have complementary habits of communication (for example, a common language) because of contact with each other and the social learning that results. Mobilization is Deutsch's term for the social and economic development of the past two or three hundred years. It involves "the growth of markets, industries, and towns, and eventually of literacy and mass communication" (p. 188). Very crudely, it is the process by which peasants migrate to cities and become clerks and factory workers. Its significance for nationalism lies in the contacts it makes possible and the need it creates for "relatively more intensive communication" (p. 126).

As already implied, assimilation, or the ability to communicate over a wide range of subjects, may increase more or less rapidly than mobilization, which determines the need for such communication. Deutsch holds that the prospects are good for the merging of different peoples (groups linked by complementary habits and facilities of communication) and the development of a common national identity among them if their ability to communicate is growing more rapidly than their need to do so. Conversely, if mobilization outruns assimilation, separatist movements and national differentiation are likely to result.

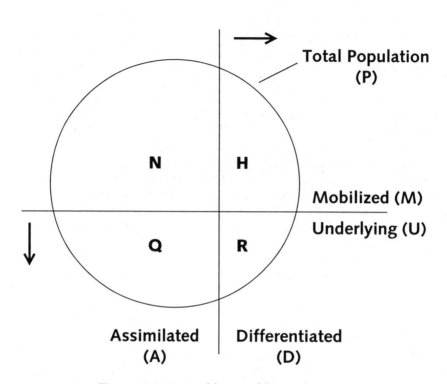

Figure A.1. Deutsch's Variables and Processes

In order to clarify the quantitative regularities he has in mind, Deutsch focuses attention on language differences and cases of linguistic assimilation or differentiation. The principles discovered in cases of this kind, he suggests, can be applied "to the social learning and unlearning of other habits of communication relevant for the waxing or waning of nationalism and nationality" (p. 125). Deutsch's very complicated analysis of linguistic assimilation or differentiation involves distinguishing nine population groups, six rates of change, and six qualitative balances. For present purposes, only a few of these need to be explained.

Deutsch divides the total population, P, of any area in two ways (figure A.1). First, he distinguishes the assimilated population, A, from the differentiated population, D. Given that language is the cultural trait of interest, the assimilated population is made up of those who speak the predominant language, the differentiated population by those who do not. Second, Deutsch distinguishes the socially mobilized part of the population, M, from the underlying population, U. This distinction, as already explained, has to do with the breadth and intensity of social intercourse. In principle, an individual could be classified as mobilized or underlying depending upon a variety of factors, such as place of residence, occupation, education, and level of political participation or involvement in the mass media. In fact, Deutsch uses urban or rural residence as his operational definition of mobilization.

Assuming sharp boundaries between these groups, any person belonging to the population in question will belong to two of the four basic groups (that is, $P = A+D$ and $P = M+U$). The remaining four groups Deutsch distinguishes represent combinations of the elementary possibilities. Thus there is a group N, made up of those who are both mobilized and assimilated: "They have been mobilized for intensive communication and assimilated to the predominant language or culture. They will be the most active carriers of this nationality and the national language; in conflicts they will form the national spearhead" (pp. 128–29). A sixth important group, H, consists of those who are mobilized but differentiated.

> They have been mobilized for intensive communication but have not been assimilated to the predominant language and culture. These persons have remained culturally or linguistically different from the members of group N, and they are frequently and acutely reminded of this difference by the intensity of social communications in which they must take part. These persons therefore are more likely than any others to experience national conflict, and they are the persons who first take part in it. We shall designate this nationally heterodox (if not "heretical") group by the letter H. The share of mobilized but differentiated persons among the total population, in our terms, H/P, is the first crude indicator of the probable incidence and strength of national conflict. (pp. 129–30)

The seventh and eighth groups are the underlying assimilated population, Q (probably from *Quelle*), and the underlying differentiated population, R (rebels or *Rivalen?*). They are important in any reckoning of the long-term strength (or vitality) of the dominant language and culture in the area in question.

Deutsch thus makes contact a cause of conflict and implies that assimilation reduces conflict. Mobilization, as Deutsch defines the concept, is equivalent to increasing intergroup contact. In Deutsch's model, an increase in mobilization, other things remaining the same, increases the mobilized but unassimilated part of the population, H, and hence the ratio H/P, his indicator of "the probable incidence and strength of national conflict." Assimilation, on the other hand, tends to reduce conflict, other things being equal, because it reduces the ratio H/P. In particular, if the assimilation of D proceeds more rapidly than their mobilization, and if assimilation occurs at least as rapidly among H as among R, then the ratio H/P will decrease, and so should the likelihood of conflict.

What determines the sizes of these different groups? Deutsch specifies four rates of natural increase (p, b, a, and d for P, M, A, and D, respectively), an assimilation rate (c, the rate at which persons born outside the assimilated group are entering it at a later time), and a mobilization rate (m, the rate of migration to towns by people born in rural areas). These rates of change determine changes in the relative sizes of A, D, M, and U—the assimilated, differentiated, mobilized, and underlying parts of the total population (pp. 148–49, 235).

Deutsch recognizes, however, that the merging and splitting of nations is not dependent solely upon population patterns. Therefore he supplements his quantitative analysis with a discussion of six qualitative or institutional balances. The first of these six is the similarity balance:

> Assimilation in general becomes easier the greater the similarity and compatibility of the mental, social, and communications equipment of the persons in both language groups; assimilation is more difficult the more different or incompatible are their linguistic or cultural habits. The similarity or dissimilarity in their vocabulary, their alphabets, and their grammatical structure can be measured. . . . Opposite traits, elements of differences or incompatibility, will of course weigh on the [dissimilarity] side of this balance. It may also happen that the linguistic similarity is very strongly in favor of assimilation, but the cultural balance is weighted toward the other side by considerable differences or partial incompatibilities in matters of value and culture. (pp. 156–57)

This passage suggests that cultural differences, too, could be treated as a variable in the analysis and that the rate of assimilation could be considered a function, in part, of this variable (the variable D in the model proposed in Chapter 5). In fact, the passage assumes behavioral relations similar to those postulated above: the greater the differences and the resulting conflicts and friction, the less likely groups will be to maintain contact with each other and consequently the lower the rate of assimilation (or the rate of reduction of cultural differences) to be expected.[3]

The third of Deutsch's six balances is the contact balance, which he defines as "the frequency and the range of communications of the average individual across linguistic or cultural barriers, as against the frequency and the range of the same person's communications within the confines of his own group." The greater the number of situations in which an individual is expected to communicate across a linguistic or cultural barrier, the greater will be the pressure on that individual to assimilate to the new language and ways of behavior. "To the extent that his time and energy are taken up by communications in his old language, with members of his own cultural group, assimilation may be retarded." These differences, Deutsch notes, "can be measured quantitatively, at least in part, by the standard methods of social communications research" (p. 158). The variable he has in mind here is essentially the same as C (the amount of contact) used in the model presented in Chapter 5.

Clearly, then, there are some important similarities between Deutsch's analysis of national consciousness and the model of ethnic conflict presented earlier. But perhaps neither of them has much to do with nationalism itself, properly understood. Both of them may be equally misleading. Their similarity alone does not suffice to establish either their merit or their relevance.

Questions about the right use of politically important terms are rarely settled by consulting dictionaries, but a few elementary observations may help to bring the problem that has just been raised into clearer focus.[4] Nations are groups, and nationalism has to do with intergroup relations. Whether nations are or are not states, they are distinguished from one another, generally speaking, by their ethnic or cultural characteristics. Different nations usually speak different languages, although there are some noteworthy exceptions (Britain and the United States, for example, or Germany and Austria). Some nations have more than one official language (Canada and Switzerland, for example). But language is plainly one of the most common ways of distinguishing one nation from another. At the same time, nations are not just linguistic groups: the differences between them typically have to do with history, culture, and kinship, not just language. To be sure, most nations have important elements of ethnic or racial diversity in their populations, and the relations between ethnic majorities and minorities are often a tension-filled issue in nationalist politics. So it is not an illusion to see nations as ethnic or cultural groups and nationalism as having something to do with ethnic consciousness or ethnocentrism.

The similarities between nationalism and ethnocentrism (or ethnic prejudice and discrimination) must not be exaggerated, of course. There are some very important differences between the goals and activities of nationalists and those of racial and religious bigots, but there are also a few similarities. A politically independent nationality has control over precisely defined boundaries through a government that is in principle superior to every other organ of society. It can limit immigration, develop economic policies that favor its own members, define treason and other capital crimes, and establish a national system of education. National in-

dependence is a kind of segregation and discrimination. National boundaries restrict the movement of people and goods and thus tend to reduce
the contacts between different nationalities and the opportunities and incentives for assimilation. Government on the basis of nationality is a kind
of discrimination designed to ensure that a particular national type is dominant, at least in the political sphere, within a given territory. When state
boundaries are aligned more or less with ethnic or national boundaries,
control of the state by representatives of the ethnic nation is facilitated and
members of other national groups can more easily be excluded from positions of influence. Practical nationalism often seems to consist of stock
arguments from debatable premises to justify excluding or subordinating
foreigners. Nationalists are sometimes called chauvinists and bigots. Some
of them seem to rationalize violent antipathies with faulty and inflexible
generalizations.

Given these similarities, one might reasonably expect that the social
scientists who study nationalism and those who study ethnic prejudice and
discrimination would pay close attention to each other's work. Ethnic conflict might be the term used to join the two fields of research.

The vast literature on nationalism, approached from the angle suggested by these conjectures, reveals two striking features. First, it contains
many detailed discussions of problems and historical developments that
have nothing directly to do with ethnocentrism or ethnic conflict as defined
by the model presented earlier or by Deutsch's theory of social mobilization
and political development. Second, it shows a surprising lack of interest in
ethnic conflict—or at least a surprising lack of clarity about its elements
and regularities. Apart from the work of Karl Deutsch, it shows almost no
interest in social scientific studies of prejudice and discrimination.

By far the most important of the distinctive topics discussed in the standard literature on nationalism is the shift from monarchy to democracy.
A simple story is often told in great detail. Long ago, before "the age of
nationalism," political life was based on ideas of natural hierarchy and
patriarchal authority. Not only did the great royal houses of Europe rule
ethnically mixed populations with which they had no particular ethnic affinities, but they ruled them as their natural superiors. A Bourbon was
more likely to marry a Habsburg (for example, Louis XVI and Marie An-
toinette) than either was to marry a commoner. From time to time countries changed rulers because of royal marriages. Sometimes whole
countries were given away as dowries. But in modern times—roughly since
the English, French, and American revolutions—political life has shifted
on its foundations. More weight now rests on the idea that all citizens are
naturally equal. Governments are now said to have been constructed out

of the individual "contractual" reasoning of their citizens about relative costs and benefits. Countries have sometimes cut the heads off monarchs who used to regard them as their private possessions, and royals have begun to marry commoners (for example, the fairy-tale marriage of Charles and Diana). This shift from dynastic principles of legitimacy to a democratic or republican basis for political life has stretched over many centuries, and its glacial advance gives it the appearance of something providential, as Tocqueville observed. It has been connected at many points with changing attitudes toward vernacular languages and with a growing sense of the political significance of other popular cultural traits—in other words, with a growing national or ethnic consciousness. These connections are discussed in detail in the literature on nationalism. The word itself, it becomes clear, can sometimes refer to the sovereignty of the people or the nation as against the sovereignty of traditional sovereigns. Nationalism can be just another word for democracy.

Now, not everything can be investigated at once. Lack of attention to ethnic conflict may be just the necessary result of paying more attention to other things. It may be the other side of the coin, the side that is not so visible or easy to document. But is it really true that those who write about nationalism tend to be unaware of something as elementary as ethnic conflict? To illustrate my suggestion, one celebrated study will have to stand for all the rest.

Benedict Anderson's *Imagined Communities* (1983) features a willingness to ignore distracting details in order to make a few things clear and a useful division of the history of nationalism into four overlapping periods, namely, creole (before about 1830, when the Americans, North and South, led not just the French but also the English in rebelling "nationally" against dynastic rule); popular-vernacular (the whole of the nineteenth century, when the polyglot European empires began to crumble because of their internal linguistic or nationality tensions, culminating in the collapse of Ottoman, Romanov, and Habsburg rule following World War I); official (from the middle of the nineteenth century to the present, when Hanoverians became Windsors, so to speak, and ruling oligarchies everywhere began to deck themselves out in "national drag," the better to placate or assimilate their rebellious subjects); and colonial (from about 1920 to the present, when decolonizing nationalism in the Third World produced multinational nations such as India, Pakistan, Bangladesh, Indonesia, Nigeria, Sri Lanka, and Vietnam).

From our present perspective, the most interesting part of Anderson's historical panorama is his description of the second phase of nationalism, the vernacular one. It provides, in effect, a model of nationalism as ethnic or linguistic conflict. By isolating this phase, Anderson cuts away the other elements of nationalism (republicanism, militarism, imperialism) to make linguistic conflict stand out more clearly. But he does not dwell on the fact that ethnic or linguistic conflict is the heart of the matter. He does not, for example, cite Deutsch's work, nor does he even line up all the elements of his own account of ethnic conflict in an orderly way.[5] All the necessary elements are present in his discussion—contact (under the rubric "print-capitalism"), cultural differences ("vernaculars"), and of course nationalism or ethnocentrism—but the closest he comes to a clear statement is when he says that what "made the new [national] communities imaginable was a half-fortuitous, but explosive, interaction between a system of production and productive relations (capitalism), a technology of communication (print), and the fatality of human linguistic diversity" (p. 46). A few similar statements are scattered through the book (see pp. 40, 49, 66, 75–76, 81, 106 and 135), but they do not suffice to override its basic theme nor even to cancel one flat declaration (discussed below) that points readers away from ethnic conflict.

Anderson's thesis is that nations must be understood as *imagined* communities. His insistence on this point is puzzling because, by his own admission, the nation is not set apart from any other relevant community (any community larger than a face-to-face group: see p. 15) by the fact that it must be imagined. Nonetheless, as imagined communities, nations are apparently best understood not in terms of what is natural or given about them but as "cultural artefacts." According to Anderson, the nation is essentially a recent, culturally heterogeneous collection of people bound together by myths about homogeneity and antiquity; nationalists are people who create these myths (the "shrunken imaginings of recent history," p. 16) or who live in their grip. Enlightened readers, one gathers, will discount or ignore altogether the substantial ethnic or cultural homogeneity of some exemplary nations—France, Germany, Greece, Hungary, Ireland, Italy, Japan, Norway, Poland, and Sweden, for example—and put aside, therefore, any thoughts about their possible relations to the processes of ethnic conflict.

The misleading declaration, which reinforces the main theme of the book, is the following: "Language is not an instrument of exclusion: in principle, anyone can learn any language. On the contrary, it is fundamentally inclusive, limited only by the fatality of Babel: no one lives long enough to learn *all* languages. Print-language is what invents nationalism, not *a* particular language per se" (p. 122). Without being simply wrong, this statement manages to point in the wrong direction. Ethnic conflict has in fact been a crucial element of nationalism, as Anderson cannot help showing, and although admittedly no particular language has "invented" nationalism, the phenomenon can hardly be understood without paying attention to the conflicts between spoken as well as written languages.

A simple model of ethnic conflict—of the processes at work in vernacular nationalism—might bring some needed clarity to Anderson's discussion and others like it. But which of the two models discussed earlier might be the more helpful, Deutsch's model of social mobilization and political development or the model of ethnic conflict presented in Chapter 5? Their similarities have already been shown. What about their differences?

Let me begin by indicating the different purposes the models were meant to serve. Deutsch worked out his analysis of nationalism in order to provide more reliable, scientifically based predictions of the growth or decline of political communities globally and in particular states or nations. His basic questions had to do with the merging and splitting of peoples. "Which ideas and attitudes have spread more widely during the last fifty years: internationalism or nationalism, constitutional government or revolution, tolerance or repression, peace or war?" (p. 15). Are the world's peoples becoming more similar to each other or more diverse? Is mankind becoming more nearly one political community, or is it becoming more fragmented and ungovernable? What are the prospects for peace and order in particular states? Can quantitative measurements be used to make reliable predictions? What does the future hold for Nigeria, for example? Will the forces drawing all its citizens together prevail over the pathological processes that are driving them apart, or will Nigeria succumb to its internal tensions? Deutsch's aim was to develop a predictive social science of nationalism and nationality that would be able to give practical guidance to those in authority—a kind of distant early warning system of nationalist storms. To this end, nationalism had to be seen not simply as a subjective state of mind but as one with "tangible roots" in social processes that could be measured and projected (p. 16). Science, he concluded, must be harnessed to serve those struggling to master "the challenge of world order and world government" (p. 193).

With this goal in mind—in order to "facilitate some prediction and control of events"—Deutsch sought a "conceptual model of the processes of nationalism and nationality" that would be operational and testable. Each of its concepts, he declared, should be "clearly specified in terms of possible observations or measurements, from which it is derived and by which it can be tested." Each should fit into "statements specific enough to exclude the possibility of certain observational data or results, so that, if these results are found, the concept clearly will have to be revised." In short, each concept should be "critical," and the model should be falsifiable (that is, testable). The model must not be "so vague and elastic as to fit all conceivable empirical results" (p. 86).

Given these practical objectives, Deutsch's quantitative reasoning was subordinate to his search for indicators. His concepts were developed with an eye to the categories used by statistical agencies. His most important quantitative relationships were presented not mathematically but verbally. The equations in his text and appendices are accounting identities (for example, $A+D = P$) or formulas useful for interpolating and extending population time series.

The empirical look of Deutsch's analysis is somewhat misleading, however. Closer inspection reveals that it has at least as much to do with searching for statistics as with analyzing data or clarifying relationships. "Furnishing frameworks for statistics which do not exist" is the way Deutsch put a likely objection. Deutsch meets this objection by insisting that today's impossible challenge may well be tomorrow's routine achievement. "It is not our purpose here to collect all these statistics, but rather to show that they can be collected and that they are worth collecting. If we succeed in showing this, then the means and manpower for the processing of the available statistics may well be found some day" (p. 127). The main task now is not to show where we are or what exists but to give directions for future research: "The center of interest is in the research that has not yet been done and that could be done by the methods here suggested" (p. 189; compare Deutsch, 1960; Russett et al., 1965).

Turning now to the model of ethnic conflict that was presented in Chapter 5, we find at the heart of it a small set of relatively simple equations. Like Deutsch's analysis of nationalism, it deals with only two groups and it provides only a partial representation of a much more complicated dynamic process—a rough, large-scale map, as it were, of a large territory. Both maps exaggerate some features of the terrain and deliberately ignore others, but only the model of ethnic conflict boldly employs variables for which no good measures can be defined, let alone found in available statistics, and it comes with the warning that the world of two groups it depicts is strictly imaginary. Yet the model of ethnic conflict is complete in the sense that all its basic relationships are spelled out. In principle the system itself determines the behavior of all its endogenous variables. Deutsch's quantitative reasoning is more open-ended: his equations are only parts of a partial representation of the phenomena of interest. Any attempt to set out his whole theory mathematically would produce something quite formidable (compare Rapoport, 1983; Zinnes and Muncaster, 1987). The model of ethnic conflict, by contrast, is simplicity itself. Those few with a severe allergy to algebra may turn away in fear or disgust, but those repelled by a properly mathematical expression of Deutsch's reasoning would be legion.

These broad contrasts may be clarified by briefly considering two more specific differences. The first has to do with the definition of assimilation. For Deutsch, it is a matter of the growth of the assimilated population A and the decline or disappearance of the differentiated population D as a result of different rates of natural increase and the flow of people between the two groups. Assimilation is defined as a condition and visualized as a one-way process. The assimilated population of a country includes its native-born citizens (who have presumably grown up speaking its dominant language as their mother tongue and learning its culture as their own) as well as those of its other citizens who have undergone the process of assimilation as usually understood. Thus Germans in Germany who speak German as their mother tongue are assimilated (with respect to language) along with migrant Poles or Russians who have learned German as a second language. Deutsch visualizes assimilation as a kind of strengthening absorption that nourishes one group numerically while necessarily (by definition) weakening or eliminating another. But those others may wish to preserve their culture and identity. Assimilation may thus be a matter of mutual accommodation rather than simple absorption. The only "border crossings" taken into account in Deutsch's analysis, however, are from the minority into the majority. Nothing is said about movements in the opposite direction or about the effects on the majority of incorporating one or more partially assimilated minorities. In these respects, the proposed statistical analysis, although it meshes with the conventions of statistical agencies, seems far from the social and psychological realities of contact between ethnic groups. In the model of ethnic conflict, by contrast, assimilation is more a matter of the amalgamation of different groups and the homogenization of their cultures or ways of life. It is measured by changes in the value of D, some kind of weighted average of all the customs and values that distinguish the people on one side of an ethnic boundary from those on the other side. Admittedly, little is said about how assimilation in this sense will come about, if it does. It might be achieved by creating a playful, postmodern pastiche of the traditional spiritual, culinary, linguistic, artistic, and sartorial resources of both groups—a kind of "shreds and patches" uniformity—but there is a presumption, in line with what Deutsch suggests, that it will come about mainly at the expense of the culture or identity of the smaller and less mobilized of the two groups.

The second specific difference worth noting has to do with the representation of nationalism or ethnic conflict. Apart from the ratio H/P, Deutsch's analysis contains no variable equivalent to E as defined in Chapter 5. His mathematical model is essentially an analysis of processes of

assimilation and differentiation, not a model of nationalism or ethnic conflict as a force affecting other variables. Only in his nonmathematical discussion does Deutsch point to the connections between the processes
described by his model and the phenomena covered by the term *nationalism.*

How one judges these differences will depend in part on how one un-
derstands the purposes of model-building. Deutsch hoped to use his model,
or one like it, to predict and control the consolidation or disintegration of
political communities. For this purpose, statistical realism was crucial. But
his hope of using scientific methods of objective observation and statistical
analysis to predict the course of national and world development, so that
policy makers could be warned about the potential danger spots and shown
how to guide the fundamental processes of social mobilization and national development into constructive channels, enabling them to master
the challenge of world order and world government—all this hopeful 1950s
social science scientism seems to have been pretty much a will-o'-the-wisp.
The United Nations now collects many statistics of the kind Deutsch was
calling for, but the future of Nigeria, or the world, remains as hidden as
before. Indeed, the keynote of the nineties seems to be crisis management,
not fine tuning. Does anyone today think that the collapse of the Soviet
Union or of Yugoslavia could have been better anticipated by giving larger
research grants to the social science moles who may have been burrowing
in their statistical archives?

The model of ethnic conflict was introduced in Chapter 5 to serve more
modest purposes. Its main purpose was only to crystallize a way of thinking
about contact and conflict. It was then used to bring out as clearly as possible the difficulties that block any straightforward statistical testing of this
way of thinking (Chapter 6). For these purposes, simplicity and complete-
ness were crucial; testability, and the kind of realism that goes with it,
were not.

Economists, like artists, it is said, fall in love with their models. My
partiality may have made me unjust to Deutsch's pioneering effort, from
which my own model obviously derives. Those students of nationalism and
ethnic conflict who have already developed the habits of economists, if not
of artists, will no doubt want to propose better models of their own. But I
am more concerned at this point with the larger number of social scientists
who may have never known the charm of a mathematical model. These
cooler heads may have been told that any model presented for their admiration should be more than just an image of perfection: they may insist
that it be demonstrably testable. They may be prepared to succumb to one
whose parameters can actually be measured using hard data, but they may
spurn one that just raises such expectations in order to dash them to the

ground. These cooler heads may be drawn to Deutsch's more testable-looking analysis of nationalism. But his model only *looks* more testable, and testability may not be the most important consideration when choosing models, as I have already shown. The real merits and shortcomings of the models on display here may have little to do with their relative testability.

The most striking, most intriguing, and perhaps most important difference between them remains to be considered. It has to do with their names. One is labeled a model of nationalism, whereas the other is called a model of ethnic conflict. This nominal difference may be more significant than it seems. But why?

Nationalism is obviously more than just ethnic or linguistic conflict, and in a world of many ethnic groups, ethnic conflict itself is a very complicated thing. Simple models of ethnic conflict may contribute to the understanding of nationalism, it seems, but the great contribution that the literature on nationalism can make to the understanding of ethnic conflict is its insistence that political factors and arrangements be given careful attention. Indeed, some scholars argue that a fundamental distinction between state and nation must always be made in any discussion of nationalism (for example, Akzin, 1964; Connor, 1994; Gellner, 1983).

The importance of doing so becomes clear even in Anderson's schematic presentation, with its emphasis on imagined communities, when he shows the differences between vernacular nationalism and official nationalism. The former is rightly seen as a popular force that often works to break states up into their all-too-real ethnic or national components. Official nationalism, by contrast, is "something emanating from the state and serving the interests of the state first and foremost" (p. 145). It is the response of dominant groups to the fissiparous tendencies of popular-vernacular agitators. It uses all the "policy levers" of compulsory state-controlled education, state-controlled propaganda, official rewriting of history, militarism, and endless affirmations of identity to conceal or overcome some awkward discrepancy between state and nation (p. 95). Although clumsy practitioners of its high arts sometimes produce explosions, official nationalism is generally a force tending to bind the citizens of a state together—by setting them against their foreign rivals. Official nationalists turn the attention of the people away from their intramural differences by getting them to focus their attention on the still greater differences that divide them from the truly strange and threatening people on the other side of the line, across the river, or over the oceans, on another continent. That those in authority can do this, and that they are often sorely tempted to do it, in order to bolster their own authority or to win re-election, is one reason why it matters a great deal how exactly the relations between political structures (or states) and ethnic differences (or nations) are arranged.

There is a fundamental practical question that is sometimes highlighted in the literature on nationalism (for example, Gellner, 1983, p. 1; Kedourie, 1961, p. 9) but that is almost always ignored in the literature on ethnic conflict, especially the whole literature on ethnic prejudice and discrimination, with its offshoots such as realistic conflict theory and social identity theory. The question is, what should be the relation between political structures and ethnic or cultural differences? For more than a century discussion of this question has centered on the so-called principle of nationalities—the boundaries of sovereign states should correspond, where possible, to the boundaries of ethnic nations. Scholars as well as statesmen have frequently debated the merits and shortcomings of this practical maxim. Its proponents see it as a solution to the problem of ethnic conflict: good fences make good neighbors (compare Kaufmann, 1996). Its critics, however, see it as a prime cause of war because, even if mixed populations could somehow be separated without trampling on human rights, doing so would just align the interests of governments and military establishments with the passions of bigots. The various arguments for and against nationalism in this sense (support for the principle of nationalities) are not easily summarized and might generally be clarified by routinely separating the question of sovereignty (whether states should be sovereign) from the question of borders (roughly, whether the populations of states should be ethnically homogeneous). At any rate, even a quick inspection of the relevant literature reveals how foolish it would be to ascribe any of the main conflicting views simply to bigotry or prejudice.

Most historians trace widespread acceptance of the principle after about 1870 to the gradual dissemination of the philosophical doctrines of the middle and late eighteenth century. Thus Kedourie (1961), for example, after laying down on his first page that "nationalism is a doctrine that pretends to supply a criterion for the determination of the unit of population proper to enjoy a government exclusively its own," goes on to argue that Immanuel Kant's critical philosophy, which made autonomy the highest moral and political good, is ultimately responsible for the rise of political movements asserting national interests and national identity. Others give more attention to Rousseau or Herder (for example, Barnard, 1965; Berlin, 1976; Cohler, 1964; Taylor, 1995), but regardless of how scholars may trace its lineage, they imply that the principle of nationalities raises more complicated philosophical questions—questions having to do with the rejection of nature as a standard for human conduct and the rise of historicism—than does simple ignorance or bigotry. Nationalism—as support for this principle—they may decry, but they do not associate it with simple ego weakness or an inability to overcome crude rationalizations. It is associated in their minds with Rousseau, Kant, and Herder.

Given the limited resources of the English language, it would be surprising if the terms *nationalism* and *ethnic conflict* were never used to mark some of the distinctions just outlined. In fact, because of the way the basic term *ethnic conflict* is commonly used, ethnic conflict is generally regarded as a problem of conflict between groups within a nation or state. The familiar examples of ethnic conflict in recent years—the ones provided by the Soviet Union, Yugoslavia, Bosnia, Rwanda, Burundi, Nigeria, and Sri Lanka—have been internal in this sense. Conflicts between nations or states, on the other hand, are seen as a different kind of problem because they are external and governed only by international law. Different terms are generally used when discussing these problems, and the main one, for present purposes, is *nationalism*. Insofar as nationalism unifies a nation against its external enemies, whereas ethnic conflict divides and weakens it, they are not at all the same. Indeed, they are opposing forces.

Opposing forces are sometimes the same force, however, and different terms can sometimes refer to the same thing. "The morning star" and "the evening star" are common, different, and slightly misleading names for the same planet. There is obviously a need, from time to time, for a distinction between internal and external conflicts. But should the distinction be made by separating nationalism from ethnic conflict? There are other possible ways of marking the difference—for example, by separating ethnic nationalism from civic nationalism or by distinguishing, as Anderson does, popular-vernacular nationalism from official nationalism.

Names often hide things. A social scientist with a taste for exploring the confusing relations between words and things might find some food for thought in the realm of nationalism and ethnic conflict. The fundamental distinction between nationalism and internationalism or humanitarianism, for example, might repay close attention. The differences some scholars have seen between the patriotism exemplified by the English and the Americans, on one hand, and the nationalism illustrated by the Germans and the Russians, on the other, might be worth investigating. More recently, as already noted, a fundamental distinction between ethnic and civic nationalism has come to the fore. Its relation to official nationalism might well be examined, and likewise the relations of both to that familiar "banal nationalism" that may sometimes be the propaganda of those in official positions but that is more often perhaps just the habits and routines of everyday life (compare Billig, 1995).

Anyone exploring these scholarly byways is likely to be struck by the many and complicated ways in which social science separates the study of patriotism and nationalism from the study of domestic prejudice and discrimination. Neglect of ethnic or linguistic conflict as a distinct theme, I have argued, is characteristic of the standard literature on nationalism, but a complementary neglect is no less characteristic of the most important literature on ethnic prejudice and discrimination, which avoids any sustained discussion of nations and nationalism.

Differences of intellectual style obviously have something to do with this scholarly separatism. The two literatures generally fall on opposite sides of an important methodological divide. On the hermeneutic or interpretive side of this divide can be found most of the literature on nationalism, which tends to be idiographic in orientation and qualitative in method. Most of it has been written by historians and political scientists who have found, generally speaking, that the best way to answer the questions that interest them is to carry out detailed historical investigations of particular cases. These studies avoid simple, clear generalizations about the nature or the causes of nationalism. They implicitly deny that it is a single thing that can be explained by reference to a few general principles. Rather, nationalism comes to light as a bewildering concatenation of circumstances, feelings, ideas, forces, and institutions that can be understood only in its particular manifestations.[6] On the other side of the methodological divide, the side of naturalism or positivism, one finds most of the social scientific studies of ethnic prejudice and discrimination. They are nomothetic in orientation: their authors try to adhere to the methodological principles of modern natural science. They aim to discover and test broad principles or laws of behavior. The studies are implicitly or explicitly quantitative.[7]

Methodological or stylistic proclivities, deep as they may be, are not the only forces at work, however. Apparently different approaches to the same problem (an economic approach, a psychological approach, a mathematical approach, an interpretive approach) often turn out, on closer inspection, to be at bottom somewhat different uses of the same reasoning power to deal with different problems. To be sure, most of the literature on nationalism is idiographic, whereas most discussions of prejudice and discrimination are nomothetic, but there are some clear exceptions to this rule. Some important studies do not conform to type. Young-Bruehl (1996), for example, verges on being an interpretive study of ethnic prejudice, whereas Deutsch's work on nationalism and social communications illustrates a nomothetic approach to a topic usually dealt with historically. His academic background, substantive interests, and empirical materials were historical, and he obviously wrote about nationalism, but his methods and aspirations are quintessentially social scientific. His main theme was really ethnic conflict. He aimed to clarify not the ideas of particular nationalists but the objective conditions for their popularity. Why is it, he asked, that nationalist ideas are sometimes widely accepted but at other times or in other places generally rejected? His overall approach and concerns were remarkably similar to those of his contemporaries who studied ethnic prejudice and discrimination, and he cited many of their publications. Many historians and other social scientists may have been put off by his aggressively scientific style—his invoking of operational definitions, explicit hypotheses, mathematical equations, and quantitative data—or by his extravagant aspirations, and this may help to explain the neglect or misunderstanding of his work in much of the literature on nationalism. But its stylistic features and lofty goals cannot have impeded its acceptance by the quantitatively minded sociologists and social psychologists who study ethnic prejudice and discrimination. Yet they are even less likely to show any interest in it. The extensive literature on the contact hypothesis contains, so far as I can recall, not a single reference to it.

If perspicuous words are the light of human minds, as Hobbes said, then it may make a difference whether an example of ethnic prejudice and discrimination is called nationalism or ethnic conflict—even if, so to speak, by either name it smells the same. How these terms should be used by social scientists is not a question that can be settled by consulting a dictionary, nor can it be settled (Humpty Dumpty–style) by simply stipulating how in fact they are going to be used. They belong to our language and politics, not to any individual author. *Ethnic conflict* is a relatively new term, not yet very well established. Its meaning is still in flux. This book as a whole is my explanation of how I think it should be used. *Nationalism*, by contrast, is a long established and practically very important political term whose meaning is not easily explained and certainly is not open to any quick redefinition. The meanings of these terms may be clarified, however, and their employment perhaps improved a little, by reflecting on how they overlap in meaning and yet remain distinct.

Notes

Introduction

1. The quotations are from *The Spirit of the Laws*, bk. 20, chs. 1 and 2 (Montesquieu, 1989, p. 338). For other important remarks about the effects of commerce, see 4, 6; 5, 6; 18, 8; 19, 27 (pp. 38, 48, 289, 328). For an overall account of Montesquieu's argument, see Pangle (1973), and for a discussion of his defense of economic interest, see Hirschman (1977). Fukuyama (1992) provides a recent example of the "Montesquieuan" perspective on ethnic conflict.

2. Factual objections have an independent force vis-à-vis empirical conjectures, but the tendency to highlight particular facts sometimes has theoretical sources. Worth noting in this connection is a recent shift of opinion among leading intellectuals. A generation or two ago, most tended to regard ethnicity and ethnic conflict as vestiges of an earlier age, destined to disappear fairly quickly, since their causes were being eliminated by philosophical and material progress. More recently this view has been challenged, not just because of its empirical shortcomings but also because of its tendency to promote an oppressive ideal of social unity. Contemporary social scientists and political theorists often shine a more flattering light on "ethnicity" and "difference" than did their predecessors, without completely obscuring the negative side of these phenomena (e.g., Young, 1990; Young-Bruehl, 1996).

With regard to American domestic politics, the shift can be dated from Glazer and Moynihan (1963) and Gordon (1964), but see also Novak (1972). Connor (1994) includes many useful studies, particularly an influential 1972 essay, "Nation-Building or Nation-Destroying?," which severely criticizes the theories of political development or modernization popular a generation ago. Since 1945, the Third World and the Middle East have provided the great laboratories for the study of ethnic conflict. Among studies dealing with these areas, Horowitz (1985) stands out because of its empirical richness and theoretical subtlety. For a recent survey of ethnic conflicts in every part of the world, see Gurr (1993b). Kaufmann (1996, p. 160), provides a list of resolved ethnic civil wars from 1944 to 1994 with estimates

233

of casualties. On Switzerland, see Vuilleumier (1987) for a brief outline and Bory (1987) or Ebel and Fiala (1983) for revealing details.

3. Hard evidence of long-term historical trends is often extremely difficult to collect, but for some good evidence of the decline of prejudice in the United States since World War II, see Schuman, Steeh, and Bobo (1985), which summarizes the results of many relevant studies. The decline of "blatant racism" shown in this study is sometimes said to have been offset by the rise of "subtle racism" (sometimes called "symbolic racism" or "modern racism"), but relevant statistical series, were they available, might well show downward trends even in the more subtle forms of specific ethnic prejudices among Americans (Steeh and Schuman, 1992; Wilson, 1994).

4. Social science theories can also be, as Elisabeth Young-Bruehl has recently argued at length, "part of the problem of prejudice, not part of its solution" (Young-Bruehl, 1996, p. 15). How to get out of what she calls "the social scientific morass" (p. 2) and "the dark wood of existing theoretical prejudices" (p. 43) is not so clear, however. It may be, as she suggests, by critiquing the "essentialism" of conventional social scientific accounts of prejudice so that we can see its diverse forms more clearly and better understand the "orecticisms" or "ideologies of desire" that oppose movements of equality. But the better route to this goal may lie through the improvement of social scientific theories that inevitably employ essences or concepts (cf. Roth, 1994). At any rate, this book, like hers, aims to convey "a sense of the territory" by providing a "preliminary map" so that others can later make their own maps on the basis of their explorations, in which they discover, as their predecessors did, "all the ways in which the terrain as we experience it defies the map that gave us an orientation" (p. 39).

5. Other competing theories could of course be used to bring out, by contrast, some of the distinctive features of contact theory, for example, the "competition theory" advanced by Susan Olzak (1992). Rather than emphasizing segregation and inequality as causes of ethnic prejudice and discrimination, she emphasizes economic competition as an explanation for ethnic collective action. Her underlying theory and statistical investigations are discussed below, but for reasons that I trust will eventually become clear, realistic conflict theory and social identity theory provide simpler and more revealing contrasts with contact theory. Other important theories that throw light on the processes involved in ethnic conflict include attribution theory (Hewstone, 1989), belief congruence theory (Insko, Nacoste, and Moe, 1983; McKirnan, Smith, and Hamayan, 1983), norm violation theory (Deridder and Tripathi, 1992), power-threat theory (Blalock, 1967), response amplification theory (Katz, Hass, and Wackenhut, 1986), similarity-attraction theory (Byrne, 1969), social accommodation theory (Giles, 1973; Giles, Coupland, and Coupland, 1991), social exchange theory (Chadwick-Jones, 1976; Cook and Emerson, 1986; Homans, 1950, 1961; Kelley, 1968), and social learning theory (Bandura, 1986). Many of the particular points emphasized in these theories are discussed in connection with the model of ethnic conflict proposed in Chapter 5.

Chapter 1: Defining Terms

1. For a recent critical discussion of Allport's *Nature of Prejudice*, see Katz (1991), which concludes: "Insofar as Gordon Allport influenced the agenda of modern social psychological research on intergroup relations, it was probably in the

direction of making negative group attitudes and stereotypes the central topic of inquiry, and the cognitive perspective (whereby ethnic categorization and stereotyping are viewed as an instance of ordinary information processing) the dominant theoretical approach. . . . This perspective fosters an overemphasis on laboratory studies of internal psychological functions to the neglect of overt actions as they unfold in naturalistic multiethnic settings. It tends to overlook the societal context of intergroup phenomena—i.e., the larger environment of class structure, political alignments, economic forces, population distributions, and the like that influence attitudes toward racial policy issues" (p. 152). Much of what follows is a further elaboration and clarification of this insight. For a brief analysis of the development of Allport's ideas, see DeCarvalho (1993). Young-Bruehl (1996) provides a very contemporary analysis of the nature of prejudices and various critical comments on Allport's book.

2. By activating latent prejudices without doing anything to reveal their error, casual contact may actually strengthen prejudices. "We can understand the reason if we examine the perceptual situation in a casual contact. Suppose that on the street or in a store one sees a visible out-group member. By the association of ideas there is likely to come to mind a recollection of rumor, hearsay, tradition, or stereotype by which this out-group is known. Theoretically, every superficial contact we make with an out-group member could by the 'law of frequency' strengthen the adverse mental associations that we have. What is more, we are sensitized to perceive signs that will confirm our stereotypes. From a large number of Negroes in a subway we may select the one who is misbehaving for our attention and disapproval. The dozen or more well-behaved Negroes are overlooked, simply because prejudice screens and interprets our perceptions. . . . Casual contact, therefore, permits our thinking about out-groups to remain on the autistic level. We do not effectively communicate with the outsider, nor he with us" (p. 264). Whether this is the mechanism underlying the "sociocultural law" or statistical generalization Allport mentions will be discussed at length below.

3. More specifically, its authors, the "Berkeley Group," explained ethnocentrism, as measured by their E scale, in terms of authoritarianism, as measured by their famous F scale. They concluded with the remarkable claim that "it would not be difficult, on the basis of the clinical and genetic studies reported in this volume, to propose a program which, even in the present cultural pattern, could produce nonethnocentric personalities. All that is really essential is that children be genuinely loved and treated as individual humans" (Adorno et al., 1950, p. 975). The book is the classic example of a reductive psychological explanation of ethnic conflict, and its influence has not altogether disappeared, despite the many criticisms leveled against its theory and methods for more than forty years (see Forbes, 1985). References to it still abound in social science journals, and its theory lives on in social psychology textbooks as well as in the underpinnings of the contact hypothesis. For some recent discussions, generally defensive in character, see Gough and Bradley (1993); Jackson (1991); Meloen (1994); Stone, Lederer, and Christie (1993); Taylor and Moghaddam (1994); and Young-Bruehl (1996).

4. These brief remarks touch on a basic issue in the interpretation of ethnic conflict. There is a long and controversial tradition in the social sciences of seeking the clashing economic interests that are assumed to lie "below" conflicts expressed in racial, ethnic, or religious terms. Horowitz (1985, pp. 105–35, 224–26) deals well

and at some length with this "materialist" approach to understanding ethnic conflict. The issue is whether ethnic conflicts, which are obviously entangled with economic conflicts, including class conflicts, can be understood as essentially masks for the conflicts between classes or other economic groupings (cf. Bonacich, 1972; Olzak, 1992). A number of important considerations speak against this view (this attempt, as Horowitz says, "to place genocide on a solid economic foundation," p. 108). For example, ostensibly class parties in many countries have ethnically defined constituencies: it seems that class masks ethnicity more often than the other way around. In addition, ethnic groups often seem surprisingly willing to sacrifice economic interests for the sake of other objectives, whereas class loyalties across ethnic boundaries are at best weak. The workers of the world did not unite against war in 1914, nor have they since. The underlying motivations for mass political behavior are of course hard to sort out, and elite manipulation of mass attitudes is a fact of life. What is important for the present, as Horowitz puts it, "is simply to hold open the prospect of alternative explanations for mass ethnic behavior and to avoid making premature judgments about the motivation of the 'common man' that must rest ineluctably on either economic competition or elite manipulation" (p. 131). The relative unimportance of economic motives in ethnic conflict is an *assumption* of the following analysis, but the analysis as a whole will, I trust, tend to justify it.

It should be noted that the neoclassical "economics of discrimination" represented by Becker and Sowell (and by Arrow, 1972, 1973) is controversial even among economists (see Cain, 1986; Leblanc, 1995; Marshall, 1974; Reich, 1981; and Thurow, 1969), because it does not seem to fit the reality of mixed work forces and little overt discrimination in wages, but persistent differences in average incomes. The most serious shortcoming of the analysis from a strictly economic standpoint is its failure to provide a strictly economic explanation for persistent discrimination—indeed, "it predicts the absence of the phenomenon it was designed to explain" (Arrow, 1972, p. 192). The theory implies that less discriminatory employers in competitive markets, because of their willingness to employ the victims of discrimination (at lower wages than they would have to pay its perpetrators), will enjoy an advantage over their more discriminatory competitors and therefore should gradually displace them, eventually equalizing the wages of the two groups. Critics stress that this implication of the theory is at odds with the easily observed fact of persistent sexual as well as racial discrimination in employment. But the neoclassical analysis may have no purpose beyond discrediting other, less satisfactory economic analyses of prejudice and discrimination: it may establish no more than the impossibility of a strictly economic explanation for these phenomena. Rigorous economic analysis may have to be complemented by a broader theory about the social and political determinants of individual tastes and choices (compare Lang, 1986).

5. Two social psychological experiments that seem to have been forgotten, Lambert, Libman, and Poser (1960) and Buss and Portnoy (1967), illustrate this basic point more clearly and simply, with more "external validity," than do the standard experiments on discrimination in minimal group situations.

6. For a discussion of its relation to contact theory, see Johnston and Hewstone (1990), who suggest that it reinforces the "cognitive" preoccupations of contemporary contact theorists.

7. Until the theory is supplemented by an explanation or explanations of the

sort indicated, it is likely to strike outsiders, as it strikes some insiders, as untestable and circular: "The foremost theoretical problem in social-identity, and later self-categorization theory is that the explanation for behaviour hinges on the concept of salience [of different identities]. When social identity is salient individuals are said to act as group members (and should they fail to, the explanation is that social identity was not salient *enough*). However, this model is somewhat descriptive, and when used for explanation is potentially tautological" (Abrams, 1992, p. 61). Trying to solve this problem in all its generality, social identity theorists sometimes tie themselves in conceptual knots (e.g., Hogg and Abrams, 1988, pp. 25–26).

8. Needless to say, different social science theories, by emphasizing different behavioral regularities, tend to support different practical remedies for practical problems. To simplify, contact theory encourages reliance upon contact in the right situations to reduce prejudice, whereas realistic conflict theory and social identity theory stress leadership and other group-level processes. In this case, as generally, theories about facts can have implications for the ranking of values. But it is a vulgar error to accept or reject an empirical theory because of one's emotional reactions to its normative implications rather than because of one's judgment of its explanatory power and the accuracy of its empirical generalizations.

Chapter 2: A Social Experiment

1. Henceforth "race" will be used without quotation marks, despite the fact that conventional ideas about distinct races have no scientific justification (Banton, 1987; Banton and Harwood, 1975; Barkan, 1992; Marks, 1995; Montagu, 1972, 1974; Patai and Patai, 1989; Webster, 1992). Physical differences are important because they mark cultural distinctions and provide a basis for different group identities. The relevant differences between black and white American culture are hard to describe apart from the details of ethnographic studies such as Kochman (1981). For more abstract formulations, see Hale-Benson (1986) and Jones (1983, 1991) and the literature they cite. For some statistical detail, see Hacker (1992).

2. Raffel (1985) reports the results of two opinion surveys of the general population of the New Castle County School District, the first in 1977 and the second in 1983. They show a high level of opposition to busing in the suburbs and a slight overall increase in opposition between 1977 and 1983 but a slight decrease among public school parents, with strikingly different trends in the city and the suburbs, suggesting different trends among black and white parents from those shown in table 2.2. "The implementation of the metropolitan school desegregation order . . . did not lead to greater support for the policy of busing to achieve school desegregation. Although suburban views toward busing became slightly less negative, city opposition increased. Ironically, those whose children were supposed to benefit most directly from the policy, city black parents, increased their opposition" (p. 259).

Chapter 3: Two Simple Correlations

1. Other reviews of this literature include Amir (1969, 1976); Brewer and Miller (1984); Ford (1986); Harrington and Miller (1992); Jackson (1993); Johnston and

Hewstone (1990); Patchen (1995); Pettigrew (1986); Riordan (1978a); Rose (1981); Stephan (1987); and Stephan and Stephan (1996).

2. The term *prejudice* will generally be used to refer to the relevant attitudes and behaviors, in conformity with the practice in the literature being reviewed. An annoying but fundamentally uninteresting problem has to do with the confusing associations of *positive* and *negative*. A negative correlation between contact and prejudice (or negative attitudes) can be taken as evidence of a positive effect of contact on (the reduction of) prejudice—and vice versa. The same correlation can be labeled either "positive" or "negative" depending upon whether the dependent variable is prejudice as conventionally understood or good intergroup relations. If an increase in intergroup negativity were for some reason desired, as in wartime, for example, then positive effects would of course become negative.

3. The opinions studied are more or less the same as those sometimes used to define modern, subtle, or symbolic racism (Kinder and Sears, 1981; McConahay, 1986; McConahay and Hough, 1976; Sears, 1988). As Sigelman and Welch (1991, p. 120) point out, the fact that these opinions are quite controversial among blacks is a good reason for doubting that they are good measures of racism among whites (unless, of course, racism simply means taking a particular position on these controversial questions of public policy).

4. As Riordan (1978, p. 323) points out, most experimental or quasi-experimental studies of contact, particularly those in education, involve "program effects" as well as "contextual" or contact effects, and more attention should be paid to program effects when generalizing about the effects of contact. The earliest quantitative study of the contact hypothesis still occasionally cited employed a before-after research design that nicely illustrates the problem. Young (1932, pp. 16–18) reports an attempt to modify the racial attitudes of sixteen white graduate students in education by having them interact with successful, cultivated blacks at tea parties, musical afternoons, and so on. Although he provides almost no details, he was evidently disappointed by the results he observed. Even if the number of experimental subjects had been greater and the results more encouraging, there would have been a difficulty deciding whether to attribute the changes observed to contact with cultivated blacks, contact with liberal professors, or general trends in attitudes due to testing or to political events. A true and rather complex experiment would have been necessary to sort out these possibilities.

5. Surprisingly, this study is almost never cited in the literature on the contact hypothesis, unlike Stouffer et al. (1949), a much weaker study that is routinely cited. Among the reasons for its unjustified neglect are no doubt the fact that it was classified Secret for fifteen years (it was first published only in 1969) and that it is difficult to summarize. It has an enormous amount of information, qualitative as well as quantitative, about attitudes toward integration and its effects on attitudes among American soldiers. Its tabulations and quotations throw light on many questions of practical interest. For a brief summary with some key tables, see Moskos (1970).

6. A similar finding is reported by Dubey (1979), who examined caste "ethnocentrism" among residents of "backward caste housing societies"—a form of public housing that mixes relatively large numbers of untouchables with some individuals from higher castes—in two states in India. Ethnocentric attitudes were related to length of residence in the mixed housing colonies but were differently related for

higher and lower castes. "The higher castes tend to become less ethnocentric toward the lower castes, while the lower castes tend to develop reverse ethnocentrism—prejudices against the higher castes" (p. 66).

7. Broad generalizations of this sort, though rarely challenged, are surprisingly difficult to prove when they are, for those who challenge them are likely to raise questions about the meaning of such emotionally loaded terms as *race* and *prejudice*. The difficulty is illustrated by Harlan (1942), one of the quantitative studies Allport (1954) cites to illustrate the "law" that "prejudice varies with the numerical density of a minority group" (p. 263). It deals with the attitudes of 502 non-Jewish college students toward Jews. The students, who were drawn from four colleges, three in the South and one in the North, were also classified by the size and location of their home communities. Northern students had on average less favorable attitudes toward Jews than southern students, and students from larger towns and cities, where Jews were a larger proportion of the population, tended to have less favorable attitudes. Using the four schools as a basis for comparison, Harlan found that favorable attitudes were inversely related to the proportion of Jewish students in each school. In short, high frequency of contact seemed to produce prejudice rather than diminish it (see also Ehrlich, 1961). But interaction with Jews—having one or more Jewish friends—was associated among these students with favorable attitudes. For some hard evidence of regional differences in attitudes in the United States, see Schuman, Steeh, and Bobo (1985).

8. Selznick and Steinberg (1969) provide a thorough analysis of the individual psychology of prejudice that highlights the education-prejudice relation. Schuman and Gruenberg (1970) report a very strong correlation (r = .90) between "white racial liberalism" and median years of education across the fifteen cities of their study. For a recent review of the relevant literature and other relevant references, see Wagner and Zick (1995).

9. The two variables are (a) the Atlas Narodov Mira index of ethnic and linguistic fractionalization mentioned earlier, calculated from census data from the early 1960s, and (b) the sum of deaths from domestic political violence between 1961 and 1967, based on reports in the *New York Times*. The distribution of the "deaths" variable is badly skewed: ninety-two of the 134 countries for which counts are available show fewer than 100 deaths, but 22 record more than 1,000 deaths, and one, Indonesia, has a total of 575,424 for the period in question. To "normalize" this distribution without ignoring the outliers altogether, the data were subjected to a logarithmic transformation (after adding 0.5 to all the values so that the logarithm of zero deaths would be defined and would have a reasonable value). If the six highest values (ten thousand or more deaths) are simply truncated, the correlation between fractionalization and the log of deaths, controlling for population, is only slightly reduced (r = .25).

Chapter 4: Situations Versus Levels of Analysis

1. Allport's (1954) presentation of the contact hypothesis featured a basic distinction between casual contact and true acquaintance. Casual contact was said to breed antagonism because it permitted the thinking of those involved to remain on an autistic level; true acquaintance was said to undermine stereotypes and thus to reduce prejudice. From a practical perspective the problem was obviously how to

foster true acquaintance without encouraging casual contact. In order to do so, one must at least be able to distinguish the two kinds of contact on some basis other than their different effects. Allport provided a list of about thirty variables, grouped under six headings, that he thought might be worth investigating as determinants of the effects of contact. "In order to predict the effects of contact on attitudes we should ideally study the consequences of each of [these] variables acting both separately and in combination," he wrote (p. 262). Out of this list a contact theory developed that features distinctions between different situations of contact (e.g., situations in which an equal status condition is or is not satisfied) rather than distinctions having to do with the persons involved (their friendliness, for example) or the background of their association (the history of relations between their groups). Social scientists such as Pettigrew seem to have emphasized situational differences because of their obvious practical importance. As Stephan and Stephan (1996, p. 63) point out, "The problem-solving orientation of the researchers led them to be interested primarily in variables that could be controlled in actual intergroup encounters." Situations of contact can in principle be controlled; personalities and histories have to be taken as given, at least initially.

A less practical kind of contact theory could be developed by shifting attention from different situations of contact to qualitatively different kinds of contact in a given situation. For example, there is obviously a difference between friendly and unfriendly contact, and these kinds of contact may have different effects on attitudes (Tzeng and Jackson, 1994). Similarly, contact between people who are disposed to meet as equals can be distinguished from contact between people disposed to struggle for status or prestige, and these two kinds of contact may have different attitudinal correlates. But there is a great difference, practically and scientifically, between our wish that people meet as equals and their wish to do so. Theories that focus on qualitatively different kinds of contact, treating other people's wishes or other dispositions as ultimate explanations, do not help us to close the gap.

Contact theory is construed here as a set of hypotheses about the situational "specification" of the statistical relation between contact and prejudice (see Lazarsfeld, 1955, and Rosenberg, 1968, for good explanations of interaction in the language of "survey analysis"). The underlying logic of the Allport-Pettigrew theory is that of the analysis of covariance, as Smith (1994) seems to have been the first to recognize clearly.

2. Further methodological reflections on the studies already summarized could suggest a fourth or fifth possibility. A line could be drawn after the observational studies of interaction in order to heighten the contrast between them and the rest of the studies of the contact hypothesis. The real (causal) correlation between contact and prejudice is always positive (more contact leads to more prejudice), one could say, but the observational studies of interaction (on one side of the line) consistently show negative correlations because of a crucial methodological weakness. These studies invite subjects to express their ethnic attitudes through their responses to questions about contact, and then they treat the contacts revealed by such responses as the causes of the causally prior attitudes. Because of this confusion of cause and effect, one could argue, such studies almost always produce results that favor the layman's contact hypothesis. But as soon as the line is crossed, the observed correlations become a mixture of positive and negative, and the farther

one moves from the line the more positive (on average) they become. They become consistently more positive (more contact, more prejudice) when the studies of proportions are reached. Some of the best studies of interaction and proximity may seem to violate this rule and thus to support the more familiar contact hypothesis, but methodological aspersions could be cast on these studies as well. For example, the truly experimental studies of interaction may demonstrate only the ability of college sophomores to "psych out" their psych professors and their willingness to help them prove the hypotheses they want to prove. Similarly, the most famous quasi-experimental studies of proximity may seem to support the conventional contact hypothesis (more contact, less prejudice), but perhaps they only show the ability of quasi-experimenters (presidents, generals, public housing directors) to influence the attitudes of their subordinates. In short, the real underlying relation between contact and prejudice—the positive correlation—may be covered over less thickly by well-designed experiments (e.g., Cook, 1969) than by poorly designed ones (e.g., Barnard and Benn, 1988), and it may come through more clearly still in studies of aggregates than in studies of individuals. The most important reasons for not pursuing this line of thought will become clearer as the reasons for emphasizing an aggregate-individual distinction are explained in Chapter 5 (see also Powers and Ellison, 1995).

3. One of the fundamental distinctions in Donald Horowitz's analysis of ethnic conflict is the distinction between systems in which different ethnic groups are "ranked" and those in which they are "unranked" in the sense that each group has a full set of social strata and there is no generally recognized hierarchy of ethnic groups (Horowitz, 1985, pp. 21–36). With respect to blacks and whites, the American South fifty years ago was a ranked system in which interracial contact partook of caste etiquette and was suffused with deference or its opposite. Ranked systems can of course become unranked, and vice versa. As Horowitz rightly observes, "among the engines of change is ethnic conflict itself" (p. 32).

For a revealing historical account of how the principles of superiority and subordination applied to the details of daily life in the South before the 1930s, see Doyle (1971). For a clear analysis of the rules that developed for the employment of black and white labor in the same firms, see Dewey (1952).

4. Even its intuitive plausibility may be challenged in light of the observation by Jackman and Crane (1986, pp. 481–82) that traditional marriage is "an intimate relationship of inequality" and that men can be very adept at discriminating against women in a friendly way. "Men, who almost uniformly experience high levels of personal contact with women, tend to express positive affective dispositions toward women, while they withhold support for the promotion of women's equality. . . . As women have long understood implicitly, intergroup friendship increases the bonds of affection with subordinates, but it does not undercut the discrimination that defines the unequal relationship between the two groups." Demeaning stereotypes can evidently survive intimacy and true acquaintance, and more generally, meeting as equals is no guarantee of a desire to remain on an equal footing: it may only set the stage for a struggle for superiority.

5. For an example of artificiality, one could hardly do better than Thompson (1993). Given the abundance of raw materials—interracial competition and cooperation in intercollegiate and professional sports—one might expect an abundance

of relevant studies of the Allport-Pettigrew competition-cooperation hypothesis. In fact such studies are scarce. The only detailed study I know of is McClendon and Eitzen (1975), which deals with interracial contact on college basketball teams. Unfortunately, the study's serious weaknesses of sampling and measurement greatly reduce the value of its results. The small attitudinal differences observed are very hard to interpret. White players on winning teams seemed to be more favorably disposed to blacks, but contact in the situation of cooperative interdependence seemed to have no relevant effects. The lack of relevant attitudinal differences among black players led the authors to the implausible conjecture that "the theory of superordinate goals is not valid for minorities such as blacks" (p. 938). In a study that compared desegregated high schools, Slavin and Madden (1979) found that individual participation on a sports team with students of another race was one of the factors that improved racial attitudes and behaviors among both blacks and whites.

Studies of American soldiers in Vietnam more detailed than any I have seen might throw an interesting light on contact theory, even if no practical purpose would be served by publishing their results. Contact with Vietnamese friends and enemies presumably affected American attitudes toward the Vietnamese, but it also seems to have been associated with a remarkably high level of racial tension among American combat soldiers, including riots and assaults on officers ("fragging"), despite their cooperative interdependence "on an equal footing in a common project of life and death importance." According to a recent book based upon lengthy interviews with Vietnam veterans, many veterans say that "there were two wars going on—one out in the boonies against the V.C., another in the rear between blacks and whites. I felt safer in the boonies." The author explains: "Virtually all combat units were racially integrated and mostly color-blind in combat, but when they came to the rear, social cohesion fell to pieces. Men segregated themselves rigidly along racial lines in the rear. . . . Racially motivated killings and riots were common in Vietnam. American soldiers in the rear were not safe *from each other*" (Shay, 1994, p. 60). Better relations in combat than in the rear can be seen as support for contact theory, but given the poor relations overall, it is rather feeble support (cf. Fiman, Borus, and Stanton, 1975; Landis, Hope, and Day, 1984).

6. These "enemies" may, however, become friends, as Slavin (1985, p. 58) points out: "Cross-race friendships formed outside cooperative groups account for some of the effects of cooperative learning on dyadic interracial friendships. *In theory, this should not happen.* After all, the teams are usually in competition with each other" (emphasis added). Theory and facts are at odds, or the facts fit another theory.

7. With respect to "cooperative learning," Slavin (1985) shrewdly observes that the assignment of students of different races or ethnicities to work together "communicates unequivocal support on the teacher's part for the idea that interracial or interethnic interaction is officially sanctioned" (p. 48). Even if nothing is said, the assignments clearly legitimize friendly contact across group lines. "The fact that the teacher assigns students to racially mixed learning groups clearly indicates teacher approval of interracial interaction" (p. 57).

8. It is sometimes forgotten that six of Allport's thirty or so contact variables have to do with the "social atmosphere surrounding the contact." Two of these six point to precisely the considerations that critics of contact theory say it neglects,

namely, "d. Is the contact perceived in terms of intergroup relations or not perceived as such? e. Is the contact regarded as 'typical' or as 'exceptional'?" (Allport, 1954, p. 263). It may nonetheless be true that contact theorists have a shortsighted understanding of the relevant contextual variables. Just as they tend to focus on "situational equal status" for the good practical reasons already explained, they may tend to focus on cooperative interdependence "in the situation," emphasizing the individuals who are in contact rather than the groups to which they belong.

A rather tangled set of quotations may provide additional insight into the underlying issues by showing how they are commonly discussed. In the introductory chapter to a book on contact and conflict, Miles Hewstone and Rupert Brown quote three passages from a collection of papers on the psychology of desegregation (Miller and Brewer, 1984) to illustrate the loose way—failing to distinguish interpersonal from intergroup contact—in which the contact hypothesis is often stated: "In a foreword [to the book in question, Lois Wladis] Hoffman [president of the Society for the Psychological Study of Social Issues, which had sponsored the collection] refers to the contact hypothesis in its simplest form as the idea that 'attitudes toward a disliked *social group will become more positive with increased interpersonal* interaction' (p. xiii, emphasis added). In apparent contradiction, the editors themselves describe, in their preface, the contact hypothesis as the idea 'that prejudice and hostility between *members of segregated groups* can be reduced by promoting the frequency and intensity of *intergroup* contact' (p. xv, emphases added). However, a few pages later, the same authors summarize the contact hypothesis as the idea that 'one's behaviour and attitudes towards *members of a disliked social category* will become more positive after direct *interpersonal* interaction with them' (p. 2). This looseness of terminology is at best careless, and at worst confusing for any reader trying to decide how best to implement a programme of intergroup contact. Such laxity also glosses over the theoretically important distinction between 'interpersonal' and 'intergroup' behaviour" (Hewstone and Brown, 1986, p. 13).

The distinction that Hewstone and Brown claimed was being neglected, despite being of fundamental importance, has to do with the salience of the relevant social categories and the perceived "typicalness" of the individuals involved in contact. "Both interpersonal and intergroup behaviour are the actions of individuals, but in one case they are the actions of individuals *qua* individuals, while in the other they are actions of individuals *qua* group members" (p. 14). How to separate the actions of individuals as individuals from their actions as group members is a baffling problem on which there is a growing social psychological literature. See Bargal (1990); Doise (1978); Granberg (1992); Sarup (1992); Tajfel (1981); and Taylor and Moghaddam (1994).

9. The relevant technical literature is not for the mathematically faint-hearted, who may shrink from the complicated notation needed to state the problem rigorously, let alone the subtle reasoning involved in exploring its intricacies. A glance at some standard references in the economics literature (e.g., Green, 1964; Nataf, 1968; Schlicht, 1985; and Theil, 1954) will quickly show what I mean. The political science and sociology literature is unfortunately not much more accessible (see Erbring, 1990; Hannan, 1971; Achen and Shively, 1995). For further examples demonstrating that the problem exists, see Robinson (1950). Alker (1969) provides a good, relatively simple explanation of its broader import.

Chapter 5: A Model of Ethnic Conflict

1. Deutsch (1966) is the immediate source of the model to be developed in this chapter, but its principles are similar to those that underlie Kevin Lang's "language theory of discrimination" (Lang, 1986). Little will be said, however, about nations or nationalism or about the different "languages" spoken by blacks and whites in the United States, since discussion of these topics would raise difficult and distracting questions best ignored at this point. Some of these questions are discussed in the Appendix on nationalism, where Deutsch's model is explained in his own terms.

2. The sociological and social psychological theories mentioned in the Introduction (note 5) throw light on the details of these processes. These theoretical resources can be supplemented by the literature on language and ethnicity such as Giles and Johnson (1981) or Edwards (1994), but particularly Giles (1977), which contains much relevant material despite having few references in its subject index to contact, conflict, discrimination, ethnocentrism, gods, prejudice, segregation, social distance, or stereotyping.

3. *Cultural differences* is an attempt to do justice, at the level of abstraction suitable for a model or theory, to the insight behind Donald Horowitz's remark about the importance of qualitative as well as quantitative differences in contact: "To ask purely objective questions, such as whether increasing intergroup contact accelerates or retards conflict, is to miss the decisive impact of the quality of that contact" (Horowitz, 1985, p. 182). The quality of contact here refers to "the psychology of group juxtapositions" because of the particular inner conflicts and uncertainties activated by particular outsiders with particular cultural traits, in other words, "the emotional concomitants of group traits and interactions." Broad differences in educational and technological advancement or backwardness are often important in relations among groups, as Horowitz shows, but many other dimensions of difference may also be important.

Following up this insight necessarily involves a move away from broad sociological or psychological generalizations toward the analysis of particular historical narratives: "If there is a group psychology, can it be understood without exploring the idiosyncratic recesses of each individual culture from which it springs?" (p. 183). This insight also has implications, as Horowitz points out, for the much-discussed "narcissism of small differences." The narcissism is certainly real, but the smallness of the relevant differences may be a bit exaggerated, the result of a failure to remember that small differences examined close up tend to look bigger than bigger differences further away (cf. Young-Bruehl, 1996). For additional quantitative evidence of the importance of cultural differences, see LeVine and Campbell (1972), pp. 177–81.

4. Readers interested in the details of the situation that has served as a model, so to speak, for my model of ethnic conflict may wish to consult Laczko (1995), Lieberson (1970), Joy (1992), or Pal (1993). For a more theoretical account of linguistic conflict that pays considerable attention to the Canadian situation, see Laponce (1987). Bashevkin (1991) and McRoberts (1988) analyze the broader context of the French-English language problem provided by Canadian nationalism. To link the Canada-Quebec case to others, it may be useful—not too misleading—to say that it corresponds, in a "first world" context, to a secessionist movement by a back-

ward group in an advanced region (compare Horowitz, 1985, pp. 230–65). Some of the complexities of the case have to do with the relatively advanced status of Montreal in relation to the rest of Quebec, together with the "external" sources of relevant in-migration. I have discussed some of the history and relevant details in two short publications (Forbes, 1993, 1996). They may be taken to illustrate, with qualifications, Horowitz's generalization that "ethnically differentiated settlers provoke a separatist response" (1985, p. 263).

5. Compare Horowitz (1985), pp. 223–24: "Symbolic claims are not readily amenable to compromise. In this, they differ from claims deriving wholly from material interest. Whereas material advancement can be measured both relatively and absolutely, the status advancement of one ethnic group is entirely relative to the status of others."

6. Ethnocentrism is often equated with provincialism and a foolish tendency to judge foreigners by domestic standards. Juvenile errors of this kind are easy to avoid in simple cases (such as blaming the British for driving on the wrong side of the road) but harder to avoid in more complicated ones in which well-established practices of another culture offend the basic principles of our own. Anthropologists have had the most practice trying to overcome ethnocentrism without falling into the trap of a self-refuting relativism. The connection with psychopathology arises from the success of Adorno et al. (1950) in imbuing social scientists with an association between ethnocentrism as provincialism and ethnocentrism as the characteristic expression of the structure of personality resulting from ego weakness (see Chapter 1, "Individualism"). In recent years ethnocentrism has had a much better press. Some eminent philosophers have presented it not as an error or a defect of character, or even as an inescapable limitation of human reason, but as a commendable pragmatic alternative to an intolerant realism rooted in fear and resentment (e.g., Rorty, 1991). For a relevant definition of xenophobia, see Breton and Breton (1995), pp. 110–11.

7. The equilibrium values of contact and ethnocentrism are:

$$C = \frac{g}{a_1 a_2 + b_1 b_2}$$

$$E_A = \frac{a_1 g}{a_1 a_2 + b_1 b_2}$$

$$E_B = \frac{b_1 g}{a_1 a_2 + b_1 b_2}$$

Given a positive value for the growth parameter, g, the equilibrium levels of contact and ethnocentrism depend on the ethnocentrism parameters (a_1, a_2, b_1, and b_2) that describe each group's tendency to respond ethnocentrically to contact with the other group. The larger these response parameters, the lower will be the resulting equilibrium level of contact. The equilibrium levels of ethnocentrism also depend in more complicated ways on these response parameters. Generally speaking, the greater the latent ethnocentrism of a group, the higher its observable level of ethnocentrism will be. Note, however, that greater latent or potential ethnocentrism in one group, by lowering the equilibrium level of contact, tends to reduce the expression of ethnocentrism by the other group: the greater a_1 and a_2, the lower will be the equilibrium value of E_B, other things being equal. Very ethnocentric neighbors save a group from having to reveal its own ethnocentrism.

Initial values of contact above or below the equilibrium value will tend to produce lower or higher values, respectively. Similarly, variations in ethnocentrism due to changes in the environment other than changes in contact will tend to produce offsetting changes in contact, increasing or reducing contact and thus gradually moving the level of contact to a new equilibrium, much as if there had been changes in the parameters a_1 and/or b_1.

Although the relation between contact and ethnocentrism described by equation (2) is inherently time-dependent, it may give rise statistically to a "timeless" relation like the one shown by the broken line in figure 5.2. Consider a system exposed to external influences and always out of equilibrium but always moving toward it. The larger the values of a_2 and b_2 in this system, the greater will be its responsiveness to external changes that directly affect only the levels of ethnocentrism (such as changes in leadership, election campaigns, the activities of interest groups, developments in the media, and similar temporary forces). Greater responsiveness means that given changes in ethnocentrism will more quickly induce larger changes in the amount of contact between the groups because of the mechanism represented by equation (2). Thus, the larger the response parameters, the greater the tendency for increases of ethnocentrism to generate a lower level of contact and, likewise, the greater the tendency for reductions of ethnocentrism to produce more contact, other things being equal. If the values of the three major variables were continually being disturbed by exogenous "shocks" that directly affected the levels of ethnocentrism but not contact, then the resulting variation in contact would be a function of the parameters a_2 and b_2, which mediate the effects of variations in ethnocentrism on variations in contact.

The unmeasured external disturbances we are now considering—political events, leadership variables, and the like—could be represented by adding disturbance terms, d, to each of the basic equations showing the dependence of ethnocentrism on contact. To simplify: $E = aC+d$. Changes in these external forces (represented by positive and negative values of d) would change the observed levels of ethnocentrism apart from any changes in contact. In effect, they would shift the solid lines in the diagrams above without changing their slopes, moving them back and forth in a northwest-southeast direction. Over a lengthy period of time, in the environment we are now imagining, many observed sets of values of contact and ethnocentrism (C_1,E_1; C_2,E_2; C_3,E_3 and so on—ignoring for the moment that there are always two values of ethnocentrism, one for each group) would tend to trace out a timeless negative functional dependence of contact on ethnocentrism like the broken line in figure 5.2. The pattern would presumably be clearer if somewhat earlier values of ethnocentrism could be related to somewhat later values of contact, but it should be apparent even with simultaneous observations, because any observed values of the "independent" variables, the ethnocentrisms, would already have had some time to affect the observed values of contact. And the larger the values of a_2 and b_2, the greater should be the "negative" responsiveness of contact to externally induced changes in ethnocentrism and the greater should be the slope of any line (or surface) describing the statistical dependence of contact on ethnocentrism—in short, the stronger the apparent *negative* correlation between contact and ethnocentrism. This correlation would be harder to detect and might be completely obscured if the system were being influenced by the external forces that directly affected only contact.

The discussion of statistical testing in Chapter 6 rests on this reasoning together with two other simplifying assumptions, which it may be helpful to spell out immediately. First, if equations (1.1) and (1.2) are true, then *average* levels of ethnocentrism (the averages of E_A and E_B) must be a simple function of levels of contact and the average value of the parameters a_1 and b_1. Second, if it can be assumed that the behavior of all groups is governed by essentially the same laws, described by equations with parameters of roughly the same size, then it is reasonable to substitute the observation of many different such groups at one time for repeated observations of the same pair of groups at different times.

To fix these ideas, assume that arrays of relevant data are available (attitude surveys, systematic observations of behavior, counts of hostile events, analyses of discriminatory laws, segregation indices, population distributions, intermarriage rates, employment statistics, trade and tourism statistics, mail flows, Internet traffic, immigration and emigration figures) for a large number of pairs of ethnic groups or nations, all collected at one time. Assume that these data are to be used to get a very rough idea of the sizes of the underlying constants (the a_1, a_2; b_1, b_2; c_1, c_2; etc.) for all the $n(n-1)/2$ pairs of n groups. An analysis of the data might have no goal beyond simply determining whether the underlying constants were significantly different from zero, on the average, for the sample of groups or countries at the time the data were collected. With this goal in mind, the equations could be rewritten so that equation (2) would now correspond to the negatively sloping broken line in the earlier diagrams:

(R1) $E_{ij} = \alpha_0 + \alpha_1 C_{ij} + e_{ij}$
(R2) $C_{ij} = \beta_0 - \beta_1 E_{ij} + e_{ij}$

The subscripts i and j would identify pairs of groups or countries (i = 1, . . . , n; j = 1, . . . , n). Since contact has no direction, it is the same for both members of a pair, $C_{ij} = C_{ji}$. One group in any pair may, however, show a higher level of ethnocentrism toward the other group in the pair than the second group shows toward the first, so in general $E_{ij} \neq E_{ji}$. Nonetheless, the predicted or expected values $\hat{E}_{ij}$ and $\hat{E}_{ji}$ must be the same, because the same equation and the same values of the independent variable, contact, are used to predict both. (A "psychological" justification for this fundamental simplification might be the fact that antipathies tend to be reciprocated. One group's dislike of another group tends to generate a reciprocal antagonism: if the **As** for some reason become less favorable toward the **Bs**, perhaps as a by-product of domestic political competition, that alone is likely to increase the **Bs'** dislike of the **As**, apart from any more basic conflict of interests or clash of cultures that may separate them.) At any rate, the regression coefficients α_0, α_1, β_0, and β_1 would no longer refer to particular groups; rather, they would be in a sense averages of the underlying constants for the sample of groups or countries, each assumed to be a slightly different expression of a common underlying pattern. The e_{ij} would be error terms with unspecified distributions about which some assumptions would have to be made.

Formidable statistical as well as data-gathering problems impede any estimation and testing of the model along the lines just indicated. Some of these will be discussed in the next chapter, but it is worth noting immediately a further broad "psychological" generalization about ethnocentrism that may justify a further statistical simplification. People tend to be undiscriminating in their hostilities: they tend to have similarly favorable or unfavorable attitudes toward *all* groups (Adorno et al., 1950, ch. 4; Forbes, 1985, ch. 8). Thus, if the **A**s dislike the **B**s for some reason, this dislike may also influence their attitude toward the **C**s and the **D**s. Ethnocentric antipathies tend to spill over from one group to another. In light of this generalization, as well as the obvious limitations of the available data, it may be unreasonable to focus attention on pairs of ethnic groups or nations and more reasonable to think of the average levels of contact and ethnocentrism of particular groups considered, so to speak, individually. This reasoning suggests the following still greater simplification of the above equations:

(R3) $E_i = \alpha_0 + \alpha_1 C_i + e_i$
(R4) $C_i = \beta_0 - \beta_1 E_i + e_i$

The variables E and C would now be average levels of ethnocentrism and contact with outsiders for the n groups or countries, and statistical "testing" would presumably focus on whether the coefficients α_1 and β_1 have "significant" positive and negative values, as postulated (cf. Quillian, 1995). Such tests would throw a little light on the basic model (as do the findings summarized in Chapter 3), but only a little, since there is now a large difference between the model itself and the regression equations serving as the basis for testing.

8. In any estimation or testing that focused on equations (1.3) and (1.4), an apparently more complicated nonlinear functional form might really be simpler to use and might produce more meaningful results. The two equations could be rewritten to resemble the Cobb-Douglas production functions often used by economists to analyze the contributions of capital and labor to the production of commodities. The general form of this function is $Q = AK^{\alpha}L^{\beta}$ where Q is physical output, A is a constant (an efficiency parameter reflecting the state of technology), K is capital input, L is labor input, and α and β are parameters. If $\alpha+\beta = 1$, then there are constant returns to scale. Twice as much labor and capital produce twice as much output. Values of $\alpha+\beta$ greater or less than one imply increasing and decreasing returns to scale, respectively. (Equations (1.3) and (1.4) above imply a fourfold increase in ethnocentrism for every doubling of contact and difference.) From a statistical standpoint, the interesting feature of all functions of the Cobb-Douglas form is that they are linear in the logarithms of the variables, so equations (1.3) and (1.4), with the additional exponential parameters, would become:

$$\log E_A = \log a_1 + a_2 \log C_t + a_3 \log D_t$$
$$\log E_B = \log b_1 + b_2 \log C_t + b_3 \log D_t$$

Assuming relevant data were available, the new parameters a_2, a_3, b_2, and b_3 (not to be confused with the constants with the same names in equations (2) and (3)) would permit some rough judgments of the relative contributions of contact and cultural differences to the "production" of ethnocentrism.

9. For example, a model that made the rate of change in D depend only upon C would imply that the system could be in equilibrium only when contact was zero

or cultural differences were zero. This seems to be the assumption underlying the generalization by Robert Park quoted earlier.

10. Further manipulation in the sense of statistical fitting, using the metric of "variance explained," which is so important in some interpretations of the social sciences, will be discussed at length in Chapter 6. For the present it may suffice to observe that government agencies and private research bureaus have yet to collect the kind of data that would be needed for any real testing and weighing of the model on the scale of R^2.

11. The standard theory about contact and conflict starts, as I have explained, from the assumption that prejudice is mainly caused by ignorance of out-groups and argues that this ignorance can be cured by "true acquaintance," which destroys stereotypes and leads to the perception of "common interests and common humanity." Recent critics have recognized that the theory is unrealistic, but they have had difficulty formulating a more realistic one. Thus Hewstone and Brown (1986) observe that "contact in cases such as these [where the groups concerned have *dissimilar* values and attitudes] is likely to reveal these differences and hence, according to the causal process alleged to underlie the contact hypothesis (i.e. similarity-attraction), should result in *less*, not more, intergroup liking" (p. 11). But as a general rule, without distinguishing levels of analysis, this inverse contact hypothesis is scarcely more satisfactory than the conventional one, as a glance at the research summarized in Chapter 3 should make clear. Incidentally, the example Hewstone and Brown use to illustrate their idea of a "shocking disconfirmation of expectations" is "when Muslim schoolgirls in the UK appear for gym lessons wearing long trousers, while everyone else is wearing shorts" (p. 10).

Chapter 6: Truth in Modeling

1. The difficulty of testing a theory increases with the number of "third variables" it suggests may be important. The rapidly increasing invulnerability of contact theory can be seen by comparing the full list of conditions in Allport (1954, pp. 262–63) with the list in Stephan (1987, pp. 24–25), but see also Amir (1976, pp. 250–51) and Hewstone and Brown (1986, pp. 36–39). As I have repeatedly noted, Allport distinguishes some thirty independent variables or conditions that (hypothetically) determine the effects of contact. "In order to predict the effects of contact upon attitudes we should ideally study the consequences of each of [these] variables acting both separately and in combination," which would be, he conceded, a task of "vast magnitude" (p. 262). Indeed, for the number of possible combinations increases exponentially with the number of relevant conditions. At the limit, even if each of twenty-nine variables had only two values (high and low, or present and absent), the total number of combinations of conditions to be investigated empirically would exceed five hundred million. Stephan (1987) distinguishes, by my count, forty-seven different independent variables, implying (by the same reasoning) about 140,000 billion possible combinations of conditions or types of contact—considerably more than one thousand times more than all the people who have ever lived. As Pettigrew noted some years ago, the contact hypothesis is a "slippery hypothesis" that is "extremely difficult to falsify definitely, for the addition of another condition or a re-specification of a condition seems all too easily possible" (1986, p. 179).

2. No reader should be scandalized if an empirically sound social scientific

model or theory is found to have a "value implication" such as "stick to your studies." The objectivity of natural science is not compromised by the value commitments of scientists or the value implications of their discoveries. No one dismisses the work of such a medical pioneer as Louis Pasteur, who discovered that germs cause disease, just because he was opposed to disease and his discoveries led to certain practical reforms, such as the pasteurization of milk and the more frequent washing of hands. The same is true of the work of the epidemiologists and laboratory scientists who demonstrated that smoking causes lung cancer. Are their discoveries to be brushed aside just because they had value commitments and their discoveries had value implications? (After the discovery of the link between smoking and lung cancer, for example, people tended to put a more negative value on cigarette smoke, and the shares of tobacco companies lost value.) Science does not demand pointless theories and, so to speak, neutered scientists, but only sound theories developed by scientists who make a clear distinction between their factual observations and their personal value preferences (compare Taylor, 1985, pp. 58–90).

3. See Duncan (1975) and Heise (1975) for good systematic introductions to the methods in question here. The statistical problem is like that of empirically estimating supply and demand functions for some commodity from data on prices and quantities traded in some market over a period of time. There is a very clear explanation of the basic problem in Kelejian and Oates (1974) and no doubt in many other similar textbooks. Austin (1991) provides a broad survey of some of the relevant statistical literature addressed to psychologists. Jackson (1996) does the same for political scientists. Readers uninterested in statistics may note that the "laws of supply and demand" that figure so prominently in economic analysis were clearly emerging in the writings of economists more than a century before any attempt was made to establish supply and demand schedules through the statistical analysis of market data, as histories of economics reveal. It is also worth noting how much difficulty the early economists had with clearly stating what now seem very simple matters. "Is it not a fact, which stares at us from the histories of all sciences, that it is much more difficult for the human mind to forge the most elementary conceptual schemes than it is to elaborate the most complicated superstructures when those elements are well in hand?" (Schumpeter, 1954, p. 602).

4. The point of critical theory, from this perspective, is to break the hold of a single model of knowledge on social scientists and philosophers. Habermas (1971, 1973, 1988), for example, distinguishes three kinds of knowledge (empirical-analytic, historical-hermeneutic, and critical) rooted in three different knowledge-constitutive interests (technical control, practical consensus, and emancipation). Benhabib (1986), Fay (1975), Geuss (1981), Held (1980), Jay (1973), Outhwaite (1994), Kortian (1980), and White (1995) provide helpful background and commentary. For related developments in the social sciences, the philosophy of science, and cultural studies, see Hiley, Bohman, and Shusterman (1991), Rouse (1987), and Sokal (1996a, 1996b).

5. Nor would there be much point trying to test it statistically. The most important variables would be very difficult to measure. For example, the most important educational variables may not be the most easily observed differences having to do with the total amount of money spent on education or the fraction of the population enrolled in schools and universities but rather the more subtle or elusive differences having to do with the content of the curriculum and the *moeurs* it sup-

ports. Crude quantitative differences in education may be less important than subtle qualitative ones. One billion dollars dedicated to the training of natural scientists and engineers may have less impact on ethnocentrism than one million spent on the teaching and research of social scientists who study the causes of prejudice and discrimination, or even one-tenth of that amount spent on a poster campaign against racism in high schools. Nonetheless, several quantitative studies have shown a strong negative relation at the individual level between schooling and ethnic prejudice, in particular Selznick and Steinberg (1969), Schoenbach et al. (1981), and Wagner and Zick (1995), but see also Jackman and Muha (1984).

6. Among philosophers of science the unqualified empiricism of the logical positivists has long since given way to a deeper appreciation of the role of theory in the scientific enterprise. Among social scientists, Kuhn (1962) had a great impact a generation ago because he showed in detail how untrue to the history of science are some of the simpler maxims of "scientific method" and how different theoretical reasoning (about "paradigms") is from the testing of simple empirical generalizations. In the writings of philosophers about these matters, the emphasis now seems to fall on considerations much broader than the "goodness of fit" of theories to facts. Charles Taylor, for example, citing MacIntyre (1977), describes practical reasoning as "a reasoning in transitions" that aims not to establish that some position is correct absolutely, or absolutely wrong, but only that it is better or worse than some other position (Taylor, 1989, p. 72; 1995, pp. 34–60). Taylor writes of transitions in "moral growth," but in MacIntyre's presentation it becomes even clearer that the crucial considerations are often of a personal character, since epistemological crises, he says, are always crises in human relationships. Like Hamlet, we are always trying to make ourselves intelligible to others, lest they think us mad. "When an epistemological crisis is resolved, it is by the construction of a new narrative which enables the agent to understand *both* how he or she could intelligibly have held his or her original beliefs *and* how he or she could have been so drastically misled by them. The narrative in terms of which he or she at first understood and ordered experience is itself made into the subject of an enlarged narrative" (MacInytre, 1977, p. 455). This enlarged narrative may provide a better account than the earlier one (given the needs of our interlocutors), but we are never in a position to claim that now we possess the simple truth and are fully rational. The criterion of a better account, including a better scientific theory, is simply that it enables us to understand its predecessors in a newly intelligible way. "It recasts the narrative which constitutes the continuous reconstruction of the scientific tradition" (p. 460). The idea that scientific reason is subordinate to and only intelligible in light of historical reason (p. 464) is also at work in Richard Rorty's influential attempts to break the traditional link between truth as a term of commendation for the views we favor and our belief that these views are commendable because they correspond to an objective reality independent of our preferences. His dictum that "there is nothing to be said about truth or rationality apart from descriptions of the familiar procedures of justification which a given society—*ours*—uses in one or another area of inquiry" (Rorty, 1991, p. 23) is worth pondering in connection with the topics discussed in this chapter.

7. Horowitz (1985), to which I have referred from time to time for support on particular points, provides a great deal of evidence that I have not tried to summarize. In his discussion of ethnic groups and the modern state, he includes some

helpful remarks about the uneasy coexistence of consanguinity and contiguity as organizing principles of modern life. The uneasiness associated with their "dialectical relationship" is at the root, he suggests, of "our reluctance to acknowledge the importance of ethnicity in politics. To the considerable extent that ethnic ties reflect the birth principle, they fall within the curtilage of those disagreeable phenomena disfavored by our ideals and therefore capable of securing only the reluctant attention reserved for distasteful subjects" (pp. 88–89).

Appendix: Nationalism

1. The literature on nationalism is immense, and some of it is quite remote in its preoccupations from the issues discussed in this book. Representative studies include Anderson (1983), Armstrong (1982), Breuilly (1994), Cobban (1969), Emerson (1960), Greenfeld (1992), Hayes (1931, 1960), Hobsbawm (1990), Ignatieff (1993), Kedourie (1961), Kohn (1944), Periwal (1995), Shafer (1955, 1972), Seton-Watson (1977), Smith (1979, 1981, 1986, 1991, 1995), and Tamir (1993). Apart from the work of Karl Deutsch, which will be discussed in detail below, Akzin (1964), Connor (1994), and Gellner (1964, 1983) are most helpful in clarifying the relation between nationalism and ethnic conflict. For additional bibliographical guidance, see Calhoun (1993), Deutsch and Merritt (1970), Smith (1973, 1983, 1992), and Williams (1994).

2. In the debate about nationalism, primordialist accounts of ethnicity and the nation collide with situationalist or constructivist accounts, and both are entangled with the distinction between ethnic and civic nationalism (see Williams, 1994). Primordialism is in a sense the nationalist's theory of nationalism, whereas constructivism is favored by social scientists eager to get behind the veil of nationalist myth-making. The basic issues are clear already in Ernest Renan's famous 1882 lecture, "Qu'est-ce qu'une nation?" (Renan, 1996). An equally famous statement of similar vintage and tendency is Lord Acton's "Nationality" (Acton, 1955).

3. Deutsch recognizes the need for more attention to some of the relationships just highlighted when he writes that "refinements [of the model] would have to include changes in the rate of assimilation c as a function of changes in the mobilization rate, and particularly as functions of the rise of the mobilized but unassimilated group H. Generally, if H is large, and its rate of growth h is also large, c may tend to decline, at least for considerable periods" (p. 239, with a correction).

4. Dictionary definitions of the two key terms, *ethnic* and *nation*, and a related one, *people*, point to some important similarities. In the dictionary I happen to have at hand, *The American Heritage Dictionary* (1970), one finds: "*ethnic:* 1. Of or pertaining to a social group within a cultural or social system that claims or is accorded special status on the basis of complex, often variable traits including religious, linguistic, ancestral, or physical characteristics. 2. Broadly, characteristic of a religious, racial, national, or cultural group. *nation:* 1. A people, usually the inhabitants of a specific territory, who share common customs, origins, history, and frequently language or related languages. *people:* 1. A body of persons living in the same country under one national government; nationality. 2. A body of persons sharing a common religion, culture, language, or inherited condition of life." An ethnic group, then, is a group distinguished from other groups in some larger social system (e.g., the global system of trade and technology) by cultural traits such as religion and

language, whereas a nation is a group set apart from others by common customs such as language and religion. The connotations of these terms are obviously different, and they are used in different contexts, but there are plainly some family resemblances among the various sets of individuals they denote.

5. Anderson's complete silence about Deutsch's communications theory is unusual, especially given his interest in "print-capitalism." Most of the literature on nationalism since the 1950s does cite Deutsch, but usually with just a bare citation or an entry in a bibliography. If his argument is summarized, it is likely to be simplified beyond recognition. Again one work will have to stand for all the rest: "[Deutsch's] approach tends to see the 'nation' in terms of a developed system of internal communication which creates a sense of common identity. . . . However, there is one crucial weakness in the approach. Intensified communications between individuals and groups can as often lead to an increase in internal conflict as to an increase in solidarity" (Breuilly, 1994, p. 406). This observation is far from the mark as an objection to Deutsch's analysis, as should be clear from the summary of it presented above.

6. Perhaps the most widely cited study in the academic literature on nationalism for the past fifty years has been *The Idea of Nationalism* (Kohn, 1944). It traces the development of relevant ideas over a period of more than two thousand years, in some twenty or thirty different national settings and discusses the theories of thinkers such as Herder and Rousseau in considerable detail. Although at the very end it quickly introduces an ethnic-civic distinction, it does not conclude with any simple generalizations about the causes of nationalism or the structure of nationalist thinking. It encourages the view that any generalization that might emerge from a comparative study of cases will be less interesting than the details of the cases compared (cf. Greenfeld, 1992).

7. Studies of social identity and intergroup relations provide good examples of the striving for generality and the belief in quantification that define positivist social science. In addition, they often illustrate with startling clarity the broader tendency among social scientists to separate the study of domestic prejudice and discrimination from the study of nations and nationalism. Proponents of these approaches write books and articles about group processes and intergroup relations liberally sprinkled with references to racism, sexism, and homophobia. They state very broad hypotheses that are meant to apply not just to racial and ethnic groups but also to gender groups, age groups, economic groups, size groups, and even families, sports teams, professional associations, government committees, and street gangs. Intergroup relations, they typically say, should call to mind "race riots, religious intolerance, rivalry between the sexes, language groups in confrontation, radical forces clashing with the establishment, civil war, the constant threat of terrorism, bitter labor disputes, and the universal preoccupation with the spread of nuclear weapons and with the environment" (Taylor and Moghaddam, 1994, p. 1). These authors go on to define "intergroup relations" as *any aspect of human interaction that involves individuals perceiving themselves as members of a social category, or being perceived by others as belonging to a social category. . . .* It is true that most often the focus is on large social categories such as race, social class, sex, religion, language, and ethnic background. However, it is our contention that any valid principles about intergroup relations apply to all social categories, regardless of type and size" (p. 6). But the books and articles read as if nations were not groups and nationalism

had nothing to do with intergroup relations. The broad hypotheses of the theory are never tested or refined by trying to square them with what is said about nations and nationalism in the literature on these topics. The problems that would immediately appear, were patriotism or nationalism to be equated psychologically with racism or homophobia, are kept away from the light of consciousness.

References

Abrams, D. (1992). "Processes of Social Identification," in *Social Psychology of Identity and the Self Concept*, ed. G. M. Breakwell, pp. 57–99. London: Academic.

Achen, C. H., and Shively, W. P. (1995). *Cross-Level Inference*. Chicago: University of Chicago Press.

Acton, J. E. E. D. (1955). "Nationality," in *Essays on Freedom and Power*, ed. G. Himmelfarb, pp. 141–70. Cleveland: World Publishing.

Adorno, T. W., Frenkel-Brunswik, E., Levinson, D. J., and Sanford, R. N. (1950). *The Authoritarian Personality*. New York: Harper & Row.

Akzin, B. (1964). *State and Nation*. London: Hutchinson.

Alker, H. R. (1969). "A Typology of Ecological Fallacies," in *Quantitative Ecological Analysis in the Social Sciences*, ed. M. Dogan and S. Rokkan, pp. 69–86. Cambridge: MIT Press.

Allen, I. L. (1983). *The Language of Ethnic Conflict: Social Organization and Lexical Culture*. New York: Columbia University Press.

Allport, F. H., et al. (1953). "The Effects of Segregation and the Consequences of Desegregation: A Social Science Statement," Appendix to Appellants' Briefs, *Brown v. Board of Education, Minnesota Law Review*, 37, 427–39.

Allport, G. W. (1954). *The Nature of Prejudice*. Reading, Mass.: Addison-Wesley.

Allport, G. W., and Kramer, B. M. (1946). "Some Roots of Prejudice," *Journal of Psychology*, 22, 9–39.

Amir, Y. (1969). "Contact Hypothesis in Ethnic Relations," *Psychological Bulletin*, 71, 319–42.

———. (1976). "The Role of Intergroup Contact in Change of Prejudice and Ethnic Relations," in *Towards the Elimination of Racism*, ed. P. A. Katz, pp. 245–308. New York: Pergamon.

———. (1992). "Social Assimilation or Cultural Mosaic?" in *Cultural Diversity and the Schools*, vol. 1, ed. J. Lynch, C. Modgil, and S. Modgil, pp. 23–26. London: Falmer.

Amir, Y., and Sharan, S., eds. (1984). *School Desegregation: Cross-Cultural Perspectives*. Hillsdale, N.J.: Lawrence Erlbaum.

Anastasopoulos, P. G. (1992). "Tourism and Attitude Change: Greek Tourists Visiting Turkey," *Annals of Tourism Research*, 19, 629–42.

Anderson, B. (1983). *Imagined Communities: Reflections on the Origins and Spread of Nationalism*. London: Verso.

Armor, D. J. (1972). "The Evidence on Busing," *Public Interest*, 28, 90–126.

———. (1995). *Forced Justice: School Desegregation and the Law*. New York: Oxford University Press.

Armstrong, J. A. (1982). *Nations Before Nationalism*. Chapel Hill: University of North Carolina Press.

Aronson, E. (1984). *The Social Animal*, 4th ed. San Francisco: W. H. Freeman.

Aronson, E., Blaney, N., Sikes, J., Stephan, C., and Snapp, M. (1978). *The Jigsaw Classroom*. Beverly Hills: Sage.

Arrow, K. J. (1972). "Models of Job Discrimination" and "Some Mathematical Models of Race in the Labor Market," in *Racial Discrimination in Economic Life*, ed. A. H. Pascal, pp. 83–102 and 187–203. Lexington, Mass.: Lexington Books.

———. (1973). "The Theory of Discrimination," in *Discrimination in Labor Markets*, ed. O. Ashenfelter and A. Rees, pp. 3–33. Princeton: Princeton University Press.

Austin, J. T. (1991). "Annotated Bibliography of Structural Equation Modelling," *British Journal of Mathematical and Statistical Psychology*, 44, 93–152.

Axelrod, R. (1970). *Conflict of Interest: A Theory of Divergent Goals with Applications to Politics*. Chicago: Markham.

———. (1984). *The Evolution of Cooperation*. New York: Basic Books.

Bandura, A. (1986). *Social Foundations of Thought and Action*. Englewood Cliffs: Prentice-Hall.

Banton, M. P. (1987). *Racial Theories*. Cambridge: Cambridge University Press.

Banton, M. P., and Harwood, J. (1975). *The Race Concept*. London: David & Charles.

Bargal, D. (1990). "Contact Is Not Enough—The Contribution of Lewinian Theory to Intergroup Workshops Involving Arab Palestinians and Jewish Youth in Israel," *International Journal of Group Tensions*, 20, 179–92.

Barkan, E. (1992). *Retreat from Scientific Racism: Changing Concepts of Race in Britain and the United States*. Cambridge: Cambridge University Press.

Barnard, F. M. (1965). *Herder's Social and Political Thought: From Enlightenment to Nationalism*. Oxford: Clarendon Press.

Barnard, W. A., and Benn, M. S. (1988). "Belief Congruence and Prejudice Reduction in an Interracial Contact Setting," *Journal of Social Psychology*, 128, 125–34.

Barrows, W. L. (1976). "Ethnic Diversity and Political Instability in Black Africa," *Comparative Political Studies*, 9, 139–70.

Barth, F., ed. (1969). *Ethnic Groups and Boundaries: The Social Organization of Cultural Difference*. Boston: Little, Brown.

Bashevkin, S. B. (1991). *True Patriot Love: The Politics of Canadian Nationalism*. Toronto: Oxford University Press.

Becker, G. S. (1957). *The Economics of Discrimination*. Chicago: University of Chicago Press.

Ben-Ari, R., and Amir, Y. (1988). "Intergroup Contact, Cultural Information, and Change in Ethnic Attitudes," in *The Social Psychology of Intergroup Conflict: Theory, Research, and Applications*, ed. W. Stroebe et al., pp. 151–65. Berlin: Springer-Verlag.

Benhabib, S. (1986). *Critique, Norm, and Utopia: A Study of the Foundations of Critical Theory*. New York: Columbia University Press.

Berlin, I. (1976). *Vico and Herder*. London: Hogarth.

Biernat, M. (1990). "Stereotypes on Campus: How Contact and Liking Influence Perceptions of Group Distinctiveness," *Journal of Applied Social Psychology*, 20, 1485–513.

Biernat, M., and Crandall, C. S. (1994). "Stereotyping and Contact with Social Groups: Measurement and Conceptual Issues," *European Journal of Social Psychology*, 24, 659–77.

Billig, M. (1995). *Banal Nationalism*. London: Sage.

Billig, M., and Tajfel, H. (1973). "Social Categorization and Similarity in Intergroup Behaviour," *European Journal of Social Psychology*, 3, 27–52.

Bizman, A., and Amir, Y. (1984). "Integration and Attitudes," in *School Desegregation: Cross-Cultural Perspectives*, ed. Y. Amir and S. Sharan, pp. 155–87. Hillsdale, N.J.: Lawrence Erlbaum.

Black, E. (1973). "The Militant Segregationist Vote in the Post-*Brown* South: A Comparative Analysis," *Social Science Quarterly*, 54, 66–84.

Black, E., and Black, M. (1973). "The Wallace Vote in Alabama: A Multiple Regression Analysis," *Journal of Politics*, 35, 730–36.

Blalock, H. M. (1957). "Per Cent Non-White and Discrimination in the South," *American Sociological Review*, 22, 677–82.

———. (1967). *Toward a Theory of Minority Group Relations*. New York: Wiley.

Bledsoe, T., Welch, S., Sigelman, L., and Combs, M. (1995). "Residential Context and Racial Solidarity among African Americans," *American Journal of Political Science*, 39, 434–58.

Blumer, H. (1958). "Race Prejudice as a Sense of Group Position," *Pacific Sociological Review*, 1, 3–7.

Bochner, S. (1982). "The Social Psychology of Cross-Cultural Relations," in *Cultures in Contact: Studies in Cross-Cultural Interaction*, ed. S. Bochner, pp. 5–44. Oxford: Pergamon.

Bogardus, E. S. (1929). *Immigration and Race Attitudes*. Boston: D. C. Heath.

Bogart, L., ed. (1992). *Project Clear: Social Research and the Desegregation of the United States Army*. New Brunswick, N.J.: Transaction.

Bonacich, E. (1972). "A Theory of Ethnic Antagonism: The Split Labor Market," *American Sociological Review*, 37, 547–59.

———. (1973). "A Theory of Middleman Minorities," *American Sociological Review*, 38, 583–94.

Bornman, E. (1992). "Factors Influencing Ethnic Attitudes in South African Work Situations," *Journal of Social Psychology*, 132, 641–53.

Bornman, E., and Mynhardt, J. C. (1991). "Social Identity and Intergroup Contact in South Africa with Specific Reference to the Work Situation," *Genetic, Social, and General Psychology Monographs*, 117, 439–62.

Bory, V. (1987). *Dehors! De la chasse aux Italiens à la peur des réfugiés, 1896–1986*. Lausanne: Pierre-Marcel Favre.

Bradburn, N. M., Sudman, S., and Gockel, G. L. (1971). *Side by Side*. Chicago: Quadrangle.

Braddock, J. H. (1985). "School Desegregation and Black Assimilation," *Journal of Social Issues*, 41(3), 9–22.

Brein, M., and David, K. H. (1971). "Intercultural Communication and the Adjustment of the Sojourner," *Psychological Bulletin*, 76, 215–30.

Breton, A. (1978). *Bilingualism: An Economic Approach*. Montreal: C. D. Howe Research Institute.

Breton, A., and Breton, M. (1995). "Nationalism Revisited," in *Nationalism and Rationality*, ed. A. Breton, G. Galeotti, P. Salmon, and R. Wintrobe, pp. 98–115. Cambridge: Cambridge University Press.

Breuilly, J. (1994). *Nationalism and the State*, 2nd ed. Chicago: University of Chicago Press.

Brewer, M. B. (1979). "The Role of Ethnocentrism in Intergroup Conflict," in *The Social Psychology of Intergroup Relations*, ed. W. G. Austin and S. Worchel, pp. 71–84. Monterey: Brooks/Cole.

———. (1981). "Ethnocentrism and Its Role in Interpersonal Trust," in *Scientific Inquiry and the Social Sciences*, ed. M. B. Brewer and B. E. Collins, pp. 345–60. San Francisco: Jossey-Bass.

Brewer, M. B., and Campbell, D. T. (1976). *Ethnocentrism and Intergroup Attitudes: East African Evidence*. New York: Halsted Press.

Brewer, M. B., and Miller, N. (1984). "Beyond the Contact Hypothesis: Theoretical Perspectives on Desegregation," in *Groups in Contact: The Psychology of Desegregation*, ed. N. Miller and M. B. Brewer, pp. 281–302. Orlando: Academic.

Brigham, J. C. (1993). "College-Students' Racial Attitudes," *Journal of Applied Social Psychology*, 23, 1933–67.

Brislin, R. W. (1968). "Contact as a Variable in Intergroup Interaction," *Journal of Social Psychology*, 76, 149– 54.

Brophy, I. N. (1946). "The Luxury of Anti-Negro Prejudice," *Public Opinion Quarterly*, 9, 456–66.

Brown, B. S., and Albee, G. W. (1966). "The Effect of Integrated Hospital Experiences on Racial Attitudes: A Discordant Note," *Social Problems*, 13, 324–33.

Brown, D. L., and Fuguitt, G. V. (1972). "Percent Nonwhite and Racial Disparity in Nonmetropolitan Cities in the South," *Social Science Quarterly*, 53, 573–82.

Brown, R. (1986). *Social Psychology*, 2nd ed. New York: Free Press.

Brown, R. J., and Turner, J. C. (1981). "Interpersonal and Intergroup Behaviour," in *Intergroup Behaviour*, ed. J. C. Turner and H. Giles, pp. 33–65. Chicago: University of Chicago Press.

Buss, A. H., and Portnoy, N. W. (1967). "Pain Tolerance and Group Identification," *Journal of Personality and Social Psychology*, 6, 106–8.

Butler, J. S., and Wilson, K. L. (1978). "*The American Soldier* Revisited: Race Relations and the Military," *Social Science Quarterly*, 59, 451–67.

Byrne, D. (1969). "Attitudes and Attraction," in *Advances in Experimental Social Psychology*, vol. 4, ed. L. Berkowitz, pp. 35–89. New York: Academic.

Cagle, L. T. (1972). "Interracial Housing: A Reassessment of the Equal- Status Contact Hypothesis," *Sociology and Social Research*, 57, 342–55.

Cain, G. C. (1986). "The Economic Analysis of Labor Market Discrimination: A Survey," in *Handbook of Labor Economics*, ed. O. Ashenfelter and R. Layard, vol. 1, pp. 693–785. Amsterdam: North Holland.

Calhoun, C. (1993). "Nationalism and Ethnicity," *Annual Review of Sociology*, 19, 211–39.

Campbell, D. T. (1965). "Ethnocentric and Other Altruistic Motives," in *Nebraska Symposium on Motivation, 1965*, Current Theory and Research on Motivation, vol. 13, ed. D. Levine, pp. 283– 311. Lincoln: University of Nebraska Press.

Campbell, D. T., and Stanley, J. C. (1966). *Experimental and Quasi-Experimental Designs for Research*. Chicago: Rand McNally.

Carithers, M. W. (1970). "School Desegregation and Racial Cleavage, 1954–1970: A Review of the Literature," *Journal of Social Issues*, 26(4), 25–47.

Carter, G. L. (1990). "Black Attitudes and the 1960s Black Riots: An Aggregate-Level Analysis of the Kerner Commission's '15 Cities' Data," *Sociological Quarterly*, 31, 269–86.

Chadwick-Jones, J. K. (1976). *Social Exchange Theory: Its Structure and Influence in Social Psychology*. London: Academic.

Cirillo, R. (1979). *The Economics of Vilfredo Pareto*. London: Frank Cass.

Clark, K. B. (1979). "The Role of Social Scientists Twenty-five Years after *Brown*," *Personality and Social Psychology Bulletin*, 5, 477–81.

Cobban, A. (1969). *The Nation State and National Self-Determination*. London: Collins.

Cohen, E. G. (1972). "Interracial Interaction Disability," *Human Relations*, 25, 9–24.

———. (1975). "The Effects of Desegregation on Race Relations," *Law and Contemporary Problems*, 39(2), 271–99.

Cohen, E. G., and Roper, S. S. (1972). "Modification of Interracial Interaction Disability: An Application of Status Characteristic Theory," *American Sociological Review*, 37, 643–57.

Cohler, A. (1964). *Rousseau and Nationalism*. New York: Basic Books.

Connor, W. (1994). *Ethnonationalism: The Quest for Understanding*. Princeton: Princeton University Press.

Cook, K. S., and Emerson, R. M. (1986). *Social Exchange Theory*. Beverly Hills: Sage.

Cook, S. W. (1962). "The Systematic Analysis of Socially Significant Events: A Strategy for Social Research," *Journal of Social Issues*, 18(2), 66–84.

———. (1969). "Motives in a Conceptual Analysis of Attitude-Related Behavior," in *Nebraska Symposium on Motivation, 1969*, ed. W. J. Arnold and D. Levine, pp. 179–235. Lincoln: University of Nebraska Press.

———. (1978). "Interpersonal and Attitudinal Outcomes in Cooperating Interracial Groups," *Journal of Research and Development in Education*, 12(1), 97–113.

———. (1979). "Social Science and School Desegregation: Did We Mislead the Supreme Court?" *Personality and Social Psychology Bulletin*, 5, 420–37.

———. (1983). "The 1954 Social Science Statement and School Desegregation: A Reply to Gerard," *American Psychologist*, 39, 819–32.

———. (1984). "Cooperative Interaction in Multiethnic Contexts," in *Groups in Contact: The Psychology of Desegregation*, ed. N. Miller and M. B. Brewer, pp. 155–85. Orlando: Academic.

———. (1985). "Experimenting on Social Issues: The Case of School Desegregation," *American Psychologist*, 40, 452–60.

———. (1990). "Toward a Psychology of Improving Justice: Research on Extending the Equality Principle to Victims of Social Injustice," *Journal of Social Issues*, 46(1), 147–61.

Corzine, J., Creech, J., and Corzine, L. (1983). "Black Concentration and Lynchings in the South: Testing Blalock's Power-Threat Hypothesis," *Social Forces*, 61, 774–96.

Crosby, F., Bromley, S., and Saxe, L. (1980). "Recent Unobtrusive Studies of Black and White Discrimination and Prejudice: A Literature Review," *Psychological Bulletin*, 87, 546–63.

Curtis, J. E., and White, P. G. (1993). "Proximity or Regional Cultures? A Reexamination of Patterns of Francophone-Anglophone Liking of Each Other," *Canadian Journal of Sociology*, 18, 303–11.

David, K. H. (1971). "Effect of Intercultural Contact and International Stance on Attitude Change Toward Host Nationals," *Psychologia*, 14, 153–57.

DeCarvalho, R. J. (1993). "Gordon W. Allport on the Nature of Prejudice," *Psychological Reports*, 72, 299–308.

Demo, D. H., and Hughes, M. (1990). "Socialization and Racial Identity among Black Americans," *Social Psychology Quarterly*, 53, 364–74.

Deridder, R., and Tripathi, R. C., eds. (1992). *Norm Violation and Intergroup Relations*. Oxford: Clarendon.

Desforges, D. M., et al. (1991). "Effects of Structured Cooperative Contact on Changing Negative Attitudes toward Stigmatized Social Groups," *Journal of Personality and Social Psychology*, 60, 531–44.

Deutsch, K. W. (1953). "The Growth of Nations: Some Recurrent Patterns of Political and Social Integration," *World Politics*, 5, 168–95.

———. (1954). *Political Community at the International Level: Problems of Definition and Measurement*. New York: Doubleday.

———. (1960). "Toward an Inventory of Basic Trends and Patterns in Comparative and International Politics," *American Political Science Review*, 54, 34–56.

———. (1961). "Social Mobilization and Political Development," *American Political Science Review*, 55, 493–514.

———. (1966). *Nationalism and Social Communication: An Inquiry into the Foundations of Nationality*, 2nd ed. Cambridge: MIT Press. First published in 1953.

———. (1969). *Nationalism and Its Alternatives*. New York: Knopf.

———. (1979). *Tides among Nations*. New York: Free Press.

Deutsch K. W., and Merritt, R. L. (1970). *Nationalism and National Development: An Interdisciplinary Bibliography*. Cambridge: MIT Press.

Deutsch, M. (1949). "An Experimental Study of the Effects of Cooperation and Competition upon Group Process," *Human Relations*, 2, 199–231.

Deutsch, M., and Collins, M. E. (1951). *Interracial Housing: A Psychological Evaluation of a Social Experiment*. Minneapolis: University of Minnesota Press.

Dewey, D. (1952). "Negro Employment in Southern Industry," *Journal of Political Economy*, 60, 279–93.

Doise, W. (1978). *Groups and Individuals: Explanations in Social Psychology*, trans. D. Graham. Cambridge: Cambridge University Press.

Dornbusch, S., and Irle, R. D. (1959). "The Failure of Presbyterian Union," *American Journal of Sociology*, 64, 352–55.

Dovidio, J. F., and Gaertner, S. L. (1991). "Changes in the Expression and Assessment of Racial Prejudice," in *Opening Doors: Perspectives on Race Relations in Contemporary America*, ed. H. J. Knopke, R. J. Morrell, and R. W. Rogers, pp. 119–48. Tuscaloosa: University of Alabama Press.

Doyle, B. W. (1971). *The Etiquette of Race Relations in the South: A Study in Social Control*. New York: Schocken. First published in 1937.

Dubey, S. N. (1979). "Positive Discrimination Policy and Ethnocentric Attitudes among the Scheduled Castes," *Public Opinion Quarterly*, 43, 60–67.

Dudziak, M. L. (1995). "Desegregation as a Cold War Imperative," in *Critical Race Theory: The Cutting Edge*, ed. R. Delgado, pp. 110–21. Philadelphia: Temple University Press.

Duncan, O. D. (1975). *Introduction to Structural Equation Models*. New York: Academic.

Dworkin, R. (1977). "Social Sciences and Constitutional Rights: The Consequences of Uncertainty," in *Education, Social Science, and the Judicial Process*, ed. R. C. Rist and R. J. Anson, pp. 20–31. New York: Teachers College Press.

Ebel, M., and Fiala, P. (1983). *Sous le consensus, la xénophobie: Paroles, argu-*

ments, contextes (1961–1981). Lausanne: Institut de Science Politique, Mémoires et documents 16.

Edwards, J. (1994). *Multilingualism.* London: Routledge.

Ehrlich, H. J. (1961). "The Swastika Epidemic of 1959–1960: Anti-Semitism and Community Characteristics," *Social Problems,* 9, 264–72

Elkin, S. L., and Panning, W. H. (1975). "Structural Effects and Individual Attitudes: Racial Prejudice in English Cities," *Public Opinion Quarterly,* 39, 159–77.

Ellis, A. L., Gunto, S. J., Weaver, C. L., and Kelso, K. A. (1992). "The Effect of Contemplated Interpersonal Contact with Union Members on Attitudes Toward Labor Unions," *Journal of Social Psychology,* 132, 411–13.

Ellison, C. G., and Powers, D. A. (1994). "The Contact Hypothesis and Racial Attitudes among Black Americans," *Social Science Quarterly,* 75, 385–400.

Emerson, R. (1960). *From Empire to Nation: The Rise to Self-Assertion of Asian and African Peoples.* Cambridge: Harvard University Press.

Erbring, L. (1990). "Individuals Writ Large: An Epilogue on the 'Ecological Fallacy,' " in *Political Analysis,* vol. 1, ed. J. A. Stimson, pp. 235–69. Ann Arbor: University of Michigan Press.

Fay, B. (1975). *Social Theory and Political Practice.* London: George Allen & Unwin.

Fenton, J. H., and Vines, K. N. (1957). "Negro Registration in Louisiana,"*American Political Science Review,* 51, 704–13.

Fiman, B. G., Borus, J. F., and Stanton, M. D. (1975). "Black-White and American-Vietnamese Relations among Soldiers in Vietnam," *Journal of Social Issues,* 31(4), 39–48.

Finchilescu, G. (1988). "Interracial Contact in South Africa Within the Nursing Context," *Journal of Applied Social Psychology,* 18, 1207–21.

Fishman, J. A. (1989). "Cross-Polity Perspective on the Importance of Linguistic Heterogeneity as a 'Contributory Factor' in Civil Strife," in J. A. Fishman, *Language and Ethnicity in Minority Sociolinguistic Perspective,* pp. 605–26. Clevedon, Eng.: Multilingual Matters.

Forbes, H. D. (1985). *Nationalism, Ethnocentrism, and Personality: Social Science and Critical Theory.* Chicago: University of Chicago Press.

———. (1993). "Canada: From Bilingualism to Multiculturalism," *Journal of Democracy,* 4(4), 69–84.

———. (1996). "Interpreting the 1993 Election," in *Party Politics in Canada,* 7th ed., ed. H. G. Thorburn, pp. 557–77. Scarborough, Ont.: Prentice-Hall Canada.

Ford, W. S. (1972). *Interracial Public Housing in Border City: A Situational Analysis of the Contact Hypothesis.* Lexington, Mass.: D. C. Heath.

———. (1973). "Interracial Public Housing in Border City: Another Look at the Contact Hypothesis," *American Journal of Sociology,* 78, 1426–47.

———. (1986). "Favorable Intergroup Contact May Not Reduce Prejudice: Inconclusive Journal Evidence, 1960–1984," *Sociology and Social Research,* 70, 256–58.

Fossett, M. A., and Kiecolt, K. J. (1989). "The Relative Size of Minority Populations and White Racial Attitudes," *Social Science Quarterly*, 70, 820–35.

Frisbie, W. P., and Neidert, L. (1977). "Inequality and the Relative Size of Minority Populations: A Comparative Analysis," *American Journal of Sociology*, 82, 1007–30.

Fukuyama, F. (1992). *The End of History and the Last Man.* New York: Free Press.

Geertz, C. (1973). *The Interpretation of Cultures: Selected Essays.* New York: Basic Books.

Gellner, E. (1964). *Thought and Change.* London: Weidenfeld and Nicolson.

———. (1983). *Nations and Nationalism.* Oxford: Basil Blackwell.

Gentry, C. S. (1987). "Social Distance Regarding Male and Female Homosexuals," *Journal of Social Psychology*, 127, 199–208.

Gerard, H. B. (1983). "School Desegregation: The Social Science Role," *American Psychologist*, 38, 869–77.

Geuss, R. (1981). *The Idea of a Critical Theory: Habermas and the Frankfurt School.* Cambridge: Cambridge University Press.

Giles, H. (1973). "Accent Mobility: A Model and Some Data," *Anthropological Linguistics*, 15, 87–105.

———. ed. (1977). *Language, Ethnicity, and Intergroup Relations.* London: Academic.

Giles, H., Coupland, J., and Coupland, N., eds. (1991). *Contexts of Accommodation: Developments in Applied Sociolinguistics.* Cambridge: Cambridge University Press.

Giles, H., and Johnson, P. (1981). "The Role of Language in Ethnic Group Relations," in *Intergroup Behavior*, ed. J. C. Turner and H. Giles, pp. 199–243. Chicago: University of Chicago Press.

Giles, H., and Saint-Jacques, B. (1979). *Language and Ethnic Relations.* New York: Pergamon.

Giles, M. W. (1977). "Percent Black and Racial Hostility: An Old Assumption Reexamined," *Social Science Quarterly*, 58, 412–17.

Giles, M. W., and Evans, A. S. (1985). "External Threat, Perceived Threat, and Group Identity," *Social Science Quarterly*, 66, 50–66.

Glaser, J. M. (1994). "Back to the Black Belt: Racial Environment and White Racial Attitudes in the South," *Journal of Politics*, 56, 21–41.

Glazer, N., and Moynihan, D. P. (1963). *Beyond the Melting Pot: The Negroes, Puerto Ricans, Jews, Italians, and Irish of New York City.* Cambridge: MIT Press.

———. (1975). "Introduction," in *Ethnicity: Theory and Experience*, ed. N. Glazer and D. P. Moynihan, pp. 1–26. Cambridge: Harvard University Press.

Goldberg, A. I., and Kirschenbaum, A. (1989). "Black Newcomers to Israel: Contact Situations and Social Distance," *Sociology and Social Research*, 74, 52–57.

Gordon, M. M. (1964). *Assimilation in American Life: The Role of Race, Religion, and National Origins*. New York: Oxford University Press.

Gough, H. G., and Bradley, P. (1993). "Personal Attributes of People Described by Others as Intolerant," in *Prejudice, Politics, and the American Dilemma*, ed. P. M. Sniderman, P. E. Tetlock, and E. G. Carmines, pp. 60–85. Stanford: Stanford University Press.

Graglia, L. A. (1976). *Disaster by Decree: The Supreme Court Decisions on Race and the Schools*. Ithaca: Cornell University Press.

Granberg, D. (1992). "Emerging Problems Individualism Cannot Solve," in *Social Judgment and Intergroup Relations: Essays in Honor of Muzafer Sherif*, ed. D. Granberg and G. Sarup, pp. 203–17. New York: Springer-Verlag.

Gray, J. S., and Thompson, A. H. (1953). "The Ethnic Prejudices of White and Negro College Students," *Journal of Abnormal and Social Psychology*, 48, 311–13.

Green, H. A. J. (1964). *Aggregation in Economic Analysis: An Introductory Survey*. Princeton: Princeton University Press.

Greenfeld, L. (1992). *Nationalism: Five Roads to Modernity*. Cambridge: Harvard University Press.

Grunbaum, W. F. (1964). "Desegregation in Texas: Voting and Action Patterns," *Public Opinion Quarterly*, 28, 604–14.

Gundlach, R. H. (1956). "Effects of On-the-Job Experiences with Negroes upon Racial Attitudes of White Workers in Union Shops," *Psychological Reports*, 2, 67–77.

Gurr, T. R. (1993a). "Why Minorities Rebel: A Global Analysis of Communal Mobilization and Conflict since 1945," *International Political Science Review*, 14, 161–201.

———. (1993b). *Minorities at Risk: A Global View of Ethnopolitical Conflicts*. Washington: United States Institute of Peace Press.

Habermas, J. (1971). *Knowledge and Human Interests*, trans. J. J. Shapiro. Boston: Beacon.

———. (1973). *Theory and Practice*, trans. J. Viertel. Boston: Beacon.

———. (1988). *On the Logic of the Social Sciences*, trans. S. W. Nicholsen and J. A. Stark. Cambridge: MIT Press.

Hacker, A. (1992). *Two Nations: Black and White, Separate, Hostile, Unequal*. New York: Charles Scribner's Sons.

Hale-Benson, J. E. (1986). *Black Children: Their Roots, Culture, and Learning Styles*, rev. ed. Baltimore: Johns Hopkins University Press.

Hamblin, R. L. (1962). "The Dynamics of Racial Discrimination," *Social Problems*, 10, 103–21.

Hamilton, D. L., and Bishop, G. D. (1976). "Attitudinal and Behavioral Effects of Initial Integration of White Suburban Neighborhoods," *Journal of Social Issues*, 32, 47–67.

Hamilton, R. F. (1972). *Class and Politics in the United States*. New York: John Wiley.

Hannan, M. T. (1971). *Aggregation and Disaggregation in Sociology*. Lexington, Mass.: Lexington Books.

Harding, J., and Hogrefe, R. (1952). "Attitudes of White Department Store Employees Toward Negro Co-Workers," *Journal of Social Issues*, 8, 18–28.

Harlan, H. H. (1942). "Some Factors Affecting Attitude Toward Jews," *American Sociological Review*, 7, 816–27.

Harrington, H. J., and Miller, N. (1992). "Research and Theory in Intergroup Relations: Issues of Consensus and Controversy," in *Cultural Diversity and the Schools*, vol. 2, ed. J. Lynch, C. Modgil, and S. Modgil, pp. 159–78. London: Falmer.

Harris, D. (1995). "Exploring the Determinants of Adult Black Identity: Context and Process," *Social Forces*, 74, 227–41.

Hawley, W. D., Banks, J. A., Padilla, A. M., Pope-Davis, D. B., and Schofield, J. W. (1995). "Strategies for Reducing Racial and Ethnic Prejudice: Essential Principles for Program Design," in *Toward a Common Destiny: Improving Race and Ethnic Relations in America*, ed. W. D. Hawley and A. W. Jackson, pp. 423–33. San Francisco: Jossey-Bass.

Hawley, W. D., and Smylie, M. A. (1988). "The Contribution of School Desegregation to Academic Achievement and Racial Integration," in *Eliminating Racism: Profiles in Controversy*, ed. P. A. Katz and D. A. Taylor, pp. 281–97. New York: Plenum.

Hayes, C. J. H. (1931). *The Historical Evolution of Modern Nationalism*. New York: Macmillan.

———. (1960). *Nationalism: A Religion*. New York: Macmillan.

Hechter, M. (1975). *Internal Colonialism: The Celtic Fringe in British National Development, 1536–1966*. Berkeley: University of California Press.

Heer, D. M. (1959). "The Sentiment of White Supremacy: An Ecological Study," *American Journal of Sociology*, 64, 592–98.

Heise, D. R. (1975). *Causal Analysis*. New York: Wiley-Interscience.

Held, D. (1980). *Introduction to Critical Theory: Horkheimer to Habermas*. Berkeley: University of California Press.

Herek, G. M. (1988). "Heterosexuals' Attitudes Toward Lesbians and Gay Men: Correlates and Gender Differences," *Journal of Sex Research*, 25, 451–77.

Herek, G. M., and Glunt, E. K. (1993). "Interpersonal Contact and Heterosexuals' Attitudes Toward Gay Men: Results from a National Survey," *Journal of Sex Research*, 30, 239–44.

Hewstone, M. (1986). *Understanding Attitudes to the European Community: A Social-Psychological Study in Four Member States*. Cambridge: Cambridge University Press.

———. (1989). *Causal Attribution: From Cognitive Processes to Collective Beliefs*. Oxford: Basil Blackwell.

Hewstone, M., and Brown, R. (1986). "Contact Is Not Enough: An Intergroup Perspective on the 'Contact Hypothesis,'" in *Contact and Conflict in Intergroup Encounters*, ed. M. Hewstone and R. Brown, pp. 1–44. Oxford: Basil Blackwell.

Hibbs, D. A. (1973). *Mass Political Violence: A Cross-National Causal Analysis*. New York: John Wiley.

Hiley, D. R., Bohman, J. F., and Shusterman, R., eds. (1991). *The Interpretive Turn: Philosophy, Science, Culture*. Ithaca: Cornell University Press.

Hirsch, E. D. (1987). *Cultural Literacy: What Every American Needs to Know*. Boston: Houghton Mifflin.

Hirschman, A. O. (1977). *The Passions and the Interests: Political Arguments for Capitalism Before Its Triumph*. Princeton: Princeton University Press.

Hobbes, T. (1960). *Leviathan, or the Matter, Forme, and Power of a Commonwealth Ecclesiasticall and Civil*, ed. M. Oakeshott. Oxford: Basil Blackwell. First published in 1651.

Hobsbawm, E. J. (1990). *Nations and Nationalism since 1780: Programme, Myth, Reality*. Cambridge: Cambridge University Press.

Hofman, J. E., and Zak, I. (1969). "Interpersonal Contact and Attitude Change in a Cross-Cultural Situation," *Journal of Social Psychology*, 78, 165–71.

Hogg, M. A., and Abrams, D. (1988). *Social Identifications: A Social Psychology of Intergroup Relations and Group Processes*. London: Routledge.

Homans, G. C. (1950). *The Human Group*. New York: Harcourt, Brace and World.

———. (1961). *Social Behavior: Its Elementary Forms*. New York: Harcourt, Brace and World.

Horkheimer, M. (1947). *Eclipse of Reason*. New York: Oxford University Press.

———. (1972). *Critical Theory: Selected Essays*, trans. M. J. O'Connell et al. New York: Seabury.

Horowitz, D. L. (1983). "Racial Violence in the United States," in *Ethnic Pluralism and Public Policy: Achieving Equality in the United States and Britain*, ed. N. Glazer and K. Young, pp. 187–211. London: Heinemann Educational Books.

———. (1985). *Ethnic Groups in Conflict*. Berkeley: University of California Press.

Hunt, C. I. (1959). "Private Integrated Housing in a Medium-Sized Northern City," *Social Problems*, 7, 196–209.

Ibrahim, S. E. M. (1970). "Interaction, Perception, and Attitudes of Arab Students Toward Americans," *Sociology and Social Research*, 55, 29–46.

Ignatieff, M. (1993). *Blood and Belonging: Journeys into the New Nationalism*. New York: Viking Penguin.

Insko, C. A., Nacoste, R. W., and Moe, J. L. (1983). "Belief Congruence and Racial Discrimination: Review of the Evidence and Critical Evaluation," *European Journal of Social Psychology*, 13, 153–74.

Irish, D. P. (1952). "Reactions of Caucasian Residents to Japanese-American Neighbors," *Journal of Social Issues*, 8, 10–17.

Jackman, M. R., and Crane, M. (1986). " 'Some of My Best Friends Are Black': Interracial Friendship and Whites' Racial Attitudes," *Public Opinion Quarterly*, 50, 459–86.

Jackman, M. R., and Muha, M. J. (1984). "Education and Intergroup Attitudes: Moral Enlightenment, Superficial Democratic Commitment, or Ideological Refinement?" *American Sociological Review*, 49, 751–69.

Jackson, J. E. (1996). "Political Methodology: An Overview," in *A New Handbook of Political Science*, ed. R. E. Goodin and H.- D. Klingemann, pp. 717–48. Oxford: Oxford University Press.

Jackson, J. W. (1991). "Authoritarian Personality Theory of Intergroup Hostility: A Review and Evaluation of the Theoretical and Empirical Literature," *International Journal of Group Tensions*, 21, 383–405.

———. (1993). "Contact Theory of Intergroup Hostility: A Review and Evaluation of the Theoretical and Empirical Literature," *International Journal of Group Tensions*, 23, 43–65.

James, H. E. O. (1955). "Personal Contact in School and Change in Intergroup Attitudes," *International Social Science Bulletin*, 7, 66–70.

Jay, M. (1973). *The Dialectical Imagination: A History of the Frankfurt School and the Institute of Social Research, 1923–1950*. Boston: Little, Brown.

Jeffries, V., and Ransford, H. E. (1969). "Interracial Social Contact and Middle-Class White Reaction to the Watts Riot," *Social Problems*, 16, 312–24.

Jenkins, J. C., and Kposowa, A. J. (1990). "Explaining Military Coups d'Etat: Black Africa, 1957–1984," *American Sociological Review*, 55, 861–75.

Johnson, D. W., Johnson, R. T., and Maruyama, G. (1984). "Goal Interdependence and Interpersonal Attraction in Heterogeneous Classrooms: A Meta-analysis," in *Groups in Contact: The Psychology of Desegregation*, ed. N. Miller and M. B. Brewer, pp. 187–212. Orlando: Academic.

Johnston, L., and Hewstone, M. (1990). "Intergroup Contact: Social Identity and Social Cognition," in *Social Identity Theory: Constructive and Critical Advances*, ed. D. Abrams and M. A. Hogg, pp. 185–210. New York: Harvester.

Jones, E. E., and Davis, K. E. (1965). "From Acts to Dispositions: The Attribution Process in Person Perception," in *Advances in Experimental Social Psychology*, vol. 2, ed. L. Berkowitz, pp. 219–66. New York: Academic.

Jones, J. (1983). "The Concept of Race in Social Psychology: From Color to Culture," in *Review of Personality and Social Psychology*, vol. 4, ed. L. Wheeler and P. Shaver, pp. 117–50. Beverly Hills: Sage.

———. (1991). "Piercing the Veil: Bi-Cultural Strategies for Coping with Prejudice and Racism," in *Opening Doors: Perspectives on Race Relations in Contemporary America*, ed. H. J. Knopke, R. J. Norrell, and R. W. Rogers, pp. 179–97. Tuscaloosa: University of Alabama Press.

Joy, R. J. (1992). *Canada's Official Languages: The Progress of Bilingualism*. Toronto: Univerisity of Toronto Press.

Kalin, R., and Berry, J. W. (1980). "Geographic Mobility and Ethnic Tolerance," *Journal of Social Psychology*, 112, 129–34.

———. (1982). "The Social Ecology of Ethnic Attitudes in Canada," *Canadian Journal of Behavioural Science*, 14, 97–109.

Kamal, A. A., and Maruyama, G. (1990). "Cross-Cultural Contact and Attitudes of Qatari Students in the United States," *International Journal of Intercultural Relations*, 14, 123–34.

Katz, I. (1991). "Gordon Allport's *The Nature of Prejudice*," *Political Psychology*, 12, 125–57.

Katz, I., Hass, R. G., and Wackenhut, J. (1986). "Racial Ambivalence, Value Duality, and Behavior," in *Prejudice, Discrimination, and Racism*, ed. J. F. Dovidio and S. L. Gaertner, pp. 35–59. New York: Academic.

Kaufmann, C. (1996). "Possible and Impossible Solutions to Ethnic Civil Wars," *International Security*, 20(4), 136–75.

Kawwa, T. (1968). "A Survey of Ethnic Attitudes of Some British Secondary School Pupils," *British Journal of Social and Clinical Psychology*, 7, 161–68.

Kedourie, E. (1961). *Nationalism*. London: Hutchinson.

Kelejian, H. H., and Oates, W. E. (1974). *Introduction to Econometrics: Principles and Applications*. New York: Harper & Row.

Kelley, H. H. (1968). "Interpersonal Accommodation," *American Psychologist*, 23, 399–410.

Kelly, J. G., Ferson, J. E., and Holtzman, W. H. (1958). "The Measurement of Attitudes Toward the Negro in the South," *Journal of Social Psychology*, 48, 305–17.

Key, V. O. (1949). *Southern Politics in State and Nation*. New York: Random House.

Kinder, D. R., and Mendelberg, T. (1995). "Cracks in American Apartheid: The Political Impact of Prejudice among Desegregated Whites," *Journal of Politics*, 57, 402–24.

Kinder, D. R., and Sears, D. O. (1981). "Prejudice and Politics: Symbolic Racism Versus Racial Threats to the Good Life," *Journal of Personality and Social Psychology*, 40, 414–31.

Kirchler, E., and Zani, B. (1995). "Why Don't They Stay at Home? Prejudices Against Ethnic Minorities in Italy," *Journal of Community and Applied Social Psychology*, 5, 59–65.

Kluger, R. (1976). *Simple Justice: The History of "Brown v. Board of Education" and Black America's Struggle for Equality*. New York: Knopf.

Knoke, D., and Kyriazis, N. (1977). "The Persistence of the Black-Belt Vote: A Test of Key's Hypothesis," *Social Science Quarterly*, 57, 899–906.

Kochman, T. (1981). *Black and White Styles in Conflict*. Chicago: University of Chicago Press.

Kohn, H. (1944). *The Idea of Nationalism*. New York: Macmillan.

Kortian, G. (1980). *Metacritique: The Philosophical Argument of Jurgen Habermas*. Cambridge: Cambridge University Press.

Kuhn, T. S. (1962). *The Structure of Scientific Revolutions* . Chicago: University of Chicago Press.

Laczko, L. S. (1995). *Pluralism and Inequality in Quebec*. Toronto: University of Toronto Press.

Laitin, D. D. (1993). "The Game Theory of Language Regimes," *International Political Science Review*, 14, 227–39.

Lambert, W. E., Hodgson, R. C., Gardner, R. C., and Fillenbaum, S. (1960).

"Evaluational Reactions to Spoken Language," *Journal of Abnormal and Social Psychology*, 60, 44–51.

Lambert, W. E., Libman, E., and Poser, E. G. (1960). "The Effect of Increased Salience of a Membership Group on Pain Tolerance," *Journal of Personality*, 28, 350–57.

Lance, L. M. (1987). "The Effects of Interaction with Gay Persons on Attitudes Toward Homosexuality," *Human Relations*, 40, 329–36.

———.(1992). "Changes in Homophobic Views as Related to Interaction with Gay Persons: A Study in the Reduction of Tensions," *International Journal of Group Tensions*, 22, 291–99.

———. (1994). "Do Reductions in Homophobia from Heterosexual Interactions with Gay Persons Continue? A Study of Social Contact Theory of Intergroup Tensions," *International Journal of Group Tensions*, 24, 423–34.

Landis, D., Hope, R. O., and Day, H. R. (1984). "Training for Desegregation in the Military," in *Groups in Contact: The Psychology of Desegregation*, ed. N. Miller and M. B. Brewer, pp. 257–78. Orlando: Academic.

Lang, K. (1986). "A Language Theory of Discrimination," *Quarterly Journal of Economics*, 101, 363–82.

Laponce, J. A. (1987). *Languages and Their Territories*, trans. A. Martin-Sperry. Toronto: University of Toronto Press.

Lazarsfeld, P. W. (1955). "Interpretation of Statistical Relations as a Research Operation," in *The Language of Social Research: A Reader in the Methodology of Social Research*, ed. P. F. Lazarsfeld and M. Rosenberg, pp. 115–25. New York: Free Press.

Leblanc, G. (1995). "Discrimination in the Labor Market," *Canadian Journal of Economics*, 28, 702–17.

LeVine, R. A., and Campbell, D. T. (1972). *Ethnocentrism: Theories of Conflict, Ethnic Attitudes, and Group Behavior*. New York: John Wiley.

Lieberson, S. (1970). *Language and Ethnic Relations in Canada*. New York: John Wiley.

———. (1981). *Language Diversity and Language Contact*. Stanford: Stanford University Press.

Longshore, D. (1982). "Social Psychological Research on School Desegregation: Toward a New Agenda," in *New Directions for Testing and Measurement*, No. 14, ed. D. J. Monti, pp. 39–52. San Francisco: Jossey-Bass.

Longshore, D., and Prager, J. (1985). "The Impact of School Desegregation: A Situational Analysis," *Annual Review of Sociology*, 11, 75–91.

MacIntyre, A. (1977). "Epistemological Crises, Dramatic Narrative, and the Philosophy of Science," *The Monist*, 60, 453—72.

MacKenzie, B. K. (1948). "The Importance of Contact in Determining Attitudes Toward Negroes," *Journal of Abnormal and Social Psychology*, 43, 417–41.

Mann, J. H. (1959). "The Effects of Inter-Racial Contact on Sociometric Choices and Perceptions," *Journal of Social Psychology*, 50, 143–52.

Marks, J. (1995). *Human Biodiversity: Genes, Race, and History*. New York: Aldine de Gruyter.

Marshall, R. (1974). "The Economics of Racial Discrimination: A Survey," *Journal of Economic Literature*, 12, 849–71.

Massey, D. S., and Denton, N. A. (1993). *American Apartheid: Segregation and the Making of the Underclass*. Cambridge: Harvard University Press.

Massey, D. S., and Hajnal, Z. L. (1995). "The Changing Geographic Structure of Black-White Segregation in the United States," *Social Science Quarterly*, 76, 527–42.

Matthews, D. R., and Prothro, J. W. (1963). "Social and Economic Factors and Negro Voter Registration in the South," *American Political Science Review*, 57, 24–44.

McClendon, McK. J. (1974). "Interracial Contact and the Reduction of Prejudice," *Sociological Focus*, 7, 47–65.

McClendon, McK. J., and Eitzen, D. S. (1975). "Interracial Contact on Collegiate Basketball Teams: A Test of Sherif's Theory of Superordinate Goals," *Social Science Quarterly*, 55, 926–38.

McConahay, J. B. (1978). "The Effects of School Desegregation upon Students' Racial Attitudes and Behavior: A Critical Review of the Literature and a Prolegomenon to Future Research," *Law and Contemporary Problems*, 42(3), 77–107.

———. (1986). "Modern Racism, Ambivalence, and the Modern Racism Scale," in *Prejudice, Discrimination, and Racism*, ed. J. F. Dovidio and S. L. Gaertner, pp. 91–125. Orlando: Academic.

McConahay, J. B., and Hough, J. C. (1976). "Symbolic Racism," *Journal of Social Issues*, 32(2), 23–45.

McIntosh, M. E., MacIver, M. A., Abele, D. G., and Nolle, D. B. (1995). "Minority Rights and Majority Rule: Ethnic Tolerance in Romania and Bulgaria," *Social Forces*, 73, 939–67.

McKirnan, D. J., Smith, C. E., and Hamayan, E. V. (1983). "A Sociolinguistic Approach to the Belief-Similarity Model of Racial Attitudes," *Journal of Experimental Social Psychology*, 19, 434–47.

McRoberts, K. (1988). *Quebec: Social Change and Political Crisis*, 3rd ed. Toronto: McClelland and Stewart.

Meer, B., and Freedman, E. (1966). "The Impact of Negro Neighbors on White Home Owners," *Social Forces*, 45, 11–19.

Meloen, J. D. (1994). "A Critical Analysis of Forty Years of Authoritarianism Research: Did Theory Testing Suffer from Cold War Attitudes?" in *Nationalism, Ethnicity, and Identity: Cross-National and Comparative Perspectives*, ed. Russell F. Farnen, pp. 127–65. New Brunswick, N.J.: Transaction.

Merton, R. K. (1957). *Social Theory and Social Structure*, rev. ed. Glencoe: Free Press.

Messick, D. M., and Mackie, D. M. (1989). "Intergroup Relations," *Annual Review of Psychology*, 40, 45–81.

Miller, N. (1981). "Changing Views about the Effects of School Desegregation: *Brown* Then and Now," in *Scientific Inquiry and the Social Sciences*, ed. M. B. Brewer and B. E. Collins, pp. 413–53. San Francisco: Jossey-Bass.

————. (1984). "Israel and the United States: Comparisons and Commonalities in School Desegregation," in *School Desegregation: Cross-Cultural Perspectives*, ed. Y. Amir and S. Sharan, pp. 237–53. Hillsdale, N.J.: Lawrence Erlbaum.

Miller, N., and Brewer, M. B., eds. (1984). *Groups in Contact: The Psychology of Desegregation*. Orlando: Academic.

Milman, A., Reichel, A., and Pizam, A. (1990). "The Impact of Tourism on Ethnic Attitudes: The Israeli-Egyptian Case," *Journal of Travel Research*, 29, 45–49.

Minogue, K. R. (1967). *Nationalism*. London: Methuen.

Mitchell, I. S. (1968). "Epilogue to a Referendum," *Australian Journal of Social Issues*, 3, 9–12.

Montagu, A. (1972). *Statement on Race: An Annotated Elaboration and Exposition of the Four Statements on Race Issued by the United Nations Educational, Scientific, and Cultural Organization*, 3rd ed. New York: Oxford University Press.

————. (1974). *Man's Most Dangerous Myth: The Fallacy of Race*, 5th ed. New York: Oxford University Press.

Montesquieu, Charles de Secondat (1989). *The Spirit of the Laws*, trans. A. Cohler, B. C. Miller, and H. S. Stone. New York: Cambridge University Press. First published in 1748.

Morris, R. T., and Jeffries, V. (1968). "Violence Next Door," *Social Forces*, 46, 352–58.

Morrison, D. G., and Stevenson, H. M. (1972a). "Cultural Pluralism, Modernization, and Conflict: An Empirical Analysis of Sources of Political Instability in African Nations," *Canadian Journal of Political Science*, 5, 82–103.

————. (1972b). "Integration and Instability: Patterns of African Political Development," *American Political Science Review*, 66, 902–27.

Moskos, C. C. (1970). *The American Enlisted Man: The Rank and File in Today's Military*. New York: Russell Sage Foundation.

Nataf, A. "Aggregation," in *International Encyclopedia of the Social Sciences*, vol. 1, ed. D. L. Sills, pp. 160–68. New York: Macmillan.

Newcomb, T. M. (1947). "Autistic Hostility and Social Reality," *Human Relations*, 1, 69–86.

Nincic, M., and Russett, B. (1979). "The Effect of Similarity and Interest on Attitudes Toward Foreign Countries," *Public Opinion Quarterly*, 43, 68–78.

Novak, M. (1972). *The Rise of the Unmeltable Ethnics: Politics and Culture in the Seventies*. New York: Macmillan.

Ogburn, W. F., and Grigg, C. M. (1956). "Factors Related to the Virginia Vote on Segregation," *Social Forces*, 34, 301–8.

Olzak, S. (1983). "Contemporary Ethnic Mobilization," *Annual Review of Sociology*, 9, 355–74.

————. (1986). "A Competition Model of Ethnic Collective Action in American

Cities, 1877–1889," in *Competitive Ethnic Relations*, ed. S. Olzak and J. Nagel, pp. 17–46. Orlando: Academic.

———. (1992). *The Dynamics of Ethnic Competition and Conflict.* Stanford: Stanford University Press.

Olzak, S., and Nagel, J. (1986). "Introduction, Competitive Ethnic Relations: An Overview," in *Competitive Ethnic Relations*, ed. S. Olzak and J. Nagel, pp. 1–14. Orlando: Academic.

Olzak, S., Shanahan, S., and West, E. (1994). "School Desegregation, Interracial Exposure, and Antibusing Activity in Contemporary Urban America," *American Journal of Sociology*, 100, 196–241.

Outhwaite, W. (1994). *Habermas: A Critical Introduction.* Stanford: Stanford University Press.

Pal, L. A. (1993). *Interests of State: The Politics of Language, Multiculturalism, and Feminism in Canada.* Montreal: McGill-Queen's University Press.

Pangle, T. L. (1973). *Montesquieu's Philosophy of Liberalism: A Commentary on "The Spirit of the Laws."* Chicago: University of Chicago Press.

Park, R. E. (1950). *Race and Culture.* New York: Free Press.

Parsons, M. A. (1985). "Parents' and Students' Attitude Changes Related to School Desegregation in New Castle County, Delaware," in *Metropolitan Desegregation*, ed. R. L. Green, pp. 185–209. New York: Plenum.

Patai, R., and Patai, J. (1989). *The Myth of the Jewish Race*, rev. ed. Detroit: Wayne State University Press.

Patchen, M. (1995). "Contact Between Ethnic Groups: When and How Does It Lead to More Positive Relations?" *International Journal of Group Tensions*, 25, 271–87.

Pearce, P. L. (1982). "Tourists and Their Hosts: Some Social and Psychological Effects of Inter-Cultural Contact," in *Cultures in Contact: Studies in Cross-Cultural Interaction*, ed. S. Bochner, pp. 199–221. Oxford: Pergamon.

Periwal, S., ed. (1995). *Notions of Nationalism.* Budapest: Central European University Press.

Pettigrew, T. F. (1957a). "Desegregation and Its Chances for Success: Northern and Southern Views," *Social Forces*, 35, 339–44.

———. (1957b). "Demographic Correlates of Border-State Desegregation," *American Sociological Review*, 22, 683–89.

———. (1959). "Regional Differences in Anti-Negro Prejudice," *Journal of Abnormal and Social Psychology*, 59, 28–36.

———. (1961). "Social Psychology and Desegregation Research," *American Psychologist*, 16, 105–12.

———. (1971). *Racially Separate or Together?* New York: McGraw-Hill.

———. (1979). "The Ultimate Attribution Error: Extending Allport's Analysis of Prejudice," *Personality and Social Psychology Bulletin*, 5, 461–76.

———. (1986). "The Intergroup Contact Hypothesis Reconsidered," in *Contact and Conflict in Intergroup Encounters*, ed. M. Hewstone and R. Brown, pp. 169–95. Oxford: Basil Blackwell.

———. (1991). "Advancing Racial Justice: Past Lessons for Future Use," in

Opening Doors: Perspectives on Race Relations in Contemporary America, ed. H. J. Knopke, R. J. Norrell, and R. W. Rogers, pp. 165–78. Tuscaloosa: University of Alabama Press.

Pettigrew, T. F., and Campbell, E. Q. (1960). "Faubus and Segregation: An Analysis of Arkansas Voting," *Public Opinion Quarterly*, 24, 436–47.

Pettigrew, T. F., and Cramer, M. R. (1959). "The Demography of Desegregation," *Journal of Social Issues*, 15, 61–71.

Pettigrew, T. F., and Meertens, R. W. (1995). "Subtle and Blatant Prejudice in Western Europe," *European Journal of Social Psychology*, 25, 57–75.

Pettigrew, T. F., Useem, E. L., Normand, C., and Smith, M. S. (1973). "Busing: A Review of 'The Evidence,' " *The Public Interest*, 30, 88–118.

Phillips, C. D. (1986). "Social Structure and Social Control: Modeling the Discriminatory Execution of Blacks in Georgia and North Carolina, 1925–1935," *Social Forces*, 65, 458–75.

Pinkney, A. (1963). "The Quantitative Factor in Prejudice," *Sociology and Social Research*, 47, 161–68.

Pizam, A., Milman, A., and Jafari, J. (1991). "Influence of Tourism on Attitudes: U.S. Students Visiting USSR," *Tourism Management*, 12, 47–54.

Popper, K. R. (1962). *Conjectures and Refutations: The Growth of Scientific Knowledge*. London: Routledge & Kegan Paul.

Posen, B. R. (1993). "The Security Dilemma and Ethnic Conflict," in *Ethnic Conflict and International Security*, ed. M. E. Brown, pp. 103–24. Princeton: Princeton University Press.

Powers, D. A., and Ellison, C. G. (1995). "Interracial Contact and Black Racial Attitudes: The Contact Hypothesis and Selectivity Bias," *Social Forces*, 74, 205–26.

Prager, J., Longshore, D., and Seeman, M. (1986). *School Desegregation Research: New Directions in Situational Analysis*. New York: Plenum.

Preston, J. D., and Robinson, J. W. (1974). "On Modification of Interracial Interaction," *American Sociological Review*, 39, 283–85.

Proshansky, H. M. (1966). "The Development of Intergroup Attitudes," in *Review of Child Development Research*, vol. 2, ed. L. W. Hoffman and M. L. Hoffman, pp. 311–71. New York: Russell Sage Foundation.

Quillian, L. (1995). "Prejudice as a Response to Perceived Group Threat: Population Composition and Anti-Immigrant and Racial Prejudice in Europe," *American Sociological Review*, 60, 586–611.

Rabushka, A. (1969). "Integration in a Multi-Racial Institution: Ethnic Attitudes among Chinese and Malay Students at the University of Malaya," *Race*, 11, 53–63.

Raffel, J. A. (1985). "The Impact of Metropolitan School Desegregation on Public Opinion: A Longitudinal Analysis," *Urban Affairs Quarterly*, 21, 245–65.

Rapoport, A. (1983). *Mathematical Models in the Social and Behavioral Sciences*. New York: Wiley.

Rawls, J. (1971). *A Theory of Justice*. Cambridge: Harvard University Press.

———. (1993). *Political Liberalism*. New York: Columbia University Press.

Ray, J. J. (1983). "Racial Attitudes and the Contact Hypothesis," *Journal of Social Psychology*, 119, 3–10.

Reed, J. S. (1972). "Percent Black and Lynching: A Test of Blalock's Theory," *Social Forces*, 50, 356–60.

———. (1980). "Getting to Know You: The Contact Hypothesis Applied to the Sectional Beliefs and Attitudes of White Southerners," *Social Forces*, 59, 123–35.

Reich, C., and Purbhoo, M. (1975). "The Effect of Cross-Cultural Contact," *Canadian Journal of Behavioural Science*, 7, 313–27.

Reich, M. (1981). *Racial Inequality: A Political-Economic Analysis*. Princeton: Princeton University Press.

Reicher, S. (1986). "Contact, Action and Racialization: Some British Evidence," in *Contact and Conflict in Intergroup Encounters*, ed. M. Hewstone and R. Brown, pp. 152–68. Oxford: Basil Blackwell.

Reigrotski, E., and Anderson, N. (1959). "National Stereotypes and Foreign Contacts," *Public Opinion Quarterly*, 23, 515–28.

Renan, E. (1996). *What Is a Nation?* trans. W. R. Taylor. Toronto: Tapir. First published in 1882.

Riordan, C. (1978a). "Equal-Status Interracial Contact: A Review and Revision of the Concept," *International Journal of Intercultural Relations*, 2, 161–85.

———. (1978b). "Developing Tolerance: A Comparison of Contextual Versus Program Effects," *International Journal of Intercultural Relations*, 2, 309–26.

———. (1987). "Intergroup Contact in Small Cities," *International Journal of Intercultural Relations*, 11, 143–54.

Roberts, H. W. (1953). "The Impact of Military Service upon the Racial Attitudes of Negro Servicemen in World War II," *Social Problems*, 1, 65–69.

Robinson, J. L. (1980). "Physical Distance and Racial Attitudes: A Further Examination of the Contact Hypothesis," *Phylon*, 41, 325–32.

Robinson, J. W., and Preston, J. D. (1976). "Equal-Status Contact and Modification of Racial Prejudice: A Reexamination of the Contact Hypothesis," *Social Forces*, 54, 911–24.

Robinson, W. S. (1950). "Ecological Correlations and the Behavior of Individuals," *American Sociological Review*, 15, 351–57.

Rogers, M., Hennigan, K., Bowman, C., and Miller, N. (1984). "Intergroup Acceptance in Classroom and Playground Settings," in *Groups in Contact: The Psychology of Desegregation*, ed. N. Miller and M. B. Brewer, pp. 213–27. Orlando: Academic.

Rorty, R. (1991). *Philosophical Papers*, vol. 1: *Objectivity, Relativism, and Truth*. Cambridge: Cambridge University Press.

Rose, A. M., Atelsek, F. J., and McDonald, L. R. (1953). "Neighborhood Reactions to Isolated Negro Residents: An Alternative to Invasion and Succession," *American Sociological Review*, 18, 497–507.

Rose, T . L. (1981). "Cognitive and Dyadic Processes in Intergroup Contact," in *Cognitive Processes in Stereotyping and Intergroup Behavior*, ed. D. L. Hamilton, pp. 259–303. Hillsdale, N.J.: Lawrence Erlbaum.

Rosen, P. L. (1972). *The Supreme Court and Social Science*. Urbana: University of Illinois Press.

Rosenberg, M. (1968). *The Logic of Survey Analysis*. New York: Basic Books.

Rosenblith, J. F. (1949). "A Replication of 'Some Roots of Prejudice,' " *Journal of Abnormal and Social Psychology*, 44, 470–89.

Rosenthal, R. (1966). *Experimenter Effects in Behavioral Research*. New York: Appleton.

Rossi, P. H., Berk, R. A., and Eidson, B. K. (1974). *The Roots of Urban Discontent: Public Policy, Municipal Institutions, and the Ghetto*. New York: Wiley.

Roth, B. M. (1994). *Prescription for Failure: Race Relations in the Age of Social Science*. New Brunswick, N.J.: Transaction.

Rothbart, M., and John, O. P. (1985). "Social Categorization and Behavioral Episodes: A Cognitive Analysis of the Effects of Intergroup Contact," *Journal of Social Issues*, 41(3), 81–104.

———. (1993). "Intergroup Relations and Stereotype Change: A Social-Cognitive Analysis and Some Longitudinal Findings," in *Prejudice, Politics, and the American Dilemma*, ed. P. M. Sniderman, P. E. Tetlock, and E. G. Carmines, pp. 32–59. Stanford: Stanford University Press.

Rouse, J. (1987). *Knowledge and Power: Toward a Political Philosophy of Science*. Ithaca: Cornell University Press.

Rule, J. B. (1988). *Theories of Civil Violence*. Berkeley: University of California Press.

Russett, B. M., Alker, H. R., Deutsch, K. W., and Lasswell, H. D. (1964). *World Handbook of Political and Social Indicators*. New Haven: Yale University Press.

St. John, N. H. (1975). *School Desegregation: Outcomes for Children*. New York: Wiley.

Sanders, J. M., and Bielby, W. T. (1980). "Revising '*The American Soldier* Revisited,' " *Social Science Quarterly*, 61, 333–36.

Sartre, J.-P. (1948). *Anti-Semite and Jew*, trans. G. J. Becker. New York: Schocken.

Sarup, G. (1992). "Sherif's Metatheory and Contemporary Social Psychology," in *Social Judgment and Intergroup Relations: Essays in Honor of Muzafer Sherif*, ed. D. Granberg and G. Sarup, pp. 55–73. New York: Springer-Verlag.

Schaefer, R. T. (1973). "Contacts Between Immigrants and Englishmen: Road to Tolerance or Intolerance?" *New Community*, 2, 358–71.

———. (1975). "Regional Differences in Prejudice," *Regional Studies*, 9, 1–14.

Schissel, B., Wanner, R., and Frideres, J. S. (1989). "Social and Economic Context and Attitudes Toward Immigrants in Canadian Cities," *International Migration Review*, 23, 289–308.

Schlicht, E. (1985). *Isolation and Aggregation in Economics*. Berlin: Springer-Verlag.

Schoenbach, P.; Gollwitzer, P.; Stiepel, G.; and Wagner, U. (1981). *Education and Intergroup Attitudes*. London: Academic.

Schoenberger, R. A., and Segal, D. R. (1971). "The Ecology of Dissent: The Southern Wallace Vote in 1968," *Midwest Journal of Political Science*, 25, 583–86.

Schofield, J. W. (1978). "School Desegregation and Intergroup Relations," in *Social Psychology of Education: Theory and Research*, ed. D. Bar-Tal and L. Saxe, pp. 329–63. New York: Wiley.

———. (1986). "Black-White Contact in Desegregated Schools," in *Contact and Conflict in Intergroup Encounters*, ed. M. Hewstone and R. Brown, pp. 79–92. Oxford: Basil Blackwell.

———. (1991). "School Desegregation and Intergroup Relations: A Review of the Literature," in *Review of Research in Education*, vol. 17, ed. G. Grant, pp. 335–409. Washington: American Educational Research Association.

———. (1993). "Promoting Positive Peer Relations in Desegregated Schools," *Educational Policy*, 7, 297–317.

———. (1995). "Promoting Positive Intergroup Relations in School Settings," in *Toward a Common Destiny: Improving Race and Ethnic Relations in America*, ed. W. D. Hawley and A. W. Jackson, pp. 257–89. San Francisco: Jossey-Bass.

Schofield, J. W., and Sagar, H. A. (1983). "Desegregation, School Practices, and Student Race Relations," in *The Consequences of School Desegregation*, ed. C. H. Rossell and W. D. Hawley, pp. 58–102. Philadelphia: Temple University Press.

Schuman, H., and Gruenberg, B. (1970). "The Impact of City on Racial Attitudes," *American Journal of Sociology*, 76, 213–61.

Schuman, H., Steeh, C., and Bobo, L. (1985). *Racial Attitudes in America: Trends and Interpretations*. Cambridge: Harvard University Press.

Schumpeter, J. A. (1954). *History of Economic Analysis*, ed. E. B. Schumpeter. New York: Oxford University Press.

Scott, G. M. (1990). "A Resynthesis of the Primordial and Circumstantial Approaches to Ethnic Group Solidarity: Towards an Explanatory Model," *Ethnic and Racial Studies*, 13, 147–71.

Sears, D. O. (1988). "Symbolic Racism," in *Eliminating Racism: Profiles in Controversy*, ed. P. A. Katz and D. A. Taylor, pp. 53–84. New York: Plenum.

Segal, B. E. (1965). "Contact, Compliance, and Distance among Jewish and Non-Jewish Undergraduates," *Social Problems*, 13, 66–74.

Sell, D. K. (1983). "Research on Attitude Change in U.S. Students Who Participate in Foreign Study Experiences: Past Findings and Suggestions for Future Research," *International Journal of Intercultural Relations*, 7, 131–47.

Selltiz, C., and Cook, S. W. (1962). "Factors Influencing Attitudes of Foreign Students Toward the Host Country," *Journal of Social Issues*, 18(1), 7–23.

Selznick, G. J., and Steinberg, S. (1969). *The Tenacity of Prejudice: Anti-Semitism in Contemporary America*. New York: Harper & Row.

Seton-Watson, H. (1977). *Nations and States: An Enquiry into the Origins of Nations and the Politics of Nationalism*. London: Methuen.

Shafer, B. C. (1955). *Nationalism: Myth and Reality*. New York: Harcourt, Brace, and World.

———. (1972). *Faces of Nationalism: New Realities and Old Myths*. Harcourt Brace Jovanovich.

Shay, J. (1994). *Achilles in Vietnam: Combat Trauma and the Undoing of Character*. New York: Scribner.

Sherif, M. (1966). *In Common Predicament: Social Psychology of Intergroup Conflict and Cooperation*. Boston: Houghton Mifflin.

Sherif, M., Harvey, O. J., White, B. J., Hood, W. R., and Sherif, C. W. (1961). *Intergroup Conflict and Cooperation: The Robbers' Cave Experiment*. Norman: University of Oklahoma Press.

Sherif, M., and Sherif, C. W. (1953). *Groups in Harmony and Tension: An Integration of Studies on Intergroup Relations*. New York: Harper & Bros.

Sigelman, L., and Welch, S. (1991). *Black Americans' Views of Racial Inequality: The Dream Deferred*. Cambridge: Cambridge University Press.

———. (1993). "The Contact Hypothesis Revisited: Black-White Interaction and Positive Racial Attitudes," *Social Forces*, 71, 781–95.

Simon, H. A. (1957). *Models of Man: Social and Rational*. New York: John Wiley.

Simpson, G. E., and Yinger, J. M. (1985). *Racial and Cultural Minorities: An Analysis of Prejudice and Discrimination*, 5th ed. New York: Plenum.

Sinha, A. K. P., and Upadhyaya, O. P. (1960). "Change and Persistence in the Stereotypes of University Students Towards Different Ethnic Groups During the Sino-Indian Border Dispute," *Journal of Social Psychology*, 52, 31–39.

Skinner, Q., ed. (1985). *The Return of Grand Theory in the Human Sciences*. Cambridge: Cambridge University Press.

Slavin, R. E. (1983). *Cooperative Learning*. New York: Longman.

———. (1985). "Cooperative Learning: Applying Contact Theory in Desegregated Schools," *Journal of Social Issues*, 41(3), 45–62.

———. (1995). "Enhancing Intergroup Relations in Schools: Cooperative Learning and Other Strategies," in *Toward a Common Destiny: Improving Race and Ethnic Relations in America*, ed. W. D. Hawley and A. W. Jackson, pp. 291–314. San Francisco: Jossey-Bass.

Slavin, R. E., and Madden, N. A. (1979). "School Practices That Improve Race Relations," *American Educational Research Journal*, 16, 169–80.

Smith, A. D. (1973). "Nationalism: A Trend Report and Annotated Bibliography," *Current Sociology*, 21(3), 1–178.

———. (1979). *Nationalism in the Twentieth Century*. New York: New York University Press.

———. (1981). *The Ethnic Revival*. Cambridge: Cambridge University Press.

———. (1983). *Theories of Nationalism*, 2nd ed. New York: Holmes and Meier.

———. (1986). *The Ethnic Origins of Nations*. Oxford: Basil Blackwell.

———. (1991). *National Identity*. London: Penguin.

———. (1992). "Nationalism and the Historians," *International Journal of Comparative Sociology*, 33, 58–80.

————. (1995). *Nations and Nationalism in a Global Era*. Cambridge, Eng.: Polity.

Smith, C. B. (1994). "Back and to the Future: The Intergroup Contact Hypothesis Revisited," *Sociological Inquiry*, 64, 438–55.

Smith, H. P. (1955). "Do Intercultural Experiences Affect Attitudes?" *Journal of Abnormal and Social Psychology*, 51, 469–77.

————. (1957). "The Effects of Intercultural Experience—A Follow-Up Investigation," *Journal of Abnormal and Social Psychology*, 54, 266–69.

Sokal, A. (1996a). "Transgressing the Boundaries: Toward a Transformative Hermeneutics of Quantum Gravity," *Social Text 46/47*, 14, 217–52.

————. (1996b). "A Physicist Experiments with Cultural Studies," *Lingua Franca: The Review of Academic Life*, 6 (May–June), 62–64.

Sowell, T. (1981). *Markets and Minorities*. New York: Basic Books.

Spangenberg, J., and Nel, E. M. (1983). "The Effect of Equal-Status Contact on Ethnic Attitudes," *Journal of Social Psychology*, 121, 173–80.

Spaulding, S., and Flack, M. J. (1976). *The World's Students in the United States: A Review and Evaluation of Research on Foreign Students*. New York: Praeger.

Spilerman, S. (1970). "The Causes of Racial Disturbances: A Comparison of Alternative Explanations," *American Sociological Review*, 35, 627–49.

————. (1971). "The Causes of Racial Disturbances: Tests of an Explanation," *American Sociological Review*, 36, 427–42.

————. (1976). "Structural Characteristics of Cities and the Severity of Racial Disorders," *American Sociological Review*, 41, 771–93.

Steeh, C., and Schuman, H. (1992). "Young White Adults: Did Racial Attitudes Change in the 1980s?" *American Journal of Sociology*, 98, 340–67.

Stephan, C. W., and Stephan, W. G. (1992). "Reducing Intercultural Anxiety through Intercultural Contact," *International Journal of Intercultural Relations*, 16, 89–106.

Stephan, W. G. (1978). "School Desegregation: An Evaluation of the Predictions Made in *Brown v. Board of Education*," *Psychological Bulletin*, 85, 217–38.

————. (1985). "Intergroup Relations," in *Handbook of Social Psychology*, 3rd ed., vol. 2, ed. G. Lindzey and E. Aronson, pp. 599–658. New York: Random House.

————. (1986). "The Effects of School Desegregation: An Evaluation 30 Years after *Brown*," in *Advances in Applied Social Psychology*, vol. 3, ed. M. J. Saks and L. Saxe, pp. 181–206. Hillsdale, N.J.: Lawrence Erlbaum.

————. (1987). "The Contact Hypothesis in Intergroup Relations," in *Group Processes and Intergroup Relations*, ed. C. Hendrick, pp. 13–40. Newbury Park, Calif.: Sage.

————. (1991). "School Desegregation: Short-Term and Long-Term Effects," in *Opening Doors: Perspectives on Race Relations in Contemporary America*, ed. H. J. Knopke, R. J. Norrell, and R. W. Rogers, pp. 100–118. Tuscaloosa: University of Alabama Press.

Stephan, W. G., and Brigham, J. C. (1985). "Intergroup Contact: Introduction," *Journal of Social Issues*, 41(3), 1–8.

Stephan, W. G., and Stephan, C. W. (1984). "The Role of Ignorance in Inter-group Relations," in *Groups in Contact: The Psychology of Desegregation*, ed. N. Miller and M. B. Brewer, pp. 229–55. Orlando: Academic.

———. (1985). "Intergroup Anxiety," *Journal of Social Issues*, 41(3), 157–75.

———. (1989). "Antecedents of Intergroup Anxiety in Asian-Americans and His-panic-Americans," *International Journal of Intercultural Relations*, 13, 203–19.

———. (1996). *Intergroup Relations*. Madison: Brown & Benchmark.

Stone, W. F., Lederer, G., and Christie, R., eds. (1993). *Strength and Weakness: The Authoritarian Personality Today*. New York: Springer-Verlag.

Stouffer, S. A., et al. (1949). *The American Soldier*, vol. 2. Princeton: Princeton University Press.

Stroebe, W., Lenkert, A., and Jonas, K. (1988). "Familiarity May Breed Con-tempt: The Impact of Student Exchange on National Stereotypes and Atti-tudes," in *The Social Psychology of Intergroup Conflict: Theory, Research and Applications*, ed. W. Stroebe et al., pp. 167–87. Berlin: Springer-Verlag.

Studlar, D. T. (1977). "Social Context and Attitudes Toward Coloured Immi-grants," *British Journal of Sociology*, 28, 168–84.

Sumner, W. G. (1906). *Folkways: A Study of the Sociological Importance of Us-ages, Manners, Customs, Mores, and Morals*. Boston: Ginn.

Tajfel, H. (1974). "Social Identity and Intergroup Behaviour," *Social Science Information*, 13(2), 65–93.

———. (1981). *Human Groups and Social Categories: Studies in Social Psy-chology*. London: Cambridge University Press.

———. (1982). "Social Psychology of Intergroup Relations," *Annual Review of Psychology*, 33, 1–29.

Tajfel, H., and Turner, J. C. (1979). "An Integrative Theory of Intergroup Con-flict," in *The Social Psychology of Intergroup Relations*, ed. W. G. Austin and S. Worchel, pp. 33–47. Monterey: Brooks/Cole.

Tamir, Y. (1993). *Liberal Nationalism*. Princeton: Princeton University Press.

Tawney, R. H. (1931). *Equality*. London: Allen & Unwin.

Taylor, C. (1985). *Philosophical Papers*, vol. 2: *Philosophy and the Human Sci-ences*. Cambridge: Cambridge University Press.

———. (1989). *Sources of the Self: The Making of the Modern Identity*. Cam-bridge: Harvard University Press.

———. (1995). *Philosophical Arguments*. Cambridge: Harvard University Press.

Taylor, C. L., and Hudson, M. C. (1972). *World Handbook of Political and Social Indicators*, 2nd ed. New Haven: Yale University Press.

Taylor, D. M., and Moghaddam, F. M. (1994). *Theories of Intergroup Relations: International Social Psychological Perspectives*, 2nd ed. Westport, Conn.: Praeger.

Taylor, S. (1979). "The Incidence of Coloured Populations and Support for the National Front," *British Journal of Political Science*, 9, 250–55.

Teahan, J. E. (1975a). "Role Playing and Group Experience to Facilitate Attitude and Value Changes among Black and White Police Officers," *Journal of Social Issues*, 31(1), 35–45.

——. (1975b). "A Longitudinal Study of Attitude Shifts among Black and White Police Officers," *Journal of Social Issues*, 31(1), 47–56.

Theil, H. (1954). *Linear Aggregation of Economic Relations*. Amsterdam: North Holland Publishing.

Thompson, L. (1993). "The Impact of Negotiation on Intergroup Relations," *Journal of Experimental Social Psychology*, 29, 304–25.

Thurow, L. C. (1969). *Poverty and Discrimination*. Washington: Brookings Institution.

Tims, A. R., and Miller, M. M. (1986). "Determinants of Attitudes Toward Foreign Countries," *International Journal of Intercultural Relations*, 10, 471–84.

Tolnay, S. E., Beck, E. M., and Massey, J. L. (1989). "Black Lynchings: The Power Threat Hypothesis Revisited," *Social Forces*, 67, 605–23.

——. (1992). "Black Competition and White Vengeance: Legal Execution of Blacks as Social Control in the Cotton South, 1890 to 1929," *Social Science Quarterly*, 73, 627–44.

Triandis, H. C., and Vassiliou, V. (1967). "Frequency of Contact and Stereotyping," *Journal of Personality and Social Psychology*, 7, 316–28.

Tsukashima, R. T., and Montero, D. (1976). "The Contact Hypothesis: Social and Economic Contact and Generational Changes in the Study of Black Anti-Semitism," *Social Forces*, 55, 149–65.

Turner, J. C., and Giles, H. (1981). "Introduction: The Social Psychology of Intergroup Behaviour," in *Intergroup Behaviour*, ed. J. C. Turner and H. Giles, pp. 1–32. Chicago: University of Chicago Press.

Tzeng, O. C. S., and Jackson, J. W. (1994). "Effects of Contact, Conflict, and Social Identity on Interethnic Group Hostilities," *International Journal of Intercultural Relations*, 18, 259–76.

Van Evera, S. (1994). "Hypotheses on Nationalism and War," *International Security*, 18(4), 5–39.

Vuilleumier, M. (1987). *Immigrants and Refugees in Switzerland: An Outline History*. Zurich: Pro Helvetia.

Wagner, U., Hewstone, M., and Machleit, U. (1989). "Contact and Prejudice Between Germans and Turks: A Correlational Study," *Human Relations*, 42, 561–74.

Wagner, U., and Machleit, U. (1986). " 'Gastarbeiter' in the Federal Republic of Germany: Contact Between Germans and Migrant Populations," in *Contact and Conflict in Intergroup Encounters*, ed. M. Hewstone and R. Brown, pp. 59–78. Oxford: Basil Blackwell.

Wagner, U., and Schonbach, P. (1984). "Links Between Educational Status and Prejudice: Ethnic Attitudes in West Germany," in *Groups in Contact: The Psychology of Desegregation*, ed. N. Miller and M. B. Brewer, pp. 29–52. Orlando: Academic.

Wagner, U., and Zick, A. (1995). "The Relation of Formal Education to Ethnic

Prejudice: Its Reliability, Validity and Explanation," *European Journal of Social Psychology*, 25, 41–56.

Watson, G. B. (1947). *Action for Unity*. New York: Harper.

Webster, S. W. (1961). "The Influence of Interracial Contact on Social Acceptance in a Newly Integrated School," *Journal of Educational Psychology*, 52, 292–96.

Webster, Y. O. (1992). *The Racialization of America*. New York: St. Martin's.

Weigel, R. H., Wiser, P. I., and Cook, S. W. (1975). "Impact of Cooperative Learning Experiences on Cross-Ethnic Relations and Attitudes," *Journal of Social Issues*, 31(1), 219–45.

Weinberg, M. (1977). *Minority Students: A Research Appraisal*. Washington: U.S. Department of Health, Education, and Welfare.

Weitz, S. (1972). "Attitude, Voice, and Behavior: A Repressed Affect Model of Interracial Interaction," *Journal of Personality and Social Psychology*, 24, 14–21.

Wells, A. S. (1995). "Reexamining Social Science Research on School Desegregation: Long- Versus Short-Term Effects," *Teachers College Record*, 96, 691–706.

Wells, J. W., and Kline, W. B. (1987). "Self-Disclosure of Homosexual Orientation," *Journal of Social Psychology*, 127, 191–97.

White, P. G., and Curtis, J. E. (1990). "Language Regions and Feelings Toward Outgroups: Analyses for 1968 and 1984," *Canadian Journal of Sociology*, 15, 441–62.

White, S. K., ed. (1995). *The Cambridge Companion to Habermas*. Cambridge: Cambridge University Press.

Whiteley, P. (1979). "The National Front Vote in the 1977 GLC Elections: An Aggregate Data Analysis," *British Journal of Political Science*, 9, 370–80.

Wilcox, J., and Roof, W. C. (1978). "Percent Black and Black-White Status Inequality: Southern Versus Non-Southern Patterns," *Social Science Quarterly*, 59, 422–34.

Wilder, D. A. (1984). "Intergroup Contact: The Typical Member and the Exception to the Rule," *Journal of Experimental Social Psychology*, 20, 177–94.

Wilder, D. A., and Thompson, J. E. (1980). "Intergroup Contact with Independent Manipulation of In-Group and Out-Group Interaction," *Journal of Personality and Social Psychology*, 38, 589–603.

Williams, R. M. (1947). *The Reduction of Intergroup Tensions*, Social Science Research Council Bulletin No. 57. New York: Social Science Research Council.

———. (1964). *Strangers Next Door: Ethnic Relations in American Communities*. Englewood Cliffs, N.J.: Prentice-Hall.

———. (1994). "The Sociology of Ethnic Conflicts: Comparative International Perspectives," *Annual Review of Sociology*, 20, 49–79.

Williams, R. M., Fisher, B. R., and Janis, I. L. (1956). "Educational Desegregation as a Context for Basic Social Science Research," *American Sociological Review*, 21, 577–83.

Wilner, D. M., Walkley, R. P., and Cook, S. W. (1955). *Human Relations in Interracial Housing*. Minneapolis: University of Minnesota Press.

Wilson, T. C. (1994). "Trends in Tolerance Toward Rightist and Leftist Groups, 1976–1988: Effects of Attitude Change and Cohort Succession," *Public Opinion Quarterly*, 58, 539–56.

Wood, P. B., and Sonleitner, N. (1996). "The Effect of Childhood Interracial Contact on Adult Antiblack Prejudice," *International Journal of Intercultural Relations*, 20, 1–17.

Worchel, S., Andreoli, V. A., and Folger, R. (1977). "Intergroup Cooperation and Intergroup Attraction: The Effect of Previous Interaction and Outcome of Combined Effort," *Journal of Experimental Social Psychology*, 13, 131–40.

Works, E. (1961). "The Prejudice-Interaction Hypothesis from the Point of View of the Negro Minority Group," *American Journal of Sociology*, 67, 47–52.

Wright, G. C. (1976). "Community Structure and Voting in the South," *Public Opinion Quarterly*, 40, 201–15.

———. (1977). "Contextual Models of Electoral Behavior: The Southern Wallace Vote," *American Political Science Review*, 71, 497–508.

Wright, Q. (1942). *A Study of War*, 2 vols. Chicago: University of Chicago Press.

Wrinkle, R. D., and Polinard, J. L. (1973). "Populism and Dissent: The Wallace Vote in Texas," *Social Science Quarterly*, 54, 306–20.

Young, D. (1932). *American Minority Peoples: A Study of Racial and Cultural Conflicts in the United States*. New York: Harper.

Young, I. M. (1990). *Justice and the Politics of Difference* . Princeton: Princeton University Press.

Young-Bruehl, E. (1996). *The Anatomy of Prejudices*. Cambridge: Harvard University Press.

Zeul, C. R., and Humphrey, C. R. (1971). "The Integration of Black Residents in Suburban Neighborhoods: A Reexamination of the Contact Hypothesis," *Social Problems*, 18, 462–74.

Zinnes, D. A., and Muncaster, R. G. (1987). "Transaction Flows and Integrative Processes," in *Communication and Interaction in Global Politics*, ed. C. Cioffi-Revilla, R. L. Merritt, and D. A. Zinnes, pp. 23–48. Beverly Hills: Sage.

Index

Aborigines, 70, 106
Acton, Lord, 252n
Adorno, T. W., 26, 235n, 245n
Afrikaner-Coloured interaction, 70, 90–91
Aggregation problem, 10, 112–13, 115, 128, 135, 136–38, 140, 166–68, 198, 203, 206, 243n
Albee, G. W., 86
Allport, Gordon, 117, 120, 132, 139, 140, 148, 197, 206; contact study of, 64–65; contact theory of, 8–9, 15, 19–22, 24, 28, 40, 47, 140–41, 198, 199–200, 239–40n, 242–43n, 249n; definition of prejudice, 15–17; dichotomizing by, 202; equality condition of, 21–22, 64, 116–21, 123, 199; law of minority density of, 20, 140, 148, 201, 235n, 239n; on thinking, 17–19, 25–27. *See also* Individualism
Allport-Pettigrew contact hypothesis, 22, 120, 123–24, 129, 240n, 242n
Amir, Yehuda, 23, 81, 83, 121, 129
Anastasopoulos, P. G., 83
Anderson, Benedict, 221–23, 227, 253n
Anderson, N., 71
Anti-Semitism, 33, 69, 119, 239n
Armor, David, 59
Army. *See* Military personnel
Aronson, E., 124, 131
Assimilation: contact and, 144–46, 164;

definition of, 144–45, 225; linguistic, 150, 215–19; social status and, 151–52, 169
Atelsek, F. J., 65–66, 88
Atlas Narodov Mira (ANM) index of heterogeneity, 109, 110, 239n
Attribution theory, 234n
Authoritarianism, 27, 202, 235n, 245n
Authoritative suggestion. *See* Experimenter effects
Autistic thinking, 17, 18–19, 31, 117

Barnard, W. A., 73, 76–77
Belief congruence theory, 234n. *See also* Cultural differences
Ben-Ari, R., 83
Benn, M. S., 73, 76–77
Berkeley Group, 26, 235n
Berry, J. W., 72, 105
Biernat, M., 66–67
Bilingualism, 33, 106, 156
Billig, M., 7, 229
Bishop, G. D., 66, 88–89
Black-white contact. *See* Interracial contact
Bledsoe, T., 68, 103
Blumer, Herbert, 27, 40, 139, 201
Bogart, L., 93
Bornman, E., 70, 90–91
Bradburn, N. M., 99, 100
Bribery, 151